Deploying SharePoint 2019

Installing, Configuring, and Optimizing for On-Premises and Hybrid Scenarios

Vlad Catrinescu
Trevor Seward

Apress®

Deploying SharePoint 2019: Installing, Configuring, and Optimizing for On-Premises and Hybrid Scenarios

Vlad Catrinescu
Greenfield Park, QC, Canada

Trevor Seward
Sultan, WA, USA

ISBN-13 (pbk): 978-1-4842-4525-5
https://doi.org/10.1007/978-1-4842-4526-2

ISBN-13 (electronic): 978-1-4842-4526-2

Managing Director, Apress Media LLC: Welmoed Spahr
Acquisitions Editor: Joan Murray
Development Editor: Laura Berendson
Coordinating Editor: Jill Balzano

Cover image designed by Freepik (www.freepik.com)

Distributed to the book trade worldwide by Springer Science+Business Media New York, 233 Spring Street, 6th Floor, New York, NY 10013. Phone 1-800-SPRINGER, fax (201) 348-4505, e-mail orders-ny@springer-sbm.com, or visit www.springeronline.com. Apress Media, LLC is a California LLC and the sole member (owner) is Springer Science + Business Media Finance Inc (SSBM Finance Inc). SSBM Finance Inc is a Delaware corporation.

For information on translations, please e-mail rights@apress.com, or visit http://www.apress.com/rights-permissions.

Apress titles may be purchased in bulk for academic, corporate, or promotional use. eBook versions and licenses are also available for most titles. For more information, reference our Print and eBook Bulk Sales web page at http://www.apress.com/bulk-sales.

Any source code or other supplementary material referenced by the author in this book is available to readers on GitHub via the book's product page, located at www.apress.com/9781484245255. For more detailed information, please visit http://www.apress.com/source-code.

Printed on acid-free paper

This book is dedicated to a few people who make working with SharePoint way more fun! Sébastien Levert, Jeff Collins, Gokan Ozcifci, Daniel Glenn, Drew Madelung, Liz Sundet, this one is for you!
– Vlad

To my wife Leana, my daughter Victoria, and my son Jameson, thank you for your love, hard work, and patience!
– Trev

Table of Contents

About the Authors

 **Vlad Catrinescu** is a SharePoint and Office 365 consultant specializing in PowerShell, SharePoint, and hybrid scenarios. As an author, MVP, Microsoft Certified Trainer, and recognized international speaker, Vlad has helped hundreds of thousands of users and IT pros across the globe to get the most out of their SharePoint and Office 365 deployments. Vlad writes the popular Absolute SharePoint Blog and is a recipient of the Top 25 Office 365 Influencers award. His contributions can also be found on other sites such as CMSWire and ComputerWorld. Vlad is very active on social media, LinkedIn, and @VladCatrinescu.

 **Trevor Seward** is an IT professional with over 20 years of experience managing the Microsoft stack. He specializes in SharePoint Server, Office 365 services, and on-premises infrastructure such as Active Directory, IIS, and virtualization. Trevor has been awarded the Office Apps and Services MVP award multiple times and has worked closely with the SharePoint product group on SharePoint Server pre-release programs. He blogs at https://thesharepointfarm.com and is active on Twitter @NaupliusTrevor.

About the Technical Reviewer

 **Thomas Vochten** is a Microsoft MVP and Office 365 solution architect. He focusses on platform architecture, planning, deployment, availability, and operations – whether on-premises or in the cloud. Thomas is a very active public speaker who travels the world to talk about implementing SharePoint and Office 365 and to prevent people from making the same expensive mistakes he did. He has a deep affection for SQL Server, teaches the occasional classroom full of IT professionals, and is getting around deploying hybrid SharePoint environments. Thomas works for Xylos, a consultancy company based in Belgium.

CHAPTER 1

Introduction to SharePoint 2019

In this chapter, we will introduce SharePoint 2019, a bit of history about where is SharePoint coming from, and Microsoft's goals for the 2019 version. We will also have a high-level overview of the new features in SharePoint 2019 as well as a few features that are deprecated, or no longer available.

A Bit of SharePoint History

SharePoint 2019 is the seventh version of SharePoint Server that Microsoft shipped to the public. First introduced in 2001, SharePoint Portal Server (the name back then) was nowhere as popular as it is now. It took a few versions, but starting with Office SharePoint Server 2007 (MOSS), SharePoint went from a CD Microsoft gave away, including 25 user licenses, to one of Microsoft's most lucrative products. After innovating SharePoint with every release ever since, there are now over 250,000 organizations, including 85% of the Fortune 500.

While for the past few years, Microsoft's primary focus has been to innovate SharePoint Online, part of Office 365, there are still many customers that use SharePoint Server for their collaboration needs, and Microsoft hasn't forgotten them. Microsoft still brings new features to the cloud first, and sometimes to the cloud only, and with every On-Premises release since SharePoint 2016, most features are packaged into a version of SharePoint On-Premises.

SharePoint Server 2016 is the first version of SharePoint Server that was "born in the cloud," and it has brought down many improvements to on-premises that were created and tested in the cloud. Some of those features include the MinRole topology, Zero Downtime Patching, common binaries and updates with Project Server and more. SharePoint 2016 brought many performance and stability improvements to on-premises, but a lot of business users were not impressed with the little number of new features aimed at business users.

V. Catrinescu and T. Seward, *Deploying SharePoint 2019*, https://doi.org/10.1007/978-1-4842-4526-2_1

Before talking about what is new in SharePoint 2019, let's take a trip back in time, and look at what were the principal features released in every version of SharePoint since the beginning. In Figure 1-1, you can view a bit of SharePoint history and the important features that each version introduced.

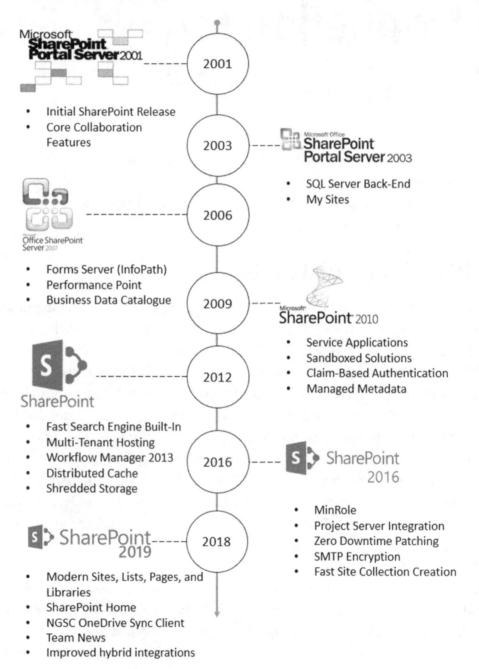

Figure 1-1. *A small history of new features in every SharePoint version*

While SharePoint Server 2019 still brings some new features for IT Professionals, most new functionality in this version is for end users. Let's look more in detail at what this version of SharePoint has to offer!

What's New in SharePoint Server 2019

If you have been following big announcements in Office 365 for the past few years, it will be quite easy to understand what Microsoft has prepared for us in SharePoint Server 2019!

Modern SharePoint Experiences

After being used by millions of users in Office 365, the most significant evolution to SharePoint in recent years has finally made it On-Premises. Modern SharePoint Experiences include Modern SharePoint Team Sites and Communication Sites, as well as the new experience in both lists and document libraries. Let's take a more in-depth look at each one of those experiences

Modern SharePoint Team Sites

The first pillar of modern SharePoint experiences is the Modern Team Sites seen in Figure 1-2. Modern Team Sites are responsive by default, include an out of the box news publishing engine, allowing users to share news with the rest of the team. Unlike Office 365 where most Modern Team Sites are connected to an Office 365 Group, on-premises Modern Team Sites do not need any integration with Exchange to function correctly.

Figure 1-2. *Modern Team Sites*

Modern SharePoint Communication Sites

The next pillar of modern SharePoint experiences is Modern Communication Sites. Communication Sites are sites that are mainly used to share news, policies, and information to the users that are included. SharePoint Server 2019 includes three different templates of Communication Sites: Blank, Topic, and Showcase. You can view a Modern Communication Site in Figure 1-3.

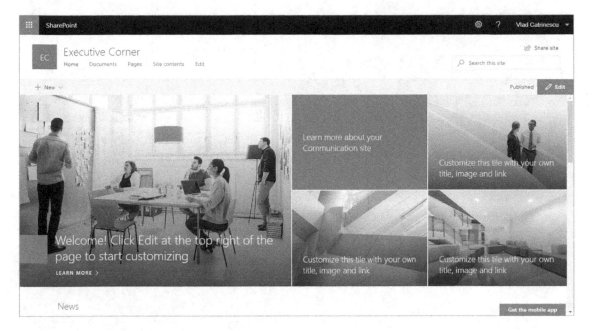

Figure 1-3. *Modern Communication Site*

Modern Lists and Libraries

Digging deeper into our sites, SharePoint Server 2019 also brings support for modern SharePoint lists and libraries. Modern SharePoint Libraries, seen in Figure 1-4, allows users to quickly view information about their documents, including permissions and metadata. Another useful Office 365 feature brought over to SharePoint 2019 are the "Move To" and "Copy To" actions, allowing users to quickly change the location of a document to a more appropriate one.

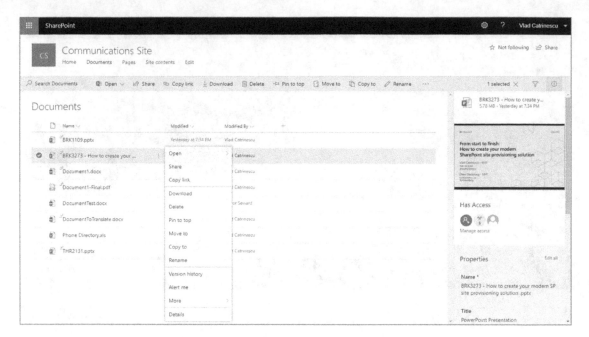

Figure 1-4. *Modern Document Library*

Modern SharePoint lists in SharePoint 2019 also include the Conditional Formatting feature seen in Figure 1-5. Conditional Formatting allows Power Users to configure different display rules for specific columns, to quickly view the status of that item.

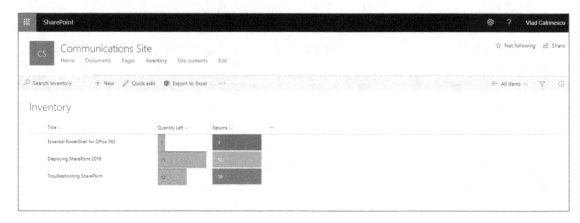

Figure 1-5. *Conditional Formatting*

Modern Search Experience

The last piece of modern SharePoint to make it On-Premises in SharePoint Server 2019 is Modern Search. The Modern Search experience, seen in Figure 1-6 makes it easier for users to find documents, list items and people inside the SharePoint environment.

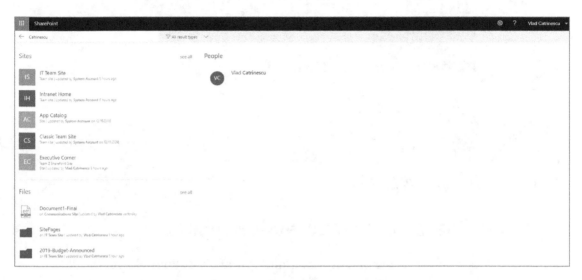

Figure 1-6. *Modern Search in SharePoint 2019*

The SharePoint Home

Our next new significant feature in SharePoint On-Premises is the SharePoint Home. The SharePoint Home, seen in Figure 1-7, brings all the news from Team Sites and Communication Sites together in a single location. All the sites you follow are also brought together, including activity from each site and quick access to your favorite sites.

Figure 1-7. *The SharePoint Home*

Improved SharePoint Framework Support

Another new feature in this version of SharePoint is that SharePoint Server 2019 now supports SharePoint Framework 1.4.1 to allow developers to create modern web parts that work for both SharePoint Online, as well as SharePoint On-Premises. With SharePoint Server 2019, developers can use Webhooks for list items, SharePoint Framework Client Side web parts and extensions in modern experiences, as well as Asset packaging and automatic JavaScript file hosting from app catalog.

OneDrive Synchronization with the New OneDrive Client

SharePoint Server 2019 allows organizations that are running on-premises SharePoint to profit from the latest improvements in OneDrive and Windows 10. SharePoint 2019 works with the latest version of OneDrive, also known as Next Generation Sync Client (NGSC) and supports the latest innovations in windows such as Files on Demand

Deprecated and Removed Features

While SharePoint Server 2019 brings us some fantastic new features, we also lost a few. Most of those features we could see coming in advance, as they have been deprecated or removed already from Office 365. In this section, we will only overview the list of features and specify the chapter in which their implications will be explained in more detail.

Note   In software terms, deprecation is a status applied to features to indicate that they should be avoided, typically because there is a better way to do the same functionality. Those features are still available in SharePoint Server 2019, mainly for backward compatibility, to give enterprises time to replace them with new tools. Those features will eventually be entirely removed from future versions of SharePoint.

Access Services 2010 and 2013

Access Services 2010 and 2013 allowed users to view Access Database files directly in the browser. Access Services 2013 also allowed users to create custom Access Applications that could be consumed through SharePoint as the one seen in Figure 1-8. While in Office 365, those services are not supported anymore, they are deprecated, but still part of SharePoint Server 2019.

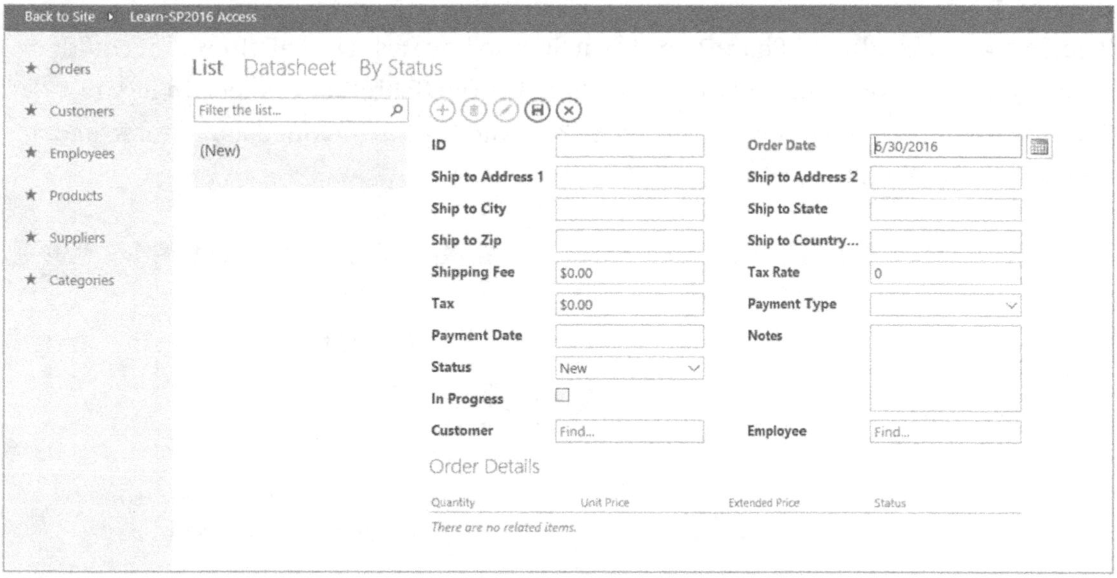

Figure 1-8. *Access Services in SharePoint 2016*

InfoPath Services

InfoPath allows Power Users and Developers to create custom forms for SharePoint lists. With InfoPath 2013 being the last version of InfoPath, the associated InfoPath Services in SharePoint 2019 are now also deprecated.

Machine Translation and Variations

The Machine Translation Service which allowed users to translate sites automatically and pages to another language is now deprecated in SharePoint Server 2019. Variations are also still supported but deprecated in this version of SharePoint.

PerformancePoint Services

PerformancePoint allowed Business Intelligence specialists to create powerful dashboards and reports and display them inside of SharePoint. With the platform relying heavily on Silverlight and more modern options available such as Power BI Server, PerformancePoint Services have been deprecated in SharePoint 2019.

Site Mailbox

The Site Mailbox allowed SharePoint Team Sites to have a shared mailbox that could be consumed by the members of the site directly from SharePoint as seen in Figure 1-9. This feature has been removed from Office 365, and it's still included, but deprecated, in SharePoint Server 2019.

Figure 1-9. *Site Mailbox*

Sandbox Solutions with Code

Sandbox solutions that include code have been removed in SharePoint Online since 2016, and the limitation now applies to SharePoint Server 2019 as well. SharePoint 2019 still allows you to create declarative sandbox solutions.

Multi-tenancy

First introduced in SharePoint 2013, multi-tenancy allowed you to use SharePoint On-Premises as a multi-tenant platform. This feature has been completely removed from SharePoint Server 2019, and customers that need this feature will need to remain on SharePoint Server 2016.

PowerPivot Gallery

With the release of more modern options such as Power BI Server On-Premises available to users, Microsoft has completely removed the PowerPivot Gallery in SharePoint Server 2019.

SSRS Integrated Mode

SharePoint-Integrated Mode SSRS Installs are no longer available in SharePoint Server 2019. You can still install SSRS in Native Mode with better integration than before.

Silverlight Rendering in Visio Services

With Silverlight being a platform of the past and support ending on October 12, 2021, Silverlight Based Rendering in Visio Services is now entirely removed from SharePoint Server 2019.

Some Notes and Next Steps

Now that we are familiar with what improvements SharePoint Server 2019 has to offer, in the next chapter, we will learn how to design our SharePoint 2019 farm topology to achieve maximum performance and stability with a variety of potential options.

As you will see throughout the book, both authors will share a lot of PowerShell scripts with you, and we all know that copying PowerShell from a book doesn't always give the best results! Most of the scripts in this book are available on GitHub at the following link: `https://github.com/Apress/deploying-sharepoint-2019`! Make sure to download them all as those scripts will be useful for your life as a SharePoint 2019 administrator!

CHAPTER 2

Designing a Physical Architecture

In this chapter, we will be reviewing physical architectures for SharePoint Server 2019, as well as networking, virtualization, and other farm considerations.

Decisions on architectures are dependent on content size, concurrent user support, overall user count, and of course monetary considerations. While this book will cover a highly available architecture with disaster recovery, many architectures remain valid for a variety of use cases and should be designed with your use case and requirements in mind.

SharePoint Server 2019 Farm Architecture

Choosing a farm architecture is a difficult decision, more so when SharePoint has never been previously deployed to the environment.

Deciding on a farm architecture largely relies on these factors:

- Monetary investments available for hardware and software licensing

- High availability and disaster recovery requirements (RTO/RPO)

- Anticipated content size

- Overall user count

- Anticipated concurrent user count

- Provisioned services

All of these play a factor in determining hardware and software requirements. For enterprises implementing a SharePoint farm for the first time, the anticipated content size and concurrent user count may not be easily determined, but there are load generation tools which this chapter will touch on to assist in determining what may be appropriate.

© Vlad Catrinescu and Trevor Seward 2019
V. Catrinescu and T. Seward, *Deploying SharePoint 2019*, https://doi.org/10.1007/978-1-4842-4526-2_2

SharePoint Server can represent a significant monetary cost. Hardware requirements are on the upper end of many Document Management Systems. Each SharePoint Server must be licensed, along with each SharePoint User. Another licensing point to consider is SQL Server, and as SharePoint Server 2019 does not support SQL Express, the only option is the licensed editions of SQL Server.

Creating a highly available SharePoint farm will also raise costs not only in initial investment, but also in operational costs. The more servers and services there are to manage, the more expensive the farm becomes over time.

Which services are provisioned in the farm will also impact performance. In a farm where you have over 500 million items to crawl, it is necessary to provision a new Search Service Application. If you have additional Search Service Applications, you may also want to provision additional SharePoint Servers to handle that load.

Microsoft introduced the concept of MinRole and Zero Downtime patching. With MinRole, customers can focus on which service applications to deploy while not having to worry about where its dependent service instances will have to be started. It also automatically starts these services when they would be stopped accidentally. MinRole provides the best service placement based on Microsoft's experience with SharePoint Online. MinRole service placement cannot be changed as it is defined in code. This may be an important consideration if you want to run any custom services within the farm. Zero Downtime patching allows for patching of a SharePoint farm without taking the farm offline, but Zero Downtime patching does not prevent any one particular server in the farm from going offline; for example, a SharePoint patch may require a reboot. This means that for effective high availability, all services within the farm must be allocated to at least two servers.

Tip   Information about each MinRole and the associated services can be found at https://docs.microsoft.com/en-us/sharepoint/administration/ description-of-minrole-and-associated-services-in-sharepoint- server-2016.

With this data in hand, a better determination can be made as to what your farm should look like.

When a server is out of compliance with a specific MinRole, it will be notated in Central Administration under Manage Servers in Farm, as shown in Figure 2-1, as well as for the specific service in Manage Services in this Farm.

Server	SharePoint Products Installed	Role	Compliant	Services Running	Status	Remove Server
CALSP01	Microsoft SharePoint Server 2019	Front-end with Distributed Cache	⊗ No (Fix)	App Management Service Business Data Connectivity Service Distributed Cache Managed Metadata Web Service Microsoft SharePoint Foundation Incoming E-Mail Microsoft SharePoint Foundation Web Application Secure Store Service User Profile Service	No Action Required	Remove Server
CALSP02	Microsoft SharePoint Server 2019	Front-end with Distributed Cache	✓ Yes	App Management Service Business Data Connectivity Service Distributed Cache Managed Metadata Web Service Microsoft SharePoint Foundation Web Application Secure Store Service User Profile Service	No Action Required	Remove Server

Figure 2-1. *Compliant role information in Central Administration*

Dedicated MinRole requires a minimum of eight servers within the SharePoint farm to keep all services highly available, while shared MinRole requires four servers. High Availability will be covered further in Chapter 17.

With the basic concepts of farm architecture, the next step in the architecture process is reviewing the hardware and software requirements for SharePoint Server 2019.

Hardware and Software Requirements

SharePoint Server 2019 hardware requirements remain largely unchanged from SharePoint Server 2013 and 2016, and any production hardware provisioned for SharePoint Server 2013 or 2016 can be used with SharePoint Server 2019, as noted in Table 2-1. These are *minimum* requirements. Production deployments often require significantly higher specifications.

Table 2-1. *Hardware Requirements*

Server	Processor	Memory	Primary Disk	Secondary Disk
SharePoint Server	4 cores, 64-bit	12–24 GB	80 GB	80 GB
SQL Server	4 cores, 64-bit	12–16 GB	80 GB	N/A
SharePoint single server farm	4 cores, 64-bit	12–24 GB	80 GB	100 GB

SharePoint Server 2019 can be installed on Windows Server 2016 Standard or Datacenter, as well as Windows Server 2019 Standard or Datacenter. SharePoint Server 2019 requires Desktop Experience; Windows Server Core and containers are not supported.

Each SharePoint Server requires the following prerequisites:

- Active Directory Rights Management Services Client 2.1

- Cumulative Update 7 for AppFabric 1.1 for Windows Server

- Microsoft .NET Framework 4.7

- Microsoft Identity Extensions

- Microsoft Information Protection and Control Client

- Microsoft ODBC Driver 11 for SQL Server

- Microsoft Sync Framework Runtime v1.0 SP1 (x64)

- SQL Server 2012 SP4 Native Client

- Visual C++ Runtime Package for Visual Studio 2012

- Visual C++ Runtime Package for Visual Studio 2017

- WCF Data Services 5.6

- Windows Server AppFabric 1.1

Supported versions of SQL Server are SQL Server 2016 and SQL Server 2017, Standard and Enterprise editions.

The choice for using SQL Server Standard or Enterprise will largely come down to what method of SQL Server High Availability will be used for the farm.

Virtualization plays an important role in today's data center as well as the cloud; next we will take a look at virtualization options, as well as restrictions with regards to SharePoint Server 2019.

Virtualization

Microsoft fully supports virtualizing SharePoint Server and SQL Server on Hyper-V and other hypervisors, such as VMware ESXi, via the Server Virtualization Validation Program at `www.windowsservercatalog.com/svvp.aspx`. For SharePoint Server, there are restrictions on supported virtualization technologies.

Virtualization is an important technology in today's world, providing greater density in the enterprise environment. It is important to thoroughly test performance of the underlying host hardware in order to properly plan the layout and configuration of virtual machines. For example, placing SQL Server virtual disks on the same LUN as a SharePoint Server may not be appropriate, or allocating a large number of vCPUs when a SharePoint Server may only require four vCPUs, thereby causing CPU oversubscription and reducing overall performance.

Virtualization Limitations and Restrictions

Dynamic memory techniques, which adjust the amount of virtual RAM allocated based on the load of the virtual machine, such as Hyper-V Dynamic Memory or VMware Memory Ballooning, are not supported by SharePoint Server. The Distributed Cache service and Search Server Service create memory allocations based on the memory available when those respective services start. If memory is removed from the system below the amount of memory allocated when the SharePoint Server has started, these two services would be unaware of that change in allocation and cannot adjust their memory quotas appropriately.

Differencing disks are virtual disks that multiple virtual machines may use as a "base." For example, a virtual disk with Windows Server 2016 and the appropriate SharePoint Server 2019 prerequisite installed could serve as that base, and each SharePoint Server virtual machine would have its own, separate virtual disk where changes would take place. This can cause performance penalties for SharePoint Server, thus Microsoft does not support them.

"Online" virtual machine backups are backups of an entire virtual machine, including virtual machine configuration as well as any virtual disks. The operating system in the virtual machine, as well as any applications, is unaware of the online backup. Microsoft does not support these operations with SharePoint Server as online backups do not happen at exactly the same time throughout the farm. This could lead to inconsistencies between farm members if the backups were to be restored, including inconsistencies between the SharePoint Servers and SQL Server databases.

Like online virtual machine backups, online checkpoints, also called snapshots, are also not supported by Microsoft for the same reason. Not only do checkpoints present the same issue of farm consistency during a checkpoint rollback, but they may lead to performance issues, as checkpoints generate a new differencing virtual disk for any changes after the checkpoint was taken.

Replication of SharePoint Server virtual machines is not supported. This includes any form of replication, such as Hyper-V Replica, VMware vSphere Replication, or even Storage Area Network (SAN) block level or file level replication.

Time synchronization services at the virtual machine level should be disabled. The Windows virtual machine will then leverage an authoritative time source within the domain, either the Active Directory Domain Controller with the PDC Emulator FSMO role, or another Domain Controller member server. This ensures time is consistent between SharePoint servers within the farm.

Networking plays a very important role with SharePoint, and next we will examine the required ports for SharePoint as well as networking bandwidth and latency limitations.

Network Requirements

Microsoft recommends the use of the Windows Firewall when possible. With this in mind, and with the potential of other firewalls between SharePoint farm members, SQL Servers, and/or Domain Controllers, it is important to make sure the appropriate ports are open for SharePoint to operate properly. SharePoint will automatically create the Windows Firewall rules when SharePoint is installed. Review Table 2-2 for the ports required by SharePoint and related services.

Table 2-2. *Ports Required for SharePoint*

Service	TCP Port	UDP Port	Protocols
Distributed Cache	22233, 22236	N/A	ICMP Type 0 (ping)
People Picker	53, 88, 135, 137–139, 389, 445, 636, 749, 750, 3268, 3269	53, 88, 137–139, 389, 445, 749	N/A
Sandbox Service	32846	N/A	N/A
Search Crawler	Web Application Ports Used (e.g., 80, 443)	N/A	N/A
Search Index	16500–16519	N/A	N/A
Service Applications	32843, 32844	N/A	N/A
SQL Server	1433 (default)	1434 (default)	N/A
WCF Services	808	N/A	N/A
User Profile Service	53, 88, 389, 5725, 1025–5000, 49152–65536	53, 88, 389, 464	N/A
SMTP	25 (default), 587 (TLS default)	N/A	N/A

SharePoint Server requires that all servers in the farm are connected with at least 1Gbps network connectivity and 1ms response time over an average of ten minutes. Latency can be measured using any preferred tool, including ping, Psping, Hrping, and others. Microsoft does expect some latency above 1 ms due to various factors, including the use of virtualization or switch fabrics adding latency. The latency limits a SharePoint member server placement to 186 miles (299 km) from each other in a vacuum; however, given that we do not live in a vacuum, the distance may be significantly reduced. Microsoft highly discourages stretched SharePoint farms, although if you do meet the requirement, they are supported.

Like SharePoint Servers in the farm, the SQL Servers must also have 1 ms or less latency to each SQL Server running in a synchronous form of replication, as well as the SharePoint servers that the SQL Servers are supporting. This means a SQL Server using AlwaysOn Availability Groups in Synchronous mode will likely need to be within a very short distance of one another.

SharePoint is heavily dependent on a healthy Active Directory forest. Domain Controllers for all domains from which SharePoint users and services reside in should be close to the SharePoint farm, preferably within 1ms RTT and connected with at least 1Gbps connectivity. Each Active Directory Domain should have two or more Domain Controllers for high availability.

Chapter 3 will discuss in further depth how Active Directory is secured for the SharePoint Server 2019 farm.

Note   Psping is a Microsoft Sysinternals Utility available from `https://docs. microsoft.com/en-us/sysinternals/downloads/psping`. Hrping is available from CFOS Software at `www.cfos.de`.

Network Load Balancers

Network Load balancers are key to providing high availability to SharePoint for your end users. While many load balancers offer SSL Offloading, this should be avoided where possible. Using SSL Offloading removes the encryption on the load balancer and sends the resulting request in clear text to the target services, such as SharePoint. SharePoint uses OAuth tokens for a variety of purposes, such as communicating with Office Online Server, Workflow Manager, and SharePoint Add-ins. OAuth tokens are plain text and rely on transport security, such as SSL, in order to remain secure. While SSL Offloading no longer provides a performance advantage in terms of CPU utilization on a server with a modern AMD or Intel processor, it can reduce the impact of the SSL handshake, which can add up to a few hundred milliseconds. Browsers will reuse the HTTP session, which may reduce the likelihood of another SSL handshake from being required. SSL Offloading may also be used for traffic inspection, looking for exploits, data validation, and so on.

In either case, explore using SSL Bridging instead of SSL Offloading. SSL Bridging decrypts the end user's SSL session at the load balancer and re-encrypts the SSL session from the load balancer to the SharePoint server. This allows the load balancer to reuse the SSL sessions and reduce the impact of any SSL handshake.

With networking requirements restrictions and load balancer options covered, we will take a look at the Active Directory service accounts that SharePoint requires.

Service Accounts

Guidance for Service Accounts varies. In this book, we will be taking the minimalist approach, which has proven performance benefits and no known security risks. There are four recommended Managed Accounts for SharePoint; the Farm Account, Service Application, Web Application Pool Account, and Claims to Windows Token Service account. In addition, non-Managed Accounts include a Crawl Account (for Search), User Profile Synchronization (for the AD Import synchronization connection), Portal Super User (for Publishing), and Portal Super Reader (for Publishing). SQL Server should leverage a Managed Service Account. Not to be confused with a SharePoint Managed Service Account, Active Directory Managed Service Accounts provide significant benefits, such as automatic password rollover, locking the account to be used with particular servers, and prevention of use of the credential to log in interactively.

Tip   Find more information on Group Managed Service Accounts at `https://docs.microsoft.com/en-us/windows-server/security/group-managed-service-accounts/group-managed-service-accounts-overview`.

Each account has a specific purpose and supports various services of the SharePoint environment as outlined in Table 2-3.

Table 2-3. *Service Account Rights*

Service Account	System/Service	Permission/Role	Notes
Farm (Timer) Service Account	SQL Server	dbcreator securityadmin	Roles are optional but recommended; database creation/security may be managed by DBA.
Farm Account	SharePoint Server	Farm Administrator Shell Administrator WSS_ADMIN_WPG Local Group WSS_ RESTRICTED_WPG_V4 Local Group WSS_WPG Local Group	On Farm creation, these permissions are assigned automatically.
SQL Server Account	SQL Server	sysadmin Perform Volume Maintenance Tasks Lock Pages in Memory	Fixed role is added automatically when the SQL Server service is configured to run as the Domain User. Perform Volume Maintenance Tasks and Lock Pages in Memory are Local Security Policy User Rights. These will allow instant initialization of database files and prevent Windows from paging out memory in use by SQL Server, respectively.
Web Application Pool Account	SharePoint Server	WSS_WPG Local Group	Other permissions may vary.
Service Application Pool Account	SharePoint Server	WSS_WPG Local Group	Other permissions may vary.

(continued)

Table 2-3. (*continued*)

Service Account	System/Service	Permission/Role	Notes
Claims to Windows Token Service Account (C2WTS)	SharePoint Server	Local Administrator User Rights Assignment: Act as part of the Operating System Impersonate a client after authentication Log on as a service	These rights must be assigned on any SharePoint Server running the C2WTS service, in addition to configuring Kerberos Constrained Delegation for external services where required. This service is often not required.
Search Crawl Account	SharePoint Web Applications	Full Read User Policy	
User Profile Synchronization Account	Active Directory	Delegated Rights: Replicate Directory Changes	Can be configured via Active Directory Users and Computers or ADSI Edit.
Portal Super User Account	SharePoint Web Applications	Full Control User Policy	
Portal Super Reader Account	SharePoint Web Applications	Full Read User Policy	

It should be noted that the Farm Account account no longer requires Local Administrator rights on any SharePoint server. This is due to the User Profile Synchronization Service (Forefront Identity Manager) no longer being part of the SharePoint Server 2019 product. The Claims to Windows Token Service account is now the only account that continues to require Local Administrator rights, but depending on the features deployed to the farm, does not necessarily need to be provisioned.

With all of the basic requirements for SharePoint Server 2019 covered, let's take a look at the various topology options available to us.

SharePoint Farm Topology Options

SharePoint topology strategies are numerous. Here we will go over the most common topologies, as well as the minimum required topology for the new "Zero Downtime" patching functionality.

Single Server Farm

A single server farm, as depicted in Figure 2-2, consists of a single SharePoint Server with SQL Server installed on the same server. It is possible that SQL Server may also be running on its own server. This farm architecture has a specific installation role named "Single Server Farm." With this role, it is not possible to add additional SharePoint Servers to the farm, although it is possible to change the role post installation to accommodate a farm expansion.

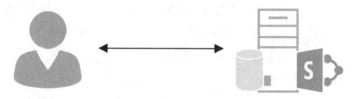

Figure 2-2. *Single server farm*

Single server farms have the disadvantage of high memory requirements in order to operate effectively, especially when SQL Server is installed on the same server. Careful memory management with SQL Server is key to acceptable performance.

Single server farms are suited to specialized roles, such as the Microsoft Identity Manager Portal, or Team Foundation Server integration, but are otherwise not recommended for production purposes due to potential significant load and lack of high availability.

If a single server farm is under consideration, it may be worth looking into leveraging SharePoint Online for the lower cost of ownership.

Three-Tier Farm

The three-tier farm is one of the most common farm types. These farms consist of a single Web Front End, single Application Server, and single SQL Server. Web Front End is simply defined as the SharePoint Server that is handling end-user traffic, while the Application Server is defined as a SharePoint Server that is not handling end-user facing traffic while typically handling most SharePoint services, such as Business Data Connectivity Services, Managed Metadata Service, and so on.

When installing SharePoint Server with the three-tier farm architecture, shown in Figure 2-3, you can choose to either use the Distribute Cache + Web Front End MinRole for the front end while the middle tier uses Application + Search or provision using the Custom role. The Custom option is the same approach to deploying a SharePoint farm as one would have taken with SharePoint Server 2010 and 2013.

For the three-tier farm architecture, it is recommended to run Distributed Cache, Microsoft SharePoint Foundation Web Application, Search Query Processing role, and Search Index Partition role on the Web Front End. This provides the best end-user experience for these services, although you may want to consider running additional services on the Web Front End for improved performance. See the Streamlined Architecture section later in this chapter.

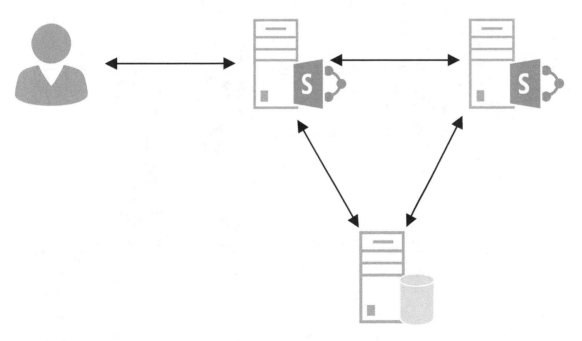

Figure 2-3. *Three-tier farm*

The Web Front End Server is where all other services will run, such as Business Data Connectivity Services, Managed Metadata Service, User Profile Service, and any other service which will not run on the Web Front End but is required within the farm. This may lower the memory requirements for the Application Server compared to the Web Front End.

Traditional Highly Available Farms

Other topologies provide basic high availability, as Figure 2-4 shows. These topologies can suffer the loss of one or more SharePoint Servers and SQL Servers while still serving users.

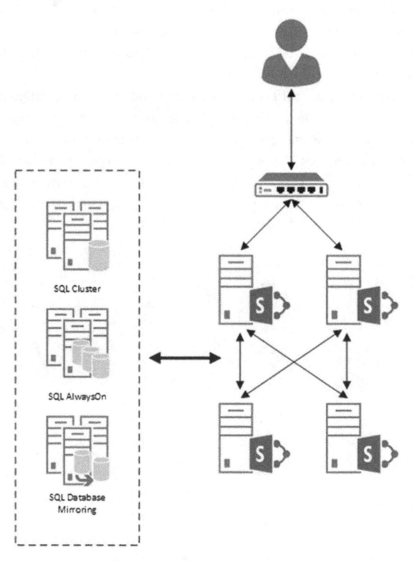

Figure 2-4. *Highly available Traditional Topology Farm*

An example of this would be two Web Front Ends, two Application Servers, and two SQL Servers using a form of high availability, such as SQL Clustering, Database Mirroring, or AlwaysOn Availability Groups with Failover Clustering.

The Web Front Ends would be behind a load balancer, such as an F5 Big-IP, HAProxy, or KEMP LoadMaster. The load balancers would detect a server failure and automatically route traffic to the available Web Front End. For Service Applications, SharePoint operates in a round-robin load balancing when two or more SharePoint Servers in the farm are running any one particular Service Instance. For example, if two SharePoint Servers are running the Managed Metadata Service and one SharePoint Server fails, the SharePoint Topology Service will automatically remove the failed SharePoint Server from the round-robin load balancing and the Managed Metadata Service would continue to be available within the farm. More information on the Topology Service and round-robin load balancing can be found later in this chapter.

MinRole Farms

Microsoft introduced the new concept of "MinRole" to SharePoint Server 2016. This is the preferred method of deployment for SharePoint farms as they automatically place services on the correct servers based on their role. With SharePoint Server 2019, the roles have not changed from SharePoint Server 2016 with Feature Pack 1. Dedicated MinRole is a set of SharePoint Server roles that are defined by the services required for that role. Roles are enforced through SharePoint code. For example, if a SharePoint Server is deployed with the "Distributed Cache" MinRole, SharePoint will automatically provision the Distributed Cache service. If other services are started that do not comply with the MinRole selected, such as the Managed Metadata Service, the SharePoint Server with the Distributed Cache MinRole will be considered out of compliance and notated as such in Central Administration.

MinRole consists of the following new installation roles:

- Distributed Cache: This role runs Distributed Cache, but does not handle end-user traffic directly.

- Web Front End: This role not only handles end-user traffic, but runs many services that require low latency for end users, such as the Managed Metadata Service, or User Profile Service.

- Application: The Application role runs what are considered non-latency-sensitive services, such as workflow or PowerPoint Conversion Service.

- Search: Search runs the specific Search roles such as the Admin or Content Processing roles.

Dedicated MinRole farms can be deployed with a minimum of four SharePoint Servers in the farm, although this provides no high availability for SharePoint. Dedicated MinRole farms comply with the Streamlined Topology, discussed later in this chapter.

Microsoft also introduced the concept of a shared MinRole farm. This consolidated services, allowing for the deployment of a minimum of 4 SharePoint servers in a highly available farm. The available roles consist of the following:

- Distributed Cache with Web Front End: This role runs Distributed Cache and services user requests. This role also runs various service instances which benefit end user performance, such as the Managed Metadata service instance.

- Application with Search: The Application role runs what are considered non-latency-sensitive services, such as workflow or PowerPoint Conversion Service. This role also runs all of the Search roles.

Use of the shared MinRole can significantly reduce cost while maintaining high availability.

Zero Downtime Farms

Zero Downtime patching requires the SharePoint farm be highly available for all services, as shown in Figure 2-5. This means there must be a minimum of eight SharePoint Servers within the farm when using dedicated MinRole and four servers when using shared MinRole.

A Zero Downtime MinRole farm would be supported by one or more highly available SQL Server configurations, such as one or more SQL Clusters or AlwaysOn Availability Groups with Failover Clustering.

The SharePoint Server 2016 Feature Pack 1 introduced the concept of shared MinRoles. These consist of the following new installation roles:

- Distributed Cache and Web Front End

- Application and Search

The enhanced MinRole options allow for smaller farms than the original MinRole options. This book will be using the shared MinRoles with a four SharePoint server deployment.

As with previous MinRoles, it is possible to convert a server from the dedicated to shared MinRoles or vice versa.

Zero Downtime patching can also be used with more traditional farms, such as a three-tier highly available farm configuration. Each server would use the Custom role with all services remaining highly available within the farm.

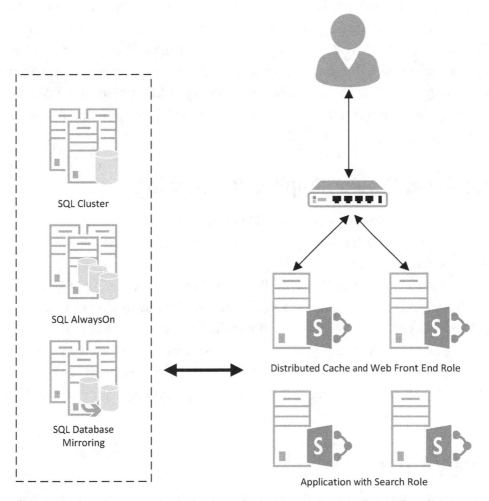

Figure 2-5. *Highly available MinRole with Zero Downtime Patching Support*

Traditional Service Application Topology

While the Traditional Topology is a topology that has been used for many years and was often deployed with SharePoint Server 2013, it is now recommended to use a MinRole deployment though it is still possible to achieve this type of topology using the Custom MinRole option.

This model follows installation of the Microsoft SharePoint Foundation Web Service on the Web Front End server. The topology may also add Distributed Cache to the Web Front End, as well.

The Application server runs all other services in this topology. This places a higher load on the Application server in comparison to other topologies, while potentially reducing the load of the Web Front End. Increased network traffic may result from this topology due to services communicating from the Application server to the Web Front End; for example, a call to a Managed Metadata field would travel from the Web Front End to the Application server, then back through the Web Front End before reaching the user's browser.

Streamlined Service Application Topology

The Streamlined Topology was born out of Microsoft's experience with SharePoint Online and is the preferred topology. This topology was introduced about a year into the SharePoint Server 2013 lifecycle.

Microsoft tiered services in the Streamlined Topology based on latency for end users. Services that required lower latency, that is, faster access for end-user requests, were placed on the Web Front Ends. Services that were not end user interactive, such as the workflow service, were placed on back-end Application servers (also called "batch" servers).

In certain conditions, this farm topology provided better performance and responsiveness for end users over the Traditional farm topology. Farms using MinRole leverage this topology.

Topology Service

The Round Robin Service Load Balancer, the core function of the Topology Service, is responsible for adding and removing available Service Application endpoints, along with endpoint availability.

The Round Robin Service Load Balancer will enumerate all Service Application Proxies in the farm and determine what endpoints are available. Each Service Instance on a SharePoint server is exposed via an endpoint.

In SharePoint Server 2013 with the Streamlined Topology configuration (and in certain scenarios, the Traditional Topology), because the Round Robin Service Load Balancer would add endpoints to the internal round-robin load balancer, it was possible that even if a particular endpoint was available on the SharePoint Server the end user was connected to, their request may be routed to another SharePoint Server in the farm. This is less than ideal, as the idea behind the Streamlined Topology was to keep end-user requests on the local SharePoint Server.

With SharePoint Server 2016, Microsoft introduced the ability for the Round Robin Service Load Balancer to keep the end-user requests on the same server when MinRole is enabled. This provides the best latency and performance for end-user requests and reduces network load between SharePoint farm member servers. This improvement continues with SharePoint Server 2019.

Hybrid Considerations

Starting with SharePoint Server 2013 with the August 2015 Cumulative Update, Hybrid Search was offered, where the Search Index is unified with a SharePoint Online Tenant Search Index. If Hybrid Search is used, the On-Premises farm does not utilize a local Search Index. This may factor into plans to reduce the number of Search Servers within the farm.

Utilizing OneDrive for Business in hybrid configuration (redirection) can also help reduce the necessary On-Premises hardware required for SharePoint and SQL Server by offloading all MySite-related activity and storage to SharePoint Online. Chapter 14 will go into further detail on Hybrid.

SQL Server Architecture

SQL Server plays a very important role for SharePoint Server 2019 performance, availability, and disaster recovery. Performance measurements of SQL Server prior to deployment are crucial in to gauge limitations of the system and determine when a scale up or scale out of SQL Server is required.

Performance

The first step is to measure the potential performance of SQL Server is the disk I/O subsystem. Microsoft has created a tool, Diskspd, to measure disk performance. This tool will provide valuable data in terms of the number of IOPS the disk subsystem is capable of supporting. Note that testing *write* performance (the DiskSpd -w switch) will cause data loss. Only test write performance on a disk with no data.

Note   Diskspd is available from Microsoft at `https://aka.ms/diskspd`.

In addition to disk, the amount of memory available to SQL Server plays a critical role in SharePoint Server performance. The more memory is available to SQL Server, the larger datasets the memory can hold and the longer SQL Server can keep those datasets in memory.

Lastly, CPU performance is crucial. Modern physical SQL Servers will typically have two sockets with four or more cores per CPU. However, in a virtual environment, be sure to allocate two or more vCPUs, depending on performance requirements. A single vCPU may lead to very poor performance in all but the very smallest of environments.

Setting an appropriate Maximum Memory value for SQL Server is important to reserve memory for the operating system and any ancillary programs running on the SQL Server. This will help prevent paging of either SQL Server memory or other process memory to disk, which may reduce overall SQL Server performance.

High Availability and Disaster Recovery

SharePoint Server supports SQL Server High Availability including SQL Server Clustering, Database Mirroring, and SQL Server AlwaysOn Availability Groups. As SQL Server Database Mirroring is deprecated, this book will focus on leveraging AlwaysOn with SharePoint Server databases. We will be reviewing AlwaysOn Availability Groups in Synchronous mode with automatic failover for a local site. SQL Server Clustering is also a valid option; however, SQL Server Clustering does not provide high availability for storage. Conversely, AlwaysOn doubles the storage requirements.

As with disk performance testing for SQL Server, we need to perform load testing for SharePoint, covered in the next section.

Load Generation/Load Testing

While having an architecture outlined is important, so is testing it! Microsoft has two primary tools for testing, Visual Studio 2013 Ultimate, Visual Studio 2015/2017 Enterprise, and the SharePoint Load Generation Tool. These Visual Studio editions include recording specific actions taken in a browser, with the ability to run multiple controllers concurrently to test many users accessing a farm at once.

The SharePoint Load Generation Tool is an add-in for Visual Studio 2013 Ultimate and Visual Studio 2015 Enterprise that performs the following tests:

- CSOM List Read and Write load test

- MySite Read and Write load test

- MySiteHost Read and Write load test

The SharePoint Load Generation Tool also has additional options for authentication and number of servers to test, and automatically records pertinent performance counters for review post-test.

Note   The SharePoint Load Generation Tool is available on the Visual Studio Gallery at `https://marketplace.visualstudio.com/items?itemName=Sh arePointTemplates.SharePointLoadGenerationTool`.

We will examine the SharePoint Server, SQL Server, Workflow Manager, and Office Online Server architecture used in this book. This farm architecture demonstrates the High Availability MinRole architecture.

Architecture in Action

The farm architecture chosen for this book, depicted in Figure 2-6, we will be using the minimum viable farm for a highly available MinRole configuration and "Zero Downtime" patching.

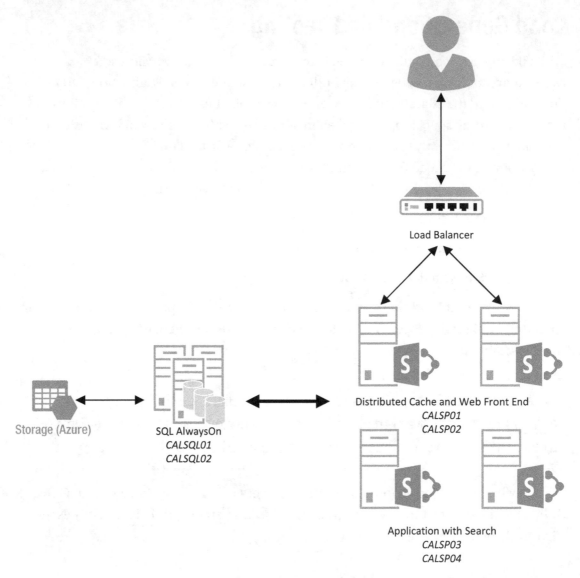

Figure 2-6. *Farm architecture chosen for this book*

The SQL Servers will be part of an Availability Group using Failover Clustering to provide an AlwaysOn Availability Group for the SharePoint Server databases. In addition, the Failover Cluster quorum will be an Azure Cloud Witness to provide automatic failover. The SharePoint servers fulfilling the Front-end role will reside behind a load balancer. This load balancer offers detection of failed hosts to provide the highest availability possible to clients. In addition to the SharePoint farm, a SharePoint Workflow Manager farm will also be provisioned with the following architecture, shown in Figure 2-7.

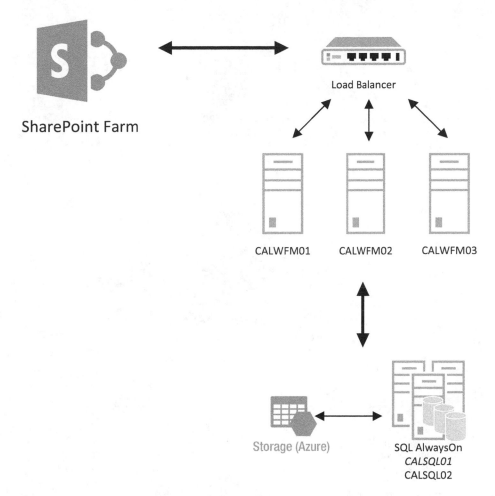

Figure 2-7. *SharePoint Workflow Manager farm*

SharePoint Workflow Manager will be covered in further detail in Chapter 10; however, SharePoint Workflow Manager can be set up with one, three, or five servers. No other valid configuration is available. In addition, Workflow Manager supports SQL Server 2016 and SQL Server 2017, hence the addition of two SQL Servers configured with an AlwaysOn Availability Group.

Lastly, the environment shown in Figure 2-8 consists of an Active Directory Rights Management Services server, Exchange Server 2016, Microsoft Identity Manager 2016, and Office Online Server in a three server highly available environment.

Active Directory
Domain Controller
CADC01

Exchange Server 2016
CAEXCH02

Office Online Server
CAOOS01
CAOOS02

SharePoint Farm

Active Directory Rights
Management Services
CARMS02

Microsoft Identity
Manager 2016
CAMIM01

Figure 2-8. *The CobaltAtom.com environment*

Next Steps

We covered some of the basic decisions required to determine what farm topology is right for your configuration and touched on a variety of viable farm topologies, along with reviewing the MinRole and Zero Downtime patching features.

In the next chapter, we will go through an end-to-end installation of SQL Server 2017 on Windows Server 2016 with a Core installation, as well as SharePoint Server 2019 in a highly available MinRole farm. The chapter will also cover security fundamentals for Active Directory, SQL Server, and SharePoint Server.

CHAPTER 3

Installing SharePoint Server 2019

In this chapter, we will learn the necessary steps for installation and configuration, from Active Directory, SQL Server, and finally to SharePoint Server 2019. We will also review basic Service Application, Web Application, and Site Collection deployment and configuration. This chapter will provide you with the knowledge to walk through each component using PowerShell as the primary deployment and configuration scripting language. Once you are finished with this chapter, you will have a fully functional, highly available SharePoint Server 2019 MinRole farm. In this chapter, some of the configurations outlined are Microsoft requirements while others are recommendations from Microsoft and the author.

Active Directory Configuration

Your Active Directory domain should consist of two or more Domain Controllers in the physical location where the SharePoint farm and SQL Servers will reside. This will provide the fastest authentication and DNS lookup performance to SharePoint. The Domain Controllers should also have a Server Authentication certificate (e.g., SSL) in order to encrypt LDAP traffic between SharePoint and the Domain Controller. These certificates are typically deployed via Active Directory Certificate Services, but you can also use a public Certificate Authority as well.

Securing Active Directory will primarily be done via Group Policy. SharePoint is provisioned in the domain LAB, which has a fully qualified domain name (FQDN) of lab.cobaltatom.com. All domain computers, with the exception of Domain Controllers, fall under the Default Domain Policy.

Review Tables 3-1 and 3-2 for the applied Group Policy Security options.

© Vlad Catrinescu and Trevor Seward 2019
V. Catrinescu and T. Seward, *Deploying SharePoint 2019*, https://doi.org/10.1007/978-1-4842-4526-2_3

Table 3-1. *Default Domain Policy Security Options*

Security Policy Name	Policy Setting
Network security: Configure encryption types allowed for Kerberos	AES128_HMAC_SHA1, AES256_HMAC_SHA1, Future encryption types
Microsoft network client: Send unencrypted password to third-party SMB servers	Disabled
Network access: Allow anonymous SID/Name translation	Disabled
Network access: Let Everyone permissions apply to anonymous users	Disabled
Domain member: Digitally encrypt or sign secure channel data (always)	Enabled
Domain member: Require strong (Windows 2000 or later) session key	Enabled
Microsoft network client: Digitally sign communications (always)	Enabled
Microsoft network server: Digitally sign communications (always)	Enabled
Network access: Do not allow anonymous enumeration of SAM accounts	Enabled
Network access: Do not allow anonymous enumeration of SAM accounts and shares	Enabled
Network security: Do not store LAN Manager hash value on next password change	Enabled
Network security: Minimum session security for NTLM SSP based (include secure RPC) clients	Require NTLMv2 session security; Require 128-bit encryption
Network security: Minimum session security for NTLM SSP based (include secure RPC) servers	Require NTLMv2 session security; Require 128-bit encryption
Domain controller: LDAP server signing requirements	Require signing
Network security: LDAP client signing requirements	Require signing
Network security: LAN Manager authentication level	Send NTLMv2 response only; Refuse LM & NTLM

Table 3-2. *Default Domain Controller Policy Security Options*

Security Policy Name	Policy Setting
Network security: Configure encryption types allowed for Kerberos	AES128_HMAC_SHA1, AES256_HMAC_SHA1, Future encryption types
Microsoft network client: Send unencrypted password to third-party SMB servers	Disabled
Network access: Allow anonymous SID/Name translation	Disabled
Network access: Let Everyone permissions apply to anonymous users	Disabled
Domain member: Digitally encrypt or sign secure channel data (always)	Enabled
Domain member: Require strong (Windows 200 or later) session key	Enabled
Microsoft network client: Digitally sign communications (always)	Enabled
Microsoft network server: Digitally sign communications (always)	Enabled
Network access: Do not allow anonymous enumeration of SAM accounts	Enabled
Network access: Do not allow anonymous enumeration of SAM accounts and shares	Enabled
Network security: Do not store LAN Manager hash value on next password change	Enabled
Network security: Minimum session security for NTLM SSP based (include secure RPC) clients	Require NTLMv2 session security; Require 128-bit encryption
Network security: Minimum session security for NTLM SSP based (include secure RPC) servers	Require NTLMv2 session security; Require 128-bit encryption
Domain controller: LDAP server signing requirements	Require signing
Network security: LDAP client signing requirements	Require signing
Network security: LAN Manager authentication level	Send NTLMv2 response only; Refuse LM & NTLM

And finally, SharePoint Server is assigned a Group Policy to disable Windows Updates. Alternatively, you may choose to deploy an enterprise patch management solution, such as Windows Software Update Services and disable SharePoint-related updates from being deployed to SharePoint servers, but allow all other forms of updates.

All computers in the domain have the Windows Firewall with Advanced Security enabled. SharePoint will make exceptions in the firewall automatically during installation, but manual exceptions can be made. For SQL Server, an exception for TCP/1433 and TCP/5022 must be made for the SQL default instance and AlwaysOn Availability Group. If using a SQL named instance, UDP/1434 must also be opened. Lastly, if the Dedicated Admin Connection is desired, open TCP/1434.

At this point we have set up basic security for Active Directory and key policies for SharePoint. In the next section, we will cover service accounts leveraged by SQL Server and SharePoint.

Service Accounts

SharePoint and SQL Server require a few service accounts in order to function. There are a variety of strategies available for the number of service accounts to use and for what function. This book will use a minimal number of service accounts to maintain the best possible performance by creating the least number of Application Pools in SharePoint. By using a single service account for Web Applications, as an example, we can deploy a single Application Pool for all Web Applications. This provides lower startup time for secondary Web Applications after the first Web Application has started up and also allows each Web Application to "share" memory. With .NET, there is very little sharable memory between processes, even if they contain the same code. As SharePoint processes can consume a significant amount of memory this provides a very large memory savings.

SQL Server will use a Group Managed Service Account (gMSA) which is a special account type in Active Directory. This functionality requires Windows Server 2012 Domain Controllers or higher. In addition, the KDS Root Key must be created prior to creating a gMSA. If a KDS Root Key has not been created, run the following PowerShell.

```
Add-KdsRootKey -EffectiveTime ((Get-Date).AddHours(-10))
```

To create the account, you will need the Active Directory Module for PowerShell installed which can be found as part of the Active Directory remote administration tools as well as the necessary rights in Active Directory to provision accounts. In this scenario, we will be creating an account named "s-sql" and granting access to the account from the associated SQL Servers. The last part of the script also adds the Service Principal Names to the account.

```
New-ADServiceAccount -Name s-sql -DNSHostName s-sql.lab.cobaltatom.
com -Enabled:$true -PrincipalsAllowedToRetrieveManagedPassword
'calsql01$','calsql02$' -ServicePrincipalNames 'MSSQLSvc/
calsql01:1433','MSSQLSvc/calsql01.lab.cobaltatom.com:1433','MSSQLSvc/
calsql02:1433','MSSQLSvc/calsql02.lab.cobaltatom.com:1433','MSSQLSvc/
calspag.lab.cobaltatom.com:1433'
```

The password for this account automatically recycles every 30 days. In addition, this account cannot be used to login interactively on any server and the account credentials are only exposed to the servers specified when creating or updating the gMSA. The gMSA can only be created with the Active Directory PowerShell Module like the above PowerShell command. Note that the SQL Server names must already be defined. In addition, this command shows how to set the Service Principle Names, negating the need to use setspn.exe.

The Service Accounts in Table 3-3 have been provisioned in Active Directory to run SQL Server and SharePoint and will be used throughout this guide.

Table 3-3. *SQL Server and SharePoint Service Accounts*

Account Name	Account Purpose
LAB\s-sql	Group Managed Service Account for SQL Server
LAB\s-farm	SharePoint Farm Account
LAB\s-svc	SharePoint Service Application Pool Account
LAB\s-web	SharePoint Web Application Pool Account
LAB\s-c2wts	Claims to Windows Token Service Account
LAB\s-spsync	User Profile Import Account
LAB\s-su	Portal Super User Account
LAB\s-sr	Portal Super Reader Account
LAB\s-crawl	Search Crawl Account

With the service accounts provisioned in Active Directory, we will look at the Power Management options that can improve performance for both SQL Server and SharePoint Server 2019.

Service Account Security

Service accounts should not be able to log into the server either locally or remotely. To set this, on each SharePoint server, run secpol.msc. Navigate to Local Policies, then User Rights Assignment. Under the policies "Deny log on locally" and "Deny log on through Remote Desktop Services," add all of the service accounts allocated for SharePoint.

BIOS and Windows Power Management

There are a few changes that can be performed on any server prior to installing SQL Server and SharePoint to increase the performance.

Taking a look at the BIOS/UEFI options for the hardware running SharePoint (whether SharePoint is installed on the physical hardware or if deploying a virtualization host that will run a SharePoint virtual machine), disabling Intel C-States (SpeedStep)/AMD Cool'n'Quiet will prevent the CPU from scaling back when not under load. In addition, disable C1E support ("enhanced halt state"), which is available on both Intel and AMD CPUs. Because SharePoint can spike in CPU load, this may cause a seesaw effect when this CPU technology is enabled. An OEM specific option, such as the HP Power Regulator Mode, may also help improve performance – for HP, setting the Power Regulator Mode to Static High Performance, and for Dell, the Power Management Mode to Maximum Performance. Lastly, disabling QPI power management will prevent throttling of lanes between multiple CPUs and physical memory.

BIOS/UEFI generally does not include an option to disable what is known as "Core Parking." Core Parking is when a specific core within a CPU is halted as it has no work. Core Parking is managed by the Operating System, and on supported Operating Systems for SharePoint Server 2019 and SQL Server, it can be disabled by setting the "Minimum Processor State" to 100%, or setting the Power Profile to "High Performance." Power Management profiles can be set via Group Policy.

With the BIOS/UEFI adjusted for best performance, we will take a brief look at antivirus configuration for SQL Server and SharePoint Server 2019. Don't forget to adjust the Power Management settings for SQL Server and SharePoint once Windows is installed!

Host-Based Antivirus

Many companies use or require host-based antivirus. SharePoint Server requires numerous antivirus exclusions in order to prevent file locking and performance problems. For example, host-based antivirus scanning the Timer Service Configuration Cache may cause the Timer Service to pause running jobs due to unexpected high activity within the folder. Microsoft outlines the required exclusions at `https://support.microsoft.com/help/952167`.

For SQL Server, exclude the SQL Server processes, MDF, LDF, and NDF file types, along with the locations where SQL Server writes logs or holds data.

Many enterprise antivirus vendors offer centralized management and configuration. If available, make generalized rules for both SQL Server and SharePoint Server 2019 to prevent the need to configure these options locally.

Next, let's start the installation and configuration process for our highly available MinRole farm, starting with the Windows configuration for SQL Server!

Windows Server Configuration for SQL Server

While SQL Server is often configured by a Database Administrator, at times the SharePoint Administrator may be responsible for provisioning the complete environment. Here we will cover the steps necessary to provision the SQL Server environment. Each section will be split between SQL Servers running on Windows Core and Windows with the Desktop Experience. We strongly recommend using Windows Core but recognize IT organizations may not have adopted Windows Core.

This farm will be utilizing SQL Server 2017 running on Windows Server 2016 using a Core installation (no GUI); however, this guide will also provide you with installation steps for a Windows Server 2016 with Desktop Experience. Windows Core installations offer increased security through a reduced attack surface, lower management overhead, and a significantly smaller footprint with up to a 75% disk space savings. While Windows Core installations are supported for SQL Server, it is not possible to use Windows Core installations with SharePoint Server.

SQL Server will be configured to use AlwaysOn Availability Groups and automatic failover via an Azure witness.

Each SQL Server has the following volumes:

- C: Operating System and SQL shared components

- M: Database data files (MDB)

- L: Database log files (LDF)

- T: TempDb data and log files

Volumes M:, L:, and T: have been formatted using ReFS (NTFS is also supported) with an allocation (cluster) size of 64Kb. SQL Server extent reads are often eight pages in size, each page being 8Kb, thus a single extent read is 64Kb in size. Matching the cluster size to the extent data read size offers the best performance.

Each SQL Server has two network adapters. The primary is for client access and data synchronization over the Availability Group. The second is for a heartbeat between the SQL Servers.

As the SQL Servers are using a Core installation, PowerShell will be the primary configuration method for each SQL Server.

Network Adapter Configuration

The steps involve getting the appropriate network adapter in PowerShell, assigning an IP address, subnet, and gateway; disable DHCP, and finally setting the DNS client addresses. The client-facing adapter will be renamed to "Intranet" while the heartbeat adapter between SQL Servers will be named "Heartbeat." The Heartbeat network adapter will be allocated a private subnet not used by other general devices on the network.

Primary "Intranet" adapter:

- CALSQL01 IP Address: 172.16.5.105

- CALSQL02 IP Address: 172.16.5.106

Use Get-NetAdapter to display all available network adapters on the system. These steps should be repeated for the secondary SQL Server.

```
$adapter = Get-NetAdapter "Ethernet 2"
$adapter | New-NetIPAddress -AddressFamily IPv4 -IPAddress 172.16.5.105
-PrefixLength 16 -Type Unicast -DefaultGateway 172.16.0.1
```

```
Set-DnsClientServerAddress -InterfaceAlias $adapter.Name -ServerAddresses
172.16.5.1
Rename-NetAdapter -Name "Ethernet 2" -NewName "Intranet"
```

Secondary "Heartbeat" adapter:

- CALSQL01 IP Address: 192.168.5.1

- CALSQL02 IP Address: 192.168.5.2

```
$adapter = Get-NetAdapter "Ethernet"
$adapter | New-NetIPAddress -AddressFamily IPv4 -IPAddress 192.168.5.1
-PrefixLength 24 -Type Unicast
Rename-NetAdapter -Name "Ethernet" -NewName "Heartbeat"
```

```
These settings may also be set via the Network and Sharing center.
```

Disable the DNS registration on the Heartbeat adapter for both servers using the following:

```
Set-DnsClient -RegisterThisConnectionAddresss $false -InterfaceAlias
"Heartbeat"
```

This prevents the Heartbeat network from performing dynamic DNS registration, which may cause a connectivity loss as AlwaysOn relies on DNS A records. To set this via the GUI, in Network and Sharing center, find the heartbeat adapter. in the "Internet Protocol Version 4 (TCP/IPv4)" properties, click on Advanced, then DNS, and deselect "Register this connection's address in DNS".

Storage Configuration

The next step will be to provision the storage for each SQL Server. For the disks "M:", "L:", and "T:", the disks will be using ReFS an allocation size of 64Kb.

Use Get-Disk to display all of the disks on the system.

```
Initialize-Disk 1 -PartitionStyle GPT
New-Partition 1 -UseMaximumSize -DriveLetter M
Format-Volume -DriveLetter M -FileSystem ReFS -AllocationUnitSize 65536
```

Repeat this process for each disk, replacing the disk number ("1" in the preceding) with the next uninitialized disk and the drive letter parameters.

This can also be accomplished in Server Manager under File and Storage Services, then selecting Volumes and configuring the Disks. From there, use the New Volume wizard using the preceding settings to provision a new drive.

Identity Configuration

The next step in the process is to rename the server, restart for the name change to take effect, finally join the server to Active Directory and reboot again.

```
Rename-Computer -NewName <value> -Restart
$cred = Get-Credential #User credentials to join the computer to the domain
Add-Computer -Credential $cred -DomainName LAB -Restart
```

```
This can also be accomplished via the System Control Panel.
```

Failover Cluster Configuration

The final step is to install the Failover Cluster service and management tools. Using PowerShell, on each server, run the following:

```
Install-WindowsFeature Failover-Clustering,NET-Framework-45-Core
-IncludeManagementTools
```

In order to create the Failover Cluster via PowerShell, the "-IncludeManagementTools" parameter is required.

Prior to creating the cluster, first test the cluster from one of the SQL Servers by running the Test-Cluster cmdlet and resolving any issues that may appear. As this cluster is not sharing storage, like a traditional failover cluster would, any storage-related warnings do not apply.

```
Test-Cluster -Node CALSQL01,CALSQL02
```

Create the cluster. The cluster name in this example is "CALSQLClus" with an IP address of 172.16.5.200, ignoring the heartbeat network and ignoring the local storage.

```
New-Cluster -Name "CALSQLClus" -Node CALSQL01,CALSQL02 -StaticAddress
172.16.5.200 -IgnoreNetwork 192.168.5.0/24 -NoStorage
```

Once the cluster has been created, it is a good idea to rename the cluster network adapters for clarity when administering the cluster. First get a list of the cluster networks as well as what subnet each cluster network is on. Based on the Address value of each cluster network adapter, rename the adapter appropriately.

```
Get-ClusterNetwork | fl *
$clusadapt = Get-ClusterNetwork -Cluster CALSQLClus -Name "Cluster Network
1"
$clusadapt.Name = "Intranet"
$clusadapt = Get-ClusterNetwork -Cluster CALSQLClus -Name "Cluster Network
2"
$clusadapt.Name = "Heartbeat"
```

To accomplish this via the GUI, run Failover Cluster Manager on one of the SQL servers. Right-click Failover Cluster Manager and select Create cluster. Under the Select Servers, add the appropriate SQL servers as shown in Figure 3-1.

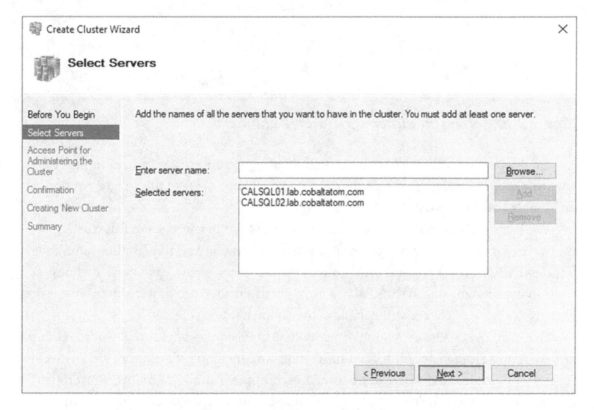

Figure 3-1. *Assigning new servers to a Failover Cluster*

The next step is to set the Cluster Name and IP Address. Using the same parameters as the preceding PowerShell, set the values as shown in Figure 3-2.

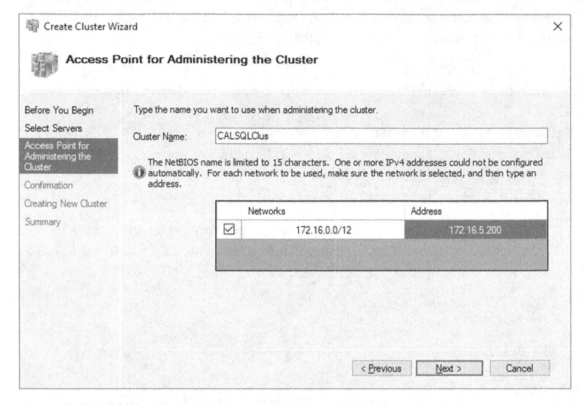

Figure 3-2. *Setting the cluster name and IP address*

On the next step, *uncheck* "Add all eligible storage to the cluster" and complete the wizard. Once completed, you will see an expected warning due to the wizard not finding an eligible disk witness.

The last step is to configure the Failover Cluster Quorum witness. For this cluster, we've chosen to use an Azure cloud witness to lower costs and administration complexity, although a SQL Server or standard Windows file share may be used as a cluster witness as well. To use an Azure cloud witness, you must provision an Azure subscription if one is not already available. We will assume that a subscription has been created.

To create the necessary resources, we will be provisioning an Azure Resource Group and an Azure Storage Account. To demonstrate both methods of doing so, first install the AzureRM module. This can be done from any computer running Windows PowerShell 5 (Windows 10 and Windows Server 2016 contain PowerShell 5 out of the box). The following commands install the AzureRM module, login to the Azure tenant, create a new Resource Group named "SqlClusterWitness", and finally an Azure Storage Account named "calsql" in US West 2 using standard local redundant storage.

```
Install-Module -Name AzureRM
Login-AzureRmAccount
$rg = New-AzureRmResourceGroup -Name 'SqlClusterWitness' -Location 'westus2'
$sa = New-AzureRmStorageAccount -ResourceGroupName $rg.ResourceGroupName
-Name 'calspag' -Location 'westus2' -SkuName Standard_LRS
```

To create the same resource via https://portal.azure.com, log into your Azure
subscription. Click Create a resource and search for Storage Account. This will bring up
the result for "Storage account – blob, file, table, queue." Enter the name of the Storage
Account, Location, set the Replication to Locally-redundant storage (LRS), and create a
new Resource group as shown in Figure 3-3.

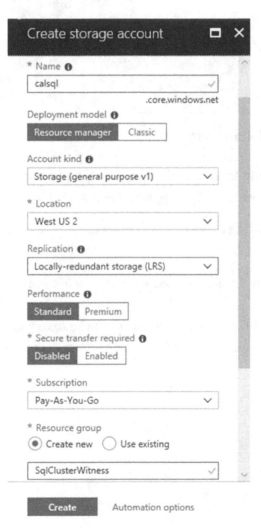

Figure 3-3. *Creating a new Storage Account for an Azure cloud witness*

> **Note**   Replication of the storage account *must* be set to Locally-redundant storage (LRS) for an Azure cloud witness.

Once the Azure witness has been created, it should look similar to Figure 3-4.

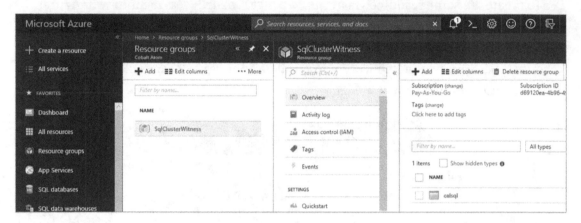

Figure 3-4. *A completed Azure witness*

Save the Storage Account name, in this case, "calsql", and retrieve the primary key. The key can be found via PowerShell using the following cmdlet.

```
Get-AzureRmStorageAccountKey -ResourceGroupName 'SqlClusterWitness' -Name 'calsql'
```

This will provide the output of two keys. We will be selecting the value for "key1". Copy the Value for key1.

The key can also be found via the Azure Portal. Navigate to your Resource Group and click the Storage Account ("calsql"). Under Access keys, copy the Key value for key1, as shown in Figure 3-5.

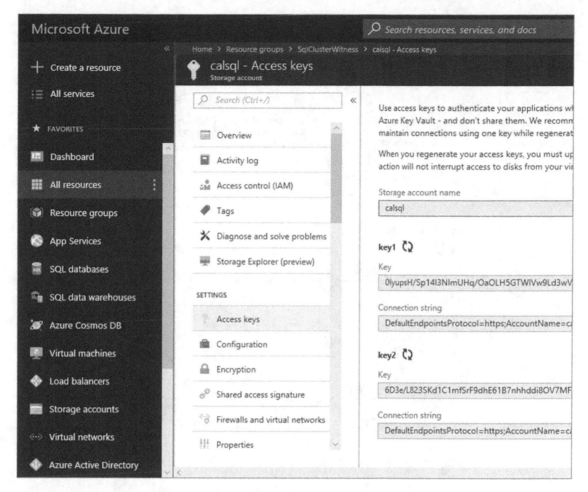

Figure 3-5. *Finding the Access keys for the Storage Account*

On the SQL Server, run the following PowerShell to set the Cluster Quorum Witness to a Cloud Witness.

```
Set-ClusterQuorum -CloudWitness -AccountName 'calsql' -AccessKey 'OlyupsH/
Sp14l3NImUHq/OaOLH5GTWlVw9Ld3wVMtLr5m9Om+kEEHvVmYcs4J39zpeM1U7a67HceyQf3bs3
uVA==' -Endpoint core.windows.net
```

This can also be accomplished via the Failover Cluster Manager. Right-click the SQL Cluster. Under More Actions, select Configure Cluster Quorum Settings. In the Configure Cluster Quorum Wizard, choose the option "Select the quorum witness," then select "Configure a cloud witness." Enter the storage account name, the value of key1 for the storage account key, as shown in Figure 3-6. The service endpoint at the time of the writing of this book does not need to be changed from the default value of core.windows.net.

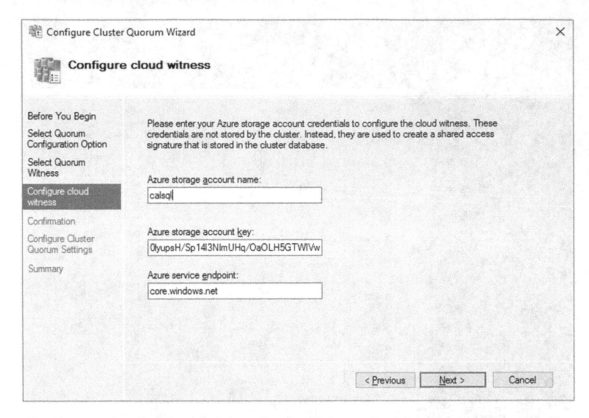

Figure 3-6. *Configuring an Azure cloud witness as the quorum*

The cluster configuration is completed and ready for the installation of SQL Server 2017.

SQL Server 2017 Installation

This section covers installing SQL Server 2017 on Windows server 2016 via command line as well as via the GUI.

For SQL Server, we will use the Enterprise edition. The SQL Server service account will a Group Managed Service Account, LAB\s-sql$.

SQL Server Installation

The SQL Server installation itself is configured via an .ini file, while the installation is processed through a batch file. The .ini file parameters must be adjusted accordingly for the specific environment.

```
[OPTIONS]
ACTION="Install"
FEATURES=SQLENGINE,REPLICATION
INSTANCENAME="MSSQLSERVER"
SQLSVCACCOUNT=LAB\s-sql$
SQLSYSADMINACCOUNTS="LAB\Domain Admins"
IAcceptSQLServerLicenseTerms="True"
QUIET="True"
UpdateEnabled="False"
ERRORREPORTING="False"
INSTANCEDIR="M:\Program Files\Microsoft SQL Server"
AGTSVCACCOUNT=LAB\s-sql$
AGTSVCSTARTUPTYPE=Automatic
SQLSVCINSTANTFILEINIT=True
SQLSVCSTARTUPTYPE=Automatic
SQLTEMPDBDIR=T:\Data
SQLTEMPDBLOGDIR=T:\Data
SQLUSERDBDIR=M:\Data
SQLUSERDBLOGDIR=L:\Logs
TCPENABLED=1
SQLCOLLATION=Latin1_General_CI_AS_KS_WS
```

Once the Configuration.ini file is created, create a SQLInstall.bat file in the same directory, specifying the environment specific installation parameters.

```
@ECHO OFF
set CDRoot=D:
@ECHO ON
%CDRoot%\Setup.exe /ConfigurationFile= Configuration.ini /Q
```

Execute SQLInstall.bat on both SQL Servers to install SQL in an unattended mode.

To accomplish this via the SQL Server Setup Wizard, follow the following prompts. Run setup.exe and in the SQL Server Installation Center, under Installation, select "New SQL Server stand-alone installation or add features to an existing installation." Completing the initial parts of the wizard, under Feature Selection, select the following feature:

```
Database Engine Services
```

Set the Instance root directory to "M:\Program Files\Microsoft SQL Server\" and leave the shared feature directories at the default paths. On the Instance Configuration, leave the settings at the defaults of "Default instance" and an Instance ID of "MSSQLSERVER". Use the Group Managed Service Account (LAB\s-sql$) for the configurable services and select the Grant Perform Volume Maintenance Task option, as shown in Figure 3-7. In the Collation tab, click Customize. Select "Windows collation designator and sort order." Select "Latin1_General" from the drop down and then check Accent-sensitive, Kana-sensitive, and finally Width-sensitive. This will set the SQL Server collation to Latin1_General_CI_AS_KS_WS.

Note   Latin1_General_CI_AS_KS_WS is not required, but recommended for the system databases, which is what we are setting here. Latin1_General_CI_AS_KS_WS is required for SharePoint databases and is set by default when SharePoint provisions databases. See `https://support.microsoft.com/help/2008668/` for additional information.

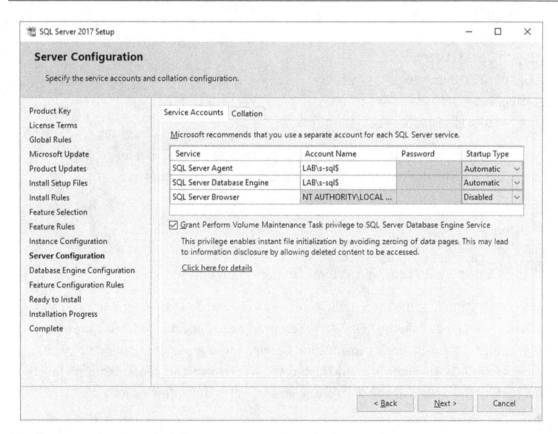

Figure 3-7. *Configuring the account settings for SQL Server*

In the Database Engine Configuration, add one or more users and/or groups to the SQL Server administrators. In this example, we have used the Domain Admins group, but you may want to use a less privledged group.

Under Data Directories, leave the Data root directory at the default. Set the User database directory to M:\Data\ and User database log directory to L:\Logs\. Finally, under TempDB, set the Data directory and Log directory to T:\Data\.

SQL Server AlwaysOn Availability Group Configuration

This section shows how to enable SQL Server AlwaysOn first via SQL PowerShell and then graphically via the SQL Server Configuration Manager.

To get started, we can quickly enable AlwaysOn via PowerShell on each SQL Server. To do this, run the following script.

```
Import-Module -Name SqlServer
Enable-SqlAlwaysOn -Path SQLSERVER:\SQL\$env:COMPUTERNAME\DEFAULT -Force
```

This script will automatically restart the SQL Server service instance for the change to take effect.

If using Windows Server with the Desktop Experience installed, AlwaysOn can be enabled via the SQL Server Configuration Manager. Running the Configuration Manager, click SQL Server Services, then right-click "SQL Server (MSSQLSERVER)" and go to Properties. On the AlwaysOn High Aavailbility tab, check the box "Enable AlwaysOn Availability Groups" as shown in Figure 3-8.

Figure 3-8. *Enabling SQL Server AlwaysOn via the Configuration Manager*

Once enabled in Configuration Manager, restart the SQL Server service instance.

The next set of tasks will be performed using SQL Server Management Studio (SSMS) on a remote workstation.

Note   SQL Server Management Studio can be downloaded from `https://docs.microsoft.com/en-us/sql/ssms/download-sql-server-management-studio-ssms`.

Connect to the primary SQL Server using Windows Authentication. We will create a temporary database to initialize the AlwaysOn Availability Group. This can be accomplished via T-SQL using the following:

```
CREATE DATABASE [aoagseed] ON PRIMARY
(NAME = N'aoagseed', FILENAME = N'M:\Data\aoagseed.mdf', SIZE = 8192KB,
FILEGROWTH = 65536KB)
 LOG ON
```

```
(NAME = N'aoagseed_log', FILENAME = N'L:\Logs\aoagseed_log.ldf',
SIZE = 8192KB, FILEGROWTH = 65536KB)
ALTER DATABASE [aoagseed] SET RECOVERY FULL
GO
USE [aoagseed]
IF NOT EXISTS (SELECT name FROM sys.filegroups WHERE is_default=1 AND name
= N'PRIMARY')
ALTER DATABASE [aoagseed] MODIFY FILEGROUP [PRIMARY] DEFAULT
```

You may also right-click the Databases node of the primary SQL Server and select New Database. Provide a name and click OK. No options need to be set.

Next, create a full backup of the database. The following T-SQL is using our default backup location but may be adjusted to any location required.

```
BACKUP DATABASE aoagseed TO DISK='M:\Program Files\Microsoft SQL Server\
MSSQL14.MSSQLSERVER\MSSQL\Backup\aoagseed.bak'
```

On each SQL Server, we must create a login for the Group Managed Service Account prior to creating the AlwaysOn Availability Group via T-SQL. To do this, run the following in SSMS while connected to each SQL Server:

```
CREATE LOGIN [LAB\s-sql$] FROM Windows
```

The next step is to create the AOAG named "CALAG". This script specifies the two SQL Servers, using Synchronious Commit, a backup preference of the Primary SQL Server, using Automatic seeding mode, and finally creates the AlwaysOn Availability Group Listener named "caspag" with an IP address of 172.16.5.201. This script requires the use of SQLCMD mode which can be set in SSMS under the Query menu by selecting "SQLCMD Mode."

To create the AOAG via SSMS, right-click the AlwaysOn High Availability node and select the New Availability Group Wizard. As shown in Figure 3-9, set the AOAG name and leave the other options at their defaults.

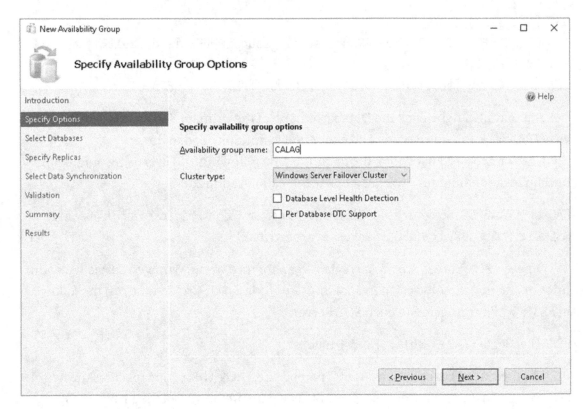

Figure 3-9. *Naming the AlwaysOn Availability Group*

Next, select the aoagseed database as shown in Figure 3-10. Verify the status is "Meets preqrequisites," otherwise take the appropriate action that the status indicates.

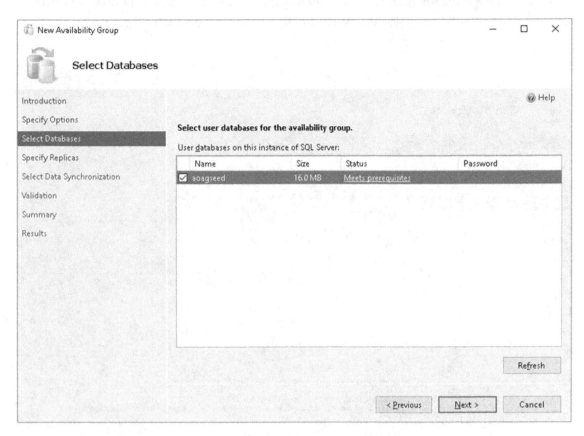

Figure 3-10. *Selecting the seed database*

In the next step, choose Add Replica and connect to the secondary SQL Server, CALSQL02 in this example. Check Automatic Failover and verify Availability Mode is seto to Synchronous commit. SharePoint Server does not use Readable Secondaries so we leave it unchecked. When the options are set correctly, it will look similar to Figure 3-11.

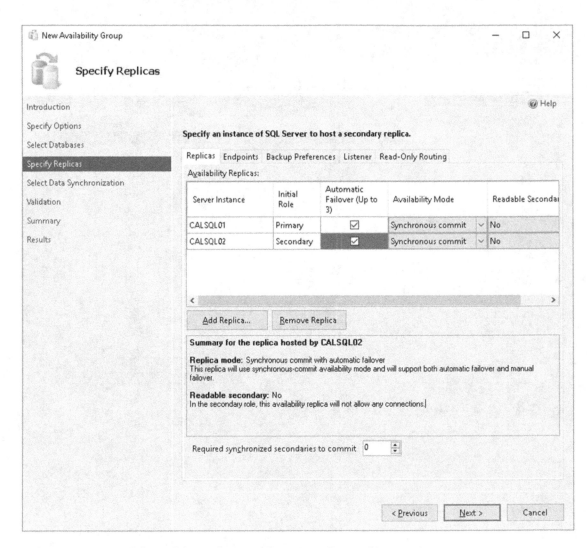

Figure 3-11. *Adding the Replica and setting the replica options*

Under Backup Preference, select the Primary as shown in Figure 3-12. The Secondary only supports Copy-only backups. These backups cannot truncate the transaction log, so we need to take our backups from the primary only.

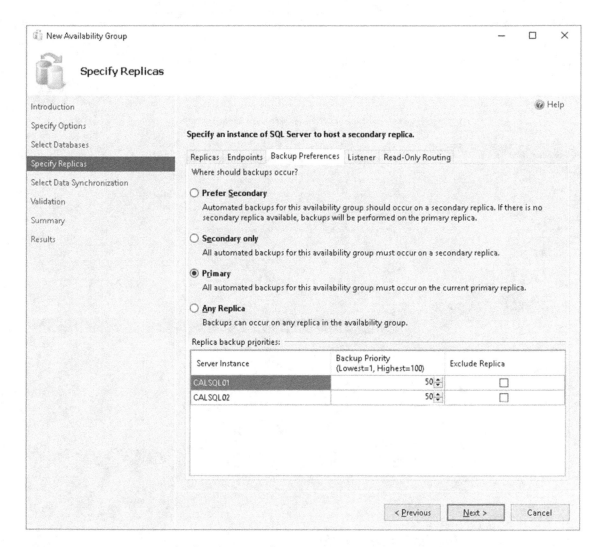

Figure 3-12. *Setting the backup preference*

The last option we need to specify is the Listener. On the Listener tab, set the Listener DNS name to a unique hostname. Set the port to 1433 and provide an unused IP address for the Listener, as shown in Figure 3-13.

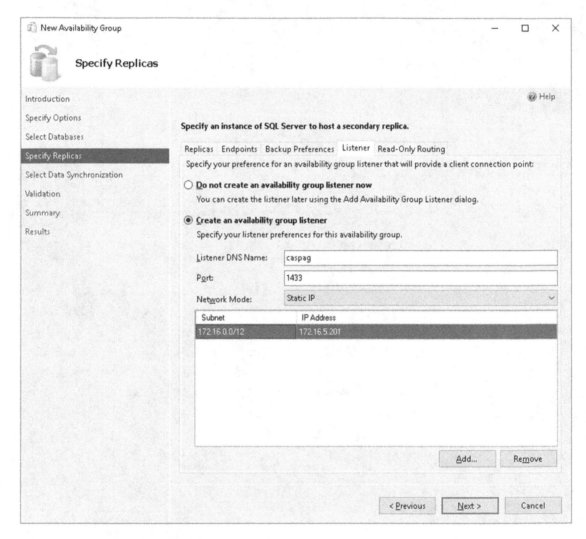

Figure 3-13. *Setting the Listener options*

The last step prior to creating the AOAG is to set the synchronization preference, as shown in Figure 3-14. In this example, we will be using Automatic seeding. Automatic seeding allows us to have SQL Server add databases to the AOAG without explicitly taking backups of the databases prior.

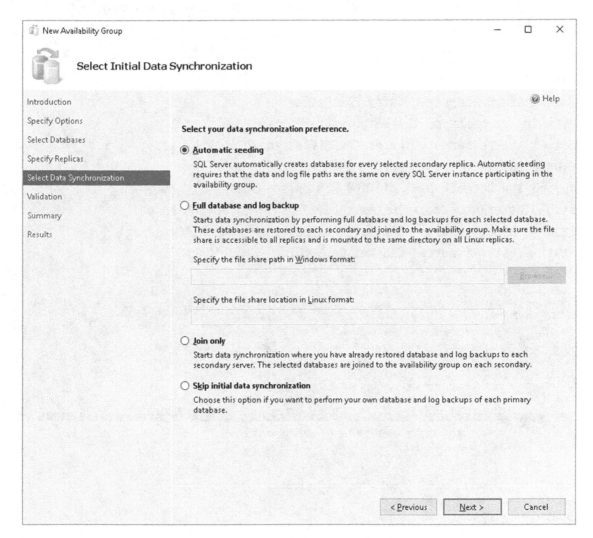

Figure 3-14. *Choosing the synchronization preference*

Complete the wizard and the AOAG will be created. The final step we will take is to set the HostRecordTTL value on the AOAG DNS A record; this sets the Time To Live on the A record to a lower value which tells clients to look at the IP of the record on a more frequent basis. This can be accomplished via PowerShell on one of the SQL Servers or remotely on a client workstation with the Failover Cluster management tools installed, as shown in Figure 3-15.

```
#Retrieve the Cluster Resources and select the Network Name owned by the
Availability Group.
Get-ClusterResource -Cluster CALSQLClus
#Set the property on the Network Name
Get-ClusterResource -Cluster CALSQLClus -Name 'CALAG_caspag' | Set-
ClusterParameter HostRecordTTL 300
#Bring the Network Name offline and online again
Stop-ClusterResource -Cluster CALSQLClus -Name 'CALAG_caspag'
Start-ClusterResource -Cluster CALSQLClus -Name 'CALAG_caspag'
Start-ClusterResource -Cluster CALSQLClus -Name 'CALAG'
```

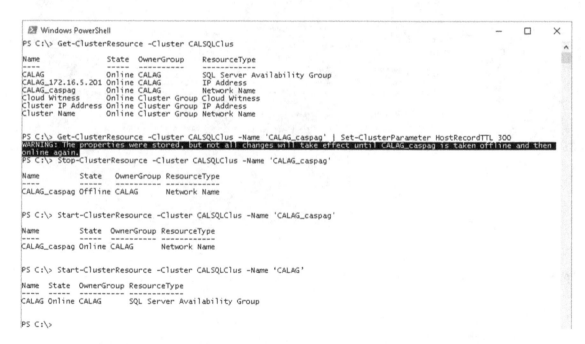

Figure 3-15. *Setting the HostRecordTTL value on the AOAG Network Name*

At this point, you may remove the temporary aoagseed database from the AlwaysOn Availability Group and delete the database from both the primary and secondary SQL Servers. This completes the AlwaysOn Availability Group.

Model Database

The model database in SQL Server is the template for all future databases created on the SQL Server. The model database initial values are not always optimal and can be adjusted with T-SQL. The initial file size will vary depending on how heavily used the environment is, and for this environment it will be set at a conservative 100MB for modeldev (data file) and modellog (log file). To complete this, on the Primary and Secondary Replica, run the following T-SQL command:

```
ALTER DATABASE [model] MODIFY FILE (NAME = modeldev, SIZE = 100MB, MAXSIZE =
UNLIMITED)
ALTER DATABASE [model] MODIFY FILE (NAME = modellog, SIZE = 100MB, MAXSIZE =
UNLIMITED)
```

Note that we are not specifying the FILEGROWTH property as SharePoint ignores this value when creating databases.

MAXDOP

Provided the account installing SharePoint has the sysadmin Fixed Role in the SQL Server instance, MAXDOP (Max Degree of Paralellism) will automatically be set. SharePoint Server 2019 will refuse to deploy if MAXDOP is not set to 1. The value of MAXDOP is how many CPUs will be used to run a single SQL statement. SharePoint has been tested to perform correctly with a MAXDOP of 1 only. If the user installing SharePoint does not have the appropriate rights on the SQL Server, the SQL Server administrator may set this value via T-SQL or through SQL Server Management Studio. It may also be necessary to manually set this value on any secondary servers in the Availability Group.

```
sp_configure 'show advanced options', 1;
GO
RECONFIGURE WITH OVERRIDE;
GO
```

```
sp_configure 'max degree of parallelism', 1;
GO
RECONFIGURE WITH OVERRIDE;
GO
```

Lock Pages in Memory

SQL Server offers functionality to lock pages in memory. Lock pages in memory allows SQL Server to tell Windows that it should not free memory allocated by SQL Server. This step is optional.

We will review three ways to accomplish this task.

NTRights.exe is shipped as part of the Windows 2003 Resource Kit Tools. This command line application can be installed on modern versions of Windows and of Windows Server 2016, still functions correctly. Run the following command line to grant the Lock Pages in Memory right to LAB\s-sql$.

```
Ntrights.exe -u LAB\s-sql$ +r SeLockMemoryPrivilege
```

Note   Windows 2003 Resource Kit Tools can be downloaded from www.microsoft.com/en-us/download/details.aspx?id=17657.

The second method is to use a PowerShell module UserRights.psm1 available from https://gallery.technet.microsoft.com/scriptcenter/Grant-Revoke-Query-user-26e259b0. Download the script to the SQL server and run it using the following method:

```
Import-Module UserRights.psm1
Grant-UserRight -Account 'LAB\s-sql$' -Right SeLockMemoryPrivilege
```

The last step is to use the Local Security Policy MMC. If you installed SQL Server on Windows Server with the Desktop Experience, open the Start menu and search for "Local Security Policy." Under Local Policies, User Rights Assignment, find the Lock Pages in Memory setting. Add LAB\s-sql$.

If you installed Windows Server using the Core installation option, you must first set this value of Lock Pages in Memory on a Windows Server running the Desktop Experience, export the policy to an INF file, and then import it onto the server running Windows Core.

Within the Local Security Policy management console, export the policy under Actions to an INF. Copy this INF to the Windows Server Core system. From there, run the following:

```
secedit.exe /configure /db secedit.sdb /cfg C:\export.INF
```

This completes the SQL Server installation. With a fully functional SQL Server AlwaysOn setup, we're ready to finally install SharePoint Server 2019!

SharePoint Server 2019 Installation

SharePoint will be set up on four servers. The setup process will consist of running the prerequisite installer in a silent mode. Once the prerequisite installer has been completed, the SharePoint binaries will be installed. A wildcard certificate for *.cobaltatom.com has been deployed to all SharePoint servers to be used for Web Applications.

Disable Insecure Transport Security Protocols

SharePoint Server 2019 supports TLS 1.2. Because of this, it is highly recommended to disable previous protocols, including SSL 3.0, TLS 1.0, and TLS 1.1. By default, SSL 2.0 is disabled in Windows Server 2016.

To disable the previous protocols, run the following PowerShell script on each SharePoint Server. This configuration change requires a reboot to take effect.

```
#Disable PCT 1.0
ni "HKLM:\SYSTEM\CurrentControlSet\Control\SecurityProviders\SCHANNEL\
Protocols\" -Name "PCT 1.0" -Value "DefaultValue" -Force
ni "HKLM:\SYSTEM\CurrentControlSet\Control\SecurityProviders\SCHANNEL\
Protocols\PCT 1.0\" -Name "Server" -Value "DefaultValue" -Force
New-ItemProperty "HKLM:\SYSTEM\CurrentControlSet\Control\SecurityProviders\
SCHANNEL\Protocols\PCT 1.0\Server\" -Name Enabled -Value 0 -PropertyType
"DWord" -Force
#Disable SSL 2.0
ni "HKLM:\SYSTEM\CurrentControlSet\Control\SecurityProviders\SCHANNEL\
Protocols\" -Name "SSL 2.0" -Value "DefaultValue" -Force
```

```
ni "HKLM:\SYSTEM\CurrentControlSet\Control\SecurityProviders\SCHANNEL\
Protocols\SSL 2.0\" -Name "Server" -Value "DefaultValue" -Force
New-ItemProperty "HKLM:\SYSTEM\CurrentControlSet\Control\SecurityProviders\
SCHANNEL\Protocols\SSL 2.0\Server\" -Name Enabled -Value 0 -PropertyType
"DWord" -Force
#Disable SSL 3.0
ni "HKLM:\SYSTEM\CurrentControlSet\Control\SecurityProviders\SCHANNEL\
Protocols\" -Name "SSL 3.0" -Value "DefaultValue" -Force
ni "HKLM:\SYSTEM\CurrentControlSet\Control\SecurityProviders\SCHANNEL\
Protocols\SSL 3.0\" -Name "Server" -Value "DefaultValue" -Force
New-ItemProperty "HKLM:\SYSTEM\CurrentControlSet\Control\SecurityProviders\
SCHANNEL\Protocols\SSL 3.0\Server\" -Name Enabled -Value 0 -PropertyType
"DWord" -Force
#Disable TLS 1.0
ni "HKLM:\SYSTEM\CurrentControlSet\Control\SecurityProviders\SCHANNEL\
Protocols\" -Name "TLS 1.0" -Value "DefaultValue" -Force
ni "HKLM:\SYSTEM\CurrentControlSet\Control\SecurityProviders\SCHANNEL\
Protocols\TLS 1.0\" -Name "Server" -Value "DefaultValue" -Force
New-ItemProperty "HKLM:\SYSTEM\CurrentControlSet\Control\SecurityProviders\
SCHANNEL\Protocols\TLS 1.0\Server\" -Name Enabled -Value 0 -PropertyType
"DWord" -Force
#Disable TLS 1.1
ni "HKLM:\SYSTEM\CurrentControlSet\Control\SecurityProviders\SCHANNEL\
Protocols\" -Name "TLS 1.1" -Value "DefaultValue"  -Force
ni "HKLM:\SYSTEM\CurrentControlSet\Control\SecurityProviders\SCHANNEL\
Protocols\TLS 1.1\" -Name "Server" -Value "DefaultValue"  -Force
New-ItemProperty "HKLM:\SYSTEM\CurrentControlSet\Control\SecurityProviders\
SCHANNEL\Protocols\TLS 1.1\Server\" -Name Enabled -Value 0 -PropertyType
"DWord" -Force
```

Prerequisite Silent Installation

To install all of the prerequisites in a silent mode, they must be downloaded from
Microsoft and placed into a directory on the SharePoint server. In this example, the
SharePoint binaries have been copied to C:\SharePoint2019, where PrerequisiteInstaller.
exe resides.

```
Start-Process "C:\SharePoint2019\ISO\PrerequisiteInstaller.exe"
-ArgumentList "/SQLNCli:`"C:\SharePoint2019\ISO\PrerequisiteInstallerFiles\
sqlncli.msi`" `
/Sync:`"C:\SharePoint2019\ISO\PrerequisiteInstallerFiles\Synchronization.msi`" `
/AppFabric:`"C:\SharePoint2019\ISO\PrerequisiteInstallerFiles\
WindowsServerAppFabricSetup_x64.exe`" `
/IDFX11:`"C:\SharePoint2019\ISO\PrerequisiteInstallerFiles\
MicrosoftIdentityExtensions-64.msi`" `
/MSIPCClient:`"C:\SharePoint2019\ISO\PrerequisiteInstallerFiles\setup_
msipc_x64.exe`" `
/KB3092423:`"C:\SharePoint2019\ISO\PrerequisiteInstallerFiles\AppFabric-
KB3092423-x64-ENU.exe`" `
/WCFDataServices56:`"C:\SharePoint2019\ISO\PrerequisiteInstallerFiles\
WcfDataServices.exe`" `
/DotNet472:`"C:\SharePoint2019\ISO\PrerequisiteInstallerFiles\NDP472-
KB4054531-Web.exe`" `
/MSVCRT11:`"C:\SharePoint2019\ISO\PrerequisiteInstallerFiles\vcredist_x64.exe`" `
/MSVCRT141:`"C:\SharePoint2019\ISO\PrerequisiteInstallerFiles\VC_redist.x64.exe`""
```

The prerequisite installer will require a single reboot. When logging back into the SharePoint Server after a reboot, the prerequisite installer will start automatically to validate the installation.

Note   The download for each prerequisite is available from the following links:

Microsoft Sync Framework Runtime v1.0 SP1 (x64) (Synchronization.msi): `http://go.microsoft.com/fwlink/?LinkID=224449`

Microsoft SQL Server 2012 SP4 Native Client (sqlncli.msi): `https://go.microsoft.com/fwlink/?LinkId=867003`

Windows Server AppFabric (WindowsServerAppFabricSetup_x64.exe): `http://go.microsoft.com/fwlink/?LinkId=235496`   Microsoft Identity Extensions (MicrosoftIdentityExtensions-64.msi): `http://go.microsoft.com/fwlink/?LinkID=252368`

WCF Data Services 5.6 Tools (WcfDataServices.exe):
http://go.microsoft.com/fwlink/?LinkId=320724

Cumulative Update 7 for Microsoft AppFabric 1.1 for Windows Server
(AppFabric-KB3092423-x64-ENU.exe):
http://go.microsoft.com/fwlink/?LinkId=627257

Active Directory Rights Management Services Client 2.1

(setup_msipc_x64.exe): http://go.microsoft.com/fwlink/?LinkID=544913

Microsoft .NET Framework 4.7 (NDP472-KB4054531-Web.exe):
https://go.microsoft.com/fwlink/?linkid=871868

Microsoft Visual C++ 2012 Redistributable (x64) (vcredist_x64.exe):
http://go.microsoft.com/fwlink/?LinkId=627156

Microsoft Visual C++ 2017 Redistributable (x64) (VC_redist.x64.exe):

https://go.microsoft.com/fwlink/?LinkId=848299

The SharePoint binaries are installed via setup.exe. Per Figure 3-16, during the installation of SharePoint Server, you will be prompted for location of where to install SharePoint as well as where to locate the Search Index. If deploying a Search Server, you may wish to locate the Index on an alternate volume dedicated to the Search Index. Consider changing the path to an alternate volume as the analysis and temporary file creation for content processing will be used for this location, regardless of the location of the Search Index. At the end of the installation, uncheck the "Run the SharePoint Products Configuration Wizard now." checkbox, as this book will guide you through using the SharePoint Management Shell to deploy SharePoint.

Figure 3-16. *Specifying the installation and Search Index location for SharePoint*

SharePoint Server 2019 has now been installed on the four farm members. We are now ready to start the SharePoint Server 2019 configuration.

Tip   It is possible to slipstream Public Updates into the base installation of SharePoint Server. See `https://go.microsoft.com/fwlink/?linkid=2003452` for information on how to complete this task.

SharePoint Server 2019 Configuration

Instead of running the SharePoint Configuration Wizard, this book will provide PowerShell scripts to configure SharePoint.

Run the SharePoint Management Shell as an Administrator on the server that will host Central Administration. In this example, it is CALSP03. The -FarmCredential parameter will be the Domain User service account, LAB\s-farm.

```
New-SPConfigurationDatabase -DatabaseName Configuration
-AdministrationContentDatabaseName Administration -DatabaseServer caspag.
lab.cobaltatom.com -Passphrase (ConvertTo-SecureString "FarmPassphrase1"
-AsPlainText -Force) -FarmCredentials (Get-Credential) -LocalServerRole
ApplicationWithSearch -SkipRegisterAsDistributedCacheHost
```

Note the use of the Availability Group Listener for the -DatabaseServer parameter. Instead of using a SQL Alias configured through cliconfg.exe on the SharePoint server, the Availability Group Listener is used. As we can add and remove SQL Servers from the Availability Group, or even move the Availability Group Listener name to another Availability Group completely, it is no longer necessary to specify a SQL Alias.

Tip   If using cliconfg.exe to create a SQL Alias, make sure to run cliconfg.exe on all SharePoint Servers in the farm. Each SharePoint server must have the same SQL Alias configured.

Additionally, note the new parameter, -LocalServerRole, which takes a value of Application, DistributedCache, WebFrontEnd, Search, Custom, ApplicationWithSearch, WebFrontEndWithDistributedCache, or SingleServerFarm. This specifies the MinRole used for the particular server. As this will be hosting Central Administration using a shared MinRole, the ApplicationWithSearch role is the appropriate choice.

The next series of cmdlet secure permissions on the files and registry entries in use by SharePoint, provision SharePoint Features, Services, and Help.

```
Initialize-SPResourceSecurity
Install-SPFeature -AllExistingFeatures
Install-SPService
Install-SPApplicationContent
```

Note   Install-SPHelpCollection is no longer required as help is now online.

Tip   You can find the definition for the ACLs Initialize-SPResourceSecurity is applying by looking at the registry! Navigate to HKEY_LOCAL_MACHINE\ SOFTWARE\Microsoft\Shared Tools\Web Server Extensions\16.0\WSS\ ResourcesToSecure\. Each resource is defined by a GUID, but under the key in the format of a GUID is a ResourceName which is the path to the item to be secured, along with the Permissions (Read (R), Write (W), Execute (E), Full Control (FC), and Change Permission (D)).

Central Administration

To configure Central Administration to use Kerberos as the authentication mechanism, a new SPN must be set on the Farm Account. The SPN will take the format of HTTP/ CentralAdminFQDN.

```
Setspn -U -S HTTP/cal.lab.cobaltatom.com LAB\s-farm
```

Tip   The SPN for a web site will always start with "HTTP" even if the site is using the SSL protocol, as HTTP is a Kerberos service, not a protocol description.

Create Central Administration using Kerberos and SSL.

```
New-SPCentralAdministration -Port 443 -WindowsAuthProvider Kerberos
-SecureSocketsLayer:$true
```

The next step is to change the default Alternate Access Mapping to align with the SPN and SSL certificate. Use Get-SPWebApplication -IncludeCentralAdministration to see what the current URL of Central Administration is, then modify it.

```
Set-SPAlternateUrl -Identity https://calsp03 -Url
https://cal.lab.cobaltatom.com
```

If a custom URL was set for Central Administration that does not include the machine name, make sure to create an A record in DNS to resolve the new hostname. In addition, validate that the IIS Site Bindings for the SharePoint Central Administration site are set correctly as shown in Figure 3-17. Because this server will only have a single IP address but will need to support multiple SSL certificates, Server Name Indication will be used. SNI is compatible with all browsers that SharePoint Server 2019 supports.

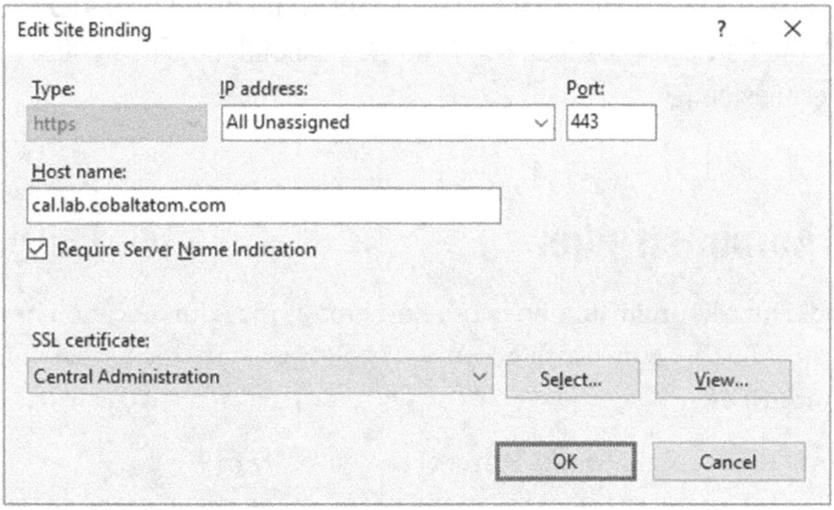

Figure 3-17. *Validating the Central Administration IIS Site Binding*

The next step is to make the Administration and Configuration databases highly available.

In order to achieve high availability for the databases, when a SharePoint database is created, you must add it to the Availability Group. This can be achieved through SQL Server Management Studio from a client computer. The first step is to take a Full Backup of the database. In this example, we will use the Configuration database, although it must be done with all databases created for the farm.

On the Primary Replica, using T-SQL, backing up the database as well as the transaction log as an Availability Group requires the use of the Full Recovery Model for each database that is part of the Availability Group. Specify the file path. Each file should have a unique name. Add the database to the Availability Group, named SPHADR in this scenario.

```
BACKUP DATABASE Configuration TO DISK='M:\Program Files\Microsoft SQL
Server\MSSQL14.MSSQLSERVER\MSSQL\Backup\Configuration.bak';
BACKUP DATABASE Administration TO DISK='M:\Program Files\Microsoft SQL
Server\MSSQL14.MSSQLSERVER\MSSQL\Backup\Administration.bak';
ALTER AVAILABILITY GROUP CALAG ADD DATABASE Configuration;
ALTER AVAILABILITY GROUP CALAG ADD DATABASE Administration;
```

Because we configured the AOAG to use automatic seeding, we do not need to take any further prerequisite actions to add the databases to the Availability Group.

To add a database through the Availability Group wizard, first take a Full Backup through the wizard, shown in Figure 3-18. Right-click the database and go to the Tasks node and then Backup. Specify the backup location that is shared and a file name, in this example, Administration.bak.

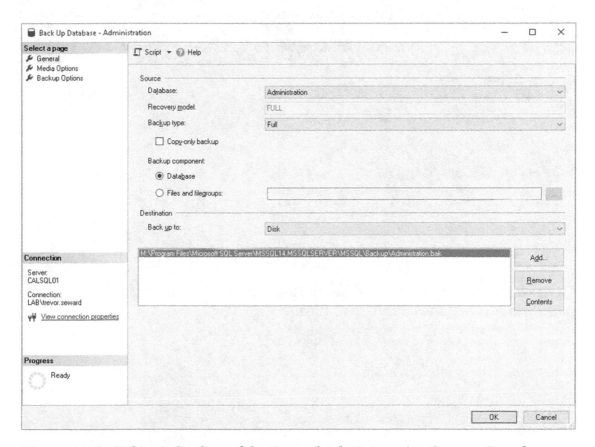

Figure 3-18. *Taking a backup of the Central Administration Content Database from SQL Server Management Studio*

To complete the addition of the database to the Availability Group, right-click the Availability Group in SQL Server Management Studio under the AlwaysOn High Availability\Availability Groups node, and then click Add Database. The status on the Select Database screen should read "Meets prerequisites" for the database to be added, shown in Figure 3-19. The next steps will be to add the database to the Availability Group using Automatic seeding as the data synchronization, shown here in Figure 3-20.

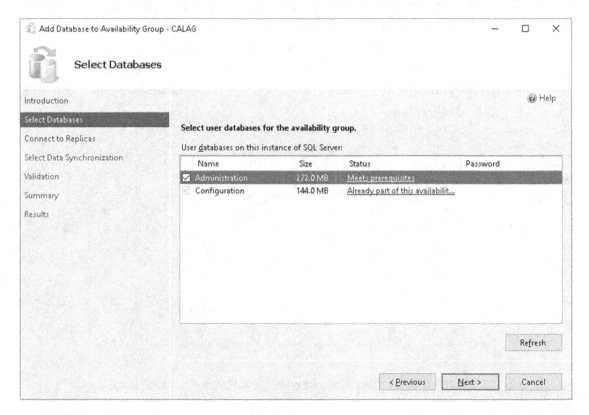

Figure 3-19. *Adding the Central Administration Content Database through the Add Database to Availability Group Wizard*

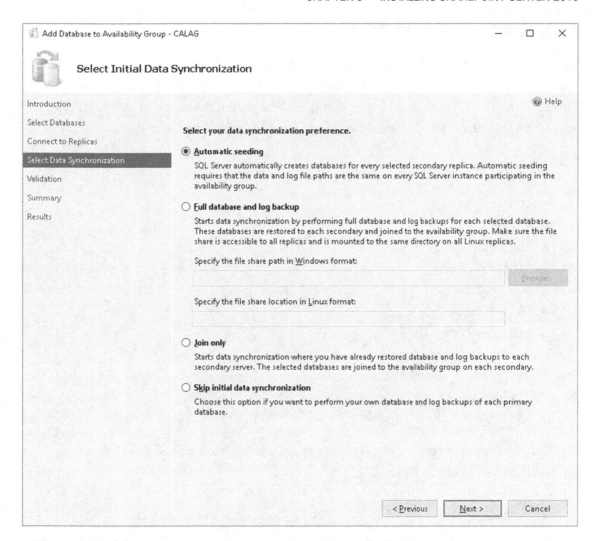

Figure 3-20. *Selecting the automatic seeding option to add the Central Administration Content Database to the AOAG*

Connect to the Secondary Replica. The Validation step will notify you of any errors that will prevent the database from being added to the Availability Group. A summary of the steps will be provided, and the last step will add the database to the Availability Group. As the databases are initially small, this process should be quick.

This completes the Availability Group configuration for the Configuration and Administration databases, but remember that all newly created databases for SharePoint, with notable exceptions you will find in this chapter, must be added to the Availability Group as they're created.

SQL Kerberos Validation

In order to validate that SharePoint is connecting to SQL Server using Kerberos, run the following script in SQL Server Management Studio while connected to the Availability Group. Note the WHERE clause specifying the first part of the name of all SharePoint servers in this farm. This WHERE clause may be dropped, if necessary.

```
SELECT
    s.session_id,
    c.connect_time,
    s.login_time,
    s.login_name,
    c.protocol_type,
    c.auth_scheme,
    s.HOST_NAME,
    s.program_name
FROM sys.dm_exec_sessions s
JOIN sys.dm_exec_connections c
ON s.session_id = c.session_id
WHERE HOST_NAME like 'CALSP%'
```

If the servers are connecting via Kerberos, the auth_scheme value will show KERBEROS, as shown in Figure 3-21.

	session_id	connect_time	login_time	login_name	protocol_type	auth_scheme	HOST_NAME	program_name
1	59	2018-07-22 14:53:55.853	2018-07-22 14:54:36.160	LAB\s-farm	TSQL	KERBEROS	CALSP03	SharePoint[OWSTIMER][1][Configuration]
2	60	2018-07-22 14:54:36.160	2018-07-22 14:54:45.170	LAB\s-farm	TSQL	KERBEROS	CALSP03	SharePoint[OWSTIMER][1][Configuration]
3	72	2018-07-22 14:54:04.083	2018-07-22 14:54:36.190	LAB\s-farm	TSQL	KERBEROS	CALSP03	SharePoint[OWSTIMER][1][Administration]

Figure 3-21. *The SharePoint Timer service connecting to the SQL Server via Kerberos*

If Kerberos has not been configured correctly on the SQL Server, the auth_scheme will display NTLM. Note that it is normal for certain connections to display as NTLM, such as if you are connected to SQL Server locally.

Note If your auth_scheme continues to display as "NTLM" after setting the SPN, verify you have restarted your SharePoint servers as well as the SQL Server service.

Adding SharePoint Servers

Adding the remaining SharePoint Servers to the farm is simple. Based on their role, only a single parameter will change, -LocalServerRole.

For the next server, CALSP04, an Application and Search server, we need to run the following cmdlet from the SharePoint Management Shell:

```
Connect-SPConfigurationDatabase -DatabaseName Configuration -DatabaseServer
caspag.lab.cobaltatom.com -Passphrase (ConvertTo-SecureString "FarmPassphrase1"
-AsPlainText -Force) -LocalServerRole ApplicationWithSearch
```

As CALSP04 will also run Central Administration, make sure to install the Central Administration SSL certificate on CALSP04.

Then the front-end servers, CALSP01 and CALSP02 with the -LocalServerRole parameter WebFrontEndWithDistributedCache.

```
Connect-SPConfigurationDatabase -DatabaseName Configuration
-DatabaseServer caspag.lab.cobaltatom.com -Passphrase (ConvertTo-
SecureString "FarmPassphrase1" -AsPlainText -Force) -LocalServerRole
WebFrontEndWithDistributedCache -SkipRegisterAsDistributedCacheHost
```

For each server, we will also need to run cmdlets to provision services, features, and set security on file system and registry objects. If the server has a role of Search, you do not need to run Install-SPApplicationContent; however, all servers in this farm use shared MinRoles which require this cmdlet to be run.

```
Initialize-SPResourceSecurity
Install-SPService
Install-SPFeature -AllExistingFeatures
Install-SPApplicationContent
```

Once the cmdlets have completed, if the SharePoint Timer Service is not started, start it via Services.msc or use the following PowerShell cmdlet:

```
Start-Service SPTimerV4
```

When all servers have been joined to the farm, validate that they have the correct services provisioned. This can be done in Central Administration by going to "Manage servers in farm" per Figure 3-22.

Server	SharePoint Products Installed	Role	Compliant	Services Running	Status	Remove Server
CALSP01	Microsoft SharePoint Server 2019	Front-end with Distributed Cache	✓ Yes	App Management Service Business Data Connectivity Service Distributed Cache Managed Metadata Web Service Microsoft SharePoint Foundation Web Application Secure Store Service User Profile Service	No Action Required	Remove Server
CALSP02	Microsoft SharePoint Server 2019	Front-end with Distributed Cache	✓ Yes	App Management Service Business Data Connectivity Service Distributed Cache Managed Metadata Web Service Microsoft SharePoint Foundation Web Application Secure Store Service User Profile Service	No Action Required	Remove Server
CALSP03	Microsoft SharePoint Server 2019	Application with Search	✓ Yes	App Management Service Business Data Connectivity Service Central Administration Managed Metadata Web Service Microsoft SharePoint Foundation Incoming E-Mail Microsoft SharePoint Foundation Web Application Microsoft SharePoint Foundation Workflow Timer Service Search Host Controller Service Search Query and Site Settings Service Secure Store Service SharePoint Server Search User Profile Service	No Action Required	Remove Server
CALSP04	Microsoft SharePoint Server 2019	Application with Search	✓ Yes	App Management Service Business Data Connectivity Service Central Administration Managed Metadata Web Service Microsoft SharePoint Foundation Incoming E-Mail Microsoft SharePoint Foundation Web Application Microsoft SharePoint Foundation Workflow Timer Service Search Host Controller Service Search Query and Site Settings Service Secure Store Service SharePoint Server Search User Profile Service	No Action Required	Remove Server

Figure 3-22. *Central Administration Manage servers in farm, showing all servers and roles*

Central Administration High Availability

To make Central Administration highly available, we need to start it on the second Application server, CALSP04. To do this, in Central Administration, navigate to Manage services on server. Select the second Application server from the Server drop-down, and then Start the Central Administration service. Once the service is started, modify the IIS binding and select the SharePoint Central Administration SSL certificate installed earlier, along with specifying the hostname of cal.lab.cobaltatom.com and ticking the SNI checkbox.

We can also start Central Administration via PowerShell. We must pass in the hostname of the SharePoint server we are going to start it on to get a reference to the specific Service Instance.

```
$si = Get-SPServiceInstance -Server CALSP04 | ?{$_.TypeName -eq 'Central
Administration'}
Start-SPServiceInstance $si
```

At this point, Central Administration is ready to be placed behind a Load Balancer. The A record for the Central Administration FQDN may now be pointed at the Load Balancer when configured.

Service Auto Provision

Services can be automatically provisioned in the farm, but each service must be set to do so. In Central Administration under Manage services in farm, note that a select few, by default, are set to Auto Provision as Figure 3-23 displays. This can be changed by clicking the Enable Auto Provision link (e.g., if you do not have plans to use a service such as Claims to Windows Token Service). Other services are auto provisioned when the Service Application is created.

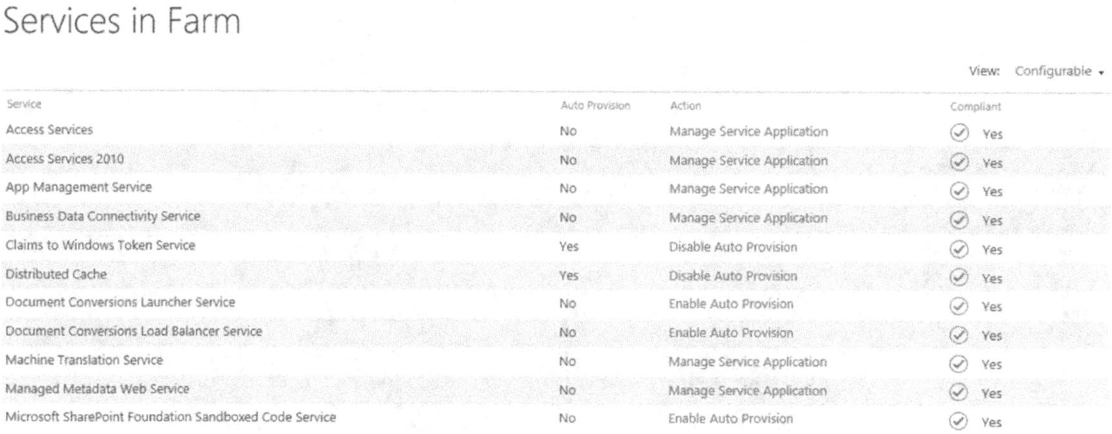

Services in Farm

Service	Auto Provision	Action	Compliant
Access Services	No	Manage Service Application	✓ Yes
Access Services 2010	No	Manage Service Application	✓ Yes
App Management Service	No	Manage Service Application	✓ Yes
Business Data Connectivity Service	No	Manage Service Application	✓ Yes
Claims to Windows Token Service	Yes	Disable Auto Provision	✓ Yes
Distributed Cache	Yes	Disable Auto Provision	✓ Yes
Document Conversions Launcher Service	No	Enable Auto Provision	✓ Yes
Document Conversions Load Balancer Service	No	Enable Auto Provision	✓ Yes
Machine Translation Service	No	Manage Service Application	✓ Yes
Managed Metadata Web Service	No	Manage Service Application	✓ Yes
Microsoft SharePoint Foundation Sandboxed Code Service	No	Enable Auto Provision	✓ Yes

View: Configurable ▾

Figure 3-23. *Services in Farm showing which services are set to Auto Provision*

The service will initially show as Processing, prior to display the outcome in the Action column, such as "Disable Auto Provision" if the Service was set to Auto Provision. Only set Auto Provision for services that will be used within the farm.

Outgoing E-Mail

Outgoing e-mail can now be configured using TLS and Windows authentication. Outgoing e-mail can be configured from Central Administration under System Settings, Configure outgoing e-mail settings, per Figure 3-24. SharePoint 2019 can use Windows authentication to connect to the SMTP host.

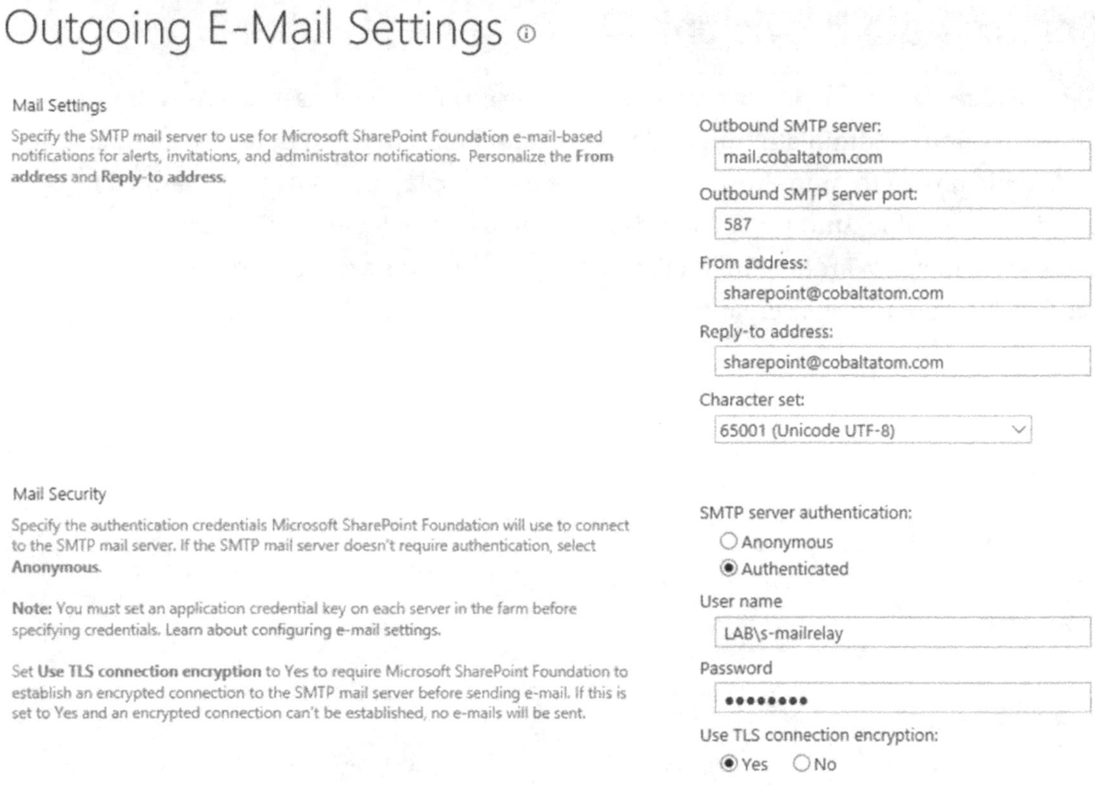

Outgoing E-Mail Settings ⓘ

Mail Settings

Specify the SMTP mail server to use for Microsoft SharePoint Foundation e-mail-based notifications for alerts, invitations, and administrator notifications. Personalize the **From** address and **Reply-to address.**

Outbound SMTP server:

mail.cobaltatom.com

Outbound SMTP server port:

587

From address:

sharepoint@cobaltatom.com

Reply-to address:

sharepoint@cobaltatom.com

Character set:

65001 (Unicode UTF-8)

Mail Security

Specify the authentication credentials Microsoft SharePoint Foundation will use to connect to the SMTP mail server. If the SMTP mail server doesn't require authentication, select **Anonymous.**

Note: You must set an application credential key on each server in the farm before specifying credentials. Learn about configuring e-mail settings.

Set **Use TLS connection encryption** to Yes to require Microsoft SharePoint Foundation to establish an encrypted connection to the SMTP mail server before sending e-mail. If this is set to Yes and an encrypted connection can't be established, no e-mails will be sent.

SMTP server authentication:

○ Anonymous
◉ Authenticated

User name

LAB\s-mailrelay

Password

••••••••

Use TLS connection encryption:

◉ Yes   ○ No

Figure 3-24 *Outgoing e-mail settings in Central Administration*

It may also be set via the SharePoint Management Shell. Prior to configuring Outgoing E-Mail with authentication, you must first set an application credential key. This can now be done with a single PowerShell cmdlet in SharePoint 2019.

```
Set-SPApplicationCredentialKey -Password (ConvertTo-SecureString
'AppCredSecret1!' -AsPlainText -Force)
```

Note   This cmdlet must be run on all SharePoint servers in the farm. The cmdlet sets a registry value which does not propagate to other SharePoint servers.

```
With the application credential key in place, it is now possible to set up
authentication for Outgoing SMTP mail.
```

```
$ca = Get-SPWebApplication -IncludeCentralAdministration | ?{$_.
IsAdministrationWebApplication -eq $true}
$senderAddr = "sharepoint@cobaltatom.com"
$replyAddr = "sharepoint@cobaltatom.com"
$smtpServer = "mail.cobaltatom.com"
$enableTls = $true
$authUser = "LAB\s-mailrelay"
$password = Read-Host -AsSecureString
$ca.UpdateMailsettings($smtpServer, $senderAddr, $replyAddr, 65001,
$enableTls, 587, $authUser, $password)
```

65001 is the default code page. The $true value is to enable TLS, and the port specified is 587.

To validate the mail settings are working successfully, mail can be sent through the SharePoint Object Model in the SharePoint Management Shell. Simply fill in the blanks, using the URL of Central Administration as the specified site.

```
$email = "recipient@cobaltatom.com"
$subject = "Email through SharePoint OM"
$body = "Message body."

$site = Get-SPSite http://centralAdministrationUrl
$web = $site.OpenWeb()
[Microsoft.SharePoint.Utilities.SPUtility]::SendEmail($web,0,0,$email,$subj
ect,$body)
```

If the result returns True, the mail has been sent successfully. If not, investigate the mail server receive connector logs for any potential errors. In addition, you can also use the Send-MailMessage cmdlet.

```
Send-MailMessage -To "recipient@cobaltatom.com" -From "sharepoint@
cobaltatom.com" -Subject "Testing Smtp Mail" -Body "Message Body"
-SmtpServer "mail.cobaltatom.com" -UseSsl -Port 587 -Credential (Get-
Credential -UserName "LAB\s-mailrelay")
```

This cmdlet bypasses the SharePoint Object Model and may provide additional diagnostic information.

Information Rights Management

Information Rights Management settings may be found in Central Administration under Security, Configure information rights management. If a Service Connection Point has been created in Active Directory for Rights Management Services (a default setting), then specify "Use the default RMS server specified in Active Directory"; otherwise, select "Use this RMS server" and enter the fully qualified domain name of the RMS cluster. If an error is encountered, validate that the RMS cluster domain name can be resolved from the SharePoint server and the Farm Account and any Web Application Pool accounts are members of the AD RMS Service Group local group on the RMS server(s).

IRM settings may also be enabled via the SharePoint Management Shell.

To set the setting "Use the default RMS server specified in Active Directory" run the following:

```
$webSvc = [Microsoft.SharePoint.Administration.
SPWebService]::ContentService
$webSvc.IrmSettings.IrmRMSEnabled = $true
$webSvc.IrmSettings.IrmRMSUseAD = $true
$webSvc.Update()
```

To specify a specific server, run the following:

```
$webSvc = [Microsoft.SharePoint.Administration.
SPWebService]::ContentService
$webSvc.IrmSettings.IrmRMSEnabled = $true
$webSvc.IrmSettings.IrmRMSUseAD = $false
$webSvc.IrmSettings.IrmRMSCertServer = "https://rms.cobaltatom.com"
$webSvc.Update()
```

When using the SharePoint Management Shell, it may take a few seconds for the results to be displayed in Central Administration.

Managed Accounts

Managed accounts are the service accounts that run SharePoint services. The Farm Account account is added by default when the SharePoint farm is created. In this farm, we have three additional managed accounts that must be registered, s-svc to run the Service Applications, s-web to run the Web Applications, and s-c2wts for the Claims to Windows Token Service.

Note   Only provision an account for the Claims to Windows Token Service if this service will be required in your farm. C2WTS is not required in most deployments.

To register Managed Accounts, run the following:

```
$cred = Get-Credential -UserName "LAB\s-svc" -Message "Managed Account"
New-SPManagedAccount -Credential $cred
```

Repeat the process for LAB\s-web and LAB\s-c2wts.

Service Application Pool

Because we will be using the minimal number of Application Pools possible in the farm, we will only create a single Application Pool for all Service Applications. This is done via PowerShell, and may also be done while creating the first Service Application in the farm. Using a single Application Pool reduces overhead as .NET processes cannot share memory even though the same binaries have been loaded into the process (e.g., Microsoft.SharePoint.dll cannot be shared between two w3wp.exe processes).

```
New-SPServiceApplicationPool -Name "SharePoint Web Services Default"
-Account (Get-SPManagedAccount "LAB\s-svc")
```

When creating Service Applications, we will now select the "SharePoint Web Services Default" Application Pool.

Diagnostic Logging

Out of the box, SharePoint logs to the Unified Logging Service (Diagnostic Logging) to "C:\Program Files\Common Files\microsoft shared\Web Server Extensions\16\ LOGS\". Logging to the C: drive may not be ideal, not only for space reasons, but also for performance due to being on the same volume as all other SharePoint web-based resources that users access. The ULS location can be moved via Central Administration under Monitoring, Configure diagnostic logging. Set the Path to a specific location, such as "E:\ULS". Note that this path must be on all SharePoint servers in the farm. In addition, you may specify the maximum number of days to retain log files as well as the maximum disk space log files can consume. It is advisable to set the maximum disk space log files can use below the volume size they reside on.

From the SharePoint Management Shell, this can be set by running the following using any or all of the parameters. Note to restrict the maximum disk space log files can use, you must specify both the -LogDiskSpaceUsageGB and -LogMaxDiskSpaceUsageEnabled:$true parameters.

```
Set-SPDiagnosticConfig -DaysToKeepLogs 7 -LogDiskSpaceUsageGB 150 -LogMaxDi
skSpaceUsageEnabled:$true -LogLocation E:\ULS
```

If moving the ULS logs to an alternate location, it is also recommended to move the Usage logs, as well. In Central Administration, under Monitoring, Configure usage and health data collection, specify the Log path to the same root directory as the ULS logs, for example, E:\ULS.

Setting this through the SharePoint Management Shell is accomplished via the following:

```
Set-SPUsageService -UsageLogLocation E:\ULS
```

Claims to Windows Token Service

As previously noted, the Claims to Windows Token Service is often not required in most SharePoint deployments. Carefully consider whether you will need or use this feature.

The Claims to Windows Token Service should always run under a dedicated account. This account is the only account that requires Local Administrator rights on the SharePoint servers where it runs. For a MinRole configuration, the Claims to Windows Token Service runs on all MinRoles. Do not configure Claims to Windows Token Service unless necessary. Many farms do not require this service.

Manually add the Claims to Windows Token Service to the Local Administrators group on each SharePoint server. In addition, using the Local Security Policy MMC (secpol.msc), add the Claims to Windows Token Service to the following User Rights Assignments, under Local Policies.

- Act as part of the operating system

- Impersonate a client after authentication

- Log on as a service

Claims to Windows Token Service must connect to data sources with Kerberos Constrained Delegation with Protocol Transition enabled. In order for the Delegation tab to appear in Active Directory Users and Computers for the Claims to Windows Token Service account, create a "dummy" SPN using setspn.exe.

```
Setspn.exe -U -S C2WTS/Dummy LAB\s-c2wts
```

To set the Claims to Windows Token Service account, use the SharePoint Management Shell.

```
$account = Get-SPManagedAccount "LAB\s-c2wts"
$farm = Get-SPFarm
$svc = $farm.Services | ?{$_.TypeName -eq "Claims to Windows Token Service"}
$svcIdentity = $svc.ProcessIdentity
$svcIdentity.CurrentIdentityType = [Microsoft.SharePoint.Administration.
IdentityType]::SpecificUser
$svcIdentity.UserName = $account.Username
$svcIdentity.Update()
$svcIdentity.Deploy()
```

Once completed, the Claims to Token Service will be running under the new identity on all SharePoint servers in the farm running the Claims to Windows Token Service.

Distributed Cache Service

The Distributed Cache service requires two modifications. The first change is to replace the Farm Admin account running the AppFabric Caching Service with the services account. The second task is to adjust the amount of memory allocated to Distributed Caching.

Tip   It is no longer necessary to set the backgroundGc=true element in the DistributedCacheService.exe.config as this is now the default setting.

To run the Distributed Cache service as the Service Application Pool account, or LAB\s-svc, execute the following commands. Distributed Cache will otherwise run as the Farm Account (LAB\s-farm) account. We will execute this change on CALSP01.

```
$acct = Get-SPManagedAccount "LAB\s-svc"
$farm = Get-SPFarm
$svc = $farm.Services | ?{$_.TypeName -eq "Distributed Cache"}
$svc.ProcessIdentity.CurrentIdentityType = "SpecificUser"
$svc.ProcessIdentity.ManagedAccount = $acct
$svc.ProcessIdentity.Update()
$svc.ProcessIdentity.Deploy()
```

If you have added the server as a Distributed Cache host, you must first stop the Distributed Cache service, remove the Distributed Cache instance, and finally add the Distributed Cache instance. This will update the account to LAB\s-svc.

```
Stop-SPDistributedCacheServiceInstance
Remove-SPDistributedCacheServiceInstance
Add-SPDistributedCacheServiceInstance
```

If multiple servers in the farm are already running Distributed Cache, use Stop-SPD istributedCacheServiceInstance prior to updating the memory value. The value can be updated via PowerShell.

```
Update-SPDistributedCacheSize -CacheSizeInMB 3096
```

On a single Distributed Cache host, run this cmdlet with a maximum value of 16384 for a server with 34GB or more RAM. In many instances, the default allocation is enough. Microsoft recommends a value of 1GB for farms with fewer than 10,000 users; 2.5GB for farms with more than 10,000 users and fewer than 10,000 users; and finally, for farms with more than 10,000 users, 16GB per server allocation (this requires 34GB RAM for Distributed Cache plus 2GB overhead).

Add Distributed Cache on any remaining servers in the farm hosting the WebFrontEndWithDistributeCache role or the DistributedCache role. This can be accomplished via PowerShell.

```
Add-SPDistributedCacheServiceInstance
$si = Get-SPServiceInstance -Server CALSP01 | ?{$_.TypeName -eq
'Distributed Cache'}
Start-SPServiceInstance $si
```

Tip   If you are using the Windows Firewall, verify the rules "AppFabric Caching Service (TCP-In)" and "Remote Service Management (NP-In)" are enabled. In addition, validate that the Remote Registry service in services.msc is in a running state.

This will complete the base changes required for the Distributed Cache service. The Distributed Cache service will be discussed further in Chapter 19 as it relates to service restarts.

With the basic services configured, we're ready to move onto Service Application setup and basic configuration.

Service Applications

Service Application creation will primarily be done via the SharePoint Management Shell, but with a few exceptions, Service Applications may also be created via Central Administration. Not all Service Applications must be provisioned on every farm. The best strategy is determining, via business requirements, to only provision Service Applications as they're required. Service Applications will typically add or activate timer jobs, which increases the load within the farm.

In this section, we will be provisioning the following Service Applications. Certain Service Applications will be covered in depth in later chapters.

- State Service

- Usage and Health Data Collection Service Application

- App Management Service

- Secure Store Service

- Business Data Connectivity Service

- Managed Metadata Service

- SharePoint Enterprise Search Service

- User Profile Service

As Service Applications are provisioned, those that require databases must have those databases added to the AlwaysOn Availability Group. The steps are the same as noted previously in this chapter and will not be covered here.

State Service

The State Service is used for the Session State management for filling out InfoPath Forms Service. If InfoPath Forms Services is not required, this Service Application is not required. This Service Application can only be configured via PowerShell.

```
$db = New-SPStateServiceDatabase -Name "StateService"
$sa = New-SPStateServiceApplication -Name "State Service" -Database $db
New-SPStateServiceApplicationProxy -Name "State Service"
-ServiceApplication $sa -DefaultProxyGroup
```

Usage and Health Data Collection Service Application

The Usage and Health Data Collection Service Application provides data collection that can be used for farm health and performance analysis via the Usage database. Note that this is a database that should not be part of the Availability Group. The data is transient. If the database becomes unavailable due to a failure of the SQL Server where the database resides, there is no end-user impact. Other Service Applications and SharePoint sites will continue running correctly. If an Availability Group is required, a new Availability Group running in Asynchronous mode should be used as the Usage database may overwhelm the Availability Group with the large number of writes to this database. If this database is a member of an Availability Group, it will prevent the Configuration Wizard from executing and the database must be removed from the Availability Group until the Configuration Wizard has completed successfully on all SharePoint servers in the farm.

The Usage database will be created automatically when the Search Service Application is created; however, the name of the database will be set to "WSS_ UsageApplication_<GUID>", which may not be desired.

This database will be created targeting the Primary Replica.

```
New-SPUsageApplication -Name "Usage and Health Data Collection Service
Application" -DatabaseServer CALSQL01 -DatabaseName Usage
```

App Management Service

The App Management Service is required for SharePoint Add-ins and Hybrid scenarios. This is the first Service Application where we will be specifying the new Service Application IIS Application Pool.

```
$sa = New-SPAppManagementServiceApplication -Name "App Management Service
Application" -DatabaseName "AppManagement" -ApplicationPool "SharePoint Web
Services Default"
New-SPAppManagementServiceApplicationProxy -Name "App Management Service
Application" -ServiceApplication $sa -UseDefaultProxyGroup
```

Secure Store Service

The Secure Store Service provides credential delegation and access to other services inside and outside of SharePoint. The -AuditlogMaxSize value is in days.

```
$sa = New-SPSecureStoreServiceApplication -Name "Secure Store Service
Application" -ApplicationPool "SharePoint Web Services Default"
-AuditingEnabled:$true -AuditlogMaxSize 7 -DatabaseName "SecureStore"
New-SPSecureStoreServiceApplicationProxy -Name "Secure Store Service
Application" -ServiceApplication $sa
```

Once the proxy has been created, set the Master Key and keep it in a safe place for Disaster Recovery purposes. The master key may be set via Central Administration, manage Service Applications. Manage the Secure Store Service Application and click Generate New Key.

Business Data Connectivity Service

Business Data Connectivity Service provides connectivity to external data sources, such as SQL databases for exposing them as External Lists.

```
New-SPBusinessDataCatalogServiceApplication -Name "Business Data
Connectivity Service Application" -DatabaseName "BCS" -ApplicationPool
"SharePoint Web Services Default"
```

> **Note**   Business Data Connectivity Service Proxy is created for you when creating the Service Application but you can change the proxy name post-deployment.

Managed Metadata Service

The Managed Metadata Service provides taxonomies for end-user consumption and SharePoint services, such as Search, User Profile Service, and more. The Managed Metadata Service should be created prior to the User Profile or Search Service.

```
$sa = New-SPMetadataServiceApplication -Name "Managed Metadata Service"
-DatabaseName "MMS" -ApplicationPool "SharePoint Web Services Default"
-SyndicationErrorReportEnabled
New-SPMetadataServiceApplicationProxy -Name "Managed Metadata Service"
-ServiceApplication $sa -DefaultProxyGroup -ContentTypePushdownEnabled
-DefaultKeywordTaxonomy -DefaultSiteCollectionTaxonomy
```

An optional parameter for New-SPMetadataServiceApplication is -HubUri, which is a Site Collection for the Content Type hub. If a Site Collection has been previously created, this option may be specified. When this option is specified, an additional parameter on New-SPMetadataServiceApplicationProxy is available, -ContentTypeSyndicationEnabled. Setting the HubUri will be covered later in this chapter.

SharePoint Enterprise Search Service

The Enterprise Search Configuration is a complex script and is often easier to complete via Central Administration. However, when created via Central Administration, the Search Server databases will have GUIDs appended to them and the Search topology will likely not fit your needs. As adjusting the Search topology requires PowerShell, it is beneficial to create the Search Service Application via PowerShell to begin with.

This PowerShell must be run from a SharePoint server running the Search or ApplicationWithSearch MinRole. In this case, the topology will be created on CALSP03.

```
Get-SPEnterpriseSearchServiceInstance -Local | Start-SPEnterpriseSearch
ServiceInstance
```

```
Get-SPEnterpriseSearchQueryAndSiteSettingsServiceInstance -Local | Start-SP
EnterpriseSearchQueryAndSiteSettingsServiceInstance
$sa = New-SPEnterpriseSearchServiceApplication -Name "Search Service
Application" -DatabaseName "Search" -ApplicationPool "SharePoint Web
Services Default" -AdminApplicationPool "SharePoint Web Services Default"
New-SPEnterpriseSearchServiceApplicationProxy -Name "Search Service
Application" -SearchApplication $sa
$si = Get-SPEnterpriseSearchServiceInstance -Local
$clone = New-SPEnterpriseSearchTopology -SearchApplication $sa
```

Create the initial topology.

```
New-SPEnterpriseSearchAdminComponent -SearchTopology $clone
-SearchServiceInstance $si
New-SPEnterpriseSearchContentProcessingComponent -SearchTopology $clone
-SearchServiceInstance $si
New-SPEnterpriseSearchAnalyticsProcessingComponent -SearchTopology $clone
-SearchServiceInstance $si
New-SPEnterpriseSearchCrawlComponent -SearchTopology $clone
-SearchServiceInstance $si
New-SPEnterpriseSearchIndexComponent -SearchTopology $clone
-SearchServiceInstance $si -IndexPartition 0 -RootDirectory F:\
SearchIndex\0
New-SPEnterpriseSearchQueryProcessingComponent -SearchTopology $clone
-SearchServiceInstance $si
```

Create the topology for the second Search Server, CALSP04.

```
Get-SPEnterpriseSearchServiceInstance | ?{$_.Server -match "CALSP04"} |
Start-SPEnterpriseSearchServiceInstance
Get-SPEnterpriseSearchQueryAndSiteSettingsServiceInstance | ?{$_.Server -match
"CALSP04"} | Start-SPEnterpriseSearchQueryAndSiteSettingsServiceInstance
$si2 = Get-SPEnterpriseSearchServiceInstance | ?{$_.Server -match "CALSP04"}
New-SPEnterpriseSearchAdminComponent -SearchTopology $clone
-SearchServiceInstance $si2
New-SPEnterpriseSearchAnalyticsProcessingComponent -SearchTopology $clone
-SearchServiceInstance $si2
```

```
New-SPEnterpriseSearchContentProcessingComponent -SearchTopology $clone
-SearchServiceInstance $si2
New-SPEnterpriseSearchCrawlComponent -SearchTopology $clone
-SearchServiceInstance $si2
New-SPEnterpriseSearchIndexComponent -SearchTopology $clone
-SearchServiceInstance $si2 -IndexPartition 0 -RootDirectory F:\
SearchIndex\0
New-SPEnterpriseSearchQueryProcessingComponent -SearchTopology $clone
-SearchServiceInstance $si2
Set-SPEnterpriseSearchTopology -Identity $clone
```

Remove the inactive topologies.

```
$sa = Get-SPEnterpriseSearchServiceApplication
foreach($topo in (Get-SPEnterpriseSearchTopology -SearchApplication $sa |
?{$_.State -eq "Inactive"})){Remove-SPEnterpriseSearchTopology -Identity
$topo -Confirm:$false}
```

Set the Crawl Account for the Search Service Application.

```
$sa = Get-SPEnterpriseSearchServiceApplication
$content = New-Object Microsoft.Office.Server.Search.Administration.
Content($sa)
$content.SetDefaultGatheringAccount("LAB\s-crawl", (ConvertTo-SecureString
"<Password>" -AsPlainText -Force))
```

Configure the same Content Source to use Continuous Crawls. While Continuous Crawls may increase CPU, memory, and/or disk usage, you won't have to be concerned with timing incremental crawls appropriately.

```
$source = Get-SPEnterpriseSearchCrawlContentSource -SearchApplication $sa
-Identity "Local SharePoint sites"
$source.EnableContinuousCrawls = $true
$source.Update()
```

The last step is to change the service account running the Search services. This can be done via Central Administration under Security. Click Configure service accounts. Change the service account to LAB\s-svc for the services "Windows Service – Search Host Controller Service" and "Windows Service – SharePoint Server Search."

User Profile Service

The User Profile Service synchronizes User and Group objects from Active Directory into the SharePoint Profile Service. This service is also responsible for managing Audiences and configuration of MySites (OneDrive). Creating the service Application may be done via PowerShell.

```
$sa = New-SPProfileServiceApplication -Name "User Profile Service
Application" -ApplicationPool "SharePoint Web Services Default"
-ProfileDBName "Profile" -SocialDBName "Social" -ProfileSyncDBName "Sync"
New-SPProfileServiceApplicationProxy -Name "User Profile Service
Application" -ServiceApplication $sa -DefaultProxyGroup
```

One thing you'll notice is that we are specifying a name for the Sync database even though the database isn't used as User Profile Synchronization Service is no longer part of SharePoint. This is because SharePoint will create it regardless, although the database will be empty with no tables.

Add the Default Content Access Account, LAB\s-crawl, to the Administrator permissions of the newly created User Profile Service Application in order to enumerate People Data for Search.

```
$user = New-SPClaimsPrincipal "LAB\s-crawl" -IdentityType
WindowsSamAccountName
$security = Get-SPServiceApplicationSecurity $sa -Admin
Grant-SPObjectSecurity $security $user "Retrieve People Data for Search Crawlers"
Set-SPServiceApplicationSecurity $sa $security -Admin
```

You may also want to consider adding additional accounts, such as SharePoint Administrators, who will need to manage the User Profile Service Application from PowerShell. In this example, we are providing a user with Full Control rights on the User Profile Service Application. The "-Admin" switch denotes the "Administrators" button in the ribbon, while the lack of the "-Admin" switch denotes the "Permissions" button in the ribbon.

```
$user = New-SPClaimsPrincipal "LAB\userName" -IdentityType
WindowsSamAccountName
$security = Get-SPServiceApplicationSecurity $sa -Admin
Grant-SPObjectSecurity $security $user "Full Control"
```

```
Set-SPServiceApplicationSecurity $sa $security -Admin
$security = Get-SPServiceApplicationSecurity $sa
Grant-SPObjectSecurity $security $user "Full Control"
Set-SPServiceApplicationSecurity $sa $security
```

Update the Search Server Service Content Source to use the SPS3S:// protocol (People Crawl over SSL, if using HTTP, use the SPS3:// protocol).

```
$sa = Get-SPEnterpriseSearchServiceApplication
$source = Get-SPEnterpriseSearchCrawlContentSource -SearchApplication $sa
-Identity "Local SharePoint sites"
$source.StartAddresses.Add("sps3s://sp-my.cobaltatom.com")
$source.Update()
```

Completing Service Application Setup

When all Service Applications are created, do not forget to add the Service Application databases, with the exception of the Usage database, to the Availability Group.

In addition, manually add the SharePoint Managed Accounts, LAB\s-farm, LAB\s-svc, LAB\s-c2wts, and LAB\s-web to the SQL Logins on the Secondary Replica or script the logins using the sp_help_revlogin stored procedure. Logins are not replicated automatically; however, during a database failover, the SQL Logins will have the appropriate rights to the databases.

Tip   Information on how to script the logins for transfer to the secondary replica is available at the Microsoft KB918992: `https://support.microsoft.com/en-us/help/918992`. Another useful PowerShell cmdlet is Copy-DbaLogin from the PowerShell module available at `https://dbatools.io/`.

Web Application Setup

Web Application configuration is straight forward with PowerShell. We will walk through creating two Web Applications, `https://sp.cobaltatom.com`, which will hold Team Sites, Portals, and so on, and `https://sp-my.cobaltatom.com`, which will contain the MySite host and user's MySites, also known as OneDrive for Business sites.

With the first Web Application, we will be creating the IIS Application Pool named "SharePoint" that both Web Applications will leverage. Both Web Applications will also be configured to use Kerberos. This requires registering two SPNs:

```
Setspn -U -S HTTP/sp.cobaltatom.com LAB\s-web
Setspn -U -S HTTP/sp-my.cobaltatom.com LAB\s-web
```

Create the Authentication Provider, enabling Kerberos, and then create the Web Application.

```
$ap = New-SPAuthenticationProvider -DisableKerberos:$false
New-SPWebApplication -Name "SharePoint" -HostHeader sp.cobaltatom.
com -Port 443 -ApplicationPool "SharePoint" -ApplicationPoolAccount
(Get-SPManagedAccount "LAB\s-web") -SecureSocketsLayer:$true
-AuthenticationProvider $ap -DatabaseName SharePoint_CDB1
```

This will take a few minutes to complete; then, we can create the MySite Web Application.

```
New-SPWebApplication -Name "SharePoint MySites" -HostHeader sp-
my.cobaltatom.com -Port 443 -ApplicationPool "SharePoint"
-SecureSocketsLayer:$true -AuthenticationProvider $ap -DatabaseName
SharePoint-My_CDB1
```

Validate the IIS Bindings are correct on all servers and that the SSL certificate has been correctly selected. SharePoint may not set the SSL certificate for you. This must be done on all servers running Microsoft SharePoint Foundation Web Application. For MinRole, this includes DistributedCache, WebFrontEnd, Application, ApplicationWithSearch, and WebFrontEndWithDistributedCache roles.

To support Publishing sites, add the Portal Super User and Portal Super Reader to the SharePoint Web Application. These accounts are used for permission comparison purposes only and the password for these accounts is not required. If there is the possibility that a Publishing site may be created on the SharePoint MySite Web Application, add the accounts there as well. We must set the initial properties on the SharePoint Web Application via the SharePoint Management Shell.

```
$wa = Get-SPWebApplication https://sp.cobaltatom.com
$wa.Properties["portalsuperuseraccount"] = "i:0#.w|LAB\s-su"
$wa.Properties["portalsuperreaderaccount"] = "i:0#.w|LAB\s-sr"
$wa.Update()
```

Adding the users to the Web Application Policy may be done through Manage Web Applications under Central Administration, or through the SharePoint Management Shell.

```
$wa = Get-SPWebApplication https://sp.cobaltatom.com
$zp = $wa.ZonePolicies("Default")
$policy = $zp.Add("i:0#.w|LAB\s-su", "Portal Super User")
$policyRole = $wa.PolicyRoles.GetSpecialRole("FullControl")
$policy.PolicyRoleBindings.Add($policyRole)
$policy = $zp.Add("i:0#.w|LAB\s-sr", "Portal Super Reader")
$policyRole = $wa.PolicyRoles.GetSpecialRole("FullRead")
$policy.PolicyRoleBindings.Add($policyRole)
$wa.Update()
```

The Farm Account account will be on the Policy for each Web Application as it was previously set as the Default Content Access Account in the Search Service. This can be removed.

When the Zone Policy has been changed, it will require an IISReset to take effect. To perform this, from the SharePoint Management Shell, run the following:

```
foreach($server in (Get-SPServer | ?{$_.Role -ne "Invalid" -and $_.Role -ne
"Search"}))
{
    Write-Host "Resetting IIS on $($server.Address)..."
        iisreset $server.Address /noforce
}
```

Add the required Managed Path, "personal" to the SharePoint MySite Web Application and remove the default "sites" Managed Path.

```
New-SPManagedPath -RelativeUrl "personal" -WebApplication https://sp-my.
cobaltatom.com
Remove-SPManagedPath -Identity "sites" -WebApplication https://sp-my.
cobaltatom.com
```

Then, enable Self-Service Site Creation.

```
$wa = Get-SPWebApplication https://sp-my.cobaltatom.com
$wa.SelfServiceSiteCreationEnabled = $true
$wa.Update()
```

These two steps are required to enable MySite creation by users. See Modern Self Service Site Creation later in this chapter for additional options.

Root Site Collections

Web Applications are required to have a root Site Collection. This is the Site Collection that resides at the path "/". For the SharePoint Web Application, we will deploy a modern Communications Site Template and for the SharePoint MySite Web Application, we will deploy the MySite Host Template.

```
New-SPSite -Url https://sp.cobaltatom.com -Template SITEPAGEPUBLISHING#0
-Name "Communications Site" -OwnerAlias "LAB\trevor.seward"
New-SPSite -Url https://sp-my.cobaltatom.com -Template SPSMSITEHOST#0 -Name
"OneDrive for Business" -OwnerAlias "LAB\trevor.seward"
```

Content Type Hub and Enterprise Search Center Configuration

In addition to these Site Collections, we will also create a Content Type Hub and an Enterprise Search Center. The Content Type Hub will be created and then configured in the Managed Metadata Service, and the Enterprise Search Center will be created and set as the Search Center URL.

The Content Type Hub can be a standard classic Team Site Template.

```
New-SPSite -Url https://sp.cobaltatom.com/sites/contentTypeHub -Template
STS#0 -Name "Content Type Hub" -OwnerAlias "LAB\trevor.seward"
```

Set the Managed Metadata Service Content Type Hub URL.

```
Set-SPMetadataServiceApplication -Identity "Managed Metadata Service"
-HubUri https://sp.cobaltatom.com/sites/contentTypeHub
```

Next, create the Enterprise Search Center using the SRCHCEN#0 template.

```
New-SPSite -Url https://sp.cobaltatom.com/sites/search -Template SRCHCEN#0
-Name "Enterprise Search Center" -OwnerAlias "LAB\trevor.seward"
```

Finally, set the Enterprise Search Center in the SharePoint Search Service.

```
$sa = Get-SPEnterpriseSearchServiceApplication
$sa.SearchCenterUrl = "https://sp.cobaltatom.com/sites/search/Pages"
$sa.Update()
```

Additional information on the Search Service Application is in Chapter 6.

MySite Configuration

To configure MySites for the User Profile Service, the only option we must set is the MySite Host. All other settings are optional, but can be found in Central Administration under Manage Service Applications in the User Profile Service Application. In the Setup MySites link are a variety of options to control the MySite configuration.

```
$sa = Get-SPServiceApplication | ?{$_.TypeName -eq "User Profile Service
Application"}
Set-SPProfileServiceApplication -Identity $sa -MySiteHostLocation https://
sp-my.cobaltatom.com
```

Modern Self-Service Site Creation

SharePoint Server 2019 introduces a new feature to allow users to provision Modern Team and Communication Sites from the MySite Host.

Enable self-service site creation on the primary Web Application, `https://sp.cobaltatom.com`.

```
$wa = Get-SPWebApplication https://sp.cobaltatom.com
$wa.SelfServiceSiteCreationEnabled = $true
$wa.Update()
```

In addition, you must provide users with at least Read access to the root Site Collection on `https://sp.cobaltatom.com`. For example, you could add the group Everyone to the root Site Collection Visitors group.

The next step is to set up self-service site creation on the MySite host Web Application.

```
$wa = Get-SPWebApplication https://sp-my.cobaltatom.com
$wa.ShowStartASiteMenuItem = $true
$wa.SelfServiceCreationAlternateUrl = "https://sp.cobaltatom.com"
$wa.Update()
```

This will allow users to create Modern Team and Communication Sites on the primary Web Application from the MySite host Web Application.

User Profile Import

The User Profile User Import supports "Active Directory Import" mode from SharePoint. While this method of import is very fast, it does not support exporting properties from SharePoint to other systems or importing pictures from Active Directory. The User Profile Service Application also supports "External Synchronization," this method requires Microsoft Identity Manager 2016.

More information about the User Profile User Import and Microsoft Identity Manager 2016 configuration are covered in Chapter 7.

With all of the basic Service Applications provisioned, we will take a brief look at Virtual Machine Templates, which will allow for faster deployment of SharePoint Server 2019.

Virtual Machine Templates

Many of the initial steps of installing SharePoint Server may be templated with virtualization technologies. When planning on using templates, a virtual machine template for SharePoint Server may have the SharePoint prerequisites installed, as well as the SharePoint binaries (setup.exe) and any Public Updates required. You cannot run the SharePoint Configuration Wizard, psconfig.exe, or PowerShell (New-SPConfigurationDatabase or Connect-SPConfigurationDatabase) prior to templating the virtual machine. Templating processes, such as Sysprep, should be run against the virtual machine prior to creating the template.

Next Steps

In this chapter, we walked through an advanced step-by-step process to install SQL Server 2017 to SharePoint Server 2019 in a highly available configuration. This should provide you with the tools required to develop your own scripts and processes to provision a highly available farm.

Next, we will discuss Authentication and Security, covering NTLM, Kerberos, and SAML authentication. In addition, we will cover transport security and firewall access rules and the Azure AD Application Proxy.

CHAPTER 4

Configuring Authentication and Security

In this chapter, we will cover the various mechanisms for authentication, authorization, and security for your SharePoint farm. NTLM, Kerberos, and SAML will be covered, along with their advantages and disadvantages throughout the farm. We'll also take a look at transport security via TLS (SSL) and IPsec. Lastly, we'll take a look at the Windows Firewall and what the best practices are for the SharePoint environment.

Authentication Methods

SharePoint Server supports a variety of authentication methods. We will cover each authentication method and their advantages and disadvantages. Authentication, also known as AuthN, is performed by IIS or services; SharePoint itself does not perform AuthN.

Basic

Basic authentication is where the user's username and password are sent in clear text to the SharePoint server. IIS performs authentication to Active Directory based on the supplied username and password. This is form of authentication is one of the least used and generally is unnecessary with the other options we have available to us. It is also not recommended to use Basic authentication without using SSL to encrypt the transport of the credentials.

© Vlad Catrinescu and Trevor Seward 2019
V. Catrinescu and T. Seward, *Deploying SharePoint 2019*, https://doi.org/10.1007/978-1-4842-4526-2_4

NTLM

Authentication via NTLM is one of the most common forms of authentication used in SharePoint environments. It requires no additional configuration on the part of SharePoint Administrators or Domain Administrators. "It just works," however, is not the most secure or performant form of authentication available to us. As the web, including SharePoint, is stateless, authentication must be performed for each request. This authentication method must perform multiple trips between the user, SharePoint (IIS) and Active Directory, increasing the amount of time it takes to authenticate. This flow is shown in Figure 4-1.

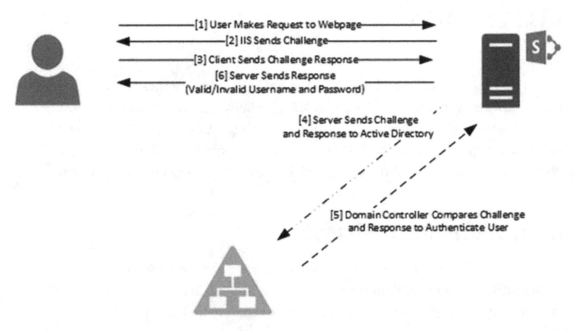

Figure 4-1. *NTLM Challenge and Response Flow*

NTLMv1 and NTLMv2 are considered insecure authentication protocols. NTLMv1 can take a matter of minutes to hours to crack an NTLM hash, while NTLMv2 may take up to 4 to 5 times longer. For highly complex NTLMv2 passwords, Rainbow Tables exist which are files that are precomputed cryptographic hash functions, reducing the amount of time it takes to reverse an NTLM hashed password into its plaintext variant. Microsoft now includes Group Policies to disable NTLM on computers that are members of Active Directory.

Kerberos

Kerberos is a modern authentication protocol in use in every Active Directory implementation. Instead of passing password hashes to and from services, Kerberos passes what are known as tickets. Certain tickets are created upon user login to the client machine and are retrieved from the Kerberos Distribution Center (KDC), which is an Active Directory Domain Controller. As shown in Figure 4-2, these tickets are steps one and two. When a user makes a request to an external service, such as SharePoint, steps three and four are executed to retrieve a Ticket Granting Service ticket (TGS). The user then sends the TGS to the target service. That service sees the ticket is valid, and in a mutual authentication scenario, the service sends information back to the client confirming the identity of the service. Each ticket has a specific lifetime, but these are generally long enough for users to not have to reauthenticate to the KDC to retrieve a new ticket. In a scenario with Active Directory domain-joined clients, this reauthentication, or retrieval of a new, valid ticket, would happen automatically.

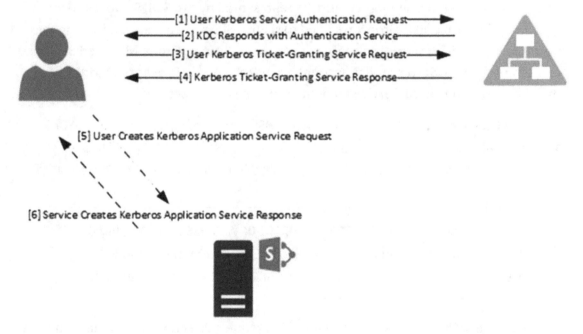

Figure 4-2. *Kerberos Ticket Flow*

There is generally a perception among administrators that Kerberos is difficult to configure and setup. Luckily, it is quite easy for IIS (and SharePoint). It simply involves creating a Service Principal Name (SPN) for the HTTP service for the Domain

User account running the IIS Application Pool. To put it simply, create an SPN for HTTP/<FQDN> for the Web Application Pool account and set the SharePoint Web Application to use Kerberos. By default, this requires Domain Administrator privileges. To use the example in this book, sp.cobaltatom.com is the FQDN of our Web Application and the Service Account assigned to it is LAB\s-web.

Using a console from any domain-joined machine, run the following command to assign the service (HTTP) to the principal (LAB\s-web):

```
setspn.exe -U -S HTTP/sp.cobaltatom.com LAB\s-web
```

The -S switch adds the SPN after searching for duplicate SPNs. Duplicate SPNs will prevent the service from functioning properly. The -U switch tells setspn.exe that the account we're assigning the HTTP service to is a user account. Lastly, while we're using SSL, the name of the service is simply "HTTP". If using a port number other than 80 or 443, specify the port number after the FQDN, in the format of FQDN:nnnn.

In addition, we created SPNs for SQL Server. The service for SQL Server is "MSSQLSvc". As our SQL implementation is represented by two SQL Servers and a SQL AlwaysOn Availability Group, we need to set five SPNs. We are also indicating the port number that SQL Server is listening on. As we are using a Group Managed Service Account for the SQL Server service account, we use the Active Directory Module for PowerShell and the Set-ADServiceAccount cmdlet instead of setspn.exe.

```
Set-ADServiceAccount -Name s-sql @{Add='MSSQLSvc/calsql01:1433','MSSQLSvc/
calsql01.lab.cobaltatom.com:1433','MSSQLSvc/calsql02:1433','MSSQLSvc/
calsql02.lab.cobaltatom.com:1433','MSSQLSvc/calspag.lab.cobaltatom.com'}
```

Tip   In the preceding example, the Add operator was used for the Service Principal Names. You can also use a Replace operator to replace the existing SPNs on the service account with the ones you define in the cmdlet parameter.

The benefit of Kerberos is the authentication request does not need to make the round trip between the User, Active Directory, back to the User, and then to the target service. The tickets are considered valid until they expire by the service the user is accessing. This also limits the potential for intercepting and decrypting tickets. Active Directory also offers, through Group Policy, encryption algorithms that currently have no known practical attacks. This includes AES256 encrypted tickets. Unlike NTLM, which may be brute-forced within a matter of hours, AES128 or AES256 encrypted tickets would take billions of years to brute-force to retrieve the plaintext password.

Kerberos does have a significant downside as it requires the client to be able to access the KDC. If the KDC is inaccessible, the client cannot retrieve a Kerberos ticket. This is best represented in an external authentication scenario, such as the user authenticating to a SharePoint site over the Internet. Without further implementation of preauthenticating reverse proxies, SharePoint, or IIS more accurately, will fall back to allow the client to authenticate over NTLM, which is undesirable.

Lastly, certain clients may be unable to connect to a Web Application using Kerberos if nonstandard ports (TCP/80 or TCP/443) are used for the Web Application. Examples include the Search Crawler as well certain browsers. This is primarily an issue when the Web Application is configured using TCP/88, the same port as Kerberos, although it is strongly recommended to only use the standard TCP/80 or TCP/443 ports.

Security Assertion Markup Language

Security Assertion Markup Language, or SAML, is a modern form of authentication which presents *claims* about a user to a service. Based on the *identity claim* contained in the SAML assertion, the service will authorize the user to the service.

SAML is a favorite with modern services due to the ability to federate with disparate services that do not have a dependency on the authentication service the user authenticates with. For example, a user may authenticate against a local Active Directory Federation Services server using NTLM or Kerberos, and due to federation, may assert their identity to a SharePoint farm running within a separate organization. Based on rules within the federation trust, SharePoint will authorize the user to access SharePoint resources. This configuration is significantly easier to manage than an Active Directory forest trust over the Internet (which would generally take place within a VPN tunnel).

One of the SAML drawbacks, as it directly relates to SharePoint, is no validation of the information entered into the People Picker. The authentication source (e.g., Active Directory), is abstracted away from SharePoint, thus SharePoint does not know where to "look" for accounts when using SAML. This is leads to a poor user experience, as it is not possible for SharePoint to validate what is a valid or invalid value.

Tip LDAPCP, a free open source project on GitHub, implements methods for SharePoint to validate the information inputted into the People Picker is valid. The validation only works when SharePoint has LDAP or LDAPS access to the target authentication service (such as Active Directory).

`https://ldapcp.com/`

SharePoint is only compatible with SAML 1.1, unlike many other services which are compatible with SAML 2.0.

Forms-Based Authentication

Forms-based authentication (FBA) is often used when using non–Active Directory identity providers, such as a SQL database data store or Active Directory Lightweight Directory Services. FBA relies on *providers* which implement the logic to authenticate the user against the data store where the username and password is held. These are often custom developed, although Microsoft does include a provider out of the box to authenticate against LDAP services. FBA is often chosen in scenarios where IT does not or cannot use Active Directory for external partners.

When a user browses to a SharePoint site with FBA enabled, they are presented with a username and password dialog box to enter their credentials. The configured authentication provider will then validate those credentials against the authentication store.

When using FBA, the username and password are transmitted over the wire in clear text. Like with Basic authentication, it is strongly recommended to use SSL to encrypt the transport of credentials. FBA also requires manual implementation in SharePoint, modifying the Membership and Role providers within the Web Application, Security Token Service, and Central Administration web.config files. These files must also contain the same configuration values across all members of the SharePoint farm.

Authorization

SharePoint performs what is known as *authorization*, or AuthZ. Authorization is where a user has already performed *authentication* (AuthN), which is performed by IIS when using Basic, NTLM, or Kerberos authentication, and in the case of SAML, the Identity Provider (e.g., ADFS). AuthN takes place when a user attempts to access a resource.

SharePoint evaluates the permissions of the resource against the permissions held by the user. If they have proper permissions, then they're authorized to access that content.

Now that we've looked at the various forms of authentication that SharePoint supports, along with the difference between authentication and authorization, let's take a look at the available transport security options we have to use with SharePoint.

Transport Security

Transport security is the act of securing, or encrypting, the information passed over the network. One of the most used forms of transport security is SSL, now known as TLS. This section will walk through TLS, IPsec, and available modern encryption protocols.

TLS

TLS, or Transport Layer Security, the replacement of SSL, or Secure Socket Layer, encrypts data as it is sent between services or between the end user and services. TLS is very important in today's modern implementation of network services in order to protect data in transit over the network.

IPsec

IPsec is a form of encrypting all data across the network without specifically implementing an encryption protocol such as TLS. IPsec, for example, would encrypt data over the network even if the user sent data to a service where the service was requesting the information in clear text. IPsec has a high barrier to entry with a significant investment into planning and security. IPsec is also only useful within an internal network, while TLS would still be required to encrypt data over the Internet.

Encryption Protocols

TLS, or SSL, have different revisions, some of which are now considered insecure. SSL has the following versions:

- SSL 2.0
- SSL 3.0

Both SSL 2.0 and SSL 3.0 are considered insecure and should be disabled server-side. TLS has the following versions:

- TLS 1.0

- TLS 1.1

- TLS 1.2

TLS 1.1 and TLS 1.2 are considered modern, and for now, secure. TLS 1.0 should be disabled if possible. SharePoint Server 2019, Office Online Server, and SharePoint Workflow Manager support disabling all protocols except for TLS 1.2.

Protocols can be disabled server-side through the registry. When these registry settings are changed, the server must be restarted in order for the change to take effect. For each protocol to disable, under the \Protocols\<Protocol Version>\Server folder, create a DWORD of "Enabled" equal to 0.

```
Windows Registry Editor Version 5.00

[HKEY_LOCAL_MACHINE\SYSTEM\CurrentControlSet\Control\SecurityProviders\
SCHANNEL\Protocols]

[HKEY_LOCAL_MACHINE\SYSTEM\CurrentControlSet\Control\SecurityProviders\
SCHANNEL\Protocols\PCT 1.0]
@="DefaultValue"

[HKEY_LOCAL_MACHINE\SYSTEM\CurrentControlSet\Control\SecurityProviders\
SCHANNEL\Protocols\PCT 1.0\Server]
@="DefaultValue"
"Enabled"=dword:00000000

[HKEY_LOCAL_MACHINE\SYSTEM\CurrentControlSet\Control\SecurityProviders\
SCHANNEL\Protocols\SSL 2.0]
@="DefaultValue"

[HKEY_LOCAL_MACHINE\SYSTEM\CurrentControlSet\Control\SecurityProviders\
SCHANNEL\Protocols\SSL 2.0\Server]
@="DefaultValue"
"Enabled"=dword:00000000
```

```
[HKEY_LOCAL_MACHINE\SYSTEM\CurrentControlSet\Control\SecurityProviders\
SCHANNEL\Protocols\SSL 3.0]
@="DefaultValue"

[HKEY_LOCAL_MACHINE\SYSTEM\CurrentControlSet\Control\SecurityProviders\
SCHANNEL\Protocols\SSL 3.0\Server]
@="DefaultValue"
"Enabled"=dword:00000000

[HKEY_LOCAL_MACHINE\SYSTEM\CurrentControlSet\Control\SecurityProviders\
SCHANNEL\Protocols\TLS 1.0]
@="DefaultValue"

[HKEY_LOCAL_MACHINE\SYSTEM\CurrentControlSet\Control\SecurityProviders\
SCHANNEL\Protocols\TLS 1.0\Server]
@="DefaultValue"
"Enabled"=dword:00000000

[HKEY_LOCAL_MACHINE\SYSTEM\CurrentControlSet\Control\SecurityProviders\
SCHANNEL\Protocols\TLS 1.1]
@="DefaultValue"

[HKEY_LOCAL_MACHINE\SYSTEM\CurrentControlSet\Control\SecurityProviders\
SCHANNEL\Protocols\TLS 1.1\Server]
@="DefaultValue"
"Enabled"=dword:00000000
```

As an alternative to implementing the registry changes on individual servers, consider using Group Policy to implement the settings.

Tip   A Group Policy ADMX file to implement these changes is freely available from `https://github.com/Nauplius/SchannelConfiguration`.

In order for Office Online Server and SharePoint Workflow Manager to be able to communicate with SharePoint Server 2019 where TLS 1.2 is enforced, use the following registry entry on the Office Online Server or Workflow Manager 1.0 server. Reboot the server once implemented.

```
Windows Registry Editor Version 5.00

[HKEY_LOCAL_MACHINE\SOFTWARE\Microsoft\.NETFramework\v4.0.30319]
"SchUseStrongCrypto"=dword:00000001
```

HTTP Strict Transport Security

HTTP Strict Transport Security (HSTS) is another form of enforcing TLS. HSTS has two primary functions:

- Redirecting clients from HTTP to SSL

- Telling clients that the site should only be accessed over SSL for all future requests

This helps prevent man-in-the-middle attacks, where, after the client has connected to the valid site, the client is "tricked" into connecting to an insecure site of the same name (e.g., via DNS poisoning). Because HSTS was enabled on the valid site, the client will refuse to connect to the invalid site, regardless if the invalid site uses SSL or HTTP. This is because HSTS also tells the client to validate the SSL certificate on the site.

HSTS has a max-age value. This value is what tells the client that for future sessions, only connect over SSL. The max-age value should be 18 weeks or greater and should be for at least as long as the site is expected to support SSL. If the site removes SSL support within the max-age timeframe, the client will refuse to connect to the site. HSTS can be set on a per–Web Application basis in SharePoint Server 2019 using the SharePoint Management Shell.

```
$wa = Get-SPWebApplication https://sp.cobaltatom.com
$wa.HttpStrictTransportSecuritySettings.IsEnabled = $true
$wa.HttpStrictTransportSecuritySettings.MaxAge = 31536000
$wa.Update()
```

The MaxAge property is a value in seconds. The default value, 31536000, is 365 days.

SSL Bridging and SSL Offloading

SSL Bridging is when a load balancer terminates the client's SSL session at the load balancer. The load balancer, in turn, decrypts the session, but resecures the session prior to connecting to the target resource, such as a SharePoint site, using SSL. This is illustrated in Figure 4-3.

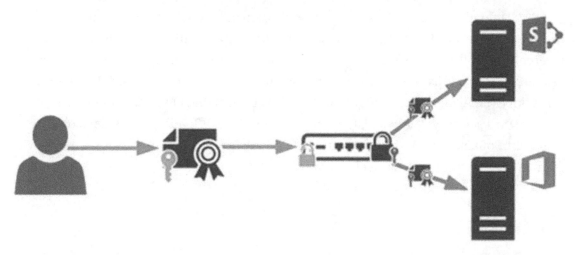

Figure 4-3. *SSL Bridging*

SSL Bridging may be used when administrators want to intercept and inspect the SSL traffic on the load balancer, want to speed up SSL session negotiation for clients (the load balancer maintains the SSL session for a longer period of time than the client would), or wants to translate the SSL or TLS protocol used by the client to a more or less strict version of the protocol.

SSL Offloading is when the load balancer decrypts a client session and then sends the information to the service over HTTP, as shown in Figure 4-4.

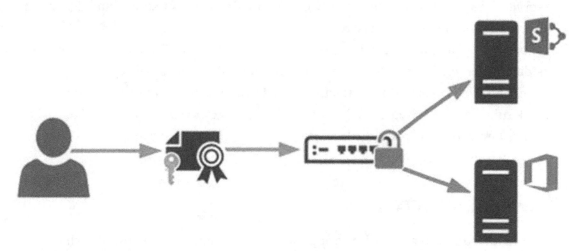

Figure 4-4. *SSL Offloading*

SSL Offloading is considered insecure as it transmits sensitive information in the clear. This may include OAuth2 tokens, which contain information that may be intercepted on the network and replayed to gain the same privileges to the requested resource (or user). As OAuth2 tokens are used between SharePoint, Office Online Server, Workflow Manager, and SharePoint Add-ins, it is critical that OAuth2 remain encrypted by transport security. If the decision is made to use SSL Offloading, consider isolating the SharePoint servers and any servers that SharePoint uses OAuth to communicate with from other networks and services.

Firewalls

Firewalls are an important aspect in network security. Firewalls provide ingress and egress rules to allow or deny traffic based on patterns, source and destination IP addresses, and so on. We will cover two types of firewalls: host-based firewalls and stand-alone firewall appliances.

Windows Firewall

The Windows Firewall is built into all modern versions of Windows. It provides a fairly extensive ruleset to allow and deny traffic based on Network Location Awareness (where the server detects if it is on a public, private, or domain network), source and destination IP address, authentication, and so on.

While it may be uncommon to use in many environments, IT departments should consider implementing it on SharePoint servers. SharePoint does create specific Windows Firewall rules during installation to make management easier. Windows Firewall rules can also be easily deployed via Group Policy to sets of servers. The Windows Firewall can present the last line of defense from an attacker who has already gained internal network access.

Firewall Appliances

Many manufactures create hardware appliances, as well as software firewalls which run on commodity hardware. These firewalls are often used as an edge firewall (the firewall between the corporate network and the DMZ as well as back channel firewalls, or firewalls used between the DMZ and internal corporate network. These firewalls are the primary line of defense for a corporate network.

DMZ

Placing web servers in a DMZ while SQL Servers and other non-web services reside in the internal network is commonplace in many environments and generally accepted as a secure option. However, as it pertains to SharePoint, this may in fact be the less secure option, as shown in Figure 4-5.

External User   **Edge Firewall**   **SharePoint DMZ**   **Back Channel Firewall**   **SharePoint**

Figure 4-5. *SharePoint in the DMZ with multiple ports open in the Back Channel Firewall*

SharePoint must have not only a port open to SQL Server, but also ports open between SharePoint Servers *and* Active Directory Domain Controllers for authentication, authorization, People Picker, as well as the User Profile Service when using AD Import. Any other integrated services, such as SharePoint Workflow Manager, Office Online Server, or hosted High Trust Add-ins must also be taken into consideration. This leads to a significant number of ports that must be opened in the back channel firewall between the DMZ and internal corporate network.

Reverse Proxies

Reverse Proxies are either preauthentication reverse proxies, such as Microsoft's Web Application Proxy, or do not provide any authentication mechanisms, such as Apache's mod_proxy or mod_ssl. Reverse proxies are typically deployed in a DMZ. Their function is to terminate the user's session, while the proxy passes the session to the services behind it. This is illustrated in Figure 4-6.

External User   **Edge Firewall**   **Reverse Proxy**   **Back Channel Firewall**   **SharePoint**

Figure 4-6. *Reverse proxies to handle external user sessions*

This allows SharePoint and related services to reside in the internal corporate network and have a single port, tcp/443 (HTTPS), as an example, open in the back channel firewall. In general, this is considered more secure versus placing SharePoint servers within the DMZ when they need access to resources within the internal corporate network.

Azure AD App Proxy

The Azure AD App Proxy is a service from Microsoft which allows communication with services behind a firewall without opening a port in the firewall. This service requires an Azure AD Basic or Premium (P1 or P2) subscription. It can be configured using pass through authentication, Windows Integrated Authentication using Kerberos Constrained Delegation, or in a Single Sign On configuration. Windows Integrated Authentication and Single Sign On configurations require that your users are synchronized with Azure AD and an SSO service is in place, such as Azure AD Connect SSO or Active Directory Federation Services.

Note   More information on App Proxy is available at `https://docs. microsoft.com/en-us/azure/active-directory/manage-apps/ application-proxy-enable`.

To configure SharePoint Server 2019 using Azure AD App Proxy with Windows authentication (Kerberos Constrained Delegation) on SharePoint, we need to first download and install the App Proxy Connector. This can be found in the Azure Portal under Azure Active Directory, then under Application proxy.

The App Proxy Connector should be installed on two or more servers with no other services running on them. The installer will ask for an account in Azure AD which has elevated rights (such as a Global Administrator or Owner). There is no further configuration required for the installation. Once installed, the Azure App Proxy Connector will register itself with Azure AD. You can validate the registration in Azure Active Directory under Application proxy, as shown in Figure 4-7.

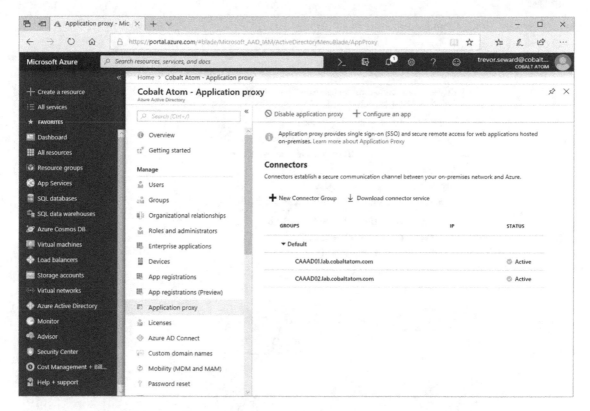

Figure 4-7. *Validating the registration of the App Proxy servers with Azure AD*

As the following configuration requires Kerberos Constrained Delegation, we must delegate the appropriate Service Principal Names to the Azure AD App Proxy computer account(s). For each Azure AD App Proxy computer object in Active Directory go to the properties of the computer object. On the Delegation tab, select Trust this computer for delegation to the specified services only then select Use any authentication protocol. We then must add the specific SPN(s) to delegate. In this case, our SPNs, HTTP/ sp.cobaltatom.com and HTTP/sp-my.cobaltatom.com are registered to the user LAB\s-web. Click the Add button and search for the s-web account. Select the SPN(s) registered to the account and click OK. The result will look like Figure 4-8.

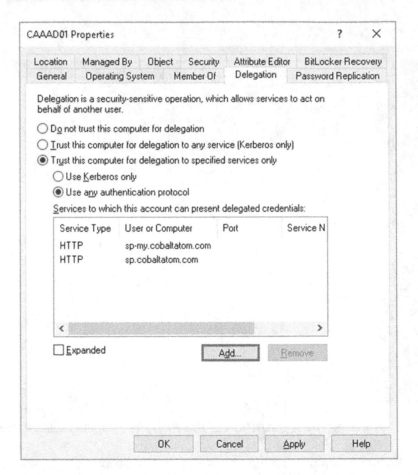

Figure 4-8. *Registering SPNs with the computer running App Proxy Connector*

The next step is to create an Enterprise Application which will point to one of the SharePoint Web Applications. In this example we will configure it for the primary Web Application, `https://sp.cobaltatom.com`.

In Azure Active Directory, navigate to Application proxy. Click the Configure an app button. Type in a logical name for the application. This is how the application will appear in the Enterprise applications within Azure Active Directory and may be how it is displayed in a tile for end users (this option is configurable).

Set the Internal Url to the same value as the URL used for the Web Application. Make sure the External Url is the same value. For Pre Authentication, if using Kerberos Constrained Delegation, set the value to Azure Active Directory. This method will present the same login experience that you may be familiar with for Office 365 and/ or Azure services. Configure the Connector Group appropriately; by default this is Default and will match the Group name containing the list of servers in the Application proxy from Figure 4-7. Set Translate URLs In Headers option to No. The other options will remain at their default values. See Figure 4-9 as an example of a full configured application. Note the informational message at the bottom of the screen. Configure your external DNS record per this message. Click Add to save the configuration to Azure AD.

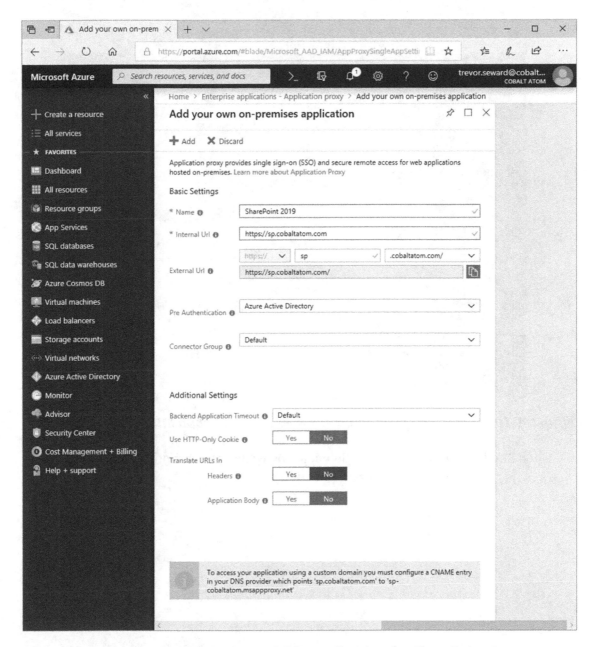

Figure 4-9. *Configuring the primary Web Application for SharePoint Server 2019 in Azure AD App Proxy*

The next step is to edit the application you just created. Click Properties and as shown in Figure 4-10, under User assignment required, select No. If you do not want the application appearing in the user App Portal or Office 365 App Launcher, select No for Visible to users. This will not impact their ability to access SharePoint on-premises.

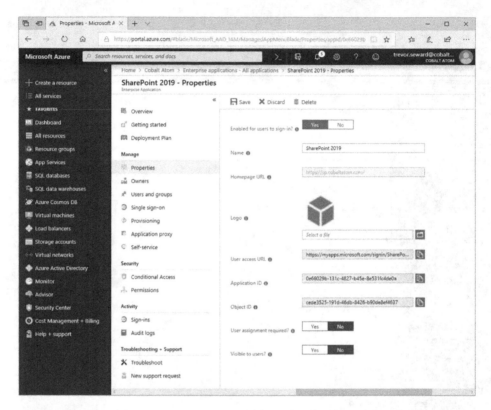

Figure 4-10. *Configuring the access properties for the application*

Click Single sign-on. Under the Select a single sign-on method as shown in Figure 4-11, select Windows Integrated Authentication.

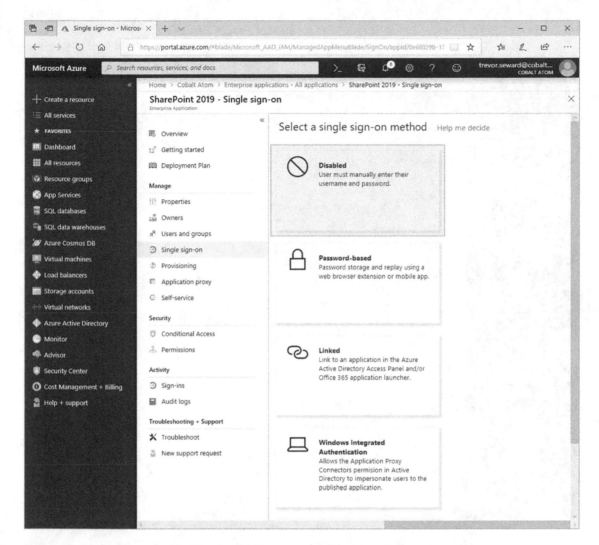

Figure 4-11. *The available single sign-on options*

After selecting Windows Integrated Authentication, you will be prompted to set the SPN for the service as shown in Figure 4-12. This is the same SPN as was set in Chapter 3; HTTP/sp.cobaltatom.com for the primary Web Application.

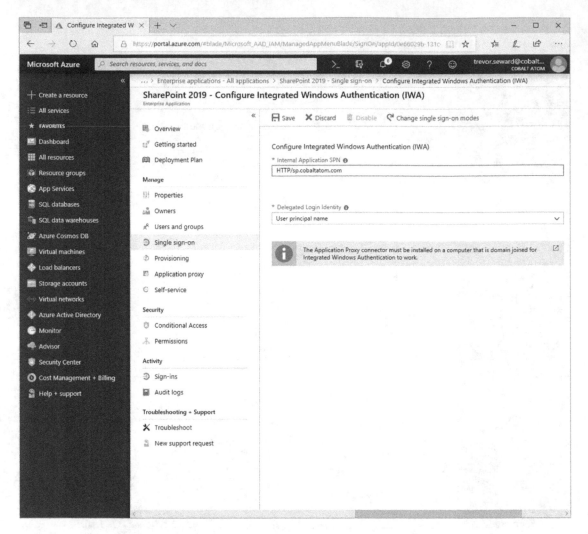

Figure 4-12. *Setting the SPN for the application*

The last step is to navigate to the Application proxy blade. Below the options we previously set in Figure 4-9 will be a new Certificate option. Upload the same certificate with private key (a PFX file) used for the primary Web Application. This completes the configuration of the application in Azure AD App Proxy. Once DNS has replicated, you will be able to use your Web Application URL to access SharePoint from anywhere without having to open any inbound ports in your corporate firewall.

Configuring Office Online Server and the SharePoint App Domain differ slightly. During the initial configuration of the application, under Pre Authentication select Passthrough instead of Azure Active Directory. This is due to Office Online Server not using any form of authentication (Office Online Server uses OAuth tokens instead) and the SharePoint App Domain not supporting Kerberos. Once the application has been created, the Single sign-on option will remain Disabled.

Tip   Make sure your internal DNS is properly configured to point to SharePoint or a load balancer if using more than one SharePoint front end. Internal DNS will be used by installed Azure App Proxy Connector to perform lookups.

Access Rules

Strict Access Rules should be created, where possible: for example, blocking client networks from directly communicating with SharePoint servers not running end-user facing roles, such as those servers which are not the WebFrontEnd role.

Likewise, rules for SQL Server should also be put in place. Only SharePoint servers, backup systems, monitoring systems, and certain administrator systems should be allowed to communicate with the SQL Server over various ports (CIFS, standard SQL ports, as two examples). Table 4-1 provides the essential inbound ports for each type of server.

Table 4-1. *Inbound Ports for Servers*

Server Type	Port Number	Notes
SQL Server	TCP/1433	Database Engine
SQL Server	TCP/1434	Optional (SQL Browser)
SQL Server	TCP/5022	Optional (Availability Group Listener)
SharePoint Server	TCP/80	Optional (if using HTTP)
SharePoint Server	TCP/443	Optional (if using SSL)
Office Online Server	TCP/80	Optional (if using HTTP)
Office Online Server	TCP/443	Optional (if using SSL)
Workflow Manager	TCP/12291	Optional (if using HTTP)
Workflow Manager	TCP/12290	Optional (if using SSL)
SharePoint Server	TCP/32843	Service Application (HTTP)

(continued)

Table 4-1. *(continued)*

Server Type	Port Number	Notes
SharePoint Server	TCP/32844	Service Application (SSL)
SharePoint Server	TCP/32845	Service Application (net.tcp)
SharePoint Server	TCP/22233	Distributed Cache
SharePoint Server	TCP/22234	Distributed Cache
SharePoint Server	ICMP (0)	Distributed Cache (Ping)
Microsoft Identity Manager	RPC Dynamic Ports	Synchronization Service
Microsoft Identity Manager	RPC Endpoint Mapper	Synchronization Service

Next Steps

We have taken a look at the available authentication and security options for SharePoint Server 2019. Next, we will learn how to set up and configure SharePoint Add-ins.

CHAPTER 5

Configuring Add-ins

In order to customize your SharePoint 2019 environment, one of the recommended options is deploying code via Add-ins (previously known as apps). With the SharePoint Framework now available in SharePoint 2019 on-premises, add-ins will be a bit less used than they were in SharePoint 2013 and 2016; however, lots of third-party vendors offer products deployed as add-ins, so it is still very important to understand how to configure the Add-ins Infrastructure in SharePoint Server 2019. Furthermore, plenty of third-party vendors offer Add-ins in the SharePoint Store, which is like Apple iTunes or Google Play, but for SharePoint.

However, compared to your smartphone, you need more than an Internet connection to install Add-ins in SharePoint. Being able to consume Add-ins in SharePoint requires some configuration not only in SharePoint, but in DNS as well.

In this chapter, you will learn how to configure a SharePoint 2019 Environment to support Add-ins as well as how to manage them by using the App Catalog.

SharePoint Add-in Architecture Overview

Before we get started configuring Add-ins for SharePoint 2019, it's important to understand the Add-in architecture, to have a preview of all the different elements we will configure in this chapter.

First, technically speaking, every Add-in you add to your SharePoint Farm becomes a subsite under the SharePoint site collection you added it under. In Figure 5-1 we can see a SharePoint Site with two Add-ins deployed.

V. Catrinescu and T. Seward, *Deploying SharePoint 2019*, https://doi.org/10.1007/978-1-4842-4526-2_5

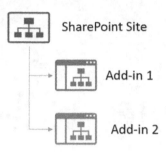

Figure 5-1. *Basic Add-in Architecture in SharePoint*

Furthermore, SharePoint Add-ins run under a different lookup zone in DNS for security reasons. If your main domain is cobaltatom.com, your *Add-in Domain* could be cobaltatomapps.com. If you plan to open your site to the Internet and allow users to connect to it without a VPN, you will need to make sure your Add-in Domain is a real public domain, and since your site will probably be using SSL (Secure Sockets Layer), you will also need a wildcard certificate on your Add-in Domain provided by a public certification authority such as DigiCert. The wildcard certificate is needed because add-in URLs are generated by SharePoint using a random ID as seen later in this chapter.

Note   Microsoft recommends using a completely new forward lookup zone and not a subdomain such as apps.cobaltatom.com. This recommendation is made to prevent Cross-Site Scripting (XSS) attacks.

The URL of each Add-in deployment is also given a unique ID. Therefore, even if we deploy the same Add-in on two different Site collections, each deployment has a different URL. The URL is composed of a prefix that you can choose, the Add-in ID, and the Add-in Domain. In Figure 5-2, we can see the same SharePoint site, with the URLs of both the site and Add-ins. For this book we will use the "app" prefix for our Add-ins.

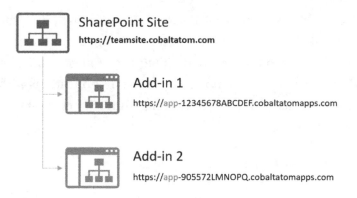

Figure 5-2. *Add-in URLs in SharePoint 2019*

We can choose the Add-in Prefix ourselves, as well as the Add-in domain; however, we cannot choose the ID that is assigned to the Add-in deployment. Therefore, that is why we need a dedicated forward lookup zone in our DNS that has a wildcard entry, so everything in our Add-in domain will point directly either to our SharePoint Server, or to the network load balancer that will forward the request to one of our SharePoint Web Front Ends. In Figure 5-3, you can see a sample of the CobaltAtom DNS, which will contain the CobaltAtom.com forward lookup zone containing all your SharePoint Sites, as well as all the servers and everything in your domain. We can also find the *CobaltAtomApps.com* forward lookup zone that simply has a wildcard entry, so everything in that forward lookup zone will go to our SharePoint Web Front End.

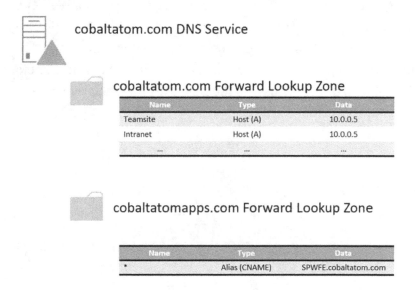

Figure 5-3. *DNS Architecture for SharePoint Add-ins*

Now that we know how we get our users to the SharePoint Server from DNS, let's take a look at how SharePoint handles those requests. In Figure 5-4, we see a user requesting an Add-in; the request goes to the DNS that directs the request to the SharePoint Server called SPWFE. However, since we do not have any Web Applications with that name, the Internet Information Services (IIS) Server running under SharePoint will not know to which site to send the request.

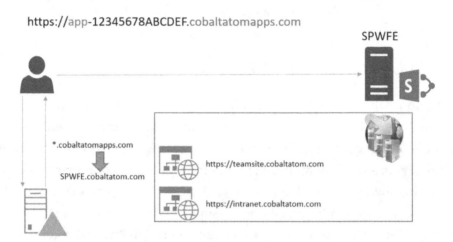

Figure 5-4. *What happens in the network when a user tries to access an Add-in*

One of the requirements we have on the SharePoint Farm for add-ins and Host Named Site Collections, which will be covered in Chapter 13, is to create a Web Application that has no host header at all. The requests to our server will automatically go to that Web Application, which will forward the request to a Service Application called the *App Management Service Application.* That application knows what Add-in belongs to what Site and will be able to direct the user to the right Add-in, in the right site. The process will then look as in Figure 5-5.

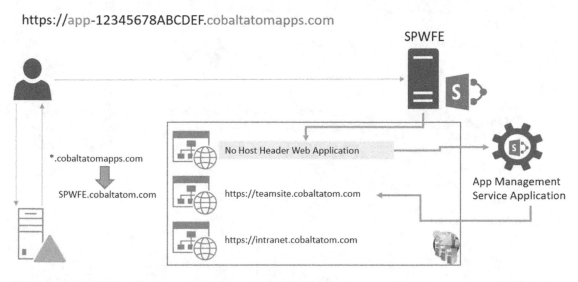

Figure 5-5. *What happens in the network when a user tries to access an Add-in*

Another Service Application that we will need to get the Add-ins working is the Subscription Settings Service Application. Now that we know what the architecture looks like, let's start to configure Add-ins for SharePoint 2019.

Configuring DNS

To configure DNS, you will need to be a Domain Administrator and have access to the DNS Manager console. First, open the DNS Console, right-click "forward lookup zones," and select "New Zone" as seen in Figure 5-6.

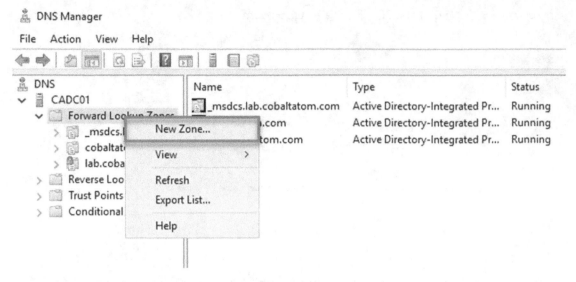

Figure 5-6. *Adding a New Zone to our DNS*

On the first screen, click "Next" as seen in Figure 5-7.

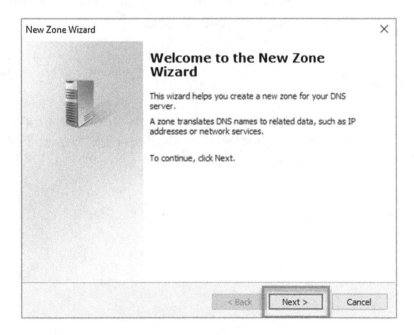

Figure 5-7. *New Zone Wizard*

The Zone must be of type "Primary Zone" and also check the "Store the zone in AD" box as seen in Figure 5-8.

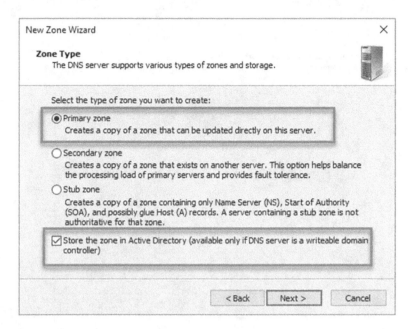

Figure 5-8. *Selecting the Zone Type*

Select if you want the data replicated to all the Domain Controllers in your domain, or in your forest. Since we only have one domain in our farm for this book, we choose the second option as seen in Figure 5-9. The option you choose here will depend on your unique organization infrastructure and you should check with your Domain Administrators if you are not sure which one to choose. If you want to make the Add-ins available via the Internet, you will also need to configure your public DNS records and reverse proxy to point in the right direction.

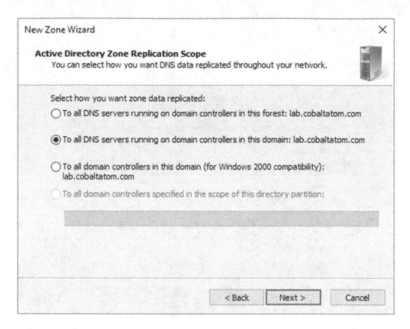

Figure 5-9. *Selecting AD Zone Replication Scope*

On the next screen you need to enter your new Add-in domain as seen in Figure 5-10.

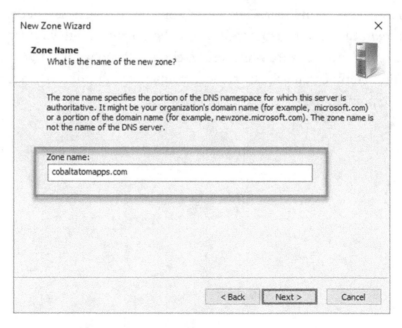

Figure 5-10. *Entering the Add-in Domain as our new Zone Name*

Lastly, select the type of Dynamic Updates for your Domain. Since there won't be any new records except the initial one, we should select "Do not allow dynamic updates" as seen in Figure 5-11.

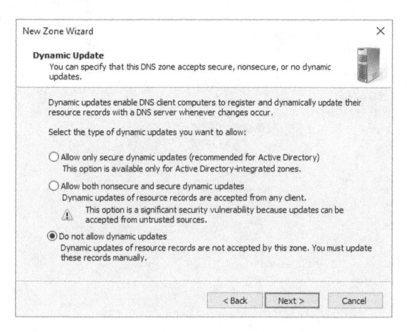

Figure 5-11. *Selecting Dynamic Update Properties*

After the zone is created, we need to create either an Alias (CNAME) or a Host (A) toward our SharePoint Servers. If you only have one SharePoint Web Front End, you can use a CNAME; however, if you use a network load balancer, you will want to use a HOST since you will probably forward your users to a Virtual IP Address. In our case, we will forward all requests for our Add-in domain to 192.168.80.10, a Virtual IP Address that goes to the load balancer, which then forwards the requests to one of our two Web Front Ends.

While still in the DNS Management Window, right-click our new forward lookup zone and select a "New Host (A or AAAA)" as seen in Figure 5-12.

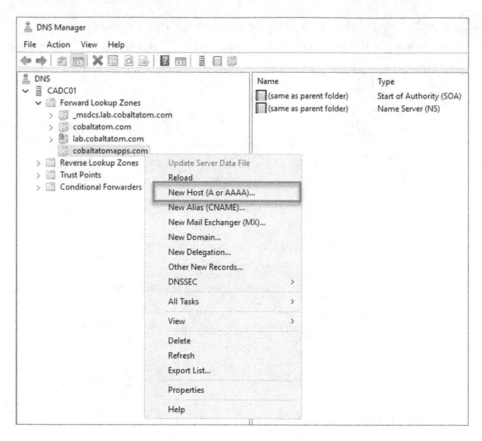

Figure 5-12. *Creating a new Host entry in DNS*

Afterward, enter a Wildcard (*) in the name, as well as the IP address you want to point it to as seen in Figure 5-13.

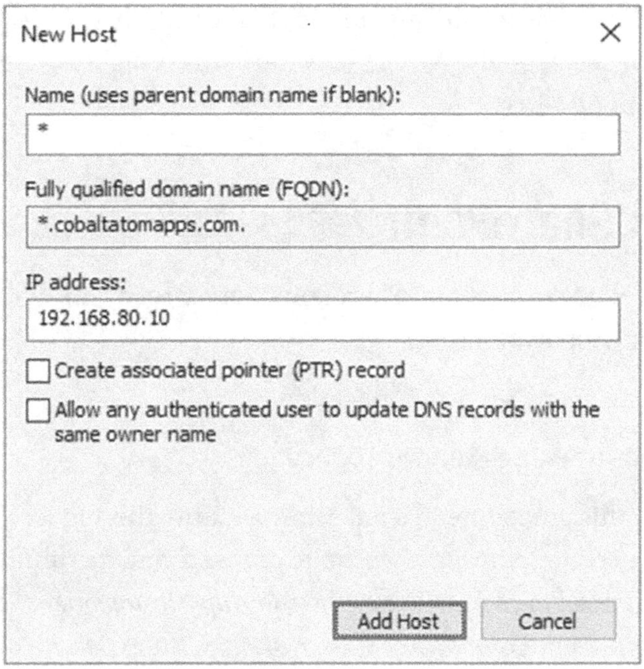

Figure 5-13. *Entering New Host Record Properties*

To test, simply do a PING request to <random word>.Add-inDomain.TLD. In my example in Figure 5-14 I used ApressRocks.CobaltAtomApps.com and the result was successful as it forwarded me to 192.168.80.10

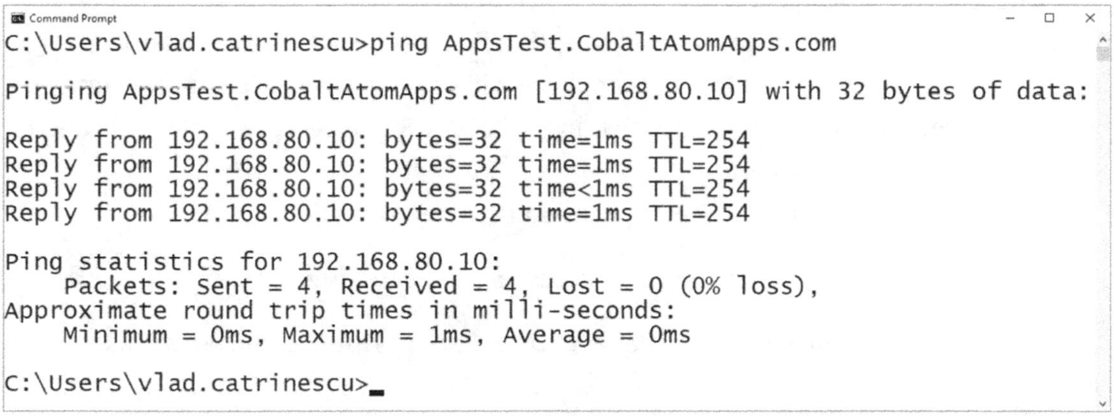

Figure 5-14. *Testing the configuration with Command Prompt*

If the ping test is successful and goes to the right IP address, it means that the DNS has been configured successfully. We can now move to configuring our SharePoint Server 2019 to accept Add-ins.

Configuring SharePoint

The first step we need to do to get our SharePoint Server ready for Add-ins is to create the two required Service Applications:

- App Management Service Application

- Subscription Settings Service Application

If you are doing this procedure in a full MinRole farm, the services will start automatically when creating the Service Applications. If you are running on a Custom mode farm, you will need to manually turn on the *App Management Service* as well as the *Microsoft SharePoint Foundation Subscription Settings Service* on at least one SharePoint Server.

Note   In a Streamlined topology it is recommended to turn on those services on all the Web Front Ends in your SharePoint Server Farm.

While the App Management Service Application can be created by both the Central Administration and PowerShell, the Subscription Settings Service Application can only be created by using PowerShell. In this book we will create both Service Applications by using PowerShell and run them both under our only Service Application Pool called *SharePoint Web Services Default*.

We first need to get our Service Application Pool and save it into a variable.

```
$apppool = Get-SPServiceApplicationPool "SharePoint Web Services Default"
```

Afterward, we create the Subscription Settings Service Application, as well as its proxy.

```
$SubscriptionSA = New-SPSubscriptionSettingsServiceApplication -
ApplicationPool $apppool -Name "Subscription Settings" -DatabaseName
SubscriptionSettings
```

```
$proxySub = New-SPSubscriptionSettingsServiceApplicationProxy –
ServiceApplication $SubscriptionSA
```

Lastly, we create the App Management Service Application as well as its proxy.

```
$AppManagementSA = New-SPAppManagementServiceApplication -ApplicationPool
$apppool -Name "App Management" -DatabaseName AppManagement
```

```
$proxyApp = New-SPAppManagementServiceApplicationProxy -ServiceApplication
$AppManagementSA
```

After the Service Applications are created and working, we need to set the Add-in Domain as well as the Add-in Prefix. This can be done in Central Administration ➤ Apps ➤ Configure App URLs as seen in Figure 5-15 or via PowerShell.

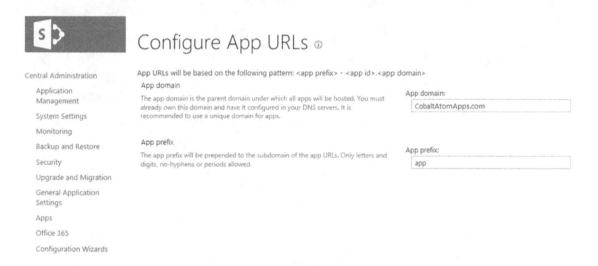

Figure 5-15. *The Configure App URL Screen in SharePoint 2019*

To do it via PowerShell, first, configure the Add-in domain using the following cmdlet:

```
Set-SPAppDomain CobaltAtomApps.com
```

And afterward set the Add-in Prefix using the following cmdlet.

```
Set-SPAppSiteSubscriptionName -Name "app" -Confirm:$false
```

The only thing that we need now is a Web Application with no host header. Without that Web Application, users will see a HTTP 404 error when trying to access an Add-in. A Web Application with no host header simply means that when you create the Web Application, you leave the "Host Header" field blank as seen in Figure 5-16.

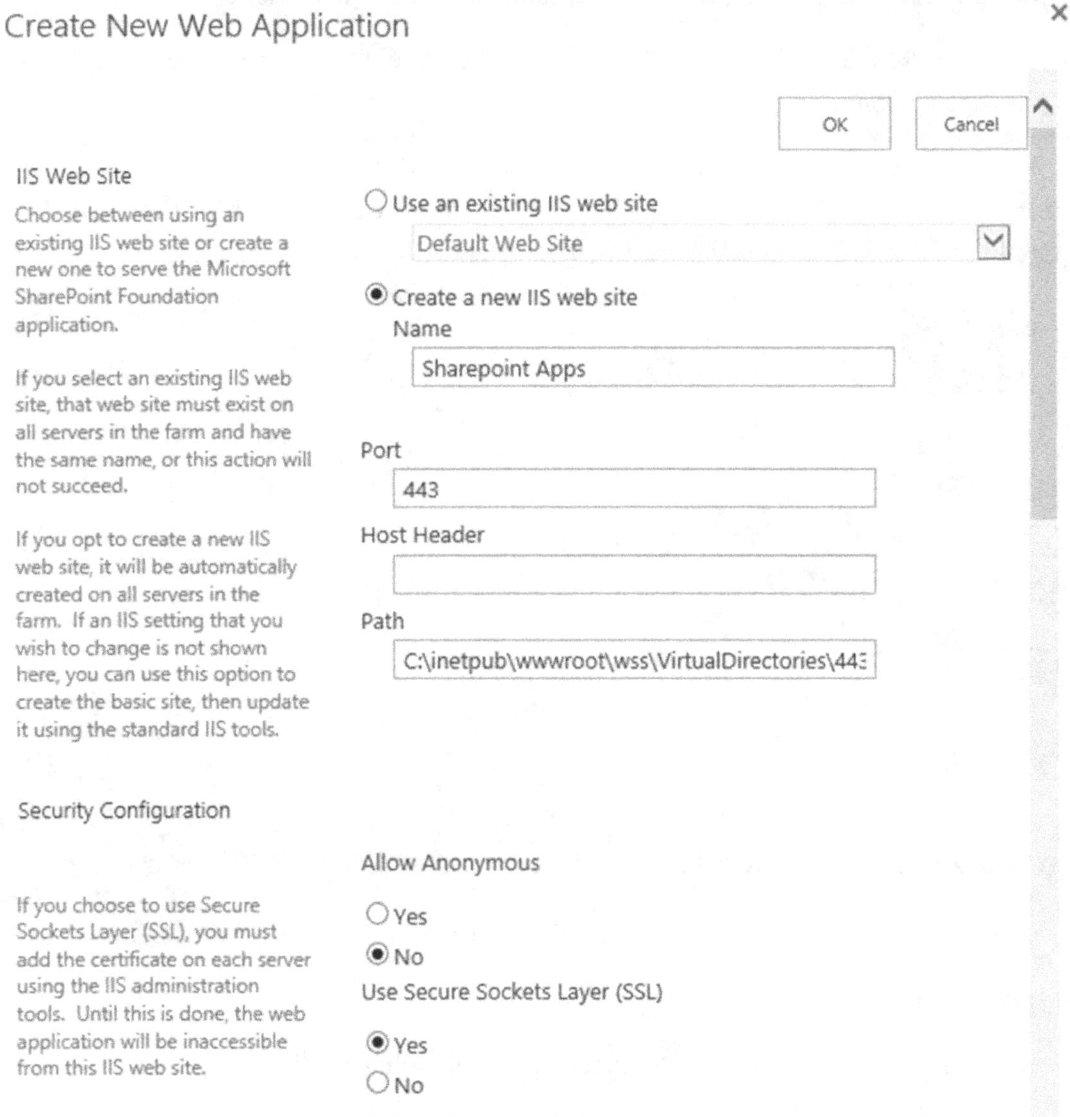

Create New Web Application ×

	OK	Cancel

IIS Web Site

Choose between using an existing IIS web site or create a new one to serve the Microsoft SharePoint Foundation application.

If you select an existing IIS web site, that web site must exist on all servers in the farm and have the same name, or this action will not succeed.

If you opt to create a new IIS web site, it will be automatically created on all servers in the farm. If an IIS setting that you wish to change is not shown here, you can use this option to create the basic site, then update it using the standard IIS tools.

○ Use an existing IIS web site
    Default Web Site

◉ Create a new IIS web site
    Name
        Sharepoint Apps

Port
    443

Host Header

Path
    C:\inetpub\wwwroot\wss\VirtualDirectories\443

Security Configuration

If you choose to use Secure Sockets Layer (SSL), you must add the certificate on each server using the IIS administration tools. Until this is done, the web application will be inaccessible from this IIS web site.

Allow Anonymous

○ Yes
◉ No

Use Secure Sockets Layer (SSL)

◉ Yes
○ No

Figure 5-16. *Creating a new Web Application in SharePoint 2019*

If you already have a Web Application using the Alternate Access Mapping of `https://servername` or an IIS site with that binding, SharePoint will not allow you to create the new Web Application on port 443. If you have setup the Central Administration on SSL as we did in this book, make sure you have deleted the default Alternate Access Mapping on it, since we created a new URL for it.

You will also need to create a root site collection on that Web Application. There is no specific template or permissions needed; however, it needs to exist for SharePoint to work properly.

Since we are using SSL, we will also need to add the certificate into IIS. To do so, you first need to import the wildcard certificate for your Add-in domain into IIS as shown in Figure 5-17.

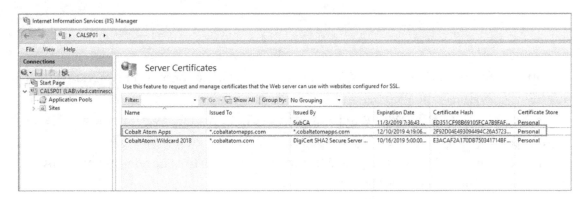

Figure 5-17. *Certificates in IIS Manager*

Afterward, you need to add a binding on the IIS Site we just created, on post 443 (SSL) and select the certificate that we just imported as shown in Figure 5-18.

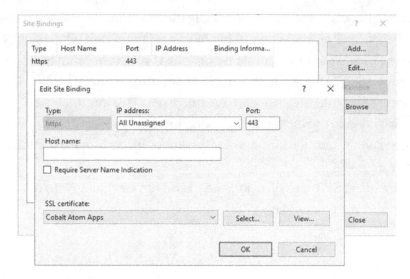

Figure 5-18. *Adding a Binding in IIS*

Due to limitations in the TLS/SSL architecture, you usually couldn't run more than one SSL site on the same Web Server because there wasn't a way in TLS to specify a "hostname" for the traffic. With Windows Server 2012 R2 and IIS8 we have Server Name Identification (SNI) on the other Web Applications, allowing this to work.

If you do not use SNI, you will have to add another IP to the SharePoint Server and redirect all Add-in requests to that IP.

Note   You need to repeat this step on every server that has the Foundation Web Application Service running. If you are running in a MinRole configuration those servers are the Front End, Distributed Cache, and Application roles. The standalone Search Role doesn't have Foundation Web Application activated; therefore, you cannot do any changes on the Search Servers.

Securing all your SharePoint sites with SSL is extremely important in SharePoint, since the OAuth token is passed in a packet on the request, and you could be subject to a man-in-the-middle attack if that token is not secured.

After this is done, you can go to the store and add an Add-in from the SharePoint Store, and everything should work!

We have now successfully configured Add-ins, but there are a few settings we can change to make the experience more enjoyable for our end users.

Post Configuration Settings

After Add-ins are configured on our SharePoint environment, there are some configurations we might need do in some cases to improve user experience, or enable extra functionality. The first one is mainly for user experience. Usually, we add our main domain, for example *.CobaltAtom.com to the Intranet zone in Internet Explorer for all our users so they don't have to enter their username and password every time they go on a SharePoint site. However, since our Add-ins run in a different domain, users will get prompted to enter their username and password each time they access an Add-in, or have an Add-in Part on a SharePoint Page as seen in Figure 5-19.

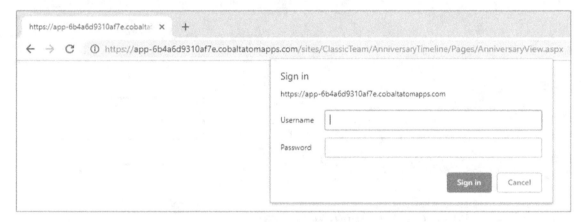

Figure 5-19. *Authentication Prompt on Add-in Domain*

Microsoft recommends not adding the Add-in Domain to our Intranet or Trusted sites zone since those zones do not provide a sufficient level of isolation of Add-ins from user data in SharePoint Sites. The consequences, as described before, are having a Windows Authentication prompt every time a user accesses an Add-in, or navigates to a page with an Add-in Part embedded.

To avoid this behavior and provide a seamless experience for your users, make sure you add the Add-in domain to the Intranet Zone of all your users, by Group Policy or any other tools you have in your organization. As a SharePoint Administrator you must decide whether to follow Microsoft's security best practices, or opt for the best end-user behavior and UX best practices.

The second setting which is a bit more SharePoint Specific is enabling users to deploy apps that require sites with Internet-facing endpoints. Those apps are greyed out by default and users cannot deploy them. If your farm is configured to allow

Internet-facing end points, you can activate the *Apps that require accessible internet facing endpoints* feature on each Web Application on which you want to enable this functionality. The feature is disabled by default as shown in Figure 5-20.

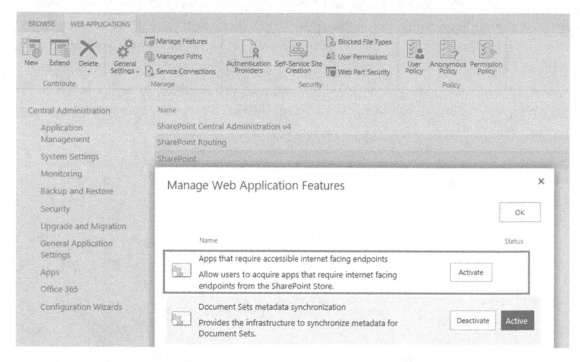

Figure 5-20. *Activating Web Application Features*

We have now successfully finished configuring Add-ins in our environment, and users can add and consume Add-ins from the SharePoint Store. In the next section, we will learn how to control what Add-ins are bought and how to distribute custom Add-ins to your users.

The App Catalog

The App Catalog is a special site collection on each Web Application that allows SharePoint Administrators to manage and control the Add-ins that are installed on the farm. By configuring an App Catalog, we can force users to get an administrator to approve all Add-in purchases, as well as upload in-house-built Add-ins and make them available to all our users.

Creating an App Catalog Site Collection

The App Catalog can be created either from the Central Administration in *Apps* ➤ *Manage App Catalog* or through PowerShell by using the *"APPCATALOG#0"* template. When creating the App Catalog through Central Administration, we need to go to the Apps section and click Manage App Catalog, and then select "Create a new app catalog site" as seen in Figure 5-21.

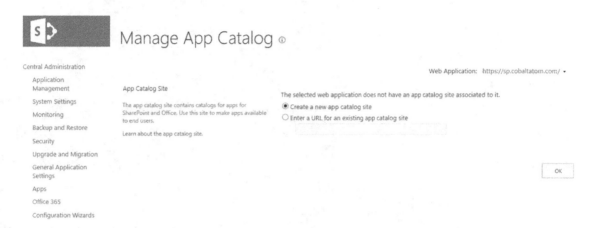

Figure 5-21. *The Manage App Catalog Page in SharePoint 2019*

The App Catalog Site creation page is very similar to a normal Site Collection creation page; the only difference is that we have a new box called "End Users" in which we enter the users that are allowed to see Add-ins from this App Catalog Site. In our scenario, we want the App Catalog to be open to all SharePoint Users, so we simply entered the Domain Users group as shown in Figure 5-22.

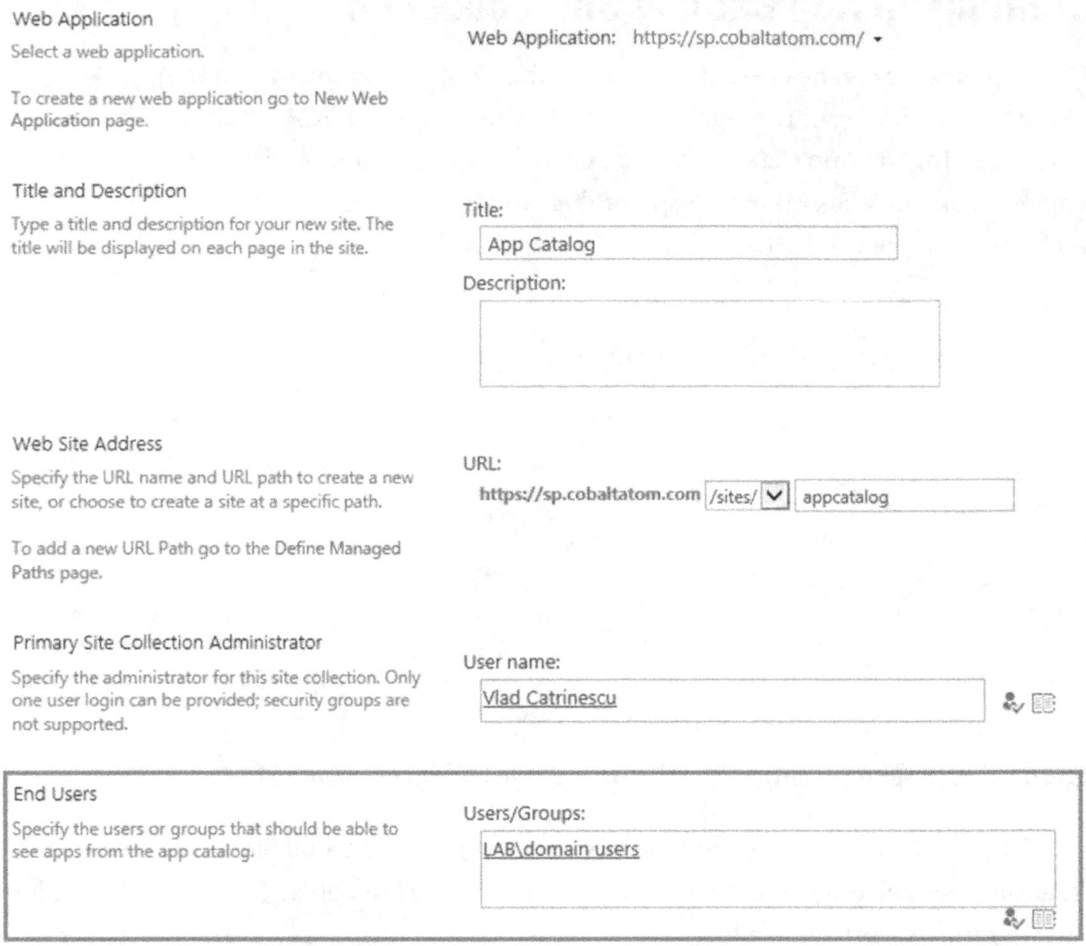

Web Application

Select a web application.

To create a new web application go to New Web Application page.

Web Application: https://sp.cobaltatom.com/ ▾

Title and Description

Type a title and description for your new site. The title will be displayed on each page in the site.

Title:

App Catalog

Description:

Web Site Address

Specify the URL name and URL path to create a new site, or choose to create a site at a specific path.

To add a new URL Path go to the Define Managed Paths page.

URL:

https://sp.cobaltatom.com /sites/ ▾ appcatalog

Primary Site Collection Administrator

Specify the administrator for this site collection. Only one user login can be provided; security groups are not supported.

User name:

Vlad Catrinescu

End Users

Specify the users or groups that should be able to see apps from the app catalog.

Users/Groups:

LAB\domain users

Figure 5-22.   *Creating a new App Catalog Site Collection*

Configure Requests

To block users from buying Add-ins from the SharePoint Store themselves and forcing them to place a request, we need to do some changes in the *Central Administration ➤ Apps ➤ Configure Store Settings* page. If we set it to No as seen in Figure 5-23, users will need to request an Add-in before being able to buy it.

SharePoint Store Settings

Web Application: https://sp.cobaltatom.com/ ▾

App Purchases
Specify whether end users can get apps from the SharePoint Store.

Should end users be able to get apps from the SharePoint Store?

◉ Yes   ○ No

App Requests
View the list used to capture app requests. Users will request apps if they aren't allowed to get apps directly from the SharePoint Store or if they prefer to request an app rather than getting it directly.

Click here to view app requests

Figure 5-23. *The SharePoint Store Settings Page in SharePoint 2019*

This change can also be done with PowerShell with the following cmdlet by replacing `https://sp.CobaltAtom.com` with the Web Application you wish to apply the change on.

```
Set-SPAppAcquisitionConfiguration -WebApplication https://sp.CobaltAtom.com
-Enable:$false
```

When you force your users to request Add-ins instead of them being able to install them themselves, the button to add an Add-in will change from "Add it" as seen in Figure 5-24 to "Request it" as seen in Figure 5-25.

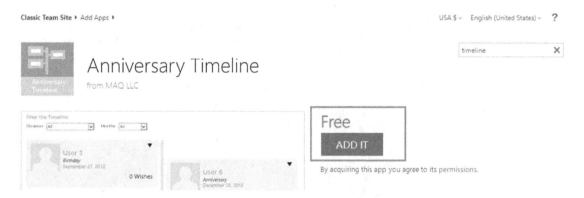

Figure 5-24. *Button when users are allowed to add Add-ins themselves*

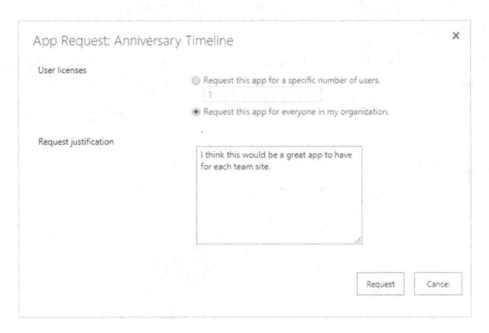

Figure 5-25. *Button when users must request an Add-in to be approved before being able to add it*

When a user requests an Add-in, they must specify how many licenses they need, or if it's for the whole organization as seen in Figure 5-26. Users also need to provide a business justification for the Add-in.

Figure 5-26. *The App Request for end users*

When an Add-in Request is done, SharePoint Server 2019 will place the request in the "App Requests" list in the App Catalog of that Web Application as seen in Figure 5-27.

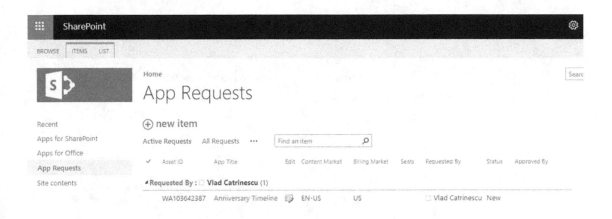

Figure 5-27. *The App Requests list in the App Catalog*

Once we click the list entry, we can see the title of the app, how many seats are required, the Justification as well as a Status field and Approver comments. Changing the Status to "Approved" will not allow the user to install the Add-in; the App Catalog admin will need to get the Add-in from the Store by clicking the "Click here to view app details and purchase or manage licenses" link as seen in Figure 5-28.

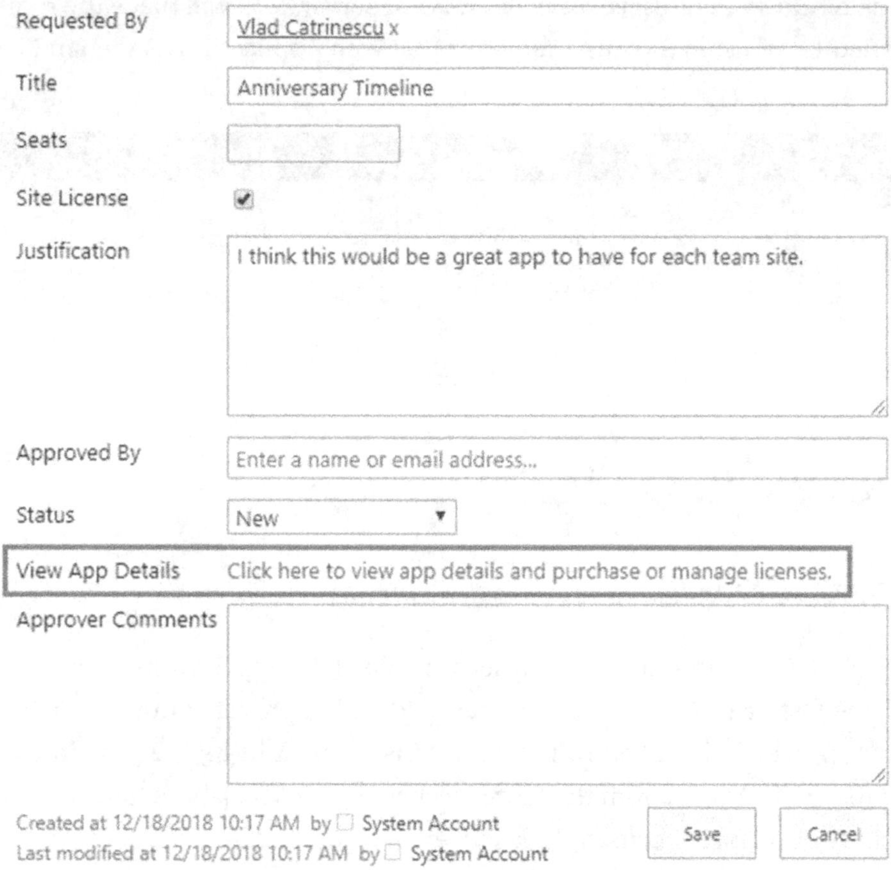

Requested By	<u>Vlad Catrinescu</u> x
Title	Anniversary Timeline
Seats	
Site License	☑
Justification	I think this would be a great app to have for each team site.
Approved By	Enter a name or email address...
Status	New ▼
View App Details	Click here to view app details and purchase or manage licenses.
Approver Comments	

Created at 12/18/2018 10:17 AM by ☐ System Account
Last modified at 12/18/2018 10:17 AM by ☐ System Account

[Save]   [Cancel]

Figure 5-28.   *The details of an Add-in Request*

Once the admin acquired the Add-in, users will be able to see the Add-in in the "Apps you can add" section in the Site Collection as seen in Figure 5-29.

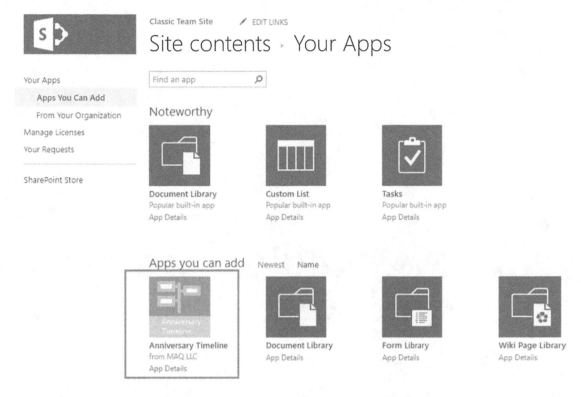

Figure 5-29. *Add-in is available on the requested Site Collection*

We have now successfully configured the App Catalog in our SharePoint 2019 Farm.

Next Steps

In this chapter, we learned how to configure our SharePoint 2019 Server Farm to allow users to consume Add-ins either from the SharePoint Store or built in-house. We also learned what the App Catalog is and how we can request an admin approval before Add-ins are added to SharePoint Sites in our organization.

In the next chapter, we will learn how to create and configure the Search Service Application!

CHAPTER 6

Configuring the Search Service Application

Search is a very important part of SharePoint, and many companies rely on the strong SharePoint Search Engine to find documents and information for their day-to-day jobs.

In this chapter, you will learn the architecture of the SharePoint Search Service Application, as well as how to configure it from both Central Administration and PowerShell.

SharePoint Search Service Application Architecture

Before starting to configure the Search Service Application, we will need to better understand the architecture and how it works internally. The SharePoint 2019 Search Engine is built on the FAST Search Engine that Microsoft acquired in 2008 from a Norwegian company then called Fast Search & Transfer ASA and has fully integrated in SharePoint since SharePoint 2013. The SharePoint Search Service Engine is broken up into six different components:

1. **Crawl Component**

   The Crawl Component is responsible for crawling different types of content such as Local SharePoint Sites, Remote SharePoint Sites, File Shares, and more. We call those Content Sources.

2. **Content Processing Component**

   The Content Processing component receives data from the Crawl component and breaks it down into artifacts that can be included in the Index. Some Search customizations such as Custom Entity Extractions are done by the Content Processing Component.

151

© Vlad Catrinescu and Trevor Seward 2019
V. Catrinescu and T. Seward, *Deploying SharePoint 2019*, https://doi.org/10.1007/978-1-4842-4526-2_6

3. **Index Component**

The Index Component is a logical representation of an index file. The Index component receives items from the Content Processing Component and writes them into an index file. For systems where there are a lot of crawled items, the Index can be split into different Index Partitions, a logical portion of the entire search index.

4. **Query Component**

The Query Processing Component is the component that interacts with the SharePoint Front End. The Query Processing Component gets the queries done by users, analyzes it and submits it to the Index Components. The Index component will then return the relevant results to the Query component, which will then return the results to the end user. The Query Component is also responsible for the Security Trimming on the search results.

5. **Analytics Processing Component**

The Analytics Processing Component creates search analytics as well as usage analytics. Those analytics are used for search relevance, generate recommendations as well as create search reports.

6. **Search Administration Component**

The Search Administration Component runs the administration tasks as well as provisioning the other Search Components.

All those components work together to offer the end-to-end search experience for your users. Unlike most Service Applications, which only have one database, the Search Service application has four different types of databases, and you can have more than one of each type in your Search Service Application, depending on your requirements. We will cover those cases and when and how to scale out your Search Service Application a bit later into this chapter. The different types of databases that you will find in the Search Service Application are as follows:

1. **Crawl Database**

   The Crawl Database contains tracking and historical information about crawled items as well as information about the last crawl times, types of crawls and durations.

2. **Search Admin Database**

   The Search Admin Database stores configuration data such as the topology, managed properties, query, and crawl rules.

3. **The Link Database**

   The Link Database stores information extracted by the Content Processing component as well as information about search clicks and popularity.

4. **The Analytics Reporting Database**

   The Analytics Reporting database stores statistics information and analytics results.

There is another data storage location, which is not a database, but log files on the server that hosts the analytics processing component. This is called the **Event Store**. The Event store holds usage events such as the number of items an item is viewed. Now that we know the components of a Search Service Application, let's see how we can create it.

It's important to remember that the Index Component is also stored on the file system and not in the database. Therefore, it's important to plan extra disk space for the servers running the Index Component.

All those search components must be hosted on a SharePoint Server that is configured as a "Search" or "Application and Search" MinRole server, or "Custom" MinRole server with the Search Services started.

Search Service Application Limitations

When planning our Search Service Application topology, we need to respect both the business requirements as well as the software boundaries of SharePoint Server 2019. Business requirements might be around index freshness as well as separation between the indexes of two different clients hosted on the same SharePoint farm. The number of items that you plan to crawl using the SharePoint Search Service application might require you to add multiple servers to your Search Topology to get around the software boundaries in SharePoint.

Tip   You can view all the SharePoint Server Software boundaries on TechNet at the following link: `https://docs.microsoft.com/en-us/SharePoint/ install/software-boundaries-and-limits-0#search-limits`.

Creating a Search Service Application

The Search Service Application can be created both from the SharePoint User Interface and from the SharePoint Management Shell. When creating the Search Service Application via Central Administration, the Search databases will have a GUID appended to them, unlike when creating the Search Service Application via PowerShell, where you have control over the database naming convention. It's also important to know that while it's possible to create the Search Service Application with Central Administration, the Search Service Application Topology can only be modified via PowerShell. Search Service Applications created with the Central Administration will host all components on a single server. For those reasons, we strongly recommend using PowerShell to create your Search Service Application. We will still cover both options of creating the Search Service Application in this chapter.

Creating a Search Service Application from Central Administration

To create a Search Service Application from the User Interface, from the Manage Service Applications page in the Central Administration, click New, and select Search Service Application as seen in Figure 6-1.

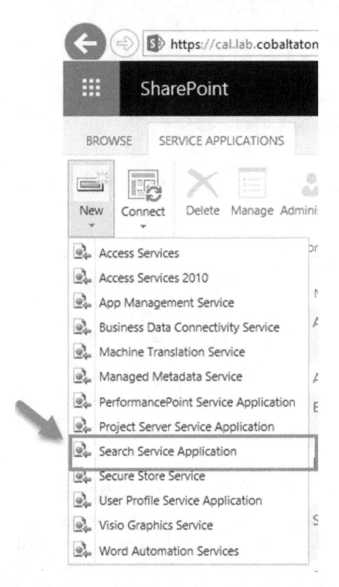

Figure 6-1. *New Search Service Application from the User Interface*

In the new Create New Search Service Application window seen in Figure 6-2, we will first have to give it a name, select if it's a normal Search Service Application or a Cloud Search Service Application, and give it the Service account that will run the Windows Search Service. In this chapter, we will not cover the Cloud Search Service Application, as this will be covered in Chapter 14. While it's possible to set a dedicated Search Service account for an extra layer of security, we recommend using the same account that runs the other services, which in our case is **Lab\s-svc**.

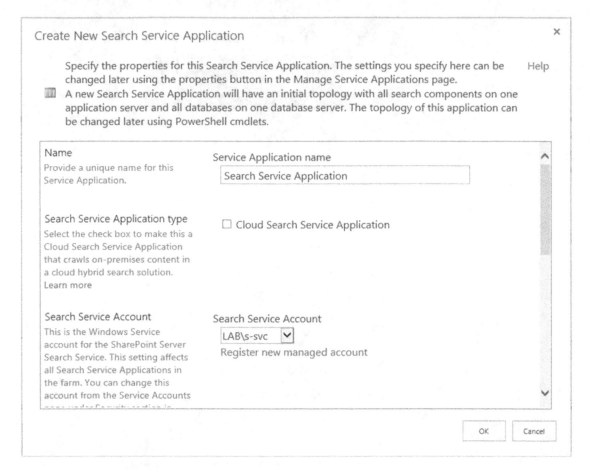

Figure 6-2. *New Search Service Application Window*

On the second part of the Create New Search Service Application Window seen in Figure 6-3, we need to select if we want to create new Service Application Pools for the Search Admin Web Service and Query and Site Settings Web Service, or use an existing one. While creating new ones could increase the isolation of the Search Service Applications, it will result in additional resources being used on your servers. In this book we recommend using the same Application Pool as the rest of your service applications, in this case "SharePoint Web Services Default", unless you have specific business or security requirements to isolate this Service Application from the other Service Applications.

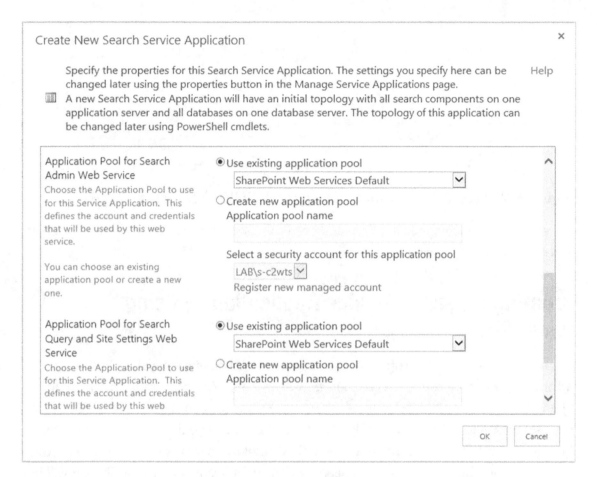

Figure 6-3. *New Search Service Application Window*

You can then click OK to create the Search Service Application. Once created, the Search Administration Page seen in Figure 6-4 will show the Search Server on which the Search Service Application activated the six components, as well as the Database Names, which have GUIDs in them because we have created this Service Application by using the user interface.

Search Application Topology

Server Name							Admin	Crawler	Content Processing	Analytics Processing	Query Processing	Index Partition 0
CALSP03							✓	✓	✓	✓	✓	✓

Database Server Name	Database Type	Database Name
caspag.lab.cobaltatom.com	Administration Database	Search_Service_Application_DB_d87437b368f648d489b17cf243fed42b
caspag.lab.cobaltatom.com	Analytics Reporting Database	Search_Service_Application_AnalyticsReportingStoreDB_2f53bb6a7c724ba28cd69a71eaaaba65
caspag.lab.cobaltatom.com	Crawl Database	Search_Service_Application_CrawlStoreDB_c8bd515f643a4484a107a9125ecb60d8
caspag.lab.cobaltatom.com	Link Database	Search_Service_Application_LinksStoreDB_45265ef3e4b249919c4c7a7b7e37a907

Figure 6-4. *Search Application Topology with GUID in Database Names*

With the Service Application created from the User Interface, let's learn how to create it from PowerShell as well.

Creating a Search Service Application by Using PowerShell

Creating a Search Service Application by using PowerShell gives the SharePoint Administrator more control. To create a new Search Service Application, you need to open the SharePoint Management Shell as an Administrator and use the `New-SPEnterp` `riseSearchServiceApplication` PowerShell cmdlet. The cmdlets will have to be run from a server that is configured in the Search MinRole, or a server that runs the Custom MinRole. Note that when creating a Search Service Application via PowerShell, it will not have an initial topology as it did when creating it by the User Interface, so it will not be usable until we modify the Search Service Application Topology, which we will cover a bit later in this chapter.

```
$sa = New-SPEnterpriseSearchServiceApplication -Name "<Service Application
Name>" -DatabaseName "<Search Database Name Prefix>" -ApplicationPool
"<Name of existing Service Application Pool>" -AdminApplicationPool "<Name
of existing Service Application Pool>"
```

In order to create a Service Application with the same settings as we did through the User Interface a bit earlier in the chapter, we would run the following PowerShell cmdlet:

```
$sa = New-SPEnterpriseSearchServiceApplication -Name "Search Service
Application 1" -DatabaseName "SearchDB" -ApplicationPool "SharePoint Web
Services Default" -AdminApplicationPool "SharePoint Web Services Default"
```

After the Search Service Application is created, we need to create the Search Service Application proxy by running the `New-SPEnterpriseSearchServiceApplicationP roxy` cmdlet. In the following cmdlet we will create a proxy named "Search Service Application Proxy" for the Search Service Application we created previously, that we saved a reference to in the $sa variable.

```
New-SPEnterpriseSearchServiceApplicationProxy -Name "Search Service
Application Proxy" -SearchApplication $sa
```

After both cmdlets finish running, we can navigate in our new Search Service Application via the User Interface, and you will notice that the Database Names do not have GUIDs in them anymore. However, since creating a Search Service Application by PowerShell does not also create an initial topology, the Search Application Topology is unable to be displayed as seen in Figure 6-5.

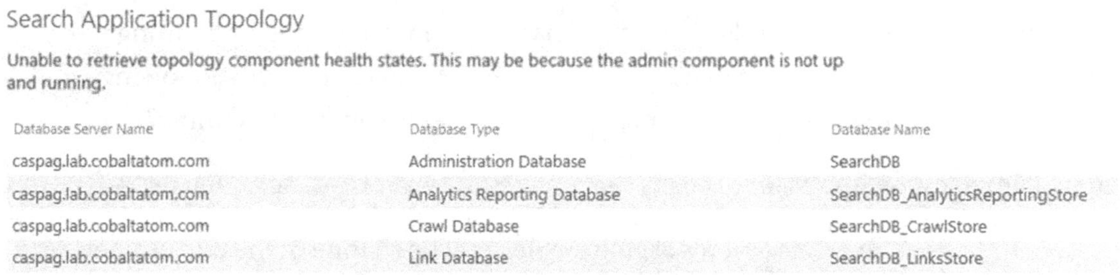

Search Application Topology

Unable to retrieve topology component health states. This may be because the admin component is not up and running.

Database Server Name	Database Type	Database Name
caspag.lab.cobaltatom.com	Administration Database	SearchDB
caspag.lab.cobaltatom.com	Analytics Reporting Database	SearchDB_AnalyticsReportingStore
caspag.lab.cobaltatom.com	Crawl Database	SearchDB_CrawlStore
caspag.lab.cobaltatom.com	Link Database	SearchDB_LinksStore

Figure 6-5. *Search Service Application created by PowerShell*

With the Service Application created, we will need to modify the Search Service Application topology to fit our needs.

Modifying the Search Service Application Topology

Modifying the Search Service Application topology can be done in a number of cases. You will need to do it when first creating your Search Service Application, as well as any time you need to change what components run on each server. Something to be aware of when modifying the Search Service Application topology using the following method is that the Index needs to be empty when changing the Search Service Application Topology. Later in this section we will learn how to change the Search Service Application Topology in a Service Application that already has items in the index.

To change the Search Topology, we first need to get the Search Service Application and save it into a variable.

```
$sa = Get-SPEnterpriseSearchServiceApplication
```

Next, we need to get the Search Service Instance of our first Search Server, called CALSP03, and save it into a variable.

```
$si = Get-SPEnterpriseSearchServiceInstance | ?{$_.Server -match "CALSP03"}
```

If you want to use a server running the Custom MinRole to host one of the Search Components, you will first have to start the Enterprise Search Service Instance. This is done by running the `Start-SPEnterpriseSearchServiceInstance` cmdlet. To start the instance, we would run the following cmdlet:

```
Start-SPEnterpriseSearchServiceInstance -Identity $si
```

You will then need to validate that the Service Instance is online by running the `Get-SPEnterpriseSearchServiceInstance` cmdlet. When running the following cmdlet and replacing CALSP03 with your server name, the status should be "Online".

```
Get-SPEnterpriseSearchServiceInstance | ?{$_.Server -match "CALSP03"}
```

We then need to create a new variable, which will be a clone of the current Active Topology in our Search Service Application. The Search Service Application can have multiple topologies; however, only one of them can be active. When modifying our topology, we will first create a clone of the active one, and after we specify its properties, we will set it to Active.

```
$clone = $sa.ActiveTopology.Clone()
```

We can then decide what components we want to enable on our first server. Here are the cmdlets for each Search Service Application Component:

- Admin: `New-SPEnterpriseSearchAdminComponent`
- Crawl: `New-SPEnterpriseSearchCrawlComponent`
- Content Processing: `New-SPEnterpriseSearchContentProcessingComponent`
- Index: `New-SPEnterpriseSearchIndexComponent`

- Query: `New-SPEnterpriseSearchQueryProcessingComponent`

- Analytics: `New-SPEnterpriseSearchAnalyticsProcessingComponent`

For all the components, we will need to give a SearchTopology parameter, which specifies the search topology we want to add this component to; in our case, it will be the search topology that is currently in the `$clone` variable. We also need to give it a Search Instance, specifying on what server we want to enable this Search Component. In our case, we will specify the $SI variable in which we saved the Search Service Instance of server CALSP03. To add all the components on Search Server CALSP03, we would run the following PowerShell code:

```
New-SPEnterpriseSearchAdminComponent -SearchTopology $clone
-SearchServiceInstance $si
New-SPEnterpriseSearchContentProcessingComponent -SearchTopology $clone
-SearchServiceInstance $si
New-SPEnterpriseSearchAnalyticsProcessingComponent -SearchTopology $clone
-SearchServiceInstance $si
New-SPEnterpriseSearchCrawlComponent -SearchTopology $clone
-SearchServiceInstance $si
New-SPEnterpriseSearchIndexComponent -SearchTopology $clone
-SearchServiceInstance $si -IndexPartition 0
New-SPEnterpriseSearchQueryProcessingComponent -SearchTopology $clone
-SearchServiceInstance $si
```

Note that by default, the Index location is on the C drive at `C:\Program Files\ Microsoft Office Servers\16.0\Data\Office Server\Applications`.

Note   The default location might have been changed during the binary Installation.

This may impact performance as Search can have a significant Disk I/O requirement. An additional impact may be the size of the index, which has the potential to cause the disk to run out of available space. In order to create your index file on a different drive, you need to specify the `RootDirectory` parameter to the `New-SPEnterpriseSearchInd exComponent` cmdlet, like we will do in the following. The folder must be empty as the cmdlet will fail otherwise.

```
New-SPEnterpriseSearchIndexComponent -SearchTopology $clone
-SearchServiceInstance $si -IndexPartition 0 -RootDirectory F:\
SearchIndex\0
```

We have added all the Search components on our first Search Server, so now it's time to add them on our second Search Server. The first thing we need to do is get the Search Service Instance of the second server and save it into a variable called $si2.

```
$si2 = Get-SPEnterpriseSearchServiceInstance | ?{$_.Server -match
"CALSP04"}
```

Note   If the server is running the Custom Role, you will need to start the Search Service Instance as we learned earlier in this section.

We will then add a new search component of each type on the second search server as well.

```
New-SPEnterpriseSearchAdminComponent -SearchTopology $clone
-SearchServiceInstance $si2
New-SPEnterpriseSearchAnalyticsProcessingComponent -SearchTopology $clone
-SearchServiceInstance $si2
New-SPEnterpriseSearchContentProcessingComponent -SearchTopology $clone
-SearchServiceInstance $si2
New-SPEnterpriseSearchCrawlComponent -SearchTopology $clone
-SearchServiceInstance $si2
New-SPEnterpriseSearchIndexComponent -SearchTopology $clone
-SearchServiceInstance $si2 -IndexPartition 0 -RootDirectory F:\
SearchIndex\0
New-SPEnterpriseSearchQueryProcessingComponent -SearchTopology $clone
-SearchServiceInstance $si2
```

Lastly, we need to set the $clone topology, as the active topology in order to see the results in our Search Service Application. This is done with the following PowerShell cmdlet:

```
$clone.Activate()
```

After the clone finishes activating, when navigating to the Search Administration page the topology will show all components on both servers with a green checkbox, meaning they are healthy as seen in Figure 6-6.

Server Name	Admin	Crawler	Content Processing	Analytics Processing	Query Processing	Index Partition 0
CALSP03	✓	✓	✓	✓	✓	✓
CALSP04	✓	✓	✓	✓	✓	✓

Database Server Name	Database Type	Database Name
caspag.lab.cobaltatom.com	Administration Database	SearchDB
caspag.lab.cobaltatom.com	Analytics Reporting Database	SearchDB_AnalyticsReportingStore
caspag.lab.cobaltatom.com	Crawl Database	SearchDB_CrawlStore
caspag.lab.cobaltatom.com	Link Database	SearchDB_LinksStore

Figure 6-6. *Search Service Application Topology*

As your search topology changes with your usage of the environment, the Search Service Application keeps a history of those topologies as Inactive. You can view them by running the following PowerShell cmdlet:

```
Get-SPEnterpriseSearchTopology -SearchApplication $sa
```

And as seen in Figure 6-7, our current Service Application has three topologies.

```
Administrator: Windows PowerShell                                      —   □   ×
PS C:\Windows\system32> Get-SPEnterpriseSearchTopology -SearchApplication $sa


TopologyId      : 02ab825f-5117-47f8-8b44-0747c81fd265
CreationDate    : 1/1/2019 2:34:00 PM
State           : Inactive
ComponentCount  : 12

TopologyId      : 843ec5bb-703b-4f7e-9b15-227e5e4848d4
CreationDate    : 1/1/2019 3:03:00 PM
State           : Inactive
ComponentCount  : 18

TopologyId      : bf053b0e-8a67-4d01-95bc-0e7942bdd5e2
CreationDate    : 1/1/2019 3:06:00 PM
State           : Active
ComponentCount  : 12
```

Figure 6-7. *Multiple Search Topologies in our Search Service Application*

This can cause confusion when trying to manage the Search Service application later on, so we can run the following PowerShell cmdlet that will loop through all the existing topologies and will delete all the inactive ones:

```
foreach($topo in (Get-SPEnterpriseSearchTopology -SearchApplication $sa |
?{$_.State -eq "Inactive"}))
{
Remove-SPEnterpriseSearchTopology -Identity $topo -Confirm:$false
}
```

When modifying a topology that already has items in the index, we need to be a bit more careful. To move your index component to another server, you first need to add the second index component to your topology, wait for the index to be replicated to the new server, and then remove the old index component. To remove a component of the Search Service Application topology, we first need to get the active topology and create a clone by using the New-SPEnterpriseSearchTopology cmdlet. The following is an example of the cmdlets:

```
$sa = Get-SPEnterpriseSearchServiceApplication
$active = Get-SPEnterpriseSearchTopology -SearchApplication $sa -Active
$clone = New-SPEnterpriseSearchTopology -SearchApplication $sa -Clone
-SearchTopology $active
```

We then need to find out the ComponentId of the Search Component that we want to remove. To see all the Component IDs, we need to run the following cmdlet:

```
Get-SPEnterpriseSearchComponent -SearchTopology $clone
```

PowerShell will output a list of all the components, and all the components will have a ComponentId. In the following example, the **IndexComponent2** running on server **CALSP04** has the ComponentId "**8bae00ce-2ca3-428d-b0bd-6356d806a23d**":

```
IndexPartitionOrdinal : 0
RootDirectory         : F:\SearchIndex\0
ComponentId           : 8bae00ce-2ca3-428d-b0bd-6356d806a23d
TopologyId            : 1e435e79-7af3-4ce3-a62f-13205aaf9e08
ServerId              : a1b3930e-18de-441c-a867-d3d0af440861
Name                  : IndexComponent2
ServerName            : CALSP04
ExperimentalComponent : False
```

Now that we know the ID, we can run the Remove-SPEnterpriseSearchComponent cmdlet and then activate our new topology. Remove the component that we targeted previously, we would run the following PowerShell cmdlets:

```
Remove-SPEnterpriseSearchComponent -Identity '8bae00ce-2ca3-428d-b0bd-
6356d806a23d' -SearchTopology $clone
$clone.Activate()
```

The Index Component from server CALSP04 will then be removed from the topology. You can then run the PowerShell cmdlets we saw earlier in this chapter to clean up the inactive Search Topologies.

To further scale out your Search Service Application, you might also want to add extra Crawl or Link databases. If we want to add another Crawl Database, we can use the **New-SPEnterpriseSearchCrawlDatabase** cmdlet and give it the Search Application and name for the new database.

```
New-SPEnterpriseSearchCrawlDatabase -SearchApplication $sa -DatabaseName
SearchDB_CrawlStore_2
```

We could also add extra Link databases using the New-SPEnterpriseSearchLinks Database cmdlet and giving the same set of parameters as we did for the crawl database.

```
New-SPEnterpriseSearchLinksDatabase -SearchApplication $sa -DatabaseName
SearchDB_LinksStore_2
```

Those databases will then appear on the on the Search Administration page on Central Administration, under the topology as seen in Figure 6-8.

Search Application Topology

Server Name	Admin	Crawler	Content Processing	Analytics Processing	Query Processing	Index Partition 0
CALSP03	✓	✓	✓	✓	✓	✓
CALSP04	✓	✓	✓	✓	✓	

Database Server Name	Database Type	Database Name
caspag.lab.cobaltatom.com	Administration Database	SearchDB
caspag.lab.cobaltatom.com	Analytics Reporting Database	SearchDB_AnalyticsReportingStore
caspag.lab.cobaltatom.com	Crawl Database	SearchDB_CrawlStore
caspag.lab.cobaltatom.com	Crawl Database	SearchDB_CrawlStore_2
caspag.lab.cobaltatom.com	Link Database	SearchDB_LinksStore_2
caspag.lab.cobaltatom.com	Link Database	SearchDB_LinksStore

Figure 6-8. *Multiple databases in our Search Service Topology*

With our topology and databases all created, it's now time to configure the Search Service Application Settings.

Configuring Search Settings

The possibilities to customize your Search Service Application to your needs are endless. In this section we will focus on the settings that you need to do when first creating your Search Service Application.

Configuring the Default Content Access Account

The first thing you need to do after creating your Search Service Application is to configure your Search default content access account. This is the service account that the Crawl Component will use to access SharePoint content. This crawl account will have read access to all your SharePoint Web Applications, so it is important to keep the credentials in a safe location. By default, when creating the Search Service Application, SharePoint will set the default content access account to the service that runs the SharePoint Search Windows Service. In order to change it, simply click the username currently in the Default Content Access account row, as seen in Figure 6-9. A window will open prompting for the username and password of this account.

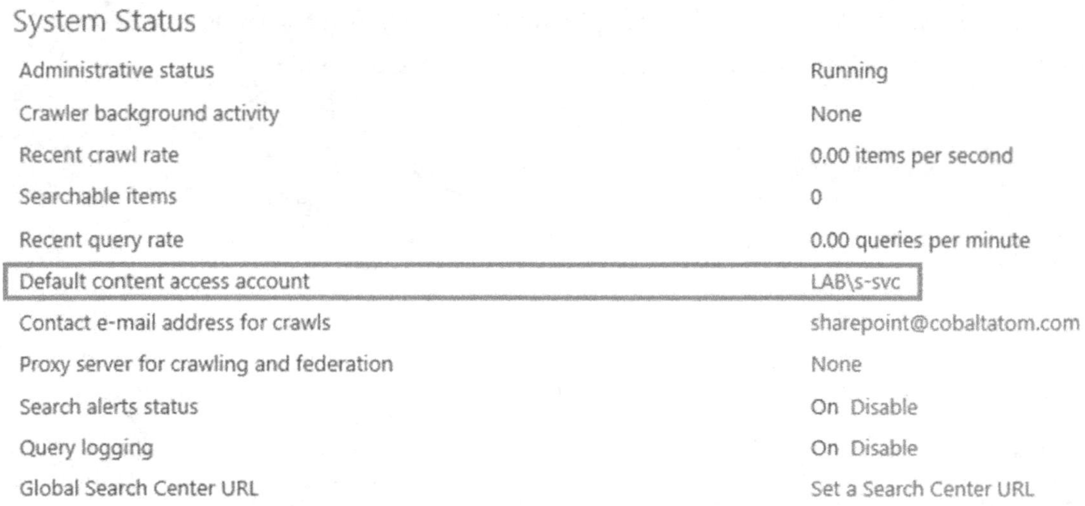

System Status

Administrative status	Running
Crawler background activity	None
Recent crawl rate	0.00 items per second
Searchable items	0
Recent query rate	0.00 queries per minute
Default content access account	LAB\s-svc
Contact e-mail address for crawls	sharepoint@cobaltatom.com
Proxy server for crawling and federation	None
Search alerts status	On Disable
Query logging	On Disable
Global Search Center URL	Set a Search Center URL

Figure 6-9. *Change Default Content Access Account*

The default content access account can also be configured via PowerShell with the following cmdlet:

```
$sa = Get-SPEnterpriseSearchServiceApplication
$content = New-Object Microsoft.Office.Server.Search.Administration.
Content($sa)
$content.SetDefaultGatheringAccount("LAB\s-crawl", (ConvertTo-SecureString
"<Password>" -AsPlainText -Force))
```

Where Lab\s-crawl is the account you want to use as default content access account. Since this account has read access to all the SharePoint content, we recommend having a dedicated service account for this purpose stated in Chapter 2.

As mentioned previously, the account will be added in the User Policy of the Web Application with Full Read permissions as seen in Figure 6-10.

Figure 6-10. *Search Crawling Account Web Application Policy*

The default content access account must also have the "Retrieve People Data for Search Crawlers" right on the User Profile Service Application, as seen in Figure 6-11. To get to the "Administrators for User Profile Service Application" page, from the Manage Service Applications page, select the User Profile Service Application, and click the Administrators button in the ribbon. This will allow the crawl account to crawl the user profiles and return this information in search.

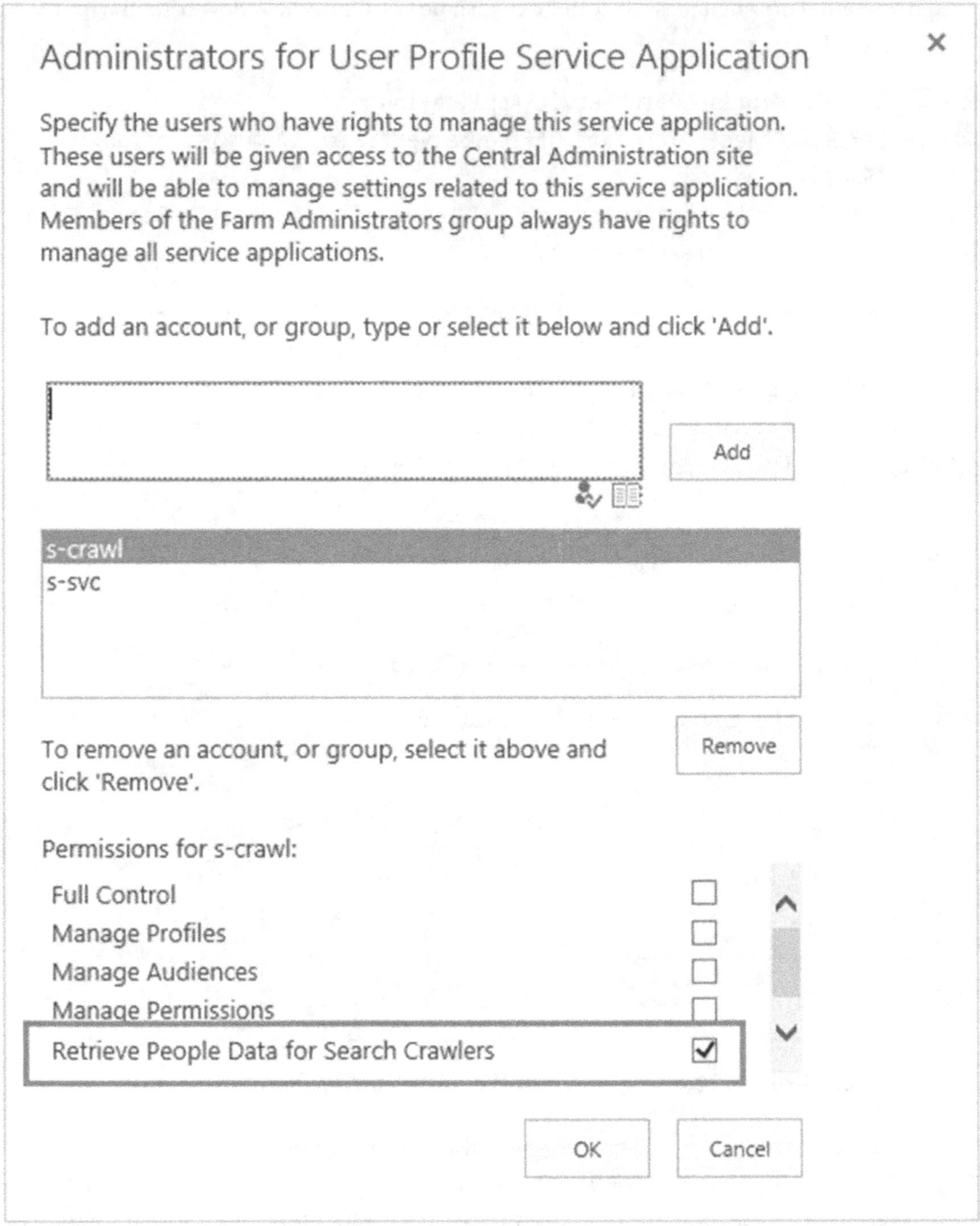

Administrators for User Profile Service Application   ×

Specify the users who have rights to manage this service application.
These users will be given access to the Central Administration site
and will be able to manage settings related to this service application.
Members of the Farm Administrators group always have rights to
manage all service applications.

To add an account, or group, type or select it below and click 'Add'.

[   ]   [Add]

s-crawl
s-svc

To remove an account, or group, select it above and   [Remove]
click 'Remove'.

Permissions for s-crawl:

Full Control   ☐
Manage Profiles   ☐
Manage Audiences   ☐
Manage Permissions   ☐
Retrieve People Data for Search Crawlers   ☑

                                          [OK]   [Cancel]

Figure 6-11. *Retrieve People Data for Search Crawlers permissions*

With the default content access account configured, it's now time to create our Content Sources.

Creating Content Sources

The next step to get our Search Service Application up and running is to create our content sources. When creating a Search Service Application, SharePoint creates a content source called *Local SharePoint sites* which contains all the Web Applications in our farm as seen in Figure 6-12.

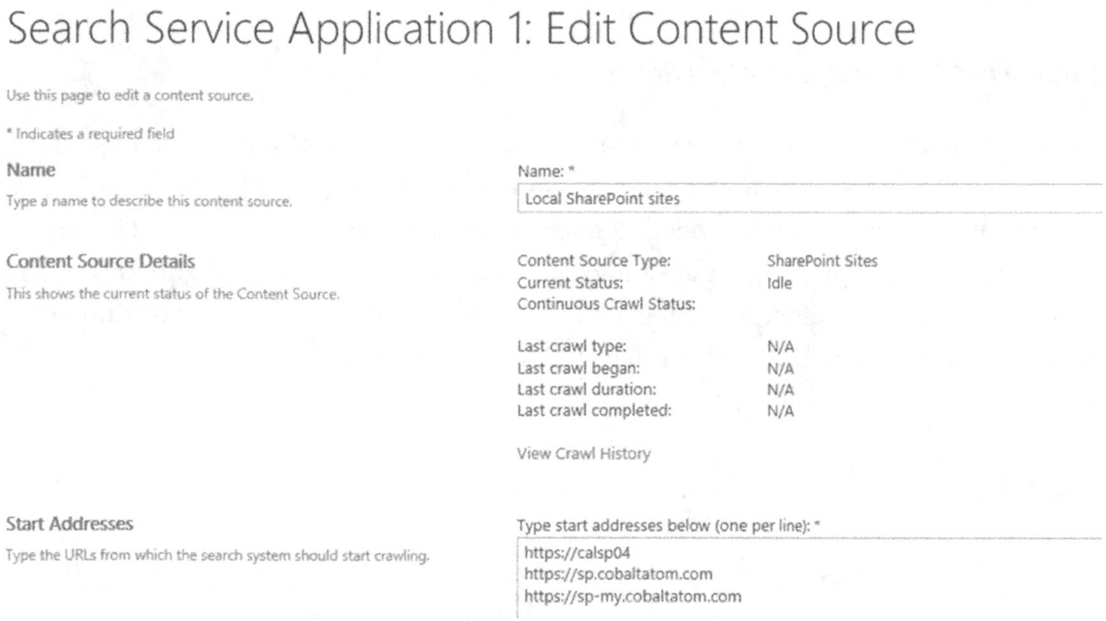

Search Service Application 1: Edit Content Source

Use this page to edit a content source.

* Indicates a required field

Name
Type a name to describe this content source.

Name: *
Local SharePoint sites

Content Source Details
This shows the current status of the Content Source.

Content Source Type:	SharePoint Sites
Current Status:	Idle
Continuous Crawl Status:	
Last crawl type:	N/A
Last crawl began:	N/A
Last crawl duration:	N/A
Last crawl completed:	N/A

View Crawl History

Start Addresses
Type the URLs from which the search system should start crawling.

Type start addresses below (one per line): *
https://calsp04
https://sp.cobaltatom.com
https://sp-my.cobaltatom.com

Figure 6-12. *Local SharePoint Sites Content Source*

You might want to split those Web Applications into different Content Sources if you want to set different crawl schedules, or create custom results based on only one Web Application. To create a Content Source, navigate to the Search Administration Page in the Central Administration and afterward in the Content Sources settings page. From the Manage Content Sources page, click the "New Content Source" page seen in Figure 6-13.

Figure 6-13. *Manage Content Sources page*

A window will open in which you can specify all the settings for the content source. First you will need to enter a name, in our example seen in Figure 6-14, the name is "SharePoint MySites." Next, we need to select what type of content is included in this Content Source. Depending on the choice of content, the available configurations later in the process will be different. Since the type of item we want to crawl in this Content Source is a SharePoint site, we have selected "SharePoint Sites."

Figure 6-14. *Add a Content Source*

The content you enter in the Start Address will depend on the crawl Settings you select in the following checkbox. The easiest to manage solution is to enter the root of the Web Application in the Start Address and select "Crawl everything under the hostname for each start address" as we did in Figure 6-15. This way, SharePoint will crawl all the Site Collections in that Web Application, and as new Site Collections get added, they will get automatically included in this content source. If you are using Host Named Site Collections, you only need to include the root Site Collection of the Web Application and SharePoint will be able to identify the other Site Collections in the same Web Applications. We will learn more about Host Named Site Collections in Chapter 13.

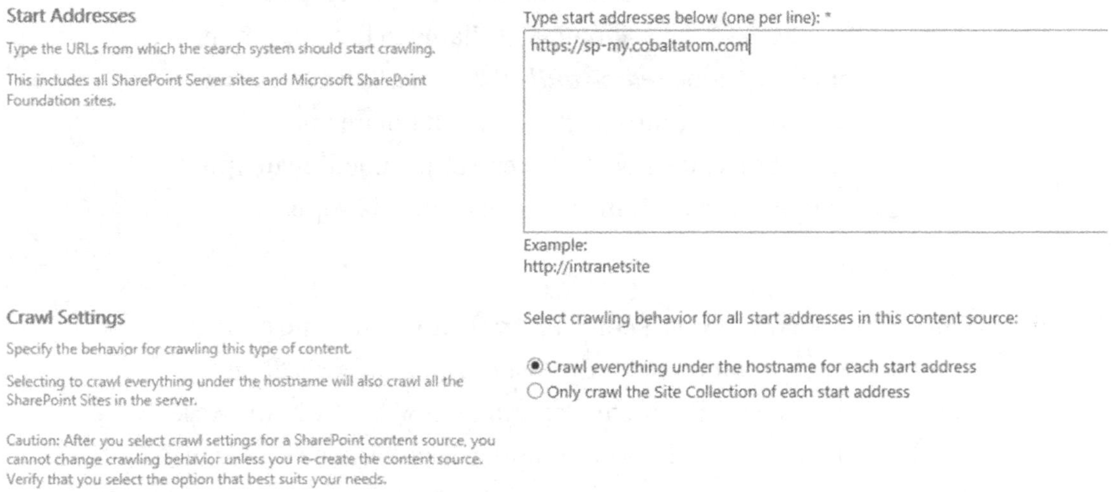

Start Addresses

Type the URLs from which the search system should start crawling.

This includes all SharePoint Server sites and Microsoft SharePoint Foundation sites.

Type start addresses below (one per line): *

https://sp-my.cobaltatom.com

Example:
http://intranetsite

Crawl Settings

Specify the behavior for crawling this type of content.

Selecting to crawl everything under the hostname will also crawl all the SharePoint Sites in the server.

Caution: After you select crawl settings for a SharePoint content source, you cannot change crawling behavior unless you re-create the content source. Verify that you select the option that best suits your needs.

Select crawling behavior for all start addresses in this content source:

◉ Crawl everything under the hostname for each start address
○ Only crawl the Site Collection of each start address

Figure 6-15. *Content Source Start Addresses and Crawl Settings*

If you want to have different Crawl Schedules between Site Collections in the same Web Application, you need to select "Only crawl the Site Collection of each start address" in the Crawl Settings and manually enter each Site Collection URL in the Start Addresses.

Lastly, you will have the options to select your crawl schedule for this content source. Your crawl schedule will depend on your business requirements as well as your search capabilities. There are two different types of schedule for your content. The first one which has been there for the last few SharePoint versions is the Incremental and Full Crawl. The second type of crawl schedule is the Continuous Crawl, which was introduced in SharePoint Server 2013. Let's look at the different types of crawls:

- **Full Crawl**

  The Full Crawl is a crawl that will crawl the entire content of your content source whether the item already exists in the index or not. The Full Crawl will not only crawl content, but also process any changes in Managed Properties, iFilters, as well as the Content Enrichment Web Service, which is a Search Feature that developers can use to customize SharePoint Search. Because the Full Crawl crawls all the content of a content source, it takes longer to finish, and it's usually run less often than the Incremental Crawl. A Full Crawl might never be scheduled and only run manually to process changes to the preceding customizations. You can minimize the number of times a Full Crawl is needed by using the built-in "Reindex Site" functionality, available in the Site Settings page of every site, under *Search and Offline Availability*. This will run a full crawl only on that specific site, and not on your whole content source, and can be useful when simply needing to update your Managed Properties or mapping of Crawled Properties.

- **Incremental Crawl**

  The Incremental Crawl is a crawl that will only index the contents that have been modified since the last time a crawl was done. The length of this crawl will directly depend on how many items were modified since you last did a crawl and is usually a lot shorter in duration than a full crawl. This crawl is usually scheduled multiple times during a day, and can also be manually started.

- **Continuous Crawl**

  Continuous Crawl is a type of that aims to keep the content as fresh as possible. Similar to the Incremental Crawl, the Continuous Crawl will only crawl items that have changed since the last crawl is finished. The main difference between Continuous Crawl and Incremental Crawl is that in Continuous Crawl mode, a crawl will start every 15 minutes, even if the last Crawl did not finish. If you want, you could customize the 15-minute crawl interval by running the following PowerShell cmdlet:

```
$sa = Get-SPEnterpriseSearchServiceApplication
$sa.SetProperty("ContinuousCrawlInterval",<TimeInMinutes>)
```

Where <TimeInMinutes> is the interval, in minutes, of how often crawls should be started. Be aware that Continuous Crawl, even with the default 15-minute delay can place a very big load on your SharePoint Infrastructure. Continuous Crawl is often used for search-based sites, where the activity of the site is highly dependent on a fresh index.

For the Content Source we created in this example, we have selected to use Continious Crawl as seen in Figure 6-16.

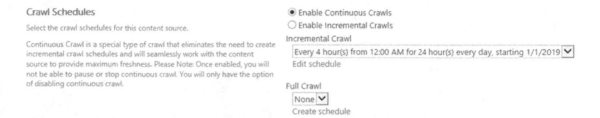

Figure 6-16. *Crawl Schedules*

To create a schedule for the Full Crawl, click the Create Schedule link under the dropbox, and a pop-up window will open allowing you to create a new schedule. As an example, we have created a schedule in Figure 6-17, where the full crawl will happen every Saturday at 2 AM.

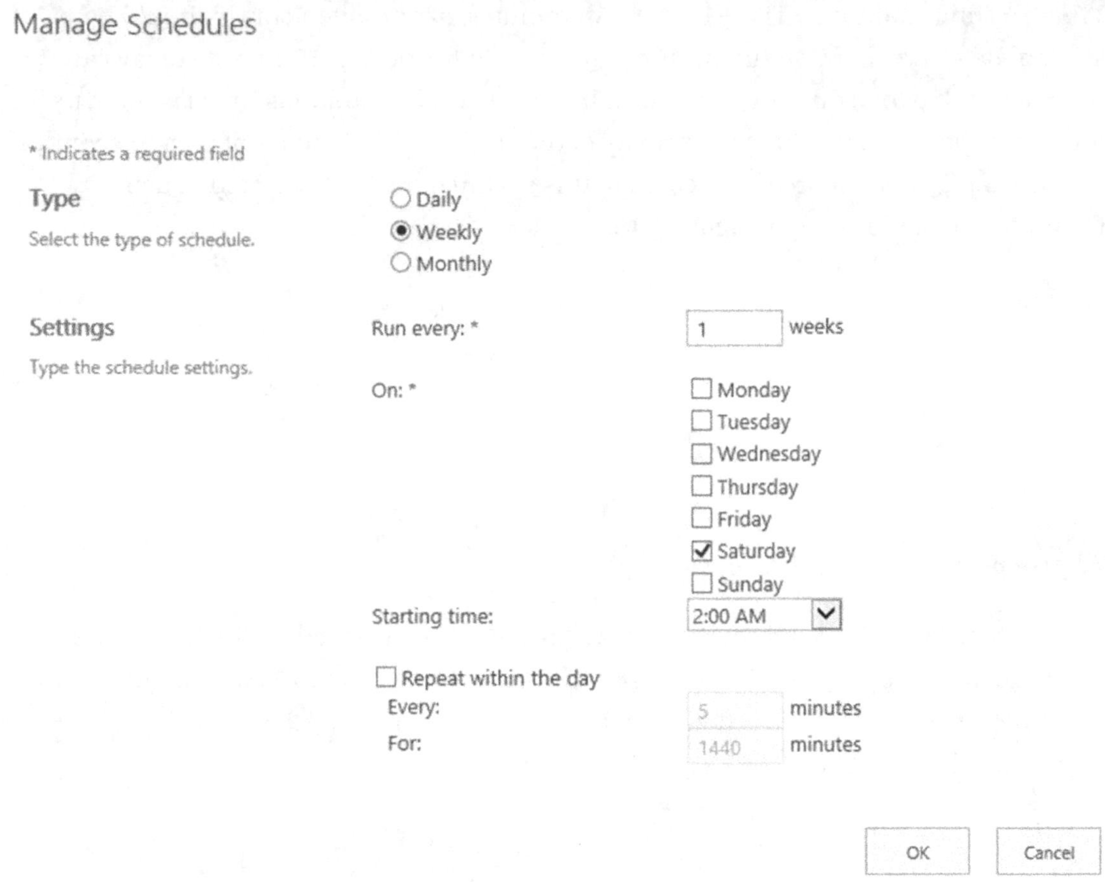

Manage Schedules

* Indicates a required field

Type
Select the type of schedule.

○ Daily
◉ Weekly
○ Monthly

Settings
Type the schedule settings.

Run every: *

1 weeks

On: *

☐ Monday
☐ Tuesday
☐ Wednesday
☐ Thursday
☐ Friday
☑ Saturday
☐ Sunday

Starting time:

2:00 AM ▾

☐ Repeat within the day
Every: 5   minutes
For: 1440   minutes

OK   Cancel

Figure 6-17. *Full Crawl Schedule*

While most Full Crawls only run very rarely, Incremental crawls probably run multiple times every day. To set a crawl schedule to repeat during the day, you need to check the "Repeat within the day" checkbox. You will then need to enter how often the crawl must be repeated and for how long. In the example in Figure 6-18, we start a crawl every 30 minutes, for 1440 minutes (24 h). Therefore, every day the crawl will run every 30 minutes.

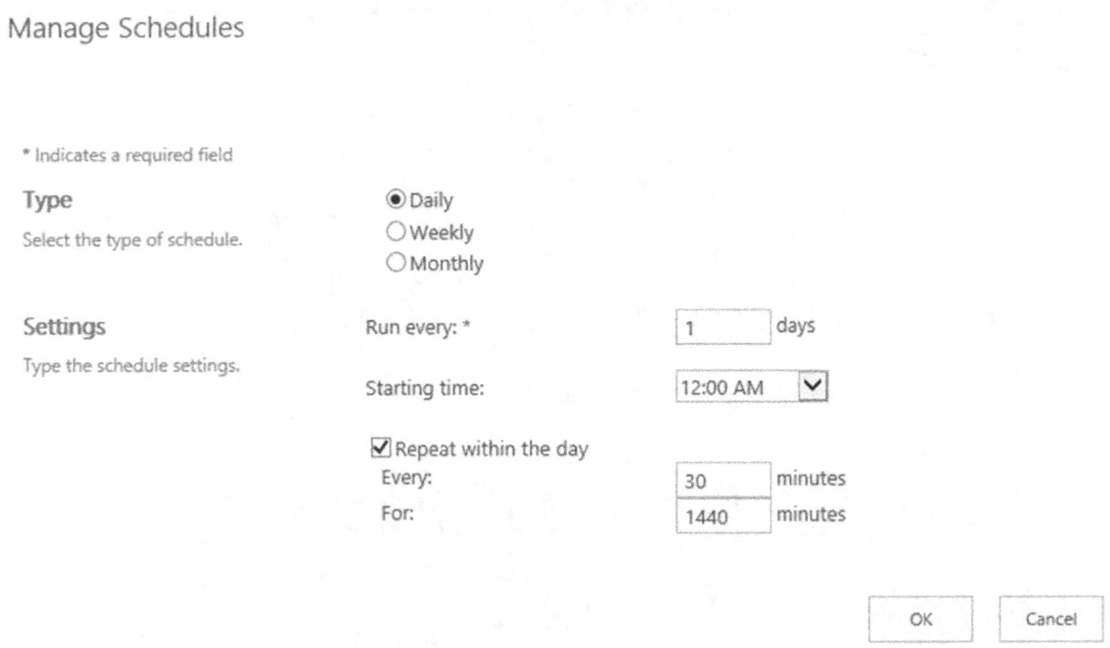

Manage Schedules

* Indicates a required field

Type
Select the type of schedule.

◉ Daily
○ Weekly
○ Monthly

Settings
Type the schedule settings.

Run every: *   1   days

Starting time: 12:00 AM   ▾

☑ Repeat within the day
Every: 30   minutes
For: 1440   minutes

OK   Cancel

Figure 6-18. *Incremental Schedule every 30 minutes*

Some companies that are located on only one time zone might only want the incremental crawls to happen during business hours, since there is usually no activity during off-hours. By changing the Start time and duration, you could set your Incremental Crawls to run every 30 minutes, from 6 AM to 6 PM, as seen in Figure 6-19. By setting the ***For*** field at 720 minutes (12 hours), no crawl will start after 6 PM, and the next incremental crawl will start at 6 AM the following day.

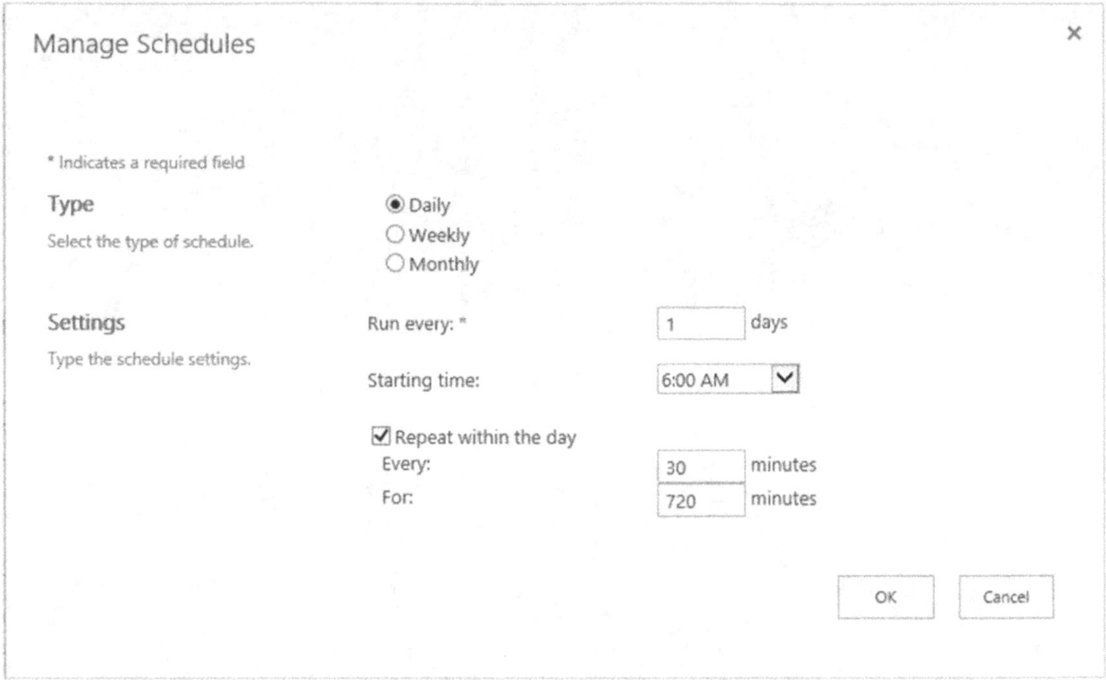

Figure 6-19. *Incremental Crawl Schedule between 6 AM and 6 PM*

In our example in Figure 6-20, we have chosen to enable continuous crawl, and do a full crawl every Saturday, starting at 2 AM.

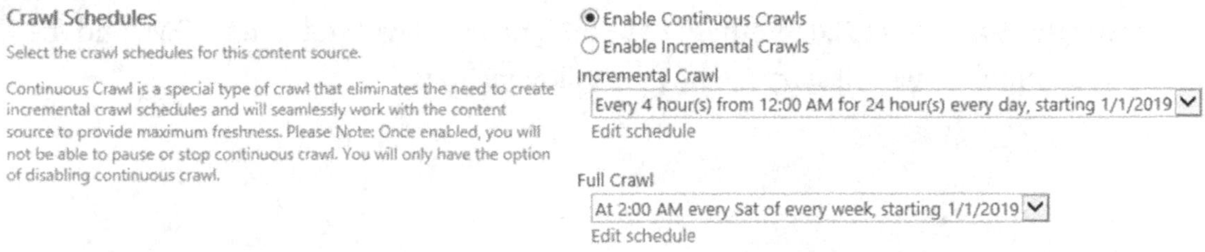

Figure 6-20. *Crawl Schedule*

After the crawl schedule is configured, simply press on OK and your new Content Source will be created. If you chose to enable Continuous Crawl, the crawl will start right away, and if you chose Incremental and Full, the crawl will start in the next scheduled period. You can always manually start the crawl from the Content Source menu as seen in Figure 6-21.

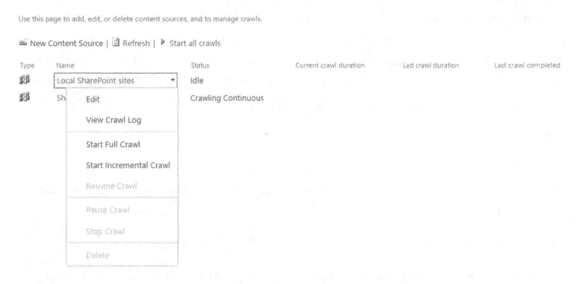

Figure 6-21. *Content Source Menu*

If Continuous Crawl is enabled, the menu will only allow you to disable Continuous crawl as seen in Figure 6-22. You will not be able to manually trigger incremental or full crawls.

Search Service Application 1: Manage Content Sources

Use this page to add, edit, or delete content sources, and to manage crawls.

New Content Source | Refresh | ▶ Start all crawls

Type	Name	Status	Current crawl duration	Last crawl duration	Last crawl completed
	Local SharePoint sites	Idle			
	SharePoint MySites ▾	Crawling Continuous			

Edit

View Crawl Log

Start Full Crawl

Start Incremental Crawl

Resume Crawl

Disable Continuous Crawl

Delete

Figure 6-22. *Content Source Menu with Continuous Crawl enabled*

Another popular type of content source you might want to create is a content source to crawl the User Profiles of users, that way important information such as names, departments, skills, and past projects will show up in the search. We have already given permission to the crawl account on the User Profile Service; we now need to create a content source to crawl People data. The content source type will still be "SharePoint Sites" as the previous example; however, what is a bit different is the Start Address we must enter. The Start Address for People Search needs to be under the following format:

```
sps3://<MySites URL>
```

Where <MySites URL> is the URL of your MySites host. If your MySites host Web Application runs on HTTPS, you will need to start it with *sps3s* instead of *sps3* as seen in the following:

```
sps3s://<MySites URL>
```

In both cases, you do not have to enter the http:// or https:// in front of the host name.

In the environment for this book, we would enter `sps3s://sp-my.cobaltatom.com` as our Start Address as seen in Figure 6-23.

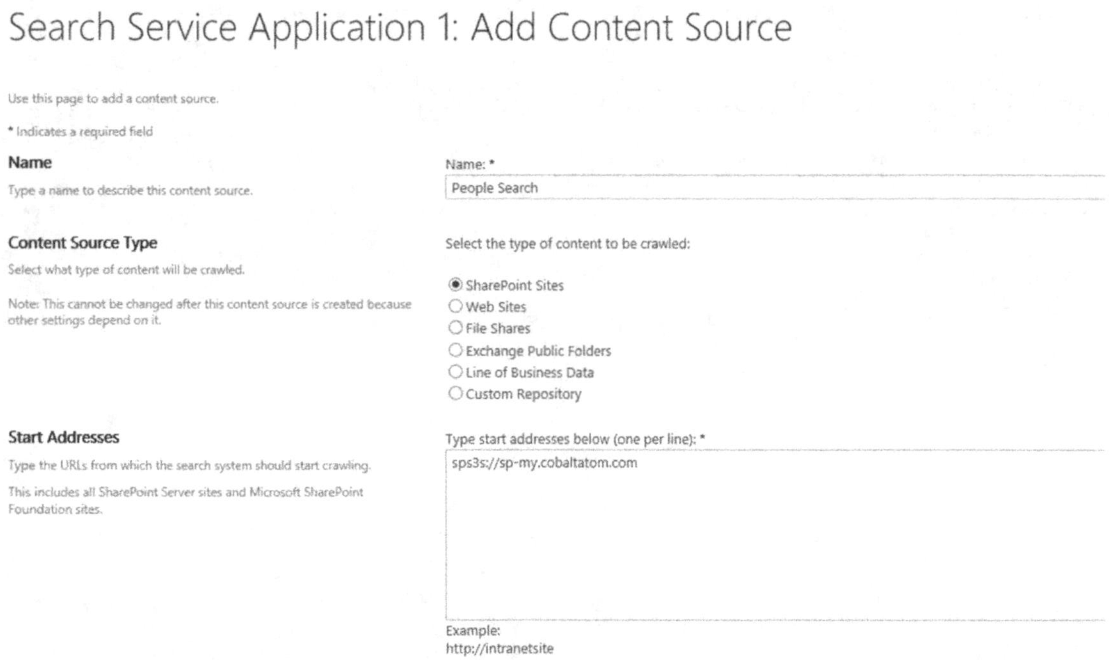

Search Service Application 1: Add Content Source

Use this page to add a content source.

* Indicates a required field

Name

Type a name to describe this content source.

Name: *

People Search

Content Source Type

Select what type of content will be crawled.

Note: This cannot be changed after this content source is created because other settings depend on it.

Select the type of content to be crawled:

◉ SharePoint Sites
○ Web Sites
○ File Shares
○ Exchange Public Folders
○ Line of Business Data
○ Custom Repository

Start Addresses

Type the URLs from which the search system should start crawling.

This includes all SharePoint Server sites and Microsoft SharePoint Foundation sites.

Type start addresses below (one per line): *

sps3s://sp-my.cobaltatom.com

Example:
http://intranetsite

Figure 6-23. *Configuring People Search*

With our content sources created, it's recommended to create an Enterprise Search Center where users can search across the whole SharePoint farm.

SharePoint Security and Search Performance

SharePoint Security and Search are highly connected because SharePoint search results are security trimmed. This means that users will only see search results that they are allowed to access and will not see any search results that they do not have permissions to. Whenever permissions change on an item, the SharePoint search engine will have to perform a crawl of that item in order to process the new permissions and calculate the Access Control List (ACL) of that item.

There are two major strategies of assigning permissions to a SharePoint site. The first one is by adding each user individually in a SharePoint group when they need access, and the second way is giving access to an Active Directory Security Group directly to the site, or placing it in a SharePoint group that has permissions on the site.

The big difference in search performance is that, each time you add a user directly to a SharePoint group, the crawler will have to do a security crawl on all the items that group has access to in order to recalculate the ACL of the site.

The first time you add an Active Directory group to a SharePoint Site, the behavior will be the same; however, when adding other users to that Active Directory group, SharePoint will not have to recalculate the ACL, since no users have been added directly in the SharePoint site. By not having to recrawl every item to recalculate the ACL, your crawls will take shorter and increase index freshness.

Lastly, when changing User Polices at the Web Application level, all the content in that Web Application will have to be recrawled for the preceding reasons. This is indicated at the top of the Policy for Web Application page seen in Figure 6-24.

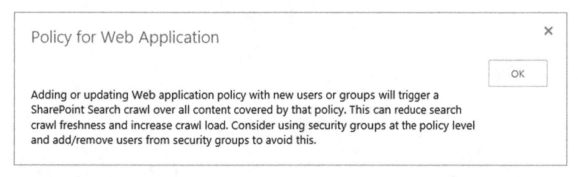

Figure 6-24. *Updating Web Application Policy will trigger a SharePoint Search Crawl*

Selecting the Search Center

Before selecting an Enterprise Search Center, you first need to create a Site Collection with the template "Enterprise Search Center," or if you create it by PowerShell, the SRCHCEN#0 template. Once that Site Collection is created, navigate to the Search Service Application Admin page and from the System Status click "Set a Search Center URL" as seen in Figure 6-25.

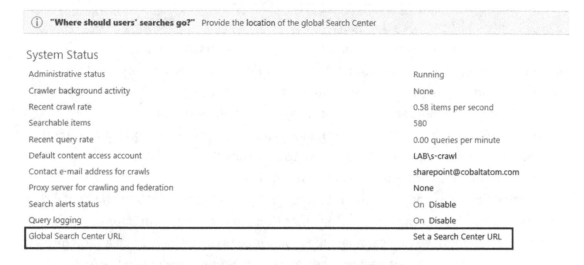

Search Service Application 1: Search Administration

(i) **"Where should users' searches go?"** Provide the location of the global Search Center

System Status

Administrative status	Running
Crawler background activity	None
Recent crawl rate	0.58 items per second
Searchable items	580
Recent query rate	0.00 queries per minute
Default content access account	LAB\s-crawl
Contact e-mail address for crawls	sharepoint@cobaltatom.com
Proxy server for crawling and federation	None
Search alerts status	On Disable
Query logging	On Disable
Global Search Center URL	Set a Search Center URL

Figure 6-25. *Set a Search Center URL link*

A pop-up window will open similar to Figure 6-26, in which you have to enter the URL of your Enterprise Search Center Site collection that you created earlier and add /pages at the end.

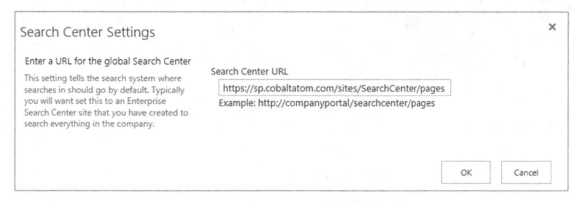

Figure 6-26. *Search Center URL*

You can also set the search center URL by using PowerShell and running the following cmdlet:

```
$ssa = Get-SPEnterpriseSearchServiceApplication
$ssa.SearchCenterUrl = "<Search Center URL>/pages"
$ssa.Update()
```

where "<Search Center URL>" is the URL to your Site Collection using the Enterprise Search Center template.

With the Search Service Application configured, let's look at how to view what was crawled, and if there were any errors while crawling content.

Analyzing Crawl Logs

The Search Service Application displays the Crawl Logs directly in the Central Administration, allowing us to see if the Search can successfully crawl our content sources and any errors that might stop content from getting to the index. This will be useful not only when setting up your Search Service Application the first time, but also as a check during regular maintenance. The Crawl logs can be accessed from the Search Administration page left navigation menu, in the Diagnostics category as seen in Figure 6-27.

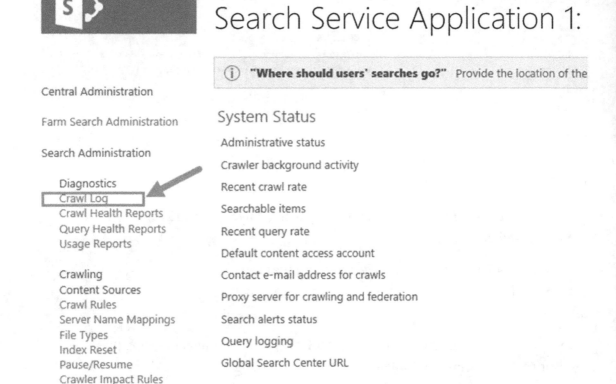

Figure 6-27. *Accessing the Crawl Log in the Search Administration Page*

The Crawl Log settings page default view seen in Figure 6-28 gives us a high-level overview of our Content Sources and the Successes and Warnings. The Successes are the number of items that have been successfully crawled, and moved to the index, while Warnings are items that could not be crawled, or were crawled, but due to certain reasons not placed in the index. The Error column includes how many individual items could not be placed in the index, while the Top Level Error column is only for critical errors that stop the crawl component from reaching an entire Content Source.

Search Service Application 1: Crawl Log - Content Source

Content Source | Host Name | Crawl History | Error Breakdown | Databases | URL View

View a summary of items crawled per content source.

| Content Source | Average Crawl Duration | | | | Summary | | | | |
	Last crawl	Last 24 hours	Last 7 days	Last 30 days	Successes	Warnings	Errors	Top Level Errors	Deletes
Local SharePoint sites	00:04:11	00:02:40	00:02:40	00:02:40	191	5	13	0	0
People Search	00:02:00	00:02:35	00:02:35	00:02:35	279	0	0	0	0
SharePoint MySites	00:02:00	00:04:21	00:04:21	00:04:21	276	4	0	0	0

Figure 6-28. *Crawl Logs page*

When clicking any of the numbers, SharePoint will show the message as well as URL for the items within that category. In Figure 6-29, we can see the three errors that we have in the SharePoint MySites content type and how many items were affected by each error. This will allow us to easily fix errors and get items in the index on the next crawl.

Search Service Application 1: Crawl Log - Error Breakdown

Content Source | Host Name | Crawl History | Error Breakdown | Databases | URL View

View crawl errors. Set filters to see errors for only a particular content source or hostname.

Filters

Content source `Local SharePoint sites`

Host `All`

[View]

Count	Error message
11	The secure sockets layer (SSL) certificate sent by the server was invalid and this item will not be crawled.
2	An unrecognized HTTP response was received when attempting to crawl this item. Verify whether the item can be accessed using your browser.

Figure 6-29. *Crawl Log – Error Breakdown for the SharePoint MySites content source*

Accumulating many errors over time will increase the size of your crawl database, since all those errors will be stored inside.

From the Crawl Logs page in the Central Administration, we can also search for specific items to find out if they have been crawled or not. This is useful when users report that their documents do not appear in search results, even if they uploaded them before the last crawl. To search the Crawl Logs, from the Crawl Log page, navigate to "URL View" in the top bar. From the URL View page, we can type an URL or hostname in the top bar and use wildcards to help us find the item we're looking for. Furthermore, we can use filters to only find the documents we are looking for. As you see in Figure 6-30, a Document in the library we searched for had a warning, and that could explain why it wouldn't appear in the search results.

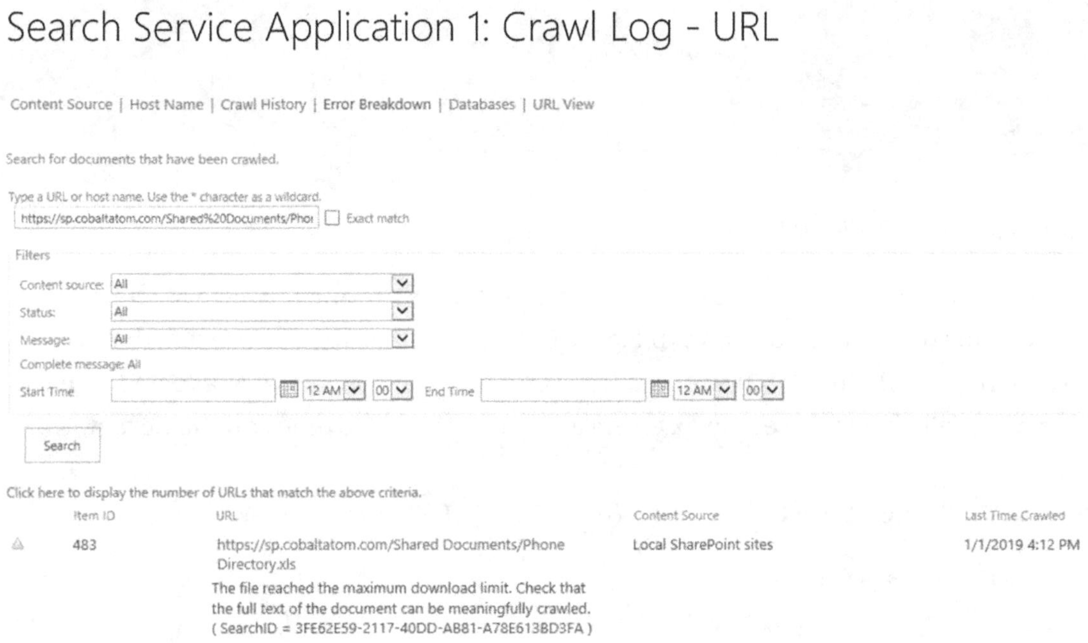

Figure 6-30. *Search Service Application Crawl Logs – URL View*

In some circumstances, to refresh our Search Results or to fix an error, we need to perform an Index Reset.

Resetting the Index

In some cases, the only way to "reset" our Search Service Application is to delete all the items in the index and recrawl all the content sources. This is called an Index reset. To do an Index Reset, navigate to the Search Administration page, and from the left navigation menu click *Index Reset* as seen in Figure 6-31.

Figure 6-31. *Index Reset button*

After resetting the index, no search results will be available until those items have been recrawled; therefore, if you have a lot of content, or you have search-dependent sites, preferably run this during off-hours. Before resetting the index, you will have the option to disable Search Alerts, in order to not send alerts to your users because new items are added to the index. If you decide to disable Search Alerts during the recrawl, remember to manually activate them after the first Full Crawl is done.

When managing a large index, resetting the index trough the User Interface can cause it to time out. The easiest way to avoid a timeout is to do an index reset by using PowerShell. An index reset can be done with the following cmdlets:

```
$sa = Get-SPEnterpriseSearchServiceApplication
$sa.reset($true, $true)
```

Where the first $true parameter is to disable Alerts, and the second $true parameter is to ignore a timeout error.

To estimate how long the Full Crawl is going to take, you could calculate the Number of Items in your index (Searchable Items) divided by Recent Crawl Rate. While this won't be an exact measure, it's a good estimate. In Figure 6-32, we have 581 items in our index and a Recent Crawl Rate of 0.26 items per second.

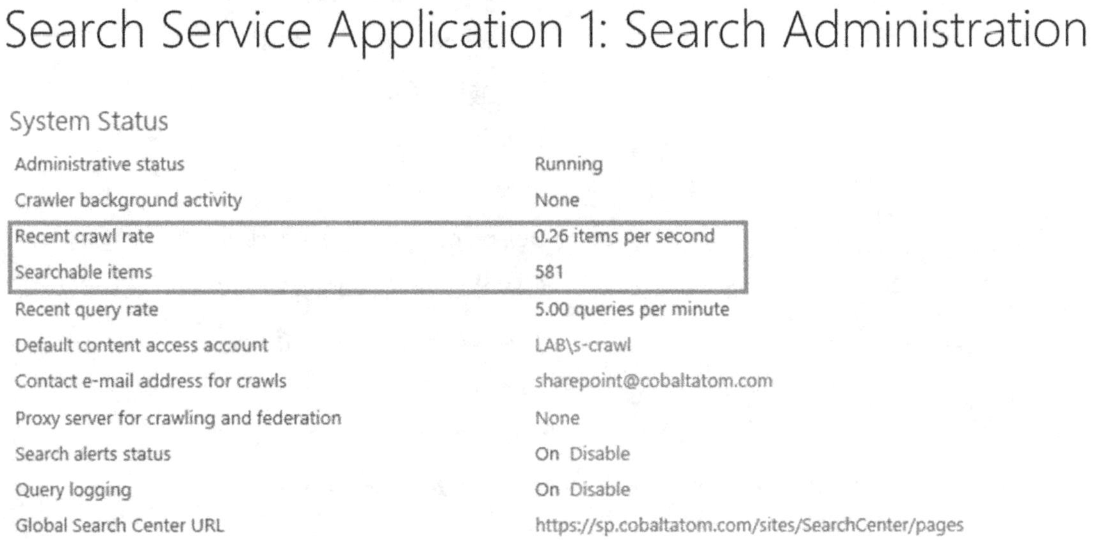

Search Service Application 1: Search Administration

System Status

Administrative status	Running
Crawler background activity	None
Recent crawl rate	0.26 items per second
Searchable items	581
Recent query rate	5.00 queries per minute
Default content access account	LAB\s-crawl
Contact e-mail address for crawls	sharepoint@cobaltatom.com
Proxy server for crawling and federation	None
Search alerts status	On Disable
Query logging	On Disable
Global Search Center URL	https://sp.cobaltatom.com/sites/SearchCenter/pages

Figure 6-32. *Calculating Full Crawl Time*

Next Steps

With the Search Service Application created and our content crawled, in the next chapter we will learn how to configure the User Profile Service application.

CHAPTER 7

Configuring the User Profile Service

The User Profile Service is one of the core services in nearly all SharePoint Server deployments. This service provides information about users, OneDrive for Business, Social features, and Audiences, among other features. In this chapter, we will go through the options available for Active Directory synchronization, OneDrive for Business On-Premises setup, Audience configuration, and finally using the OneDrive Next Gen Sync Client.

Initial Configuration

We performed an initial configuration of the User Profile Service Application in Chapter 3, where we created the User Profile Service Application and set up the MySite Host with a/personal/ wildcard Managed Path and enabled Self-Service Site Creation. We need to set up the User Profile Import from Active Directory into SharePoint. SharePoint Server 2019 only includes Active Directory Import (AD Import), unlike SharePoint Server 2010 and 2013 which included the User Profile Synchronization Service. The UPSS was based on Forefront Identity Manager. AD Import has a few limitations, primarily that it is import only, which means no writing back of attributes to Active Directory, no deletion of User Profiles for users who have been removed or disabled in Active Directory, and it does not import user profile pictures. While photo import can be accomplished via PowerShell, if any of these are scenarios which your farm requires, consider implementing Microsoft Identity Manager 2016 which will be discussed in further detail later in this chapter.

© Vlad Catrinescu and Trevor Seward 2019
V. Catrinescu and T. Seward, *Deploying SharePoint 2019*, https://doi.org/10.1007/978-1-4842-4526-2_7

The User Profile Synchronization Service Account, in this case, LAB\s-spsync, must have "Replicating Directory Changes" permission on the Active Directory domain we are synchronizing with. To grant this right, right-click the root of the domain in the Active Directory Users and Computers MMC, then proceed to start the Delegation Wizard. In the first step, add the synchronization account (LAB\s-spsync), then create a Custom Task to Delegate. For the Active Directory Object Type, leave the default option of "This folder, existing objects in this folder, and creation of new objects in this folder." selected. In the last step, select the permissions named "Replicating Directory Changes," as shown in Figure 7-1. This completes the delegation process.

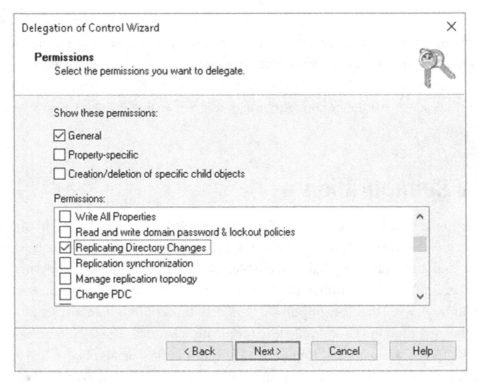

Figure 7-1. *Adding the appropriate permissions in Active Directory for the synchronization account*

If the NetBIOS domain name does not match the Fully Qualified Domain Name, that is, if the NetBIOS name was EXAMPLE while the Fully Qualified Domain Name was CORP. COMPANY.COM, an additional step is necessary using ADSI Edit (adsiedt.msc). While not the case for this environments domain, using ADSI Edit, connect to the Configuration Naming Context. As shown in Figure 7-2, right-click the Configuration node (shown as "CN=Configuration,DC=LAB,DC=COBALTATOM,DC=COM"), and select Properties (note if using Microsoft Identity Manager, complete this step regardless of a mismatch between the NetBIOS name and FQDN). From here, select the Security tab, add the synchronization account, and grant the same permissions, as shown in Figure 7-3.

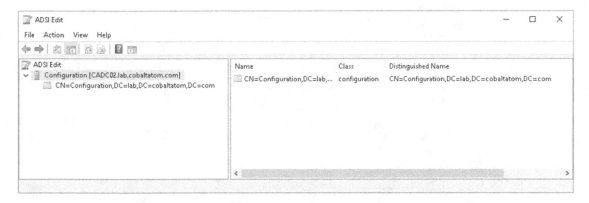

Figure 7-2. *Using ADSI Edit while connected to the Configuration Naming Context*

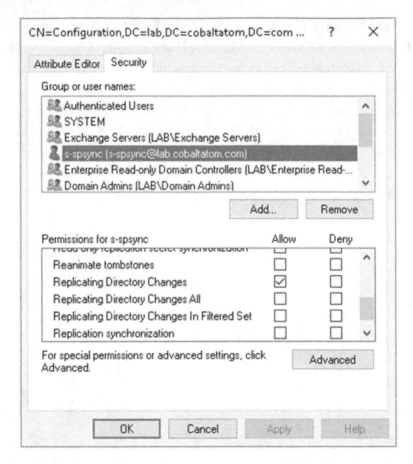

Figure 7-3. *Adding the synchronization account with the "Replicating Directory Changes" permission*

Once completed, we can continue creating the synchronization connection from SharePoint Central Administration.

Navigating in Central Administration to Manage Service Applications, click the User Profile Service Application previously created. Go into Configure Synchronization Connections and click Create New Connection. There should only be a single connection per Active Directory Forest. Provide a relevant Connection Name, such as the name of the Forest. You'll note the only available option for Type is now AD Import. Provide the fully qualified domain name for the root domain of the forest, and the account name in DOMAIN\Username format and enter the password. Because we've deployed Active Directory Certificate Servers and our Domain Controller has a valid Server Authentication certificate, we will change the port number to 636 and check the

Use SSL-secured connection. If the Domain Controllers do not have certificates installed, such as a Domain Controller or Kerberos Authentication certificate from a Microsoft Active Directory Certificate Services server, leave the default port of 389 and Use SSL unchecked. We also do not want disabled users being imported and will check that box as well. Add an LDAP filter if necessary; for example, to filter out Computer Objects, the filter would be as follows:

`(!objectClass=computer)`

The connection configuration is complete, as shown in Figure 7-4.

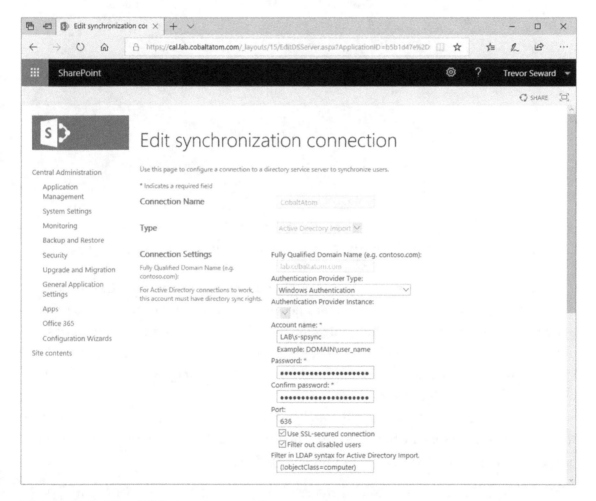

Figure 7-4. *The AD Import connection*

Click Populate Containers. Unlike the previous User Profile Synchronization Service import, AD Import will import all objects into the User Profile Service. It is recommended that you only select the specific containers you need, namely those containing Users and Groups. Groups will be imported for use in Audiences.

As our Organization Unit structure is not complicated, we will only be selecting a few containers as shown in Figure 7-5.

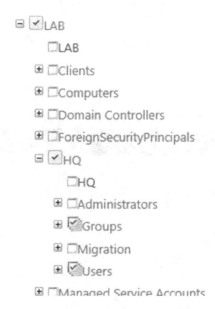

Figure 7-5. *Selecting the Organization Units to import Users and Groups*

Once the OU selection is complete, click OK and the Synchronization Connection will be created. Go back to the Manage Profile Service page, and click Start Profile Synchronization. Start a Full Synchronization. The time it takes for this import varies depending on the number of objects you are synchronizing. The synchronization will start shortly and under the Synchronization Status on the right hand side, you will see it change to Synchronizing when refreshing your browser.

If you do not see additional profiles after the import process has completed, check the ULS logs on the server where the timer job ran. Using the SharePoint Management Shell, we can get the timer job and examine the history entries.

```
$job = Get-SPTimerJob | ?{$_.TypeName -like "*.UserProfileADImportJob"}
$job.HistoryEntries | Select -First 1
```

Here, examine the ServerName value for the last location the timer job ran on. Convert the Start and End time from UTC to your local time zone.

```
$historyEntry = $job.HistoryEntries | Select -First 1
$historyEntry.StartTime.ToLocalTime()
$historyEntry.EndTime.ToLocalTime()
```

Once you've gathered the appropriate ULS entries, examine them for "DirSync import failed." Here, you will see a stack trace that will contain the error message. For example:

```
ActiveDirectory Import: DirSync import failed: ScanDirSyncChanges: Exception
thrown by Dirsync request: page 0, LdapServer 'CADC01.LAB.COBALTATOM.
COM:636', rootDn 'DC=LAB,DC=COBALTATOM,DC=COM', exception 'System.
DirectoryServices.Protocols.LdapException: The search filter is invalid.
```

In this particular case, we know that we must edit our LDAP filter as the syntax is incorrect. Other errors might include connectivity issues, such as timeouts or incorrect permissions. There are many free tools to validate LDAP syntax available on the Internet that you may want to use prior to adding a new filter.

Once the filter has been fixed, rerun your AD Import and validate the appropriate users are imported to the User Profile Service.

The synchronization connection may also be configured using PowerShell, with the Add-SPProfileSyncConnection cmdlet.

```
$sa = Get-SPServiceApplication | ?{$_.TypeName -eq "User Profile Service
Application"}
Add-SPProfileSyncConnection-ProfileServiceApplication $sa
-ConnectionForestName "lab.cobaltatom.com" -ConnectionDomain "LAB"
-ConnectionUserName "s-spsync" -ConnectionPassword (ConvertTo-SecureString
"<Password>" -AsPlainText -Force) -ConnectionPort 636 -ConnectionUseSSL
$true -ConnectionUseDisabledFilter $true -ConnectionSynchronizationOU
"OU=Employees,DC=LAB,DC=COBALTATOM,DC=COM"
```

This will create the same synchronization connection as shown in the preceding; however, if any additional Organization Units are needed, or an additional LDAP filter is required, add them through Central Administration. Note that the -ConnectionUserName parameter expects only the sAMAccountName, not the full DOMAIN\Username value.

With the AD Import configuration complete, let's take a look at the second option for importing User Profiles.

External Identity Manager Configuration

Configuring an external identity manager requires a significantly larger time investment. There is the Microsoft Identity Manager, which supports Active Directory and the SharePoint User Profile service, along with many other directory types and custom solutions.

The initial configuration requires changing the User Profile Service Application to use an External Identity Manager. This is set through the Configure Synchronization Settings in the User Profile Service Application, as shown in Figure 7-6. Select the "Enable External Identity Manager" option.

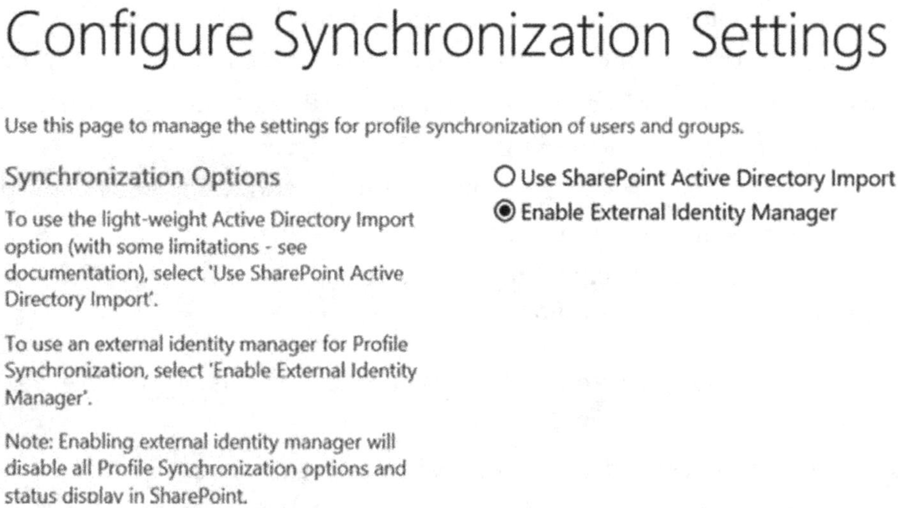

Configure Synchronization Settings

Use this page to manage the settings for profile synchronization of users and groups.

Synchronization Options

To use the light-weight Active Directory Import option (with some limitations - see documentation), select 'Use SharePoint Active Directory Import'.

To use an external identity manager for Profile Synchronization, select 'Enable External Identity Manager'.

Note: Enabling external identity manager will disable all Profile Synchronization options and status display in SharePoint.

○ Use SharePoint Active Directory Import
◉ Enable External Identity Manager

Figure 7-6. *Enabling External Identity Manager for SharePoint Server 2016*

When set, on the User Profile Service Application will display that it is now using an External Identity Manager, as shown in Figure 7-7.

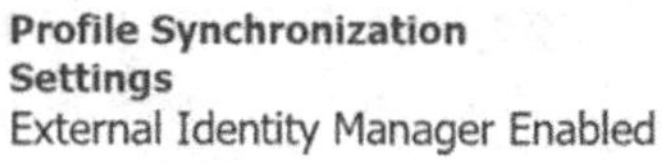

Profile Synchronization Settings
External Identity Manager Enabled

Figure 7-7. *The External Identity Manager is enabled for this User Profile Service Application*

With Microsoft Identity Manager, we only need to install the Synchronization Service. This service provides inbound and outbound synchronization between many different directory and business data platforms.

Microsoft provides install documentation for Microsoft Identity Manager (MIM). MIM should be installed on a dedicated server, if possible.

Note   Documentation for the Microsoft Identity Manager 2016 installation is available from `http://aka.ms/UserProfileMIMSync`.

To install MIM on Windows Server 2016 using the SQL Server 2016 AlwaysOn Failover Cluster Instance, the MIM server must first have the .NET 3.5 Framework and SQL 2008 R2 or 2012 Native Client installed. In addition, to support the SharePoint Connector, MIM must have at minimum build of 4.3.2064.0, but consider using Service Pack 1 and post-Service Pack 1 patches.

Note   Build 4.3.2064.0 is available from `https://support.microsoft.com/help/3092179`.

Install the Forefront Identity Manager Connector for SharePoint User Profile Store, available from `www.microsoft.com/en-us/download/details.aspx?id=41164`, on the MIM server. This is the Management Agent, which will connect to the SharePoint User Profile Service.

The User Profile Sync MIM solution includes a PowerShell Module, SharePointSync. psm1, to set up the Active Directory and SharePoint Management Agents. This will run on the MIM server.

Note   The User Profile Sync solution is available from `https://github.com/OfficeDev/PnP-Tools/tree/master/Solutions/UserProfile.MIMSync`.

From an elevated PowerShell console, navigate to the extracted location of the module. To configure this will require two accounts, the account previously created with Replicate Directory Changes as well as the Farm Administrator account to connect to the User Profile Service.

```
$syncCred = Get-Credential "LAB\s-spsync"
$farmCred = Get-Credential "LAB\s-farm"
Import-Module C:\SharePointSync\SharePointSync.psm1
Install-SharePointSyncConfiguration -Path C:\SharePointSync -ForestDnsName
"LAB.COBALTATOM.COM" -ForestCredential $syncCred -OrganizationalUnit "OU=HQ
,DC=LAB,DC=COBALTATOM,DC=COM" -SharePointUrl https://cal.lab.cobaltatom.com
-SharePointCredential $farmCred
```

Prior to running the synchronization, you must set the password for the synchronization account on the "ADMA" Management Agent. Using the Synchronization Service Manager, go to the Management Agents tab. Double-click the "ADMA" Management Agent. Click the "Connect to Active Directory Forest" section and enter the password for the synchronization account, as shown in Figure 7-8. Click OK to save the machines.

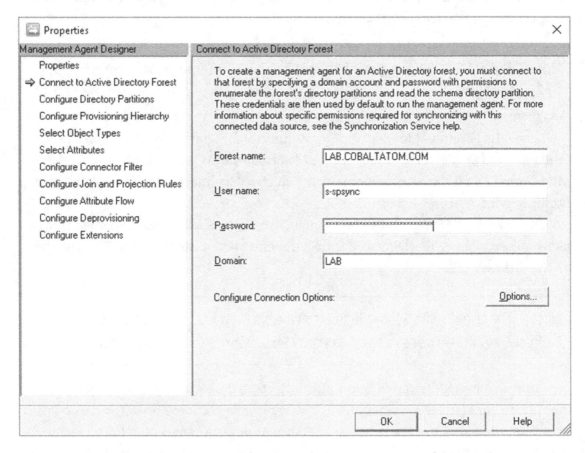

Figure 7-8. *Setting the password for the Active Directory synchronization account in the Active Directory Management Agent*

As our initial configuration of SharePoint enforces the use of TLS 1.2, we must import the following registry entries and reboot the MIM server prior to starting the initial synchronization process.

```
Windows Registry Editor Version 5.00
[HKEY_LOCAL_MACHINE\SOFTWARE\Microsoft\.NETFramework\v2.0.50727]
"SchUseStrongCrypto"=dword:00000001
[HKEY_LOCAL_MACHINE\SOFTWARE\Wow6432Node\Microsoft\.NETFramework\v2.0.50727]
"SchUseStrongCrypto"=dword:00000001
[HKEY_LOCAL_MACHINE\SOFTWARE\Microsoft\.NETFramework\v4.0.30319]
"SchUseStrongCrypto"=dword:00000001
[HKEY_LOCAL_MACHINE\SOFTWARE\Wow6432Node\Microsoft\.NETFramework\v4.0.30319]
"SchUseStrongCrypto"=dword:00000001
```

The synchronization can be run through PowerShell after importing the SharePointSync.psm1 file.

```
Start-SharePointSync -Confirm:$false
```

Monitoring the synchronization process can be done from the Synchronization Service Manager, which is installed at C:\Program Files\Microsoft Forefront Identity Manager\2010\Synchronization Service\UIShell\miisclient.exe. The Operations tab will show the progress of the two Management Agents, ADMA (Active Directory), and SPMA (SharePoint). Any errors will be notated in the Status column.

When a full synchronization has completed, you may then start using delta synchronization. Again, using the SharePointSync.psm1 module, run the following:

```
Start-SharePointSync -Delta -Confirm:$false
```

The delta process should be faster than the full synchronization. Note that, like the previous User Profile Synchronization Service, any changes to properties require a full synchronization to take place. In Figure 7-9, we see a Full Import process completed successfully and a subsequent Delta Import completing successfully.

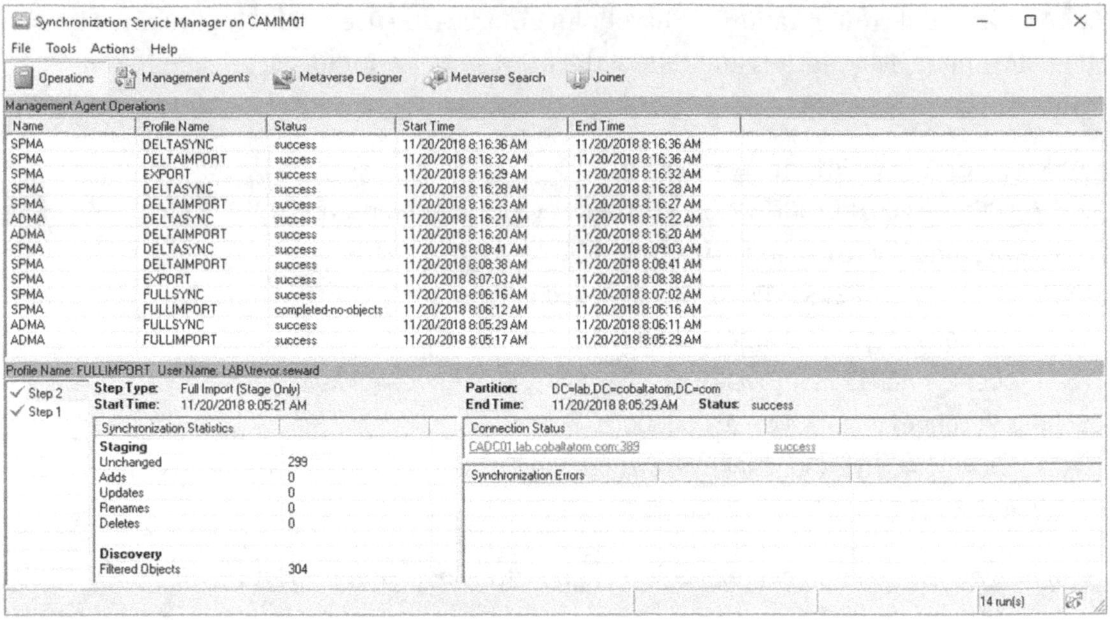

Figure 7-9. *A Full run followed by a Delta run*

While this process will import profile photos, the profile photos will need to be converted to the small, medium, and large photos. In order to do this, set up a Scheduled Task that runs the following cmdlet on the MySite Host. This must be run on a SharePoint server in the farm which is running the User Profile Service instance by a user who has administrative rights on the User Profile Service Application and Shell Admin rights.

```
Add-PSSnapin Microsoft.SharePoint.PowerShell -EA O
Update-SPProfilePhotoStore -MySiteHostLocation https://sp-my.cobaltatom.com
-CreateThumbnailsForImportedPhotos 1
```

This cmdlet may take some time to complete depending on the number of user profile photos that need to be converted.

Configuring Additional Import Properties

To configure additional import properties to import into SharePoint, it will require modification of the User Profile Service in SharePoint, the SharePoint Management Agent, and the Active Directory Management Agent in Microsoft Identity Manager. We will be creating a property named "Company" which pulls from the Active Directory attribute named "company."

In the User Profile Service Application, under Manage User Properties, create the property with the applicable settings, or in our case, a string with a 64-character limit. The limit of the value may be found in the Active Directory Schema Manager MMC. In order to view the Active Directory Schema, you must first register schmmgmt.dll.

```
regsvr32.exe C:\Windows\System32\schmmgmt.dll
```

From there, open mmc.exe and add the snap-in named "Active Directory Schema." In the Attributes node, find the target attribute, or company in this case. Viewing the attribute properties will tell you the constraints of the attribute, as shown in Figure 7-10.

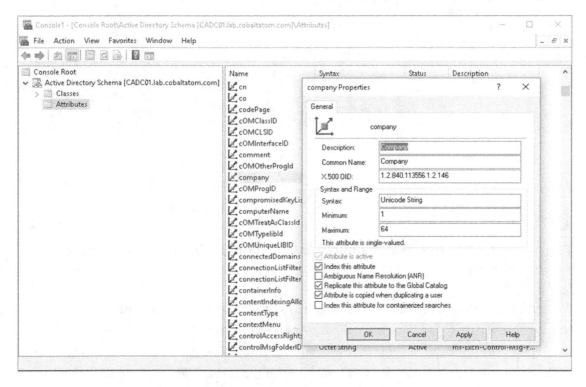

Figure 7-10. *Using the Active Directory Schema manager, showing the company attribute*

In Microsoft Identity Manager Synchronization Service Manager, navigate to the Management Agents tab. Open the Active Directory Domain Services Management Agent (named ADMA). Under Select Attributes, select the appropriate Active Directory attribute, or "company" in our case. The next step is to configure the Attribute Flow. Select the appropriate object type, or in this case, the Object Type of "user" which flows to the Object Type of "person," as shown in Figure 7-11.

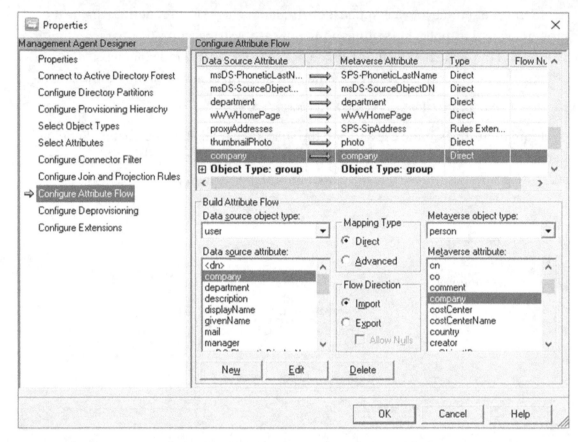

Figure 7-11. *Creating an attribute flow for "company" in the Active Directory Management Agent*

Once completed, the next step is to refresh the schema on the SharePoint Management Agent. On the Management Agents tab, right-click the SharePoint Management Agent and select Refresh Schema. You will be prompted for the password of the user configured to connect to Central Administration. The schema update will take a few seconds to complete. At this point, it is time to edit the new Company attribute to import it into SharePoint, so edit the SharePoint Management Agent and navigate to Select Attributes. Select the new "Company" attribute, then move onto Configure Attribute Flow. We are modifying the Object Type user from the Object Type person. Add a new flow for Company as shown in Figure 7-12. Note that we must select "Allow Nulls" as this property may not have a value for each user in the directory.

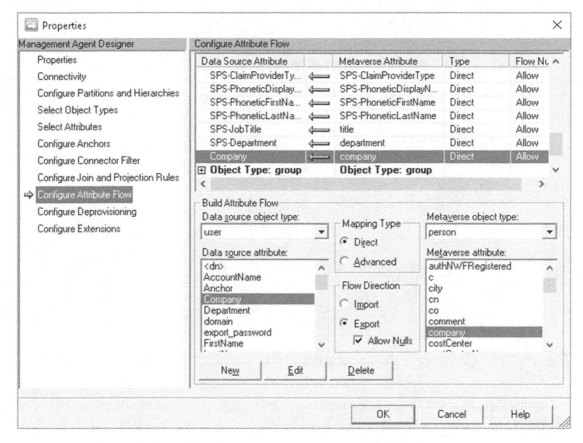

Figure 7-12.   *Importing the company attribute into SharePoint*

Now, run a full import, and that's it! The new Company attribute will be populated for users who have that property populated in Active Directory.

Configuring Export Properties

To *export* properties, we'll allow users to enter their own Home Phone number. We need to create a new User Profile Service property of a string, with a length of 256 characters, which matches the value of the homePhone attribute as viewed through the Active Directory Schema Manager. As we want to write this attribute, we must provide our synchronization service account, LAB\s-spsync, with the ability to write back this attribute to user accounts in Active Directory. For this, we will again start the Delegation Control Wizard via Active Directory Users and Computers, choosing the synchronization service account and a custom task to delegate. We will only delegate control to User objects, and the right to write to the Home Phone attribute, as shown in Figure 7-13.

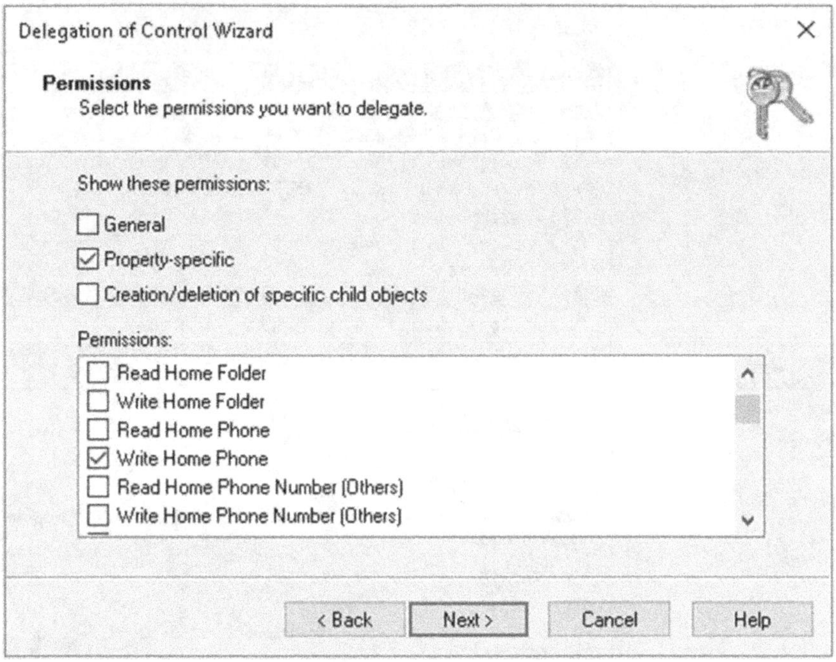

Figure 7-13.   *Granting LAB\s-spsync with Write access to the Home Phone attribute*

Working backward, in the Microsoft Identity Manager Synchronization Service Manager, modify the SharePoint Management Agent. Select the HomePhone attribute under Select Attribute, then configure an attribute flow to *import* the attribute HomePhone from SharePoint to the metaverse for user objects, as shown in Figure 7-14. The directional arrow points from the SharePoint Management Agent into the Microsoft Identity Manager metaverse.

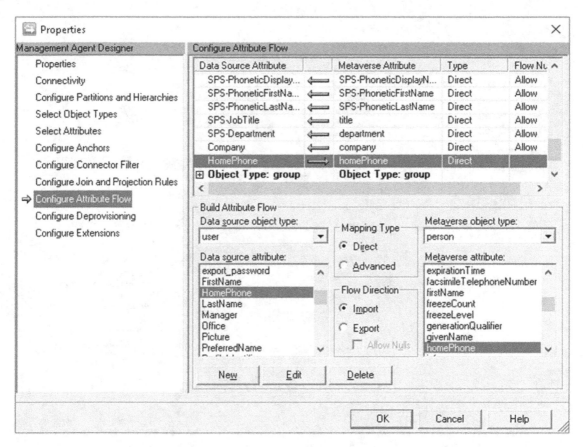

Figure 7-14. *Importing the HomePhone attribute from SharePoint into the metaverse*

Tip   If you created a custom User Profile Property, refresh the SharePoint Management Agent Schema, otherwise it will not appear in the Select Attributes list.

Moving onto the Active Directory Management Agent, again select the homePhone attribute from Select Attributes. Under Configure Attribute Flows, for the Object Type of user, *export* the homePhone attribute from the metaverse into the homePhone attribute in Active Directory, allowing for nulls (as not all users may have populated the field), as shown in Figure 7-15.

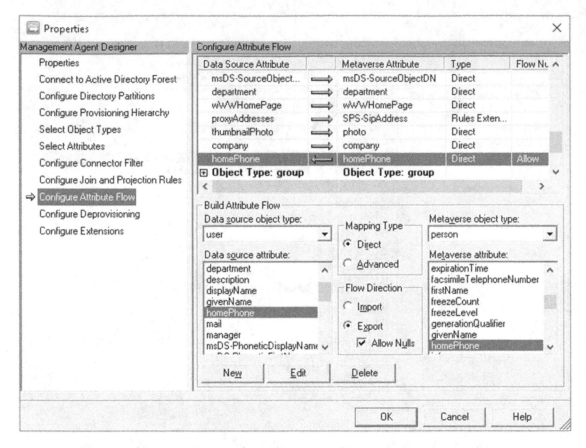

Figure 7-15. *Exporting homePhone from the metaverse into Active Directory*

The setup of the Management Agents does not create an *Export* attribute flow for Active Directory. This means, by default, we cannot write attributes in Active Directory. To configure an Export run profile, under the Management Agents tab, highlight the Active Directory Management Agent and select Configure Run Profiles. Create a new profile named Export and for the Step type, select Export. Complete the run profile. When you click Run for the Active Directory Management Agent, Export is now an option. Run the export, and if the permissions are configured correctly, the homePhone attribute will be written with the value inputted by a user from their User Profile in SharePoint.

The ADMA Export run profile may also be started with PowerShell by importing the SharePointSync.psm1 and using Start-ManagementAgent.

```
Import-Module .\SharePointSync.psm1
Start-ManagementAgent -Name ADMA -RunProfile Export
```

Now that we know how to import and export profiles from and to SharePoint Server, let's take a look at custom properties that may not exist within the metaverse.

Custom Properties

In order to support custom properties from either Active Directory or the SharePoint User Profile Service, it may be necessary to create a new attribute within the Microsoft Identity Manager metaverse. This can be accomplished under the Metaverse Designer. The object type will most likely be "person." When highlighting person, the existing attributes belonging to that object type in the metaverse will appear below. From here, it is possible to add additional attributes to the metaverse, or create *new* attributes within the metaverse, as seen in Figure 7-16. Once the attribute has been added to the metaverse, it is treated like any other attribute in terms of synchronization to and from the Management Agents.

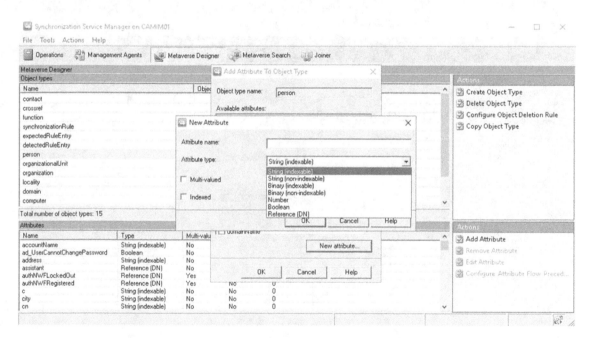

Figure 7-16. *Adding a new attribute to the Microsoft Identity Manager metaverse*

With our custom property in Microsoft Identity Manager created, take a brief look at Audiences and how to configure them within SharePoint.

Audiences

Audiences are used to scope certain content, such as SharePoint webparts, to a certain set of users. Audiences are powerful in that they allow a variety of rules to be created to define who should belong to them. One caveat with audiences is that they are not security boundaries. Content hidden by an audience is still viewable by a client. Audiences, by default, are also only compiled once per week on Saturday at 1 AM. This can be adjusted to be more frequent, although was set specifically to one day per week for performance considerations.

In order to configure an audience, the audience is created under Manage Audiences within the User Profile Service Application. Here you will define the rules that scope the audience to specific users. In this example, as seen in Figure 7-17, we are creating a Project Managers audience containing all users who have a job title of "Project Manager."

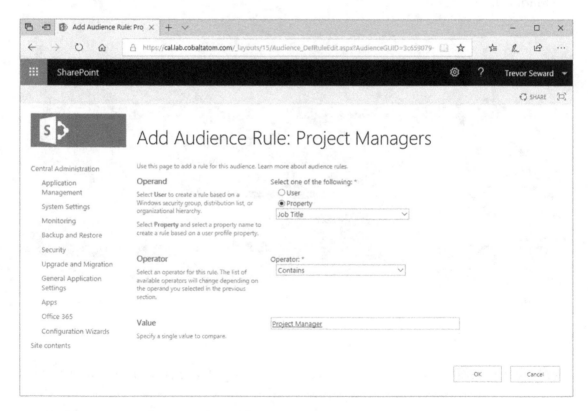

Figure 7-17. *A newly created Audience*

When compiled, as shown in Figure 7-18, the number of members will be displayed that match the rule(s) along with any errors that occurred during audience compilation. At this point, the audience can be used on SharePoint content to scope the content to the specific set of users.

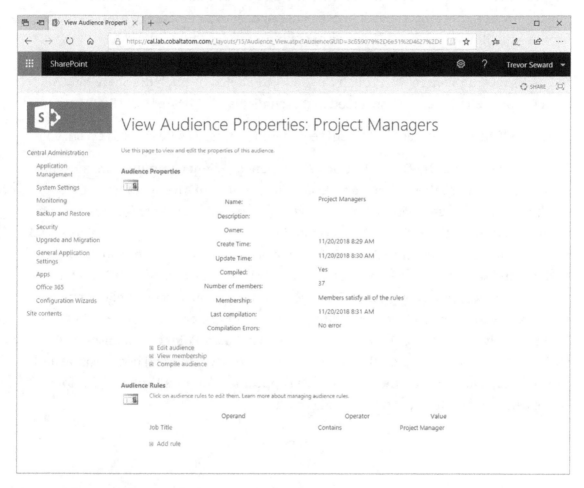

Figure 7-18. *The compiled Project Managers audience*

OneDrive for Business

OneDrive for Business, also known as a MySite, is a location where the user can upload documents to for personal use and limited sharing. This is also a location where the user can update their User Profile and create posts within their blog. Two notable features no longer available are the Company Newsfeed, which is now read-only, Tasks, or the task aggregation feature available in SharePoint Server 2013 as the Work Management Service Application is no longer available.

The MySite settings were configured in Chapter 3, but can be further adjusted from the User Profile Service Application under Setup My Sites. For example, you may add a Preferred Search Center or change the Site Naming Format. Note that changing the Site Naming Format will cause all MySite Site Collections to migrate to the new naming format, which may be a disk I/O heavy operation.

Recently Shared Items is a new feature for SharePoint On-Premises that displays the items recently shared with you. It can only be enabled through the SharePoint Management Shell. The URL specified in this cmdlet is the MySite Host URL.

```
Enable-SPFeature "RecentlySharedItems" -Url https://sp-my.cobaltatom.com
```

To configure the OneDrive Next Gen Sync client on client computers, we must first get the Group Policy files (ADMX and ADML) from the OneDrive sync client. These can be found in %LocalAppData%\Microsoft\OneDrive\<ClientVersion>\adm. Copy OneDrive.admx to the SYSVOL Policy Definitions (e.g. \\lab.cobaltatom.com\SYSVOL\ lab.cobaltatom.com\Policies\PolicyDefinitions) and the OneDrive.adml to the en-US folder in the same location (copy other language ADML files as required). With the two files copied, open Group Policy Management and edit an existing policy or create a new policy to apply the OneDrive settings. Under Computer Configuration, Policies, Administrative Templates, OneDrive, edit the policy "SharePoint on-premises server URL and tenant folder name". Set the URL to the OneDrive (MySite) host location and provide a logical name for the folder as it will appear in Windows Explorer (this folder name can be any value), as shown in Figure 7-19.

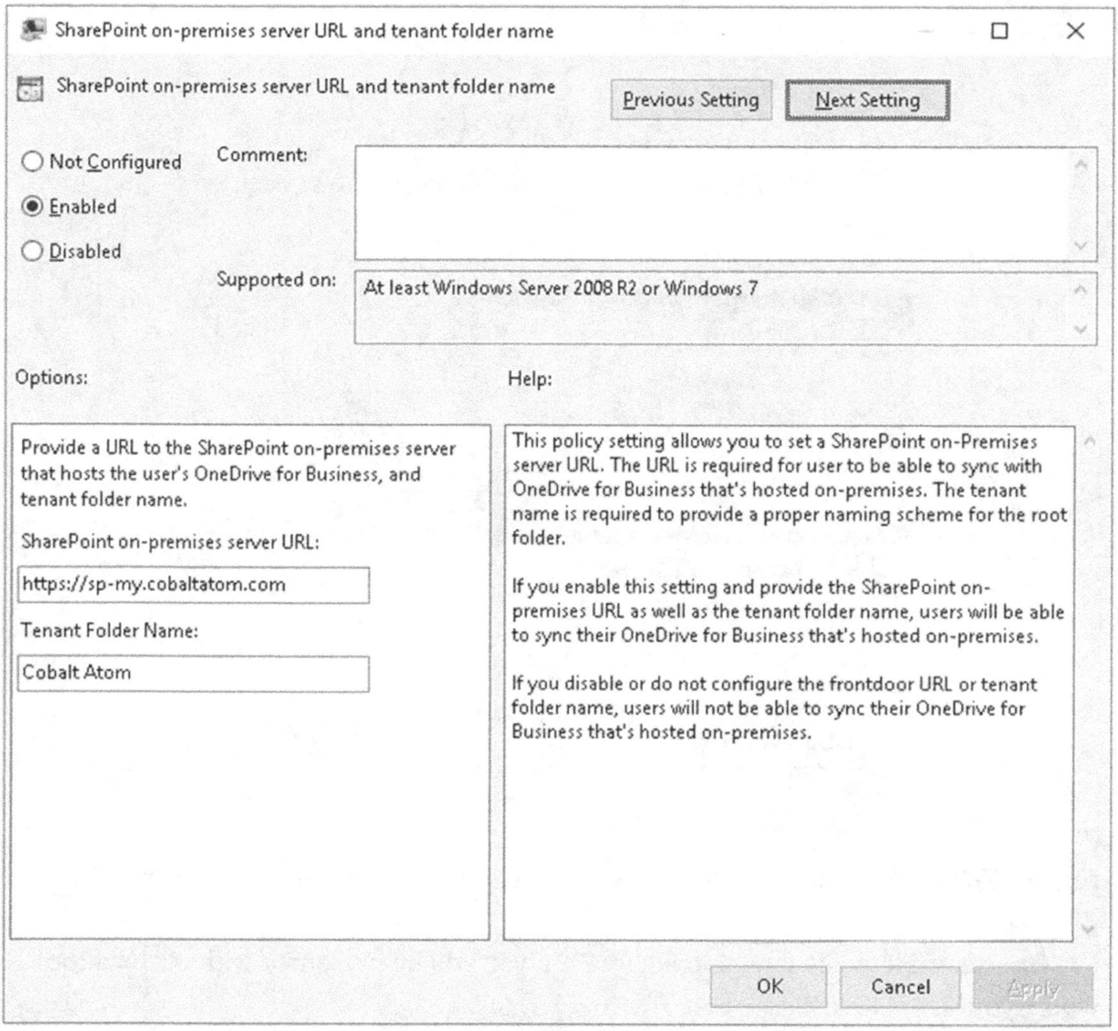

Figure 7-19. *Setting the OneDrive host location and providing a folder name*

When OneDrive starts, instead of entering an e-mail address, you will enter your Windows login information, as shown in Figure 7-20.

Figure 7-20. *Logging into OneDrive when used with SharePoint Server 2019*

Once completed as shown in Figure 7-21, you will be presented with the location where your OneDrive files reside.

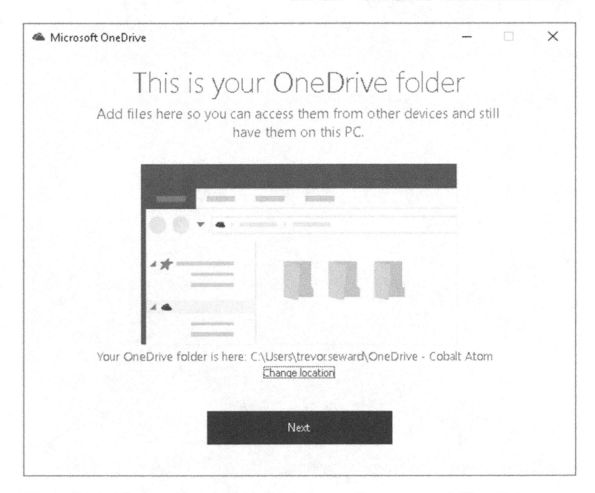

Figure 7-21. *The completion of the OneDrive configuration with SharePoint Server 2019*

As with SharePoint Online, it is also possible to synchronize document libraries using the OneDrive Next Gen Sync client with SharePoint Server 2019. Simply hit the "Sync" button in the document library command bar and OneDrive will automatically configure the synchronization process for you.

Next Steps

In this chapter, we covered the User Profile Service Application, including how to manage AD Import as well as working with Microsoft Identity Manager. In the next chapter, we will be looking at productivity Service Applications, such as Access Services, Managed Metadata, and others.

CHAPTER 8

Configuring Productivity Service Applications

In previous chapters, we have already learned how to configure some Service Applications such as Search and User Profile as well as the App Management and Subscription Service Applications.

SharePoint Server 2019 includes other Service Applications that add many other features to SharePoint 2019 which can increase your users' productivity.

In this chapter, we will learn to configure the Managed Metadata Service Application, Business Connectivity Services, Word Automation Services, PowerPoint Automation Service, Visio Graphics Service, Machine Translation Services, and lastly Access Services.

Managed Metadata Service Application

The Managed Metadata Service Application is one of the most popular Service Applications that are deployed with SharePoint. This Service Application makes it possible to use managed metadata and share content types across site collections and Web Applications. Managed Metadata is a central repository that stores your information taxonomy in a hierarchical view. There are two ways to create this Service Application, Central Administration or PowerShell.

To create the Managed Metadata Service Application using the Central Administration, from the Manage Service Applications Page, click New on the ribbon, then select Managed Metadata Service Application. A window will open similar to Figure 8-1, in which you have to enter the name of your Managed Metadata Service Application as well as the database server and Database name you want to deploy it on.

© Vlad Catrinescu and Trevor Seward 2019
V. Catrinescu and T. Seward, *Deploying SharePoint 2019*, https://doi.org/10.1007/978-1-4842-4526-2_8

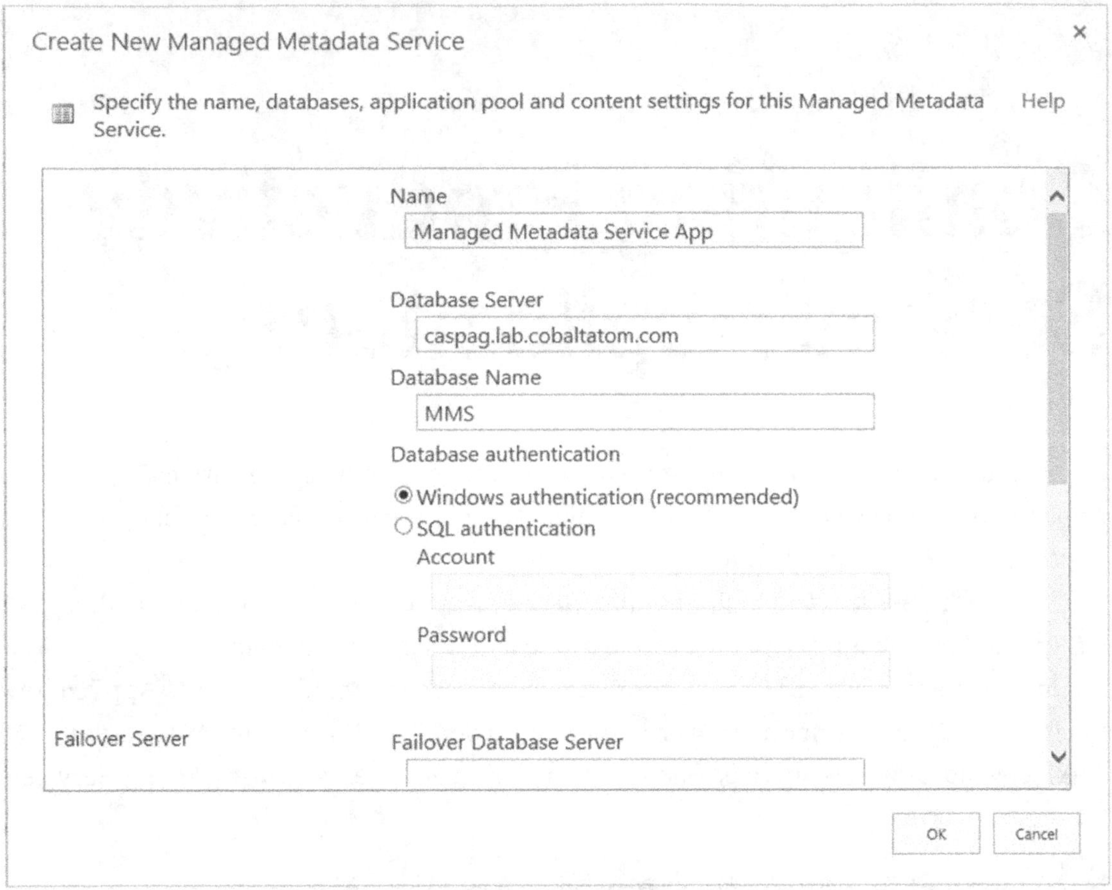

Figure 8-1. *Create New Managed Metadata Service Part 1*

Scrolling down to the end of the New Managed Metadata Service window seen in
Figure 8-2, we need to select which Application Pool to host this Service Application on.
Unless you have business requirements requiring this Service Application to be isolated
from others, we recommend putting it in the same Service Application Pool as the rest
of your Service Applications for a better resource management and server performance.
In our environment, this application pool is named SharePoint Web Services Default.
Lastly, you can optionally enter the Content Type hub URL. The Content Type Hub is
a central location where you can manage and publish your content types. Other Site
Collections can subscribe to this hub and pull down the published content types and
even receive updates when you update Content Types in the Content Type Hub. There
is no special Site Collection template for the Content Type hub, and it's usually a Team
Site template which is used for the Content Type Hub. The Content Type hub can also

be configured after the Managed Metadata Service Application has been created. The *Report Syndication import errors from Site Collections using this service application* will report import errors in the Content type publishing error log, accessible from the Site Collection Site Settings page.

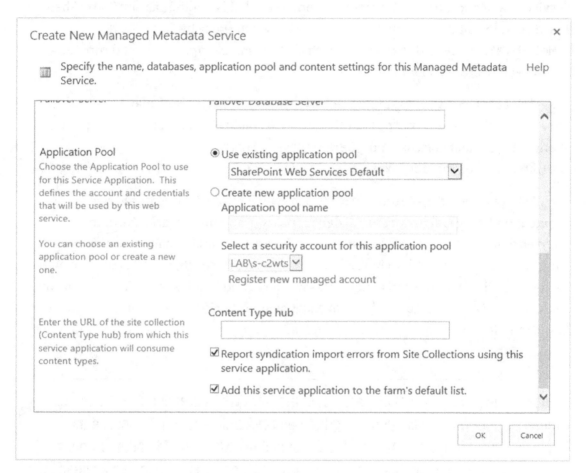

Figure 8-2. *Create a New Managed Metadata Service Application Part 2*

Lastly, you can click OK and the Service Application will be created. The Managed Metadata Service Application can also be created by PowerShell using the New-SPMetadataServiceApplication cmdlet. To create the Service Application with the same settings used when we created it using Central Administration, we would run the following cmdlet in an elevated SharePoint Management Shell:

```
$sa = New-SPMetadataServiceApplication -Name "Managed Metadata Service"
-DatabaseName "MMS" -ApplicationPool "SharePoint Web Services Default"
-SyndicationErrorReportEnabled
```

When creating the Service Application by the UI, SharePoint will also create the Service Application Proxy automatically; however, that is not the case by PowerShell. The next step will be to create the Service Application proxy by using the New-SPMetadataServiceApplicationProxy cmdlet. In our example, we would run the following PowerShell cmdlet:

```
New-SPMetadataServiceApplicationProxy -Name "Managed Metadata
Service Proxy" -ServiceApplication $sa -DefaultProxyGroup
-ContentTypePushdownEnabled -DefaultKeywordTaxonomy
-DefaultSiteCollectionTaxonomy
```

We have added the -DefaultProxyGroup switch to specify that this Service Application Proxy will be part of the default proxy group for the farm. Next, the -ContentTypePushdownEnabled switch specifies that existing instances of changed content types in subsites and libraries will be updated. The -DefaultKeywordTaxonomy switch specifies that Enterprise Keywords will be stored in this service application, and lastly the -DefaultSiteCollectionTaxonomy switch specifies that when users create Managed Metadata Columns in a Site Collection, the term will be saved in this Service Application.

Note   The preceding options are not in the form when creating the Managed Metadata Service Application using the Central Administration. To access those options from the Central Administration, select the Managed Metadata Service Proxy from the Manage Service Application Page, and click Properties as seen in Figure 8-3.

Figure 8-3. *Manage Metadata Service Proxy Properties*

For both options of creating the Service Application, if you are running a farm that uses the MinRole model, the Managed Metadata Service will be automatically started on all the servers running the Web Front End, or Application Roles. If you are running in a Custom mode farm, make sure to manually start the Managed Metadata Web Service on at least one server in your farm.

With the Managed Metadata Service Application created, you can now create Managed Terms that users can use throughout your SharePoint farm. To configure the Content Type Hub, you can create a Site Collection with a Team Site template that will be used for this purpose. We have created it using the following PowerShell cmdlet:

```
New-SPSite -Url https://sp.cobaltatom.com/sites/ContentTypeHub -Template
STS#0 -Name "Content Type Hub " -OwnerAlias "LAB\vlad.catrinescu"
```

Afterward, run the `Set-SPMetadataServiceApplication` to specify the Content Type Hub URL with the `-HubUri` parameter:

```
Set-SPMetadataServiceApplication -Identity "Managed Metadata Service"
-HubUri https://sp.cobaltatom.com/sites/ContentTypeHub
```

With the Managed Metadata Service Application configured, we will configure the Business Connectivity Service Application Next.

Business Data Connectivity Service

The Business Data Connectivity Service, often referred to as BCS, is a Service Application that allows SharePoint Administrators to display data from other data sources directly into SharePoint Server 2019. By using SharePoint Designer users can connect to an external data source such as a SQL Server database, and expose that information as an External List in SharePoint. Developers can also create External Content Types in Visual Studio that connect to more types of data sources, such as an OData Source. A Business Data Connectivity Service Application can be created either from the Central Administration, or through PowerShell.

To create the Business Data Connectivity Service Application by the Central Administration, from the Service Applications Page, click New on the ribbon, and Business Data Connectivity Service Application. A window will open similar to Figure 8-4, in which you have to enter the name of your Business Data Connectivity Service Application as well as the database server and Database name you want to deploy it on.

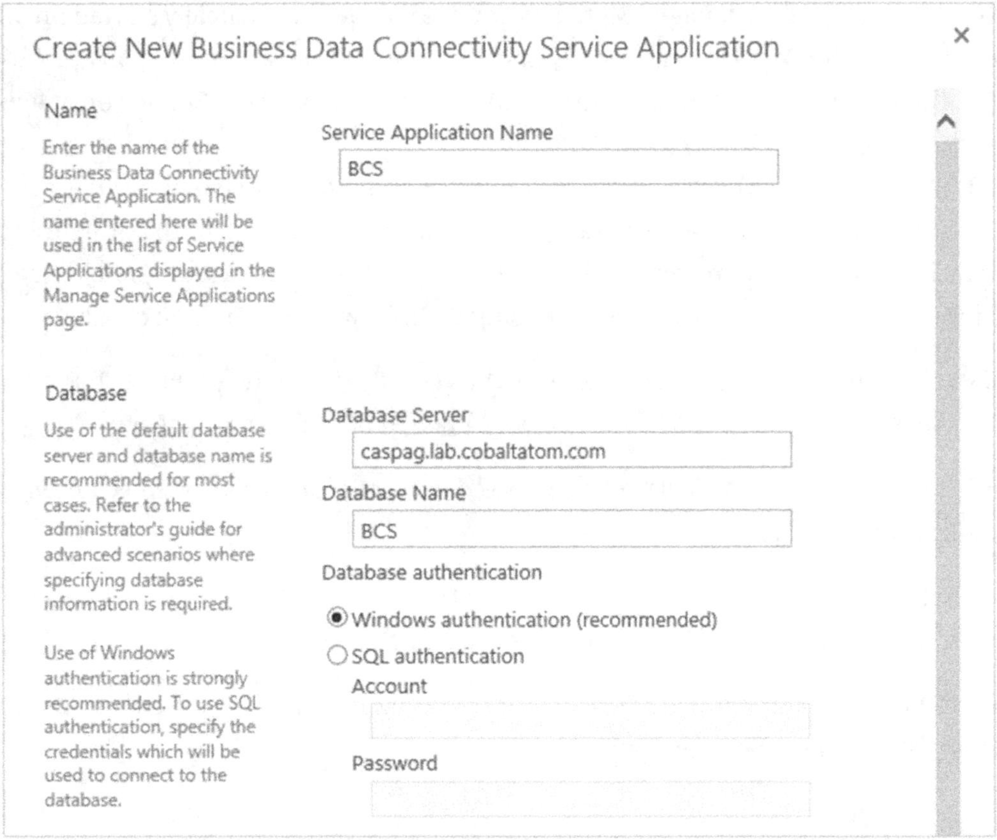

Figure 8-4.   *Create a New Business Data Connectivity Service Application*

Scrolling down to the end of the New Business Data Connectivity Service Application window seen in Figure 8-5, we need to select which Application Pool to host this Service Application on. Unless you have business requirements requiring this Service Application to be isolated from others, we recommend putting it in the same Service Application Pool as the rest of your Service Applications for a better resource management and server performance. Simply press on OK to create the Service Application.

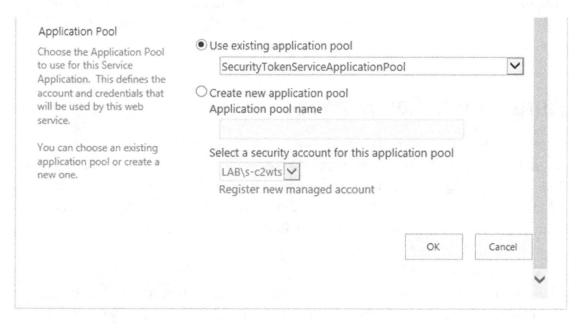

Figure 8-5. *Select an Application Pool for the Business Data Connectivity Service Application*

To create the Service Application by PowerShell, we need to use the New-SPBus inessDataConnectivityServiceApplication PowerShell cmdlet from an elevated SharePoint Management Shell. We need to specify the name of the Service Application, the Database name, and the Service Application Pool. To create a Service Application like the one we would have created by the User Interface, we would run the following PowerShell cmdlet:

```
New-SPBusinessDataCatalogServiceApplication -Name "BCS" -DatabaseName "BCS"
-ApplicationPool "SharePoint Web Services Default"
```

If you are running SharePoint 2019 in a MinRole farm, the Business Data Connectivity Service will be automatically started on all the servers running the Web Front End or the Application roles. If you are running a farm using the Custom MinRole, you will need to start the Business Data Connectivity Service on at least one server in your SharePoint Server farm.

Your users can now create External Content Types by using SharePoint Designer to connect to external systems. For an example of how a developer can create an External Content Type by using an OData Service, you can refer to Chapter 14, the section on Hybrid Business Connectivity Services. Next, we will configure Word Automation Services.

Word Automation Services

The Word Automation Services Service Application is a Service Application that automatically converts documents supported by the Word client application into formats such as PDF and XPS. In a simpler way to explain it, the Word Automation Services takes the "Save As" functionality of the Word client and replicates the functionality on SharePoint. A Word Automation Service Application can be created either through the User Interface, or through PowerShell.

To create a Word Automation Service Application, from the Central Administration on the Manage Service Applications page, click New on the Ribbon and select Word Automation Services. A window similar to Figure 8-6 will open in which you will have to enter the name and Application Pool and select whether to add this Service Application to the farm default Proxy list. Like previous Service Applications, unless you have business requirements for this Service Application to be isolated from the rest, we recommend you deploy it in the same Service Application Pool as the rest of your Service Applications.

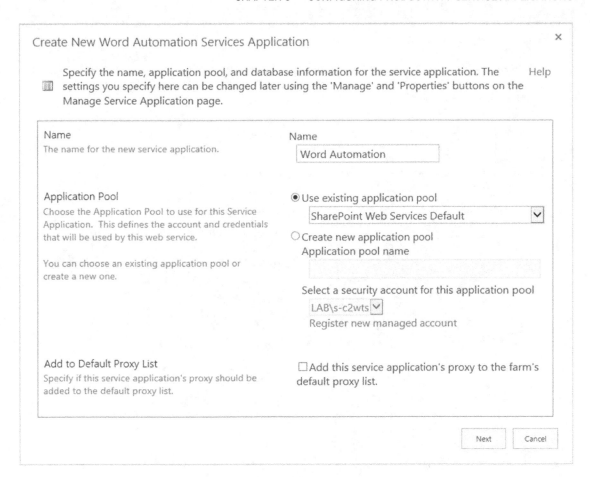

Figure 8-6. *Create a New Word Automation Services Application*

After clicking Next, SharePoint will ask you for the Database Server as well as the Database Name as seen in Figure 8-7.

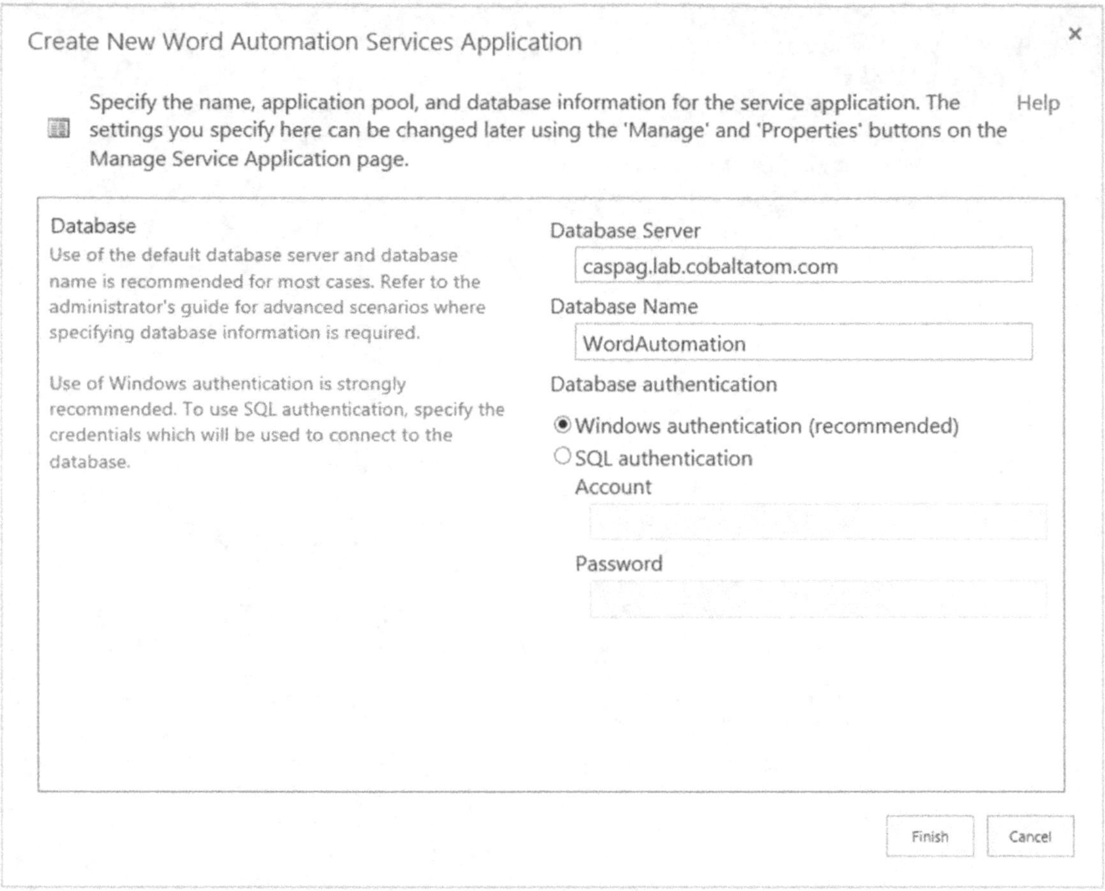

Figure 8-7. *Word Services Application Database Option*

After clicking OK, the Service Application will be created. To create a Word Automation Services Application with PowerShell, we will use the `New-SPWordConversionServiceApplication` cmdlet from an elevated SharePoint Management Shell. To create a Service Application like the one we would have created in the preceding screenshots, we would have used the following PowerShell cmdlet:

```
New-SPWordConversionServiceApplication -Name "Word Automation"
-DatabaseName "WordAutomation" -ApplicationPool "SharePoint Web Services
Default" -Default
```

The Word Automation Services can only be used via Code and not by the User Interface; therefore, it is a bit trickier to test, but we can test it by calling functions directly from PowerShell. To test Word Automation Services, we have uploaded a document called "Document1.docx", which we want to convert to PDF with the name "Document1-Final.pdf". We will first load the assembly required to call Word Automation Services functions.

```
Add-Type -Path 'C:\Windows\Microsoft.NET\assembly\GAC_MSIL\Microsoft.Office.
Word.Server\v4.0_16.0.0.0__71e9bce111e9429c\Microsoft.Office.Word.Server.dll'
```

We then create new Object of type `ConversionJobSettings` specifying the Output format is PDF.

```
$jobSettings = New-Object Microsoft.Office.Word.Server.Conversions.
ConversionJobSettings
$jobSettings.OutputFormat = "PDF"
```

We then create a new object of type `ConversionJob` and give it our Service Application Proxy Name, in our case Word Automation, as well as the `$jobsettings` object. We then set the `$Job.Usertoken` to the SharePoint SPWeb where the document is stored.

```
$job = New-Object Microsoft.Office.Word.Server.Conversions.ConversionJob
("Word Automation", $jobSettings)
$job.UserToken = (Get-SPWeb https://sp.cobaltatom.com).CurrentUser.UserToken
```

Lastly, we add the properties for the file that we want converted. We give it the URL to the Word Document, as well as the URL to the future PDF document, which does not exist yet. We then Start the Job.

```
$job.AddFile("https://sp.cobaltatom.com/Shared%20Documents/Document1.docx",
"https://sp.cobaltatom.com/Shared%20Documents/Document1-Final.pdf")
$job.Start()
```

The Word Automation Services job runs asynchronous, meaning that we won't know when it will run directly from PowerShell; however, we can force the job to run right away by starting the Word Automation timer job.

```
Start-SPTimerJob  "Word Automation"
```

If we put it all together, the script looks like this:

```
Add-Type -Path 'C:\Windows\Microsoft.NET\assembly\GAC_MSIL\Microsoft.
Office.Word.Server\v4.0_16.0.0.0__71e9bce111e9429c\Microsoft.Office.Word.
Server.dll'
```

```
$jobSettings = New-Object Microsoft.Office.Word.Server.Conversions.
ConversionJobSettings
$jobSettings.OutputFormat = "PDF"
$job = New-Object Microsoft.Office.Word.Server.Conversions.
ConversionJob("Word Automation", $jobSettings)
$job.UserToken = (Get-SPWeb https://sp.cobaltatom.com).CurrentUser.UserToken
$job.AddFile("https://sp.cobaltatom.com/Shared%20Documents/Document1.docx",
"https://sp.cobaltatom.com/Shared%20Documents/Document1-Final.pdf")
$job.Start()
Start-SPTimerJob  "Word Automation"
```

To see the status of the job, run the following PowerShell cmdlet where "Word Automation" is the name of your Word Automation Services Application:

```
new-object Microsoft.Office.Word.Server.Conversions.
ConversionJobStatus("Word Automation", $job.JobId,$null);
```

Initially, it will show as InProgress since we force started the Timer Job as seen in Figure 8-8.

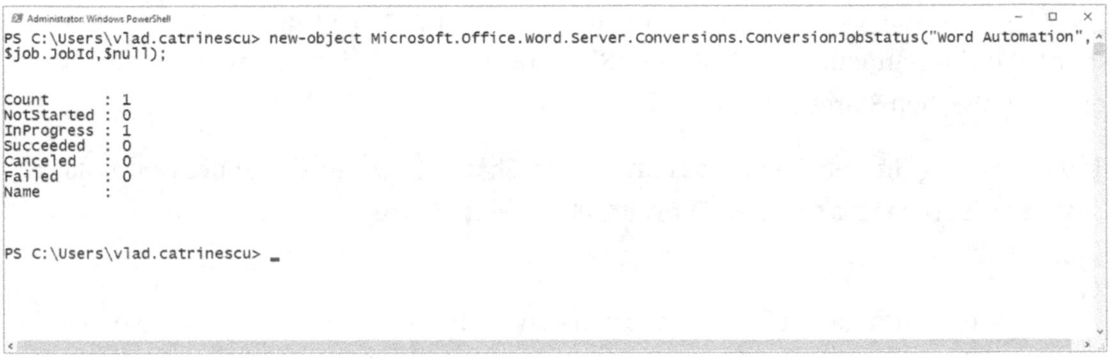

Figure 8-8. *Word Automation Job in Progress*

Once the job is completed, it will either show as Succeeded or Failed. If everything was configured correctly, it should show as Succeeded as seen in Figure 8-9, and you should see your PDF document in your document library.

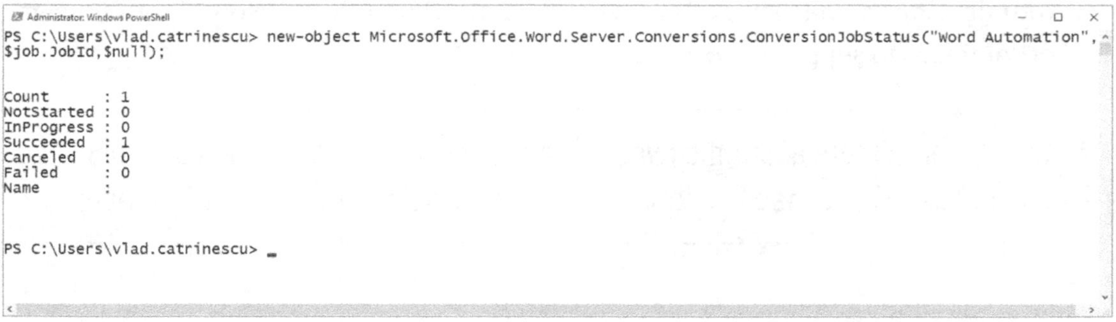

```
Administrator: Windows PowerShell                                                    –  □  ×
PS C:\Users\vlad.catrinescu> new-object Microsoft.Office.Word.Server.Conversions.ConversionJobStatus("Word Automation",
$job.JobId,$null);


Count        : 1
NotStarted   : 0
InProgress   : 0
Succeeded    : 1
Canceled     : 0
Failed       : 0
Name         :



PS C:\Users\vlad.catrinescu> _
```

Figure 8-9. *Word Automation Job Succeeded*

In a MinRole farm configuration, the Word Automation Service will automatically be started on all the servers that have the Application Role. If you are running a farm using Custom Roles, you will need to start it manually on at least one server in the farm.

PowerPoint Automation Service

The PowerPoint Automation Service is very similar to the Word Automation Service that we just talked about, but it's for PowerPoint files instead of Word files. The PowerPoint Automation Service allows developers to create solutions that will convert PowerPoint Files to formats such as PDF, JPG, PNG, or XPS.

Unlike the Word Automation Service, the PowerPoint Automation Service can only be created via PowerShell and not by the Central Administration. We will need to use the New-SPPowerPointConversionServiceApplication cmdlet from an elevated SharePoint Management Shell. We need to give it a name, as well as the Service Application Pool in which it should be deployed.

```
$sa = New-SPPowerPointConversionServiceApplication -Name "PowerPoint
Conversion Service" -ApplicationPool "SharePoint Web Services Default"
```

After the Service Application is created, we will create a PowerPoint Conversion Service Application Proxy by using the New-SPPowerPointConversionServiceApplicationProxy cmdlet and adding it to the default group with the -AddToDefaultGroup switch.

```
New-SPPowerPointConversionServiceApplicationProxy "PowerPoint Conversion
Service Proxy" -ServiceApplication $sa –AddToDefaultGroup
```

Your developers will then be able to use the PowerPoint Conversion APIs to convert PowerPoint files to supported formats.

Note   To learn more about the available APIs, check out the resources on MSDN: https://msdn.microsoft.com/en-us/library/office/FP179894.aspx/.

Visio Graphics Service

The Visio Graphics Service Application allows user to visualize Visio diagrams directly in the browser, without needing the client application installed. Furthermore, users could consume those Visio files directly on their mobile devices.

Note   Only PNG based rendering is available in SharePoint Server 2019 as Silverlight rendering was completely removed in SharePoint 2019.

The Visio Graphics Service Application can either be created from the Central Administration, or from PowerShell. To create a Visio Graphics Service Application from the Central Administration, navigate to the Service Application Management page, click New in the Ribbon and select Visio Graphics Service Application. A window similar to Figure 8-10 will open, in which you will need to input the Service Application name, choose to create a new Application Pool or use an existing one, and finally create a Visio Graphics Service Application Proxy. We recommend using the same Service Application pool as the rest of the Service Application, unless you have a business requirement to isolate this Service Application from the rest.

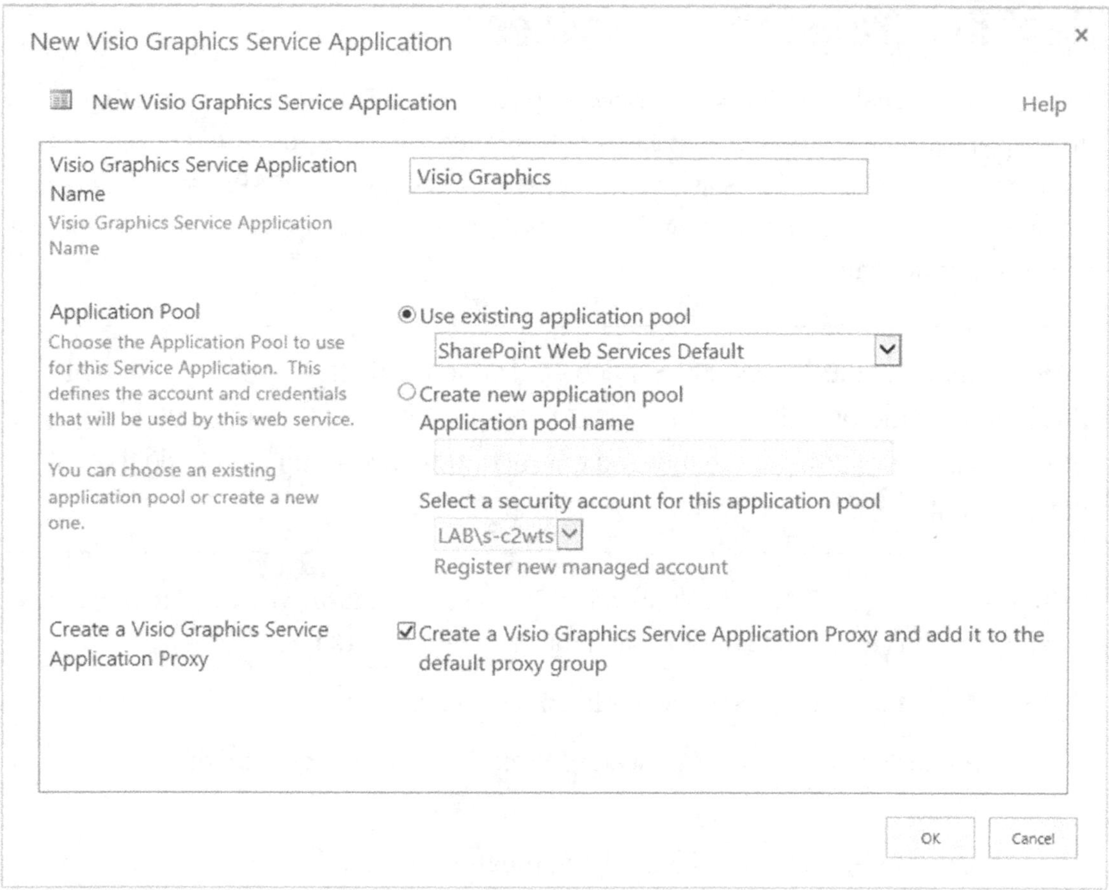

New Visio Graphics Service Application   ✕

🖾   New Visio Graphics Service Application   Help

Visio Graphics Service Application Name	Visio Graphics
Visio Graphics Service Application Name	

Application Pool

Choose the Application Pool to use for this Service Application. This defines the account and credentials that will be used by this web service.

You can choose an existing application pool or create a new one.

◉ Use existing application pool

SharePoint Web Services Default ▾

○ Create new application pool
Application pool name

Select a security account for this application pool
LAB\s-c2wts ▾
Register new managed account

Create a Visio Graphics Service Application Proxy

☑ Create a Visio Graphics Service Application Proxy and add it to the default proxy group

OK   Cancel

Figure 8-10. *New Visio Graphics Service Application*

The Visio Graphics Service Application can also be created by using the New-SPVisioServiceApplication cmdlet from an elevated SharePoint Management Shell. To create a Visio Graphics Service, we need to specify the Service Application name, Application Pool, and the switch to add it to the default Proxy group.

```
$sa = New-SPVisioServiceApplication -Name "Visio Graphics" -ApplicationPool
"SharePoint Web Services Default" -AddToDefaultGroup
```

To test the Service Application, simply upload a Visio Diagram into SharePoint, and when clicking the document, it will open in the browser, instead of downloading it to the computer.

Machine Translation Services

The Machine Translation Services Service Application is a Service Application that allows users and developers to translate not only sites, but their content as well, to other languages. The Machine Translation Services is interacted through APIs, and the users do not have a "Translate Document" button, unless of course, their developers created a custom action for them.

Note   The Machine Translation Service Application is deprecated in SharePoint 2019. You should only use it for backward compatibility if you were using it in past versions of SharePoint, but we do not recommend starting new projects that depend on it!

Before creating the Machine Translation Service Application, you need to make sure the following Service Applications exist in the SharePoint 2019 farm:

- App Management Service Application (seen in Chapter 5)

- A User Profile Service Application Proxy in the Default Group of the Farm

- The SharePoint Farm has access to the Internet

The Machine Translation Service Application can be created either from the Central Administration or by PowerShell. To create the machine Translation Service Application via the Central Administration, navigate to the Manage Service Application page, from the Ribbon click New, and select Machine Translation Service.

A Window will open similar to Figure 8-11, in which you will have to enter the Name of the Service Application as well as selecting whether to create a new Service Application pool or not. We recommend using the same Application pool as for the previous service applications, unless there is a business requirement to isolate this Servicer Application.

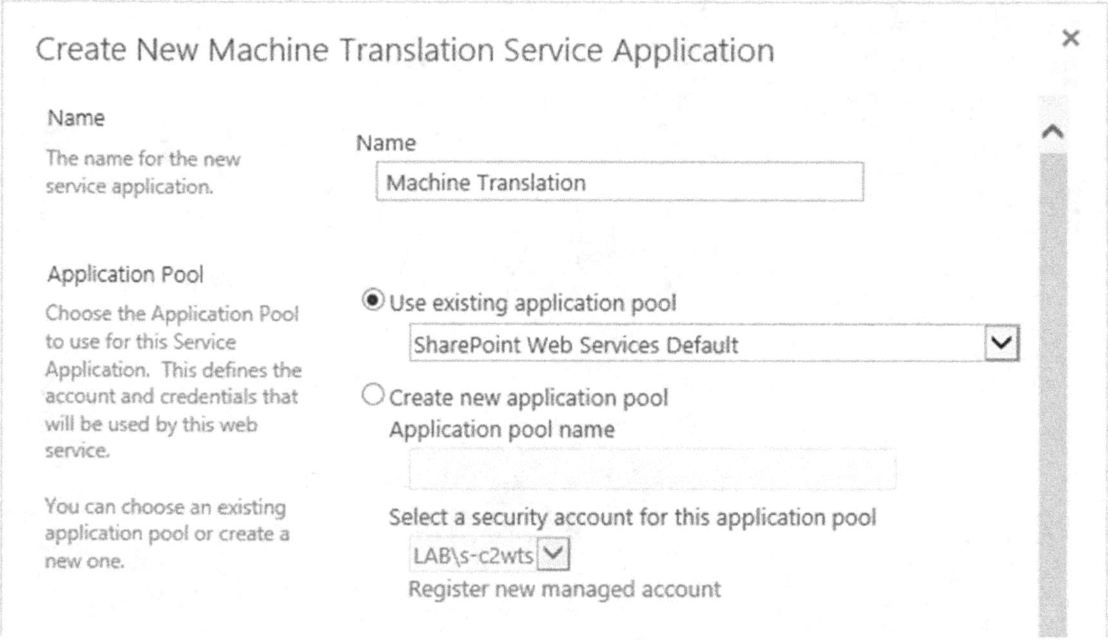

Figure 8-11. *New Machine Translation Service Application Name and Application Pool*

Finally, we must enter the Database Server and name for our Machine Translation database as seen in Figure 8-12.

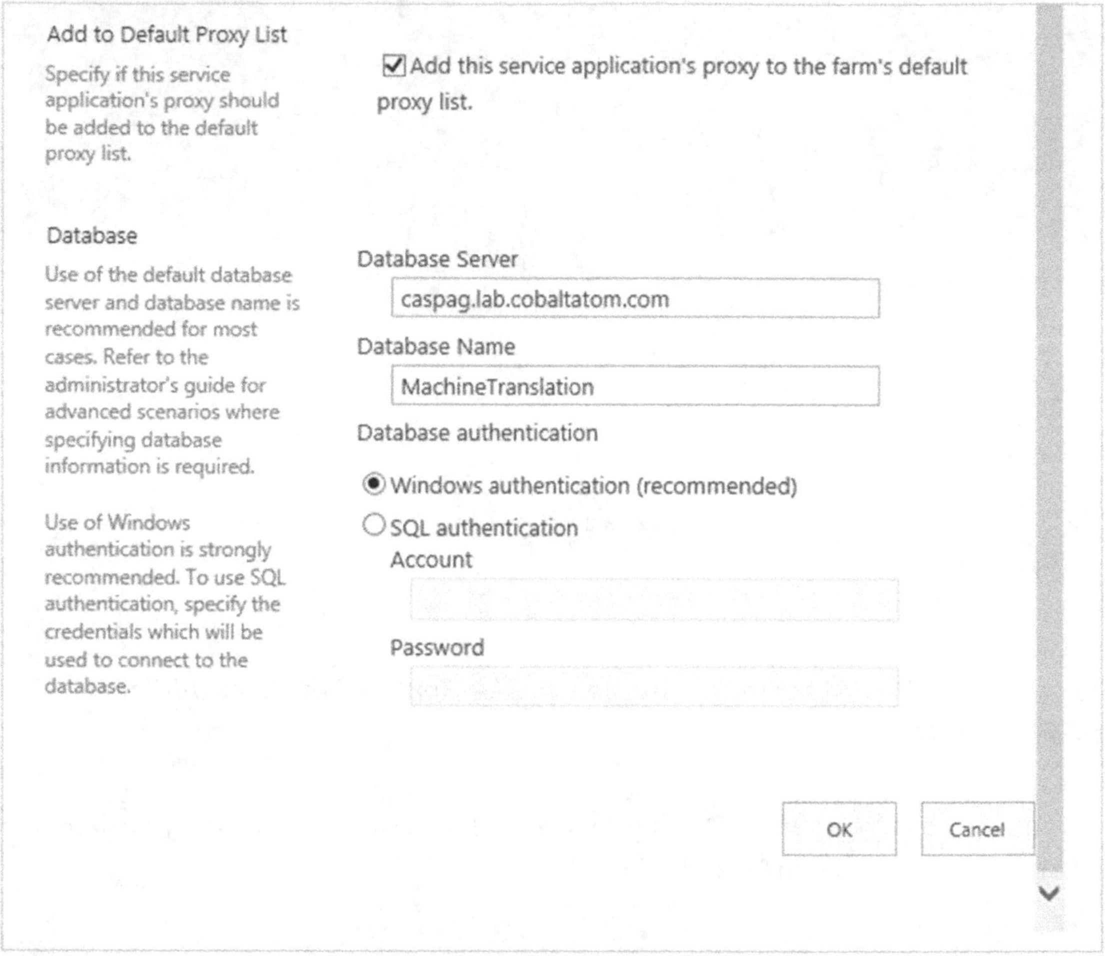

Add to Default Proxy List

Specify if this service application's proxy should be added to the default proxy list.

☑ Add this service application's proxy to the farm's default proxy list.

Database

Use of the default database server and database name is recommended for most cases. Refer to the administrator's guide for advanced scenarios where specifying database information is required.

Use of Windows authentication is strongly recommended. To use SQL authentication, specify the credentials which will be used to connect to the database.

Database Server

caspag.lab.cobaltatom.com

Database Name

MachineTranslation

Database authentication

◉ Windows authentication (recommended)

○ SQL authentication

Account

Password

OK   Cancel

Figure 8-12. *New Machine Translation Service Application*

To create the Machine Translation Service Application via PowerShell, you must use the New-SPTranslationServiceApplication cmdlet from an elevated SharePoint Management Shell. To create the Machine Translation Service Application with the same settings as in the preceding screenshot, we would run the following PowerShell command:

```
New-SPTranslationServiceApplication -Name "Machine Translation"
-DatabaseName "MachineTranslation" -ApplicationPool "SharePoint Web
Services Default" -Default
```

With the Machine Translation Service Application created, your developers can now create code that uses the Machine Translation Service.

Tip   To learn more about the Machine Translation Services APIs, visit the page on MSDN: `https://docs.microsoft.com/en-us/sharepoint/dev/general-development/machine-translation-services-in-sharepoint`.

Access Services 2010

SharePoint Server 2019 includes two different Access service applications. The first one is called "Access Services 2010", while the second one is "Access Services 2013".

Note   Both Access Services 2010 and 2013 are considered deprecated in SharePoint Server 2019 and are only included for compatibility purposes. You should only use it for backward compatibility if you were using it in past versions of SharePoint, but we do not recommend starting new projects that depend on it!

Access Services 2010 is a Service Application that allows users to modify and publish in SharePoint 2019, an access Web Database that was previously created in SharePoint 2010. Users can view the published web database without having Access installed locally; however, they need the Office application in order to modify the database structure.

To create the Access Services 2010 Service Application from Central Administration, navigate to the Manage Service Applications page, click New in the Ribbon, and select Access Services 2010. As seen in Figure 8-13, you will have to enter a name for the Service Application, select the Service Application Pool we created earlier for those Service Applications, and select whether this Service Application will be in the default proxy list.

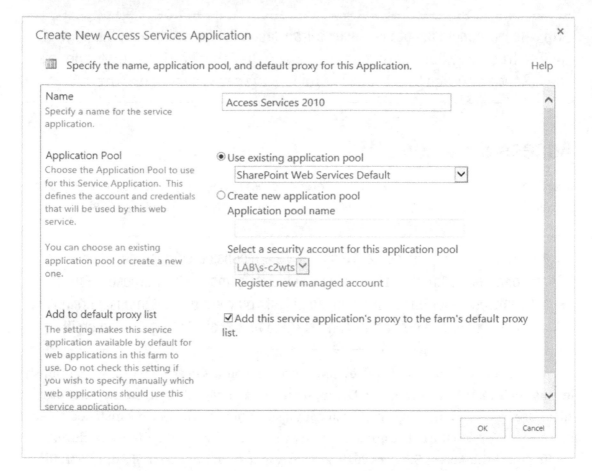

Figure 8-13. *New Access Services 2010 Service Application*

This can also be done by PowerShell with the New-SPAccessServiceApplication cmdlet from an elevated SharePoint Management Shell. In order to create a Service Application with the same parameters as before, we would run the following cmdlet:

```
New-SPAccessServiceApplication -Name "Access Services 2010"
-ApplicationPool "SharePoint Web Services Default" –Default
```

With the Access 2010 Service Application created, let's look at the Access App Services 2013 version.

Access Services 2013

Access Apps for SharePoint are a type of database that you build in Access, and use and share with others as an app in SharePoint directly in the browser. Access Services 2013 is a more advanced Service Application that allows you to create Access apps and track data such as contacts, orders, and so on. Access Services 2013 is a bit more complicated to configure compared to the other Service Applications and will require installing extra prerequisites.

Before starting to configure Access Services, the following Service Applications need to be configured:

- Secure Store Service

- App Management Service

- Microsoft SharePoint Foundation Subscription Settings Service

- Access Services 2010

Your App environment must also be configured as we covered in Chapter 5.

First, since the account running Access Services 2013 requires more SQL permissions than the other Service Applications, we will create a new service account dedicated for this service application. In our environment, the account we created has the username LAB\s-access. Since this account will be used to run an Application Pool, we will register it as a managed account by running the following PowerShell cmdlet:

```
$cred = Get-Credential -UserName "LAB\s-access" -Message "Managed Account"
New-SPManagedAccount -Credential $cred
```

We will then create a new Service Application Pool called "SharePoint Access App Services" in which we will run the Service Application.

```
New-SPServiceApplicationPool -Name "SharePoint Access App Services"
-Account (Get-SPManagedAccount "LAB\s-access")
```

After the Service Application is created, we need to modify a setting in IIS that will be unique to this Service Application. Navigate to the IIS Application Pools, and from Advanced Settings, change "Load User Profile" to True, as seen in Figure 8-14.

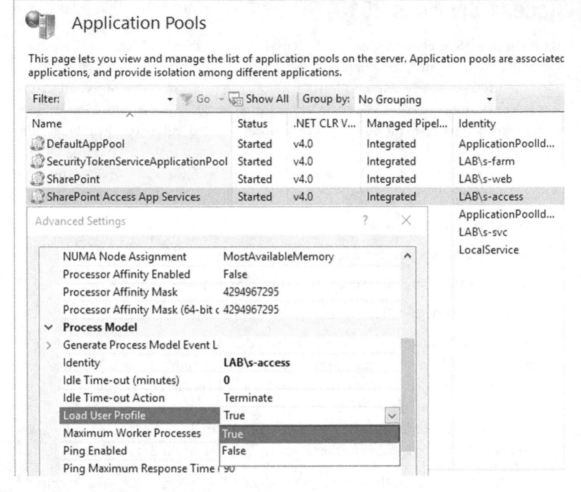

Figure 8-14. *Load User Profile Setting in IIS*

Note   Remember to make this change on all the servers where the App Pool is present.

Next we need to make sure our new Service Account has rights to the other content databases, since that is where the Access Apps will be created. This is done by the following PowerShell cmdlets:

```
$w = Get-SPWebApplication https://sp.cobaltatom.com
$w.GrantAccessToProcessIdentity("LAB\s-access")
$w.Update()
```

Remember to repeat this step for every Web Application where you wish to host Access Apps. Lastly, the service account must have Read/Write permission to the config cache folder located at `C:\ProgramData\Microsoft\SharePoint\Config` on every server.

After those permissions are done, we need to install prerequisites from the SQL Server Feature Pack on our SharePoint servers. This is only required on the servers on which you will run the Access Services SharePoint service; however, we recommend installing those prerequisites on all the servers in your farm. This will make your farm more flexible if you decide to change roles in the future. In a MinRole configuration, Access Services are automatically started on all the servers running the Web Front End role. The Prerequisites are

- Microsoft SQL Server Local DB (SQLLocalDB.msi)

- Microsoft SQL Server Data-Tier Application Framework (Dacframework.msi)

- Microsoft SQL Server Native Client (sqlncli.msi)

- Microsoft SQL Server Transact-SQL ScriptDom (SQLDOM.MSI)

- Microsoft System CLR Types for Microsoft SQL Server (SQLSysClrTypes.msi)

After the prerequisites are installed, we need to configure SQL Server for Access Services. The SQL Server you use needs to have the following Instance features:

- Database Engine Services

- Full-Text and Semantic Extractions for Search

- Client Tools Connectivity

If those features weren't installed when originally creating the Instance, you can add them afterward from the SQL Server Installation Center.

Next, we need to create a new login in your SQL Server from SQL Server Management Studio as seen in Figure 8-15.

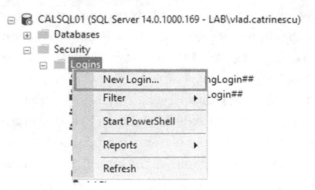

Figure 8-15. *New Login in SQL Server*

On the General Tab, write the username of the Access service account, and from the *Server Roles* tab, select *dbcreator* as well as *securityadmin* as seen in Figure 8-16.

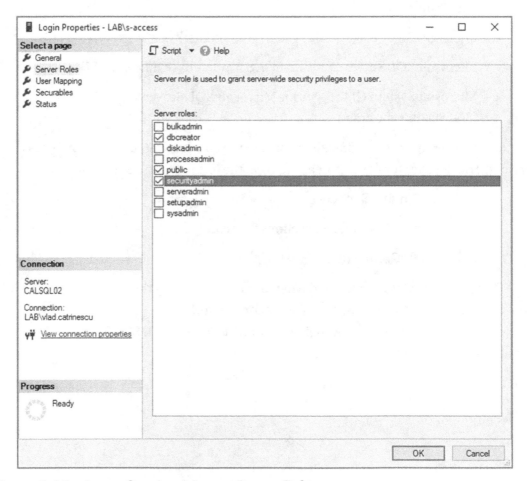

Figure 8-16. *Access Service Account Server Roles*

Since this account will also have to run some stored procedures on the Configuration database, in the User Mapping tab, give this account the *SPDataAccess* permission as seen in Figure 8-17.

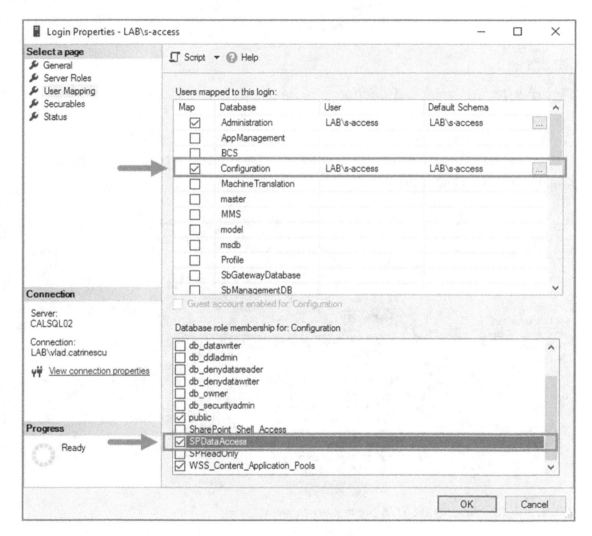

Figure 8-17. *SPDataAccess on the Config Database*

We then need to go to the SQL Server Properties and, from the Security Tab, enable mixed authentication mode (SQL Server and Windows) as seen in Figure 8-18.

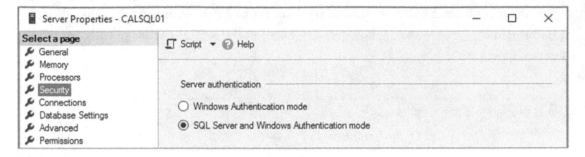

Figure 8-18. *Mixed SQL Authentication mode*

Afterward, from the Advanced Tab, we need to change the "Enable Contained Databases" and "Allow Triggers to Fire Others" to True and set the Default Language to English as seen in Figure 8-19.

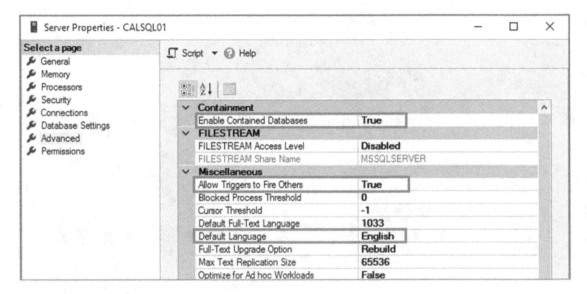

Figure 8-19. *Advanced SQL Server properties*

Lastly, we need to configure SQL Server protocols. Both the TCP/IP and Named Pipes protocols must be enabled. This can be done from the SQL Server Configuration Manager as seen in Figure 8-20.

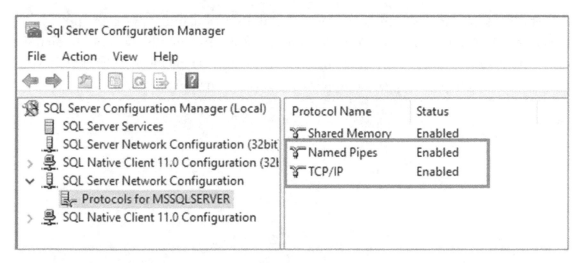

Figure 8-20. *Protocols for SQL Server*

For those changes to take effect, you need to restart the SQL Server Engine Service. After SQL Server is configured, you must enable the following ports through the firewall:

- TCP 1433

- TCP 1434

- UDP 1434

With all the prerequisites configured, it's time to create the Access Service Application.

Tip   Remember to make the configuration changes on all your SQL Servers part of the farm.

To create the Access Services 2013 Service Application we would use the New-SPAccessServicesApplication cmdlet, notice the extra **s** in Services compared to the PowerShell cmdlet for the Access 2010 Service Application. To create a Service Application with the name Access App Services in our Service Application pool dedicated for Access Services, we would run the following cmdlet:

```
New-SPAccessServicesApplication -Name "Access App Services"
-ApplicationPool "SharePoint Access App Services" -Default
```

The last step is to navigate to the Central Administration, into the Access App Services 2013 Service Application. At the bottom of the configuration window, open the New Application Database Server configuration group, and type the SQL Server that you want to use for the Access Services App Databases as seen in Figure 8-21.

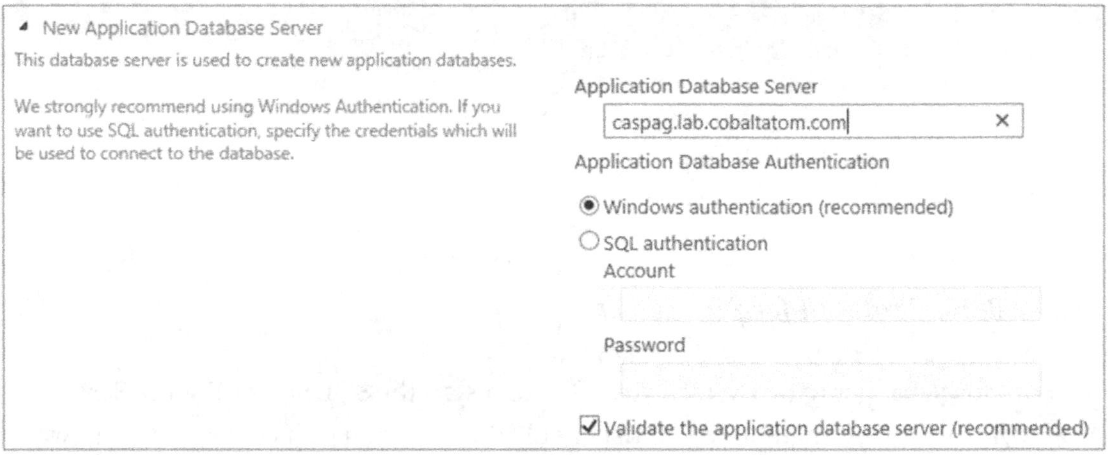

Figure 8-21. New Application Database Server

After the Application Database Server is configured, we can test the Service Application from a client that has Access 2013 or higher installed. From Access, create a new Custom Web App as seen in Figure 8-22. When prompted, enter the URL of a Site Collection to which you have contribute access.

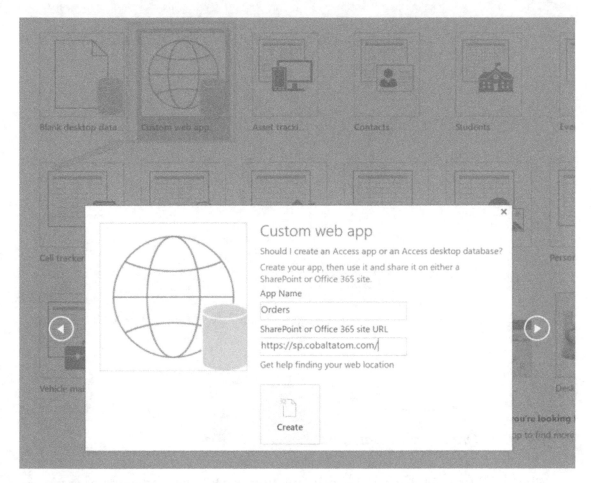

Figure 8-22. *New Custom Web App*

In our example seen in Figure 8-23, we have created an Access App by using the default Orders template.

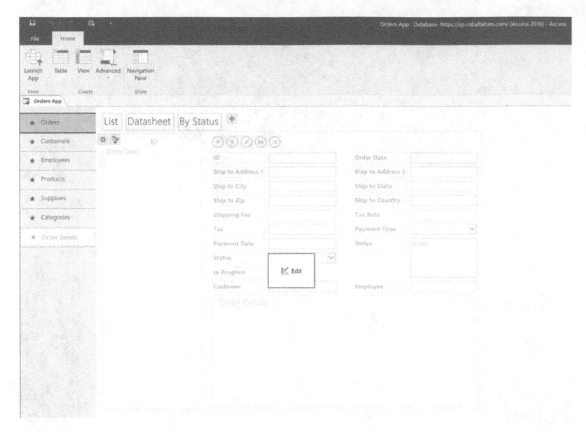

Figure 8-23. *Orders Access Database*

When ready to publish, click "Launch App" from the Ribbon, and the App should open in SharePoint 2019 as seen in Figure 8-24.

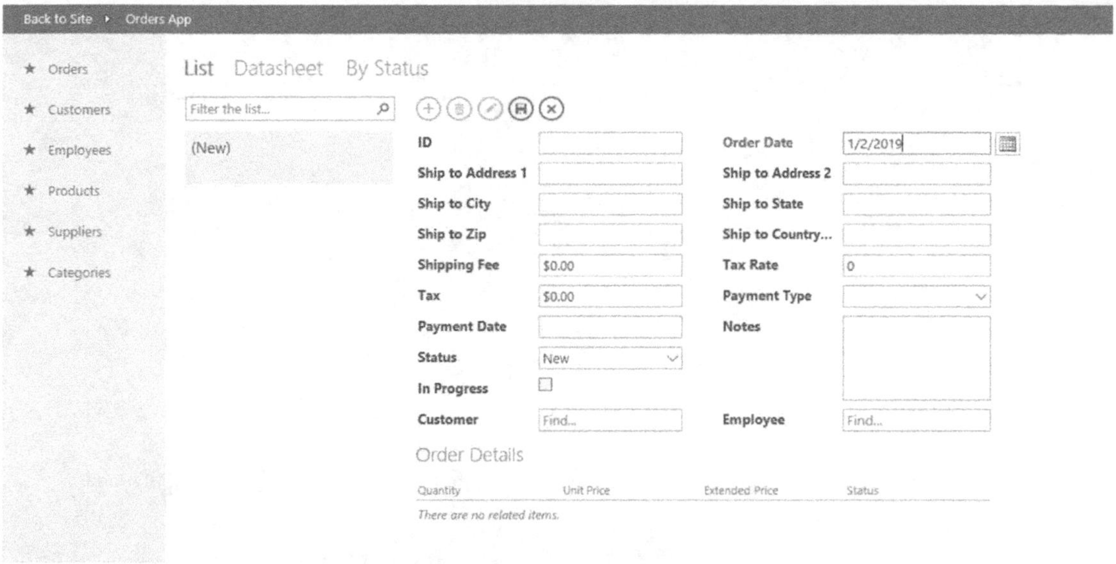

Figure 8-24. *Access App in SharePoint*

Access Services has successfully been configured. As a SharePoint Admin, it's important to understand that each App creates its own database in SQL Server; therefore, it's important to make sure new App databases are added to your SQL Maintenance plan and to your SQL AlwaysOn availability group or mirroring.

Next Steps

In this chapter, we learned how to deploy the productivity Service Applications in SharePoint Server 2019 both by the Central Administration and by using PowerShell. In the next chapter, we will look at how to install and configure Office Online Server to allow our users to view, edit, and create Office documents directly in the browser.

CHAPTER 9

Configuring Office Online Server for SharePoint 2019

Office Online Server, previously named Office Web Apps, is a server that allows users to view and edit Office documents such as Word, Excel, PowerPoint, and OneNote directly from the browser. Office Online Server also allows users to view PDF documents in the browser and convert Office documents to PDF.

It's important not to get confused in Microsoft's choice of name for the product. Even if it's called Office *Online* Server, the product is fully On-Premises and does not require a connection to Office 365 or any Office 365 licenses.

Furthermore, Office Online Server isn't only for SharePoint! Office Online Server can add features to Exchange Server 2016 / 2019 as well as Skype for Business Server 2015 / 2019. We will not cover those features, or how to enable them in this book; however, it is important to know that the investments you make in Office Online Server aren't only for SharePoint, but for Exchange and Skype for Business as well.

There are multiple reasons to deploy Office Online Server other than the ability to view and edit Office documents from the browser. With Excel Services gone since SharePoint Server 2016, you need Office Online Server in order to view Excel Dashboards. Furthermore, Office Online Server enables additional features such as Durable Links. Office Online Server is an evergreen product, so we do not have an Office Online Server 2016 and Office Online Server 2019; it's simply Office Online Server with an update becoming available every three to four months. The minimum version of Office Online Server for SharePoint Server 2019 is November 2018; however, it's always recommended to install the latest version available.

© Vlad Catrinescu and Trevor Seward 2019
V. Catrinescu and T. Seward, *Deploying SharePoint 2019*, https://doi.org/10.1007/978-1-4842-4526-2_9

Office Online Server Architecture Overview

Before we get start configuring Office Online Server, it's important to understand the Office Online Server architecture in order to understand what we will install and configure in this chapter.

Office Online Server is in a way similar to SharePoint Server as we need one or more Office Online Servers to create an Office Online Server Farm. This farm can serve one, or multiple SharePoint, Exchange and Skype for Business deployments. In Figure 9-1, we can see an Office Online Server farm consisting of three servers that serve two different SharePoint Farms as well as an Exchange deployment and a Skype for Business deployment.

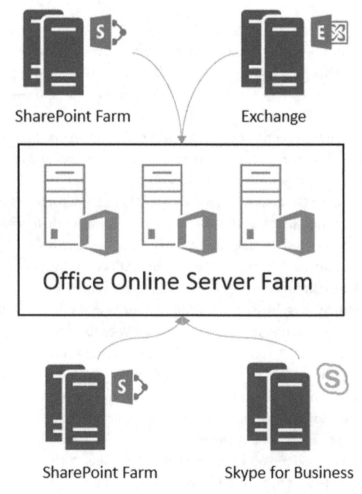

Figure 9-1. *High-Level Overview of Office Online Server Architecture*

An Office Online Server Farm can be made accessible through two different URLs. We call the first one the Internal URL, and the second one the External URL as seen in Figure 9-2. The URLs can be either HTTP or HTTPS, and at least one of the URLs is mandatory. Office Online Server allows you to configure either the Internal URL, the External URL, or both. When configuring the Internal and External URLs, you have the choice to configure them either on HTTP or HTTPS. Since our SharePoint Server will use HTTPS, we will configure Office Online Server to use HTTPS as well. Securing your Office Online Server with SSL is extremely important, since the OAuth token is passed in a packet on the request, and you could be subject to a man-in-the-middle attack if that token is not secured. You can set up Office Online Server on HTTPS even if your SharePoint sites are running on HTTP.

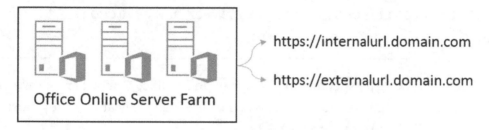

Figure 9-2. *Office Online Server Internal and External URL*

Office Online Server uses only three ports to communicate between servers and with SharePoint, Exchange, and Skype for Business. Those ports are described in Table 9-1.

Table 9-1. *Office Online Server Ports*

Port	Function
80	HTTP traffic
443	HTTPS traffic
809	Traffic between Office Online Servers

To enhance security, you can block the ports that you do not use. For example, if your Office Online Server farm will be only made of one server and be accessible via SSL, you only need port 443.

The minimum hardware requirements for Office Online Server are the same as for SharePoint Server 2019 and outlined in Table 9-2.

Table 9-2   *Office Online Server Minimum Requirements*

CPU	RAM	Disk
64-bit, 4 cores	12 GB	80 GB for system drive

Office Online Server supports the 64-bit versions of Windows Server 2012 R2 and Windows Server 2016. The *Server with Desktop Experience* feature needs to be enabled as Office Online Server cannot run on Windows Server core.

Note   At the time of writing this book, Office Online Server running on Windows Server 2019 was not supported. Always check the latest supported operating systems at `https://docs.microsoft.com/en-us/officeonlineserver/plan-office-online-server`.

From a networking perspective, all the servers in an Office Online Server Farm must be in the same forest, and in order to use Business Intelligence Features, they must be in the same forest as the users who will use them.

Office Online Server must be installed on its own dedicated server. It can run on both Physical as well as in a Virtual Machine running on Hyper-V or VMware. Office Online Server cannot be installed on the same machine as Exchange, SharePoint, and Skype for Business, SQL, Domain Controller, or any server that has Office installed.

Note   At the time of writing this book, the Office Online Server license prohibits enterprises installing Office Online Server on physical hardware they do not own, therefore making it impossible to use Office Online Server in Azure, AWS, or any other provider. Check with your Microsoft Licensing Expert before deploying Office Online Server on any machines you do not own.

If you plan to have more than one Office Online Server in your farm, you will need a load balancer that supports the following features:

- SSL Offloading or SSL Bridging

- Enabling client affinity or front-end affinity

- Layer 7 routing

Furthermore, if you plan to open Office Online Server to the Internet for SharePoint or Exchange, you will also need a reverse proxy in order to securely make it available to external users.

If you plan to use SSL, the certificate must come from a trusted Certificate Authority and include the fully qualified domain name (FQDN) of your Office Online Server farm URL in the SAN (Subject Alternative Name). Furthermore, the FQDN of every server in your Office Online Server farm must be in the SAN of the certificate. The certificate we used in our book can be seen in Figure 9-3 and has office.cobaltatom.com as the Issued To, which is both our Internal and External URL and also has servers *CALOS1* and *CALOS2* in the SAN in their FQDN format.

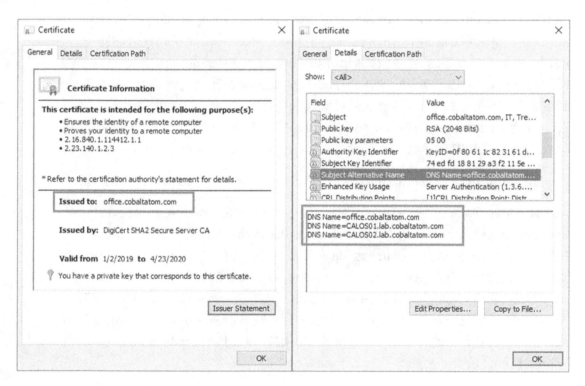

Figure 9-3. *Office Online Server Certificate*

Installing Office Online Server

Now that we know the Office Online Server architecture, let's start installing it. We first need to install the following prerequisites:

- NET Framework 4.5.2

- Visual C++ Redistributable for Visual Studio 2015

Afterward, we need to activate the required Windows Server Features and Roles. This can be achieved with the following PowerShell script, which **will require a reboot.**

For **Windows Server 2012 R2** run the following in an elevated PowerShell window:

```
Add-WindowsFeature Web-Server,Web-Mgmt-Tools,Web-Mgmt-Console,Web-
WebServer,Web-Common-Http,Web-Default-Doc,Web-Static-Content,Web-
Performance,Web-Stat-Compression,Web-Dyn-Compression,Web-Security,Web-
Filtering,Web-Windows-Auth,Web-App-Dev,Web-Net-Ext45,Web-Asp-Net45,Web-
ISAPI-Ext,Web-ISAPI-Filter,Web-Includes,InkandHandwritingServices,NET-
Framework-Features,NET-Framework-Core,NET-HTTP-Activation,NET-Non-HTTP-
Activ,NET-WCF-HTTP-Activation45,Windows-Identity-Foundation
```

For **Windows Server 2016** run the following in an elevated PowerShell window:

```
Add-WindowsFeature Web-Server,Web-Mgmt-Tools,Web-Mgmt-Console,Web-
WebServer,Web-Common-Http,Web-Default-Doc,Web-Static-Content,Web-
Performance,Web-Stat-Compression,Web-Dyn-Compression,Web-Security,Web-
Filtering,Web-Windows-Auth,Web-App-Dev,Web-Net-Ext45,Web-Asp-Net45,Web-
ISAPI-Ext,Web-ISAPI-Filter,Web-Includes,NET-Framework-Features,NET-
Framework-45-Features,NET-Framework-Core,NET-Framework-45-Core,NET-HTTP-
Activation,NET-Non-HTTP-Activ,NET-WCF-HTTP-Activation45,Windows-Identity-
Foundation,Server-Media-Foundation
```

After the reboot, the following prerequisites need to be installed:

- Microsoft.IdentityModel.Extention.dll

After all prerequisites are successfully installed, you can open the Office Online Server Setup.exe from the binaries you got either from MSDN or the Volume Licensing Center.

After accepting the terms, select where you want to install the Office Online Server binaries as seen in Figure 9-4.

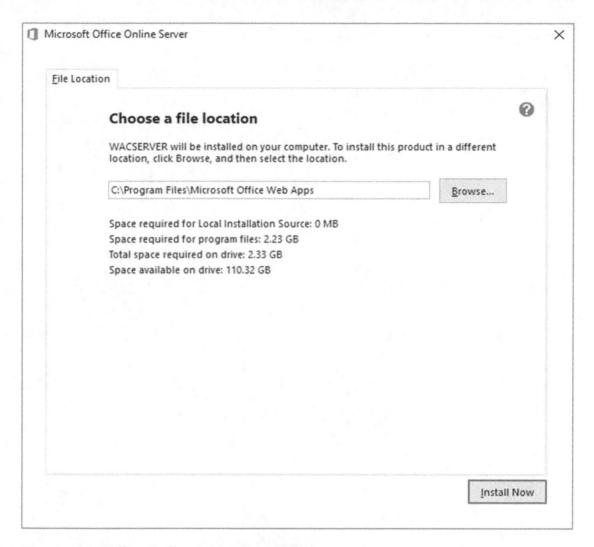

Figure 9-4. *Office Online Server Installation*

Location of the log files as well as cache location can be specified later when creating the Office Online Server farm. Click Next, until you get a screen similar to Figure 9-5 indicating that the installation has finished.

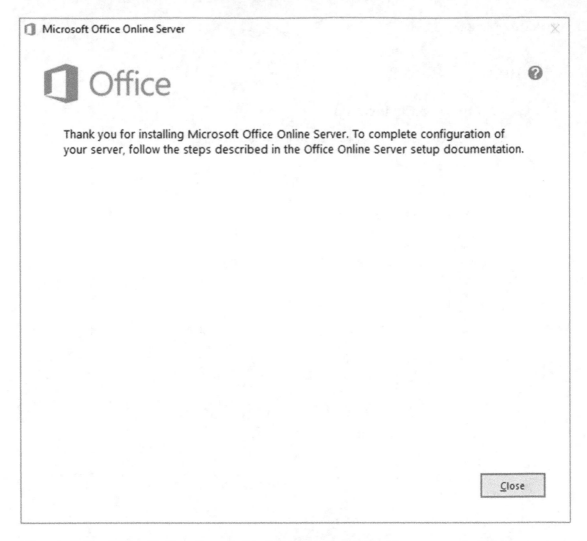

Figure 9-5. *Office Online Server Installation Confirmation*

With the installation of the Office Online Server binaries complete, it's now time to install any Language Packs that you might want to offer to you users. For the Multilanguage UI to work, the language pack must be installed both on the Office Online Server, as well as on your host (SharePoint, Exchange, or Skype for Business).

Since our farm is not created at this point, installing Public Updates or Language Packs is as simple as starting the installer and clicking Next until it's done. As Public Updates also include updates for the Language Packs, make sure to install the base Language Packs before installing Public Updates. By installing the base Language Packs before the Public Updates, all the language related updates in the Public Updates will be applied.

After your Office Online Server(s) are on the update level you want and have the required Language Packs for your business, it's now time to create the Office Online Server farm.

Creating the Office Online Server Farm

Unlike most Microsoft products, Office Online Server does not have a user interface at all and the only way to manage it is by Windows PowerShell. Furthermore, unlike other Office Server products such as SharePoint, there is no "Office Online Management Shell" that you will find on your computer; the required module manage Office Online Server will be loaded by default every time you open PowerShell.

To create the farm, we need to run the `New-OfficeWebAppsFarm` PowerShell cmdlet. Office Web Apps is the old name of Office Online Server in the 2013 suite of Office Servers. You will see that most of the PowerShell cmdlets to manage Office Online Server still refer to Office Web Apps.

Note   Make sure to always run PowerShell as an administrator when changing Office Online Server configurations.

Before running the PowerShell to create our farm, there are a few things we need to plan. The first item to plan is what the URL will be that the consuming services (SharePoint, Exchange, or Skype for Business) will use to connect to the Office Online Server farm. From a SharePoint-only point of view, you could only have one URL if you want, since SharePoint can only use one of them, but not both. If you also plan to connect Skype for Business and Exchange to your Office Online Server Farm, they will sometimes need the External URL. A good example is when doing a Skype for Business meeting and sharing a PowerPoint presentation. Skype for Business will connect external users to the external URL of your office Online Server Farm. Something to consider is that to enable full functionality, the External URL must be accessible from the Internet. Some of the features are Document Previews from Outlook on the Web (formerly known as Outlook Web App), Skype for Business PowerPoint Presentations with external users, and document previews in Office 365 Search Results when using Cloud Hybrid Search.

Publishing both the Internal and External URL by using Secure Sockets Layers (SSL) is highly recommended for security reasons; both SharePoint and Exchange server can consume Office Online Server via HTTP. The only reasons that make it mandatory for you to publish it under SSL are as follows:

1. You have at least one SharePoint site that will be using HTTPS. If your SharePoint sites are using HTTPS, you will need it for your Office Online Server as well.

2. You plan to connect Office Online Server to Skype for Business. Skype for Business only connects to Office Online Server if the latter is using https.

While in this book we recommend SSL Bridging for security, Office Online Server also supports SSL Offloading. SSL Offloading is not recommended because the traffic between the Load Balancer and your Office Online Server will not be encrypted, and you can be subject to a man-in-the-middle attack. If you plan to use SSL up to the Office Online Server, either by using pass through or SSL bridging on your Network Load Balancer, make sure to import the certificate into IIS on every server of your Office Online Server Farm. Make sure the certificate has a Friendly Name in IIS, as that's what we will need to use in our PowerShell cmdlet.

Note   It is mandatory that the certificate have a Friendly Name, and this Friendly Name *cannot* contain an asterisk.

This certificate must also be trusted by the SharePoint Server Farm. If the certificate is from a Certification Authority such as DigiCert that is included by default in the Root Certification Authorities in Windows, it will work without doing any special configurations. However, if using a Self-Signed Certificate or an authority that is not in the root authority cert store by default, make sure to add it as a trusted certificate in the SharePoint Central Admin ➤ Security ➤ Manage Trust. Make sure to add the root certificate and not the end Certificate. You can view an example in Figure 9-6.

Figure 9-6. *Establish Trust Relation in the SharePoint 2019 Central Administration*

You could also do this by running the following PowerShell cmdlets from an elevated SharePoint Management Shell:

```
$trustCert = Get-PfxCertificate <C:\Certs\OOSRootCert.cer>
New-SPTrustedRootAuthority "OOSRootCert" -Certificate $trustCert
```

The following is the cmdlet we used in our environment to create the Office Online Server Farm:

```
New-OfficeWebAppsFarm -InternalUrl "https://office.cobaltatom.com" -ExternalUrl
"https://office.cobaltatom.com" -CertificateName "OOSCert" –EditingEnabled
```

where

- **InternalURL** is the Internal URL of the Office Online Server farm.

- **ExternalURL** is the External URL of the Office Online Server farm, and as you see, you can select the same URL for both Internal and External URLs. This is what we did in our lab.

- **CertificateName** is the Friendly Name of my Certificate in IIS.

- **EditingEnabled** is a switch that tells Office Online Server that users are allowed not only to view documents with it, but also to create and modify documents in SharePoint directly in the browser. As soon as you choose this switch, you will be prompted to approve that you have the right licenses.

Note   If you plan to use Office Online Server on HTTP you need to add the –AllowHttp switch. If you plan to use SSL Offloading, you need to pass the –SSLOffloaded switch.

The New-OfficeWebAppsFarm cmdlet has many parameters that are important to select the features you want to activate in your Office Online Server Farm. You can view those features on TechNet at the following link: https://docs.microsoft.com/en-us/powershell/module/officewebapps/new-officewebappsfarm?view=officewebapps-ps or by running the following PowerShell cmdlet:

```
Get-Help New-OfficeWebAppsFarm -Online
```

After running the command, PowerShell will configure everything needed to get the farm configured. To validate the configuration was successful, point your DNS A record or host file to the server you just configured the farm on and navigate to the Internal or External URL + /hosting/discovery. In this case that URL would be https://office.cobaltatom.com/hosting/discovery/. If everything works as planned, you should see an XML file similar to Figure 9-7.

Figure 9-7. *Discovery XML File*

After we successfully configured our first machine in the Office Online Server farm, you need to install the same binaries on all the other machines in the Office Online Server farm, and if using an SSL Certificate, make sure you also import that into IIS. After the binaries are installed, simply run the following cmdlet:

```
New-OfficeWebAppsMachine -MachineToJoin CALOS01.lab.cobaltatom.com
```

Where in the MachineToJoin Parameter, you give it the FQDN of the first Office Online Server in the farm. In our case, that FQDN is CALOS01.Lab.cobaltatom.com.

Repeat the New-OfficeWebAppsMachine cmdlet on all the servers you want to join to the Office Online Server Farm. After you finish adding all the servers in the farm, run the following cmdlet to validate their health status:

```
(Get-OfficeWebAppsFarm).Machines
```

The output should be all the servers in your Office Online Server farm, with a health status of healthy.

SSL Configuration

As we have enforced the use of TLS 1.2 for SharePoint, we must enable strong crypto as outlined in Microsoft Security Advisory 2960358. Per the advisory, it may be necessary to enable TLS 1.2 support via a registry entry. Save the following text as a UseStrongCrypto. reg and import it into each Office Online Server. Once imported, restart each Office Online Server in your farm.

```
Windows Registry Editor Version 5.00

[HKEY_LOCAL_MACHINE\SOFTWARE\Microsoft\.NETFramework\v4.0.30319]
"SchUseStrongCrypto"=dword:00000001
```

Connecting Office Online Server with SharePoint 2019

After our Office Online Server Farm is up and running, we need to connect it to SharePoint Server 2019. The Process is pretty straightforward. From any SharePoint Server in the farm, run the following cmdlet to create the binding from SharePoint 2019 to Office Online Server:

```
New-SPWOPIBinding -ServerName office.cobaltatom.com
```

If you are using Office Online Server on HTTP, you would need to add the –AllowHTTP switch, as in the following example:

```
New-SPWOPIBinding -ServerName office.cobaltatom.com –AllowHTTP
```

Furthermore, if you use Office Online Server over HTTP, you also need to configure the Security Token Service to allow connections over HTTP. You can do this by running the following PowerShell Script:

```
$config = (Get-SPSecurityTokenServiceConfig)
$config.AllowOAuthOverHttp = $true
$config.Update()
```

The Server name you need to give is the FQDN of the URL you want SharePoint Server to use to access Office Online Server, without any http or https in front. After that is successfully finished, we will need to tell SharePoint how to correctly call this URL. SharePoint Server knows four WOPI Zones:

- Internal-http

- Internal-https (default)

- External-http

- External-https

The difference between the zones is the way that SharePoint calls the Office Online Server URL we gave it. In the Internal Zone, SharePoint will do a call on the short name. Since the default is internal-https, it would call our Office Online Server on $https://office$; however, we might have errors because our certificate SAN is $https://office.cobaltatom.com$. That is why we need to set it to external-https by using the following cmdlet:

```
Set-SPWOPIZone -zone "external-https"
```

Lastly, you need to enable the Excel SOAP API for scheduled data refresh with Excel Online. To enable the Excel SOAP API, run the following Windows PowerShell cmdlet and replace the URL with your Office Online Server farm URL:

```
$Farm = Get-SPFarm
$Farm.Properties.Add("WopiLegacySoapSupport", "https://office.cobaltatom.
com /x/_vti_bin/ExcelServiceInternal.asmx")
$Farm.Update()
```

To test that the connection was successfully configured, navigate to any SharePoint Site and open an Office document. That document should open in the browser and you should be able to go through the entire document. Test Office Online Server with all of the supported Office document types, including editing functionality, if enabled.

One of the features of Office Online Server is document previews directly in the search results, as seen in Figure 9-8.

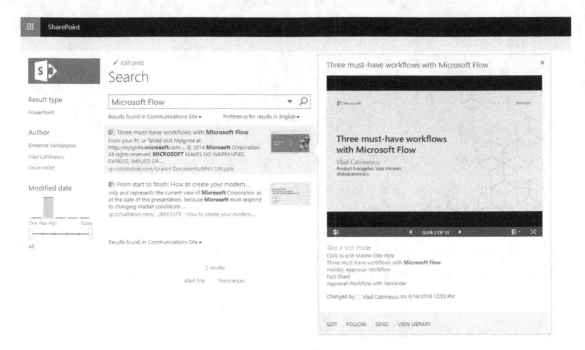

Figure 9-8. *Office Documents Preview in Office Online Server*

In order to enable this functionality, you will need to do a Full Crawl on your Content Sources and the previews will work afterward. With everything setup, let's learn how to maintain Office Online server, and how to debug it in case something goes wrong.

Office Online Server Maintenance

As a SharePoint Administrator, you might also be tasked with debugging and patching Office Online Server. Luckily, Office Online Server allows us to use tools we are already used to, since Office Online Server also has a ULS Log, and it works almost exactly the same as the SharePoint one. To find out the location of your Office Online, simply run the following PowerShell cmdlet:

```
(Get-OfficeWebAppsFarm).LogLocation
```

Note   By default, the Office Online Server log location is at C:\ProgramData\ Microsoft\OfficeWebApps\Data\Logs\ULS.

ULS log viewing tools such as UlsViewer will also work with Office Online Server as seen in Figure 9-9.

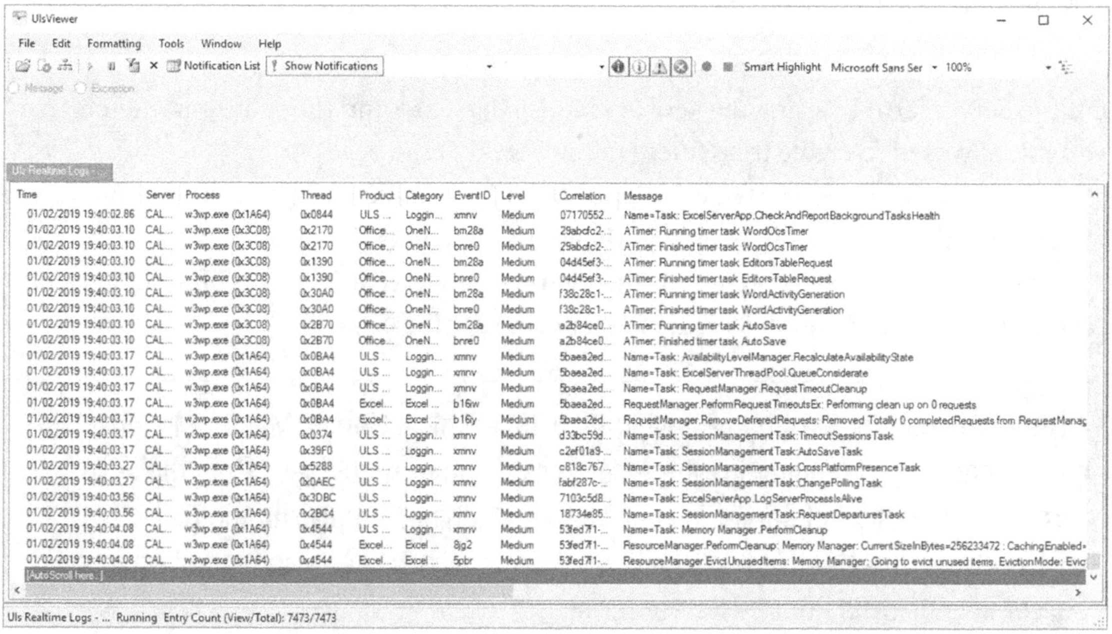

Figure 9-9. Viewing ULS logs with UlsViewer

You can also get more details in the ULS log files by changing the Log Verbosity. The Lowest level is VerboseEX, which will output everything, and the highest level is Unexpected, which will only show critical errors. To change the Log Verbosity in your Office Online Server farm, run the following cmdlet:

```
Set-OfficeWebAppsFarm -LogVerbosity Verbose
```

Note   A reboot of every machine in the Office Online Server farm is required for the Log Verbosity to be changed.

Patching Office Online Server

Patching Office Online server is very different from patching SharePoint Server. In order to apply patches to an Office Online Server machine, it needs to be removed from the Office Online Server farm it is part of. If you are patching a Single Server Office Online

Server Farm, you simply have to remove the server from the farm by using the following PowerShell cmdlet:

`Remove-OfficeWebAppsMachine`

After the machine is removed, you can apply the patch, and then recreate the Office Online Server farm by using the `New-OfficeWebAppsFarm` and the same parameters that you initially used to create this Office Online Server Farm.

Patching a Multi-Server Office Online Server Farm adds an extra layer of complexity. In order to keep Office Online Server availability, you must first remove one of the servers from the load balancer pool, and afterward remove it from the Office Online server farm by using the `Remove-OfficeWebAppsMachine` cmdlet.

Note   You cannot start by removing the Office Online Server Master Machine as this can only be removed when there are no other machines left in the farm. To find out what server is your Master Machine, simply run the `Get-OfficeWebAppsMachine | Select MasterMachineName` cmdlet on any server in your Office Online Server farm.

Once you remove a server from the farm, apply the patches on it, and then recreate the farm by using the `New-OfficeWebAppsFarm` cmdlet and the same parameters that you initially used to create this Office Online Server Farm. Point the Load Balancer only to this server, so users will use the server with the patched version of Office Online Server.

Remove the other Office Online Servers from the old farm, apply the patches, and then join them to this server by running the `New-OfficeWebAppsMachine` cmdlet.

Finally, add the remaining servers in the load balancer to load balance the charge.

Next Steps

With Office Online Server successfully configured, in the next chapter we will learn how to configure Workflow Manager in order to provide modern workflows in SharePoint 2019.

CHAPTER 10

Workflow Manager

Workflow Manager is an external system to SharePoint Server but is leveraged for advanced workflows created through SharePoint Designer 2013 or Visual Studio. Workflow Manager is designed to run in a separate Workflow Manager "farm," although it can be colocated on SharePoint.

Initial Setup

In our topology design, Workflow Manager 1.0 will be installed on CALWFM01, CALWFM02, and CALWFM03 for a highly available farm. Workflow Manager supports an architecture of one, three, or five servers in a Workflow Manager farm. No other farm configuration is valid.

The SharePoint farm will consume Workflow Manager via the DNS name "calwfm. lab.cobaltatom.com" which is a virtual IP on a load balancer in front of the three Workflow Manager servers. The load balancer must be listening on TCP port 12290. A trusted SSL certificate, in this case a wildcard certificate, is used during the Workflow Manager configuration. This certificate should contain a Common Name of the wildcard DNS domain that will be used for the Workflow Manager endpoint as well as the Subject Alternative Names of the Workflow Manager servers and finally, the last Subject Alternative Name should match the Common Name of the certificate. Install this certificate on all Workflow Manager servers. The certificate must also be trusted by the SharePoint farm. Workflow Manager 1.0 supports SQL Server 2016 and SQL Server 2017. This installation will be using SQL Server 2017 with the AlwaysOn Listener of "caspag. lab.cobaltatom.com".

Workflow Manager is installed via the Web Platform Installer (WebPI), which is run on each of the Workflow Manager servers.

© Vlad Catrinescu and Trevor Seward 2019
V. Catrinescu and T. Seward, *Deploying SharePoint 2019*, https://doi.org/10.1007/978-1-4842-4526-2_10

> **Tip**   WebPI requires an Internet connection in order to download the applicable
> products. WebPI can be downloaded from www.microsoft.com/web/
> downloads/platform.aspx. Not covered in this chapter is an Offline Installation
> of Workflow Manager. Offline Installation instructions are available at https://
> docs.microsoft.com/en-us/previous-versions/dotnet/workflow-
> manager/jj906604(v%3dazure.10).

In this installation, we will be starting with Service Bus. Search for and select
"Windows Azure Pack: Service Bus 1.1 with TLS 1.2 Support" only, as shown in
Figure 10-1. This will also install other dependencies, as required.

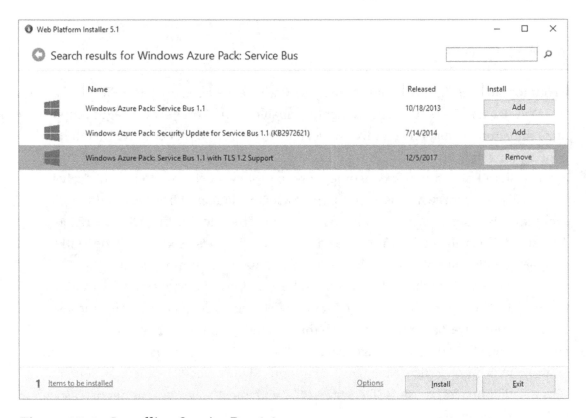

Figure 10-1. *Installing Service Bus 1.1*

Once the installation of the Service Bus 1.1 components has completed, search for
"Workflow Manager" in the Web Platform Installer. Find and select "Workflow Manager 1.0
Refresh (CU2)," as shown in Figure 10-2.

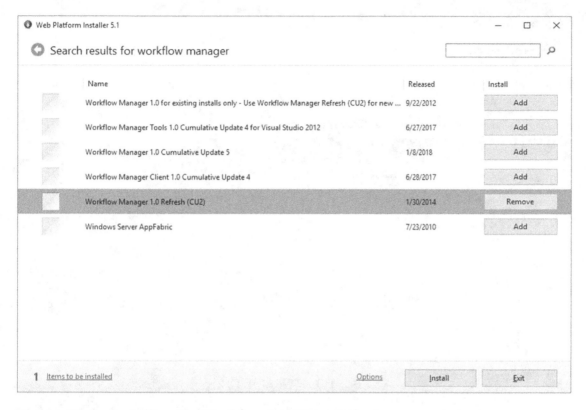

Figure 10-2. *Installing the Workflow Manager Refresh*

Once the Workflow Manager 1.0 Refresh (CU2) package has completed installing, you may be asked to run the Workflow Manager wizard. Instead, close out the wizard and then close and reopen the Web Platform Installer. This is done in order for the Web Platform Installer to detect that Service Bus 1.1 and Workflow Manager 1.0 are installed.

Again, search for "Workflow Manager". Find and select "Workflow Manager 1.0 Cumulative Update 5" as shown in Figure 10-3 and install it. Close the Workflow Manager wizard, if prompted, as well as the Web Platform Installer.

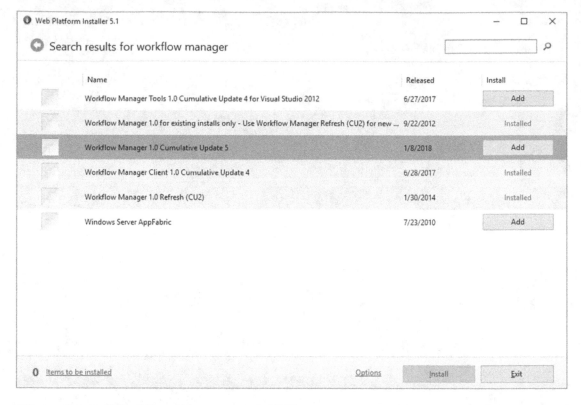

Figure 10-3. *Workflow Manager 1.0 CU3*

During the installation process, the Windows Fabric V1 RTM and IIS components will also be installed automatically.

Repeat the installation steps for the remaining two Workflow Manager servers.

Prior to deploying Workflow Manager, add the Service Account as a Local Administrator to each Workflow Manager server.

To create the Workflow Manager farm, we will be using the following PowerShell script, CreateWFMFarm.ps1:

```
$ErrorActionPreference = "Stop"
$ra = ConvertTo-SecureString "Password1!" -AsPlainText -Force
$certThumbprint = '8E6DC4D0A2DEA825EA49AF2C3BEA5ABE46AEC432'$admins =
'BUILTIN\Administrators'
$svcAcct = 's-wfm@LAB'
$mgUsers = 's-wfm@LAB','trevor.seward@LAB','vlad.catrinescu@LAB'
$baseConnectionString = 'Data Source=caspag.lab.cobaltatom.com;Integrated
Security=True;Encrypt=False;Initial Catalog='
```

```
$sbConnString = $baseConnectionString + 'SbManagementDB;'
$sbGateConnString = $baseConnectionString + 'SbGatewayDatabase;'
$sbMsgConnString = $baseConnectionString + 'SBMessageContainer01;'
$wfConnString = $baseConnectionString + 'WFManagementDB;'
$wfInstConnString = $baseConnectionString + 'WFInstanceManagementDB;'
$wfResConnString = $baseConnectionString + 'WFResourceManagementDB;'
```

The variables that must be adjusted in this script for your particular deployment are as follows:

- `$ra`

  - This variable contains the password of the RunAs account. Note this script uses the same RunAs account for the Service Bus and Workflow Manager farms.

- `$certThumbprint`

  - This contains the certificate thumbprint from the valid SSL certificate in use by the Workflow Manager farm.

Tip   You can find the certificate thumbprint by running dir `cert:\LocalMachine\My` in PowerShell.

- `$svcAcct`

  - This is the RunAs, or Service Account of the Service Bus and Workflow Manager farms. Note this script uses a single account to run both services.

- `$mgUsers`

  - This is a comma-separated list of users in the format of username@DOMAIN that will have administrative rights over the Service Bus and Workflow Manager farms.

- `$baseConnectionString`

  - This variable contains the SQL Server AlwaysOn Availability Group fully qualified domain name. Alternatively, it can be adjusted to use a SQL Alias or SQL Server Name, as well as Instance Name if required.

All other variables may be left as they are.

```
Add-Type -Path "C:\Program Files\Workflow Manager\1.0\Workflow\Artifacts\
Microsoft.ServiceBus.dll"

Write-Host "Creating Service Bus farm..."
New-SBFarm -SBFarmDBConnectionString $sbConnString `
    -InternalPortRangeStart 9000 -TcpPort 9354 -MessageBrokerPort 9356
-RunAsAccount $svcAcct -AdminGroup $admins `
    -GatewayDBConnectionString $sbGateConnString -FarmCertificateThumbprint
$certThumbprint `
    -EncryptionCertificateThumbprint $certThumbprint
-MessageContainerDBConnectionString $sbMsgConnString
```

New-SBFarm creates the ServiceBus farm and ServiceBus databases.

```
Write-Host "Creating Workflow Manager farm..."
New-WFFarm -WFFarmDBConnectionString $wfConnString `
    -RunAsAccount $svcAcct -AdminGroup $admins -HttpsPort 12290 -HttpPort
    12291 `
        -InstanceDBConnectionString $wfInstConnString `
    -ResourceDBConnectionString $wfResConnString
-OutboundCertificateThumbprint $certThumbprint `
        -SslCertificateThumbprint $certThumbprint `
    -EncryptionCertificateThumbprint $certThumbprint

Write-Host "Adding host to Service Bus farm..."
Add-SBHost -SBFarmDBConnectionString $sbConnString -RunAsPassword $ra
-EnableFirewallRules $true
```

Likewise, New-WFFarm creates the Workflow Manager farm and databases. The next step, Add-SBHost, adds this server to the ServiceBus farm.

```
Try
{
    New-SBNamespace -Name 'WorkflowDefaultNamespace' -AddressingScheme
'Path' -ManageUsers $mgUsers
    Start-Sleep -s 90
}
```

```
Catch [system.InvalidOperationException] {}

$SBClientConfiguration = Get-SBClientConfiguration -Namespaces
'WorkflowDefaultNamespace'
Write-Host "Adding host to Workflow Manager Farm..."
Add-WFHost -WFFarmDBConnectionString $wfConnString -RunAsPassword $ra
-EnableFirewallRules $true `
    -SBClientConfiguration $SBClientConfiguration
Write-Host "Completed."
$ErrorActionPreference = "Continue"
```

These last pieces of the script create the ServiceBus namespace along with add this server to the Workflow Manager farm.

Once the farm is created, one at a time, we will add the remaining two Workflow Manager servers to the farm using the ConnectWFMFarm.ps1 script. For these two servers, the PowerShell script is slightly shorter. The script adds the server to the ServiceBus farm and then to the Workflow Manager farm.

```
$ErrorActionPreference = "Stop"
$ra = ConvertTo-SecureString "Password1!" -AsPlainText -Force
$mgUsers = 's-wfm@LAB','trevor.seward@LAB','vlad.catrinescu@LAB'
$baseConnectionString = 'Data Source=caspag.lab.cobaltatom.com;Integrated
Security=True;Encrypt=False;Initial Catalog='
$sbConnString = $baseConnectionString + 'SbManagementDB;'
$wfConnString = $baseConnectionString + 'WFManagementDB;'

Add-Type -Path "C:\Program Files\Workflow Manager\1.0\Workflow\Artifacts\
Microsoft.ServiceBus.dll"

Write-Host "Adding host to Service Bus Farm..."
Add-SBHost -SBFarmDBConnectionString $sbConnString -ExternalBrokerUrl
"sb://$($farmDomain)" -RunAsPassword $ra -EnableFirewallRules $true
-Verbose
$ErrorActionPreference = "Continue"

try
{
```

```
    $SBClientConfiguration = Get-SBClientConfiguration -Namespaces
'WorkflowDefaultNamespace' -Verbose
}
Catch [system.InvalidOperationException] {}

Write-Host -ForegroundColor Yellow "Adding host to Workflow Manager Farm..."

Add-WFHost -WFFarmDBConnectionString $wfConnString -RunAsPassword $ra
-EnableFirewallRules $true `
    -SBClientConfiguration $SBClientConfiguration -Verbose
Write-Host -ForegroundColor Green "Completed."
$ErrorActionPreference = "Continue"
```

As with the CreateWFMFarm.ps1 script, the same variables are available to be adjusted, except for $svcAcct and $certThumbprint. Note that when adding additional servers, it will stop and start the Service Bus and dependent services on the any existing Workflow Manager servers which are part of the farm.

The output of Get-SBFarm will be similar to Figure 10-4 and Get-WFFarm will be similar to Figure 10-5.

Figure 10-4. *The output of the Get-SBFarm cmdlet*

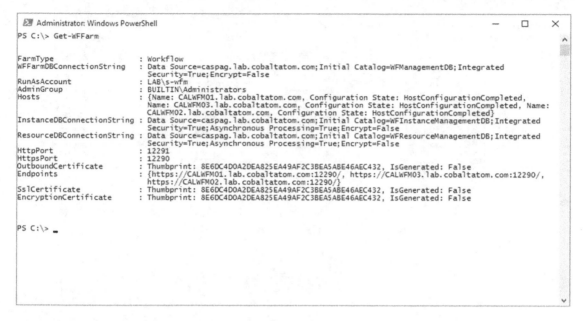

Figure 10-5. *The output of the Get-WFFarm cmdlet*

When the deploy has been completed, verify that the following services are running on each farm member:

- Service Bus Gateway

- Service Bus Message Broker

- Service Bus Resource Provider

- Windows Fabric Host Service

- Workflow Manager Backend

In addition, verify the status of the services via Get-SBFarmStatus, as shown in Figure 10-6, and Get-WFFarmStatus, as shown in Figure 10-7.

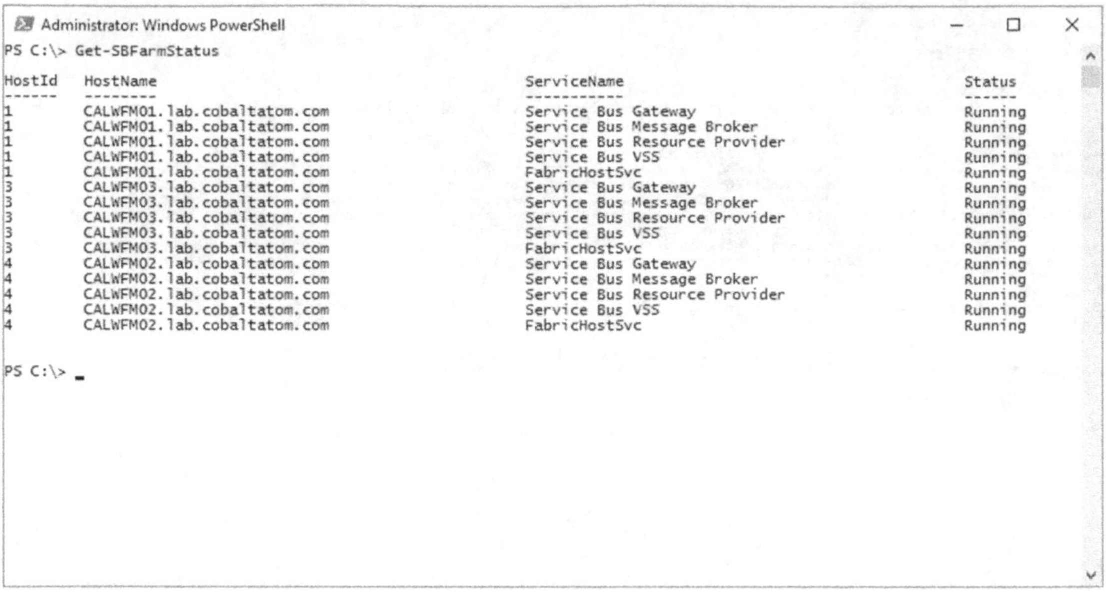

Figure 10-6. *The output of Get-SBFarmStatus*

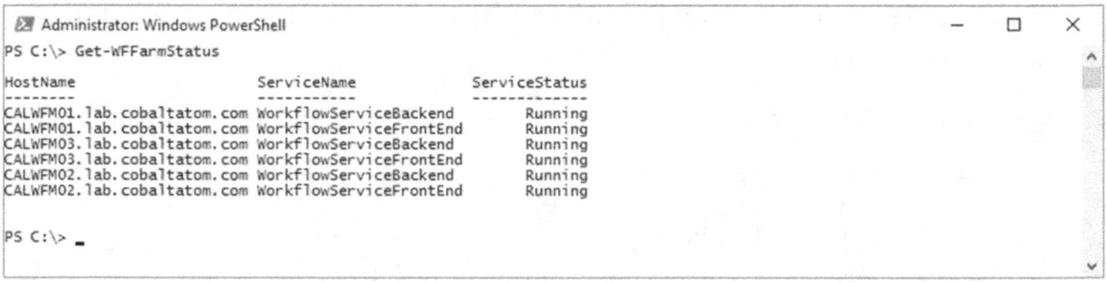

Figure 10-7. *The output of Get-WFFarmStatus*

The final step in the Workflow Manager configuration is to add the databases to the Availability Group on the SQL Server 2016 AlwaysOn Availability Group. Take a full backup of three Service Bus and three Workflow Manager databases:

- SbGatewayDatabase

- SbManagementDB

- SBMessageContainer01

- WFInstanceManagementDB

- WFManagementDB

- WFResourceManagementDB

Add the databases to the remaining replicas, and then add the Service Bus and Workflow Manager service account to the secondary node logins.

SSL Configuration

As we have enforced the use of TLS 1.2 for SharePoint, we must enable strong crypto via a registry entry. Save the following text as a UseStrongCrypto.reg and import it into each Workflow Manager server. Once imported, restart each Workflow Manager server.

```
Windows Registry Editor Version 5.00

[HKEY_LOCAL_MACHINE\SOFTWARE\Microsoft\.NETFramework\v4.0.30319]
"SchUseStrongCrypto"=dword:00000001
```

Now that the Workflow Manager farm setup has been completed, we will move onto configuring and testing the SharePoint Server 2019 integration with Workflow Manager.

SharePoint Server Workflow Manager Integration

Prior to configuring the integration with Workflow Manager in the SharePoint farm, you must install the Workflow Manager Client. The client can be downloaded directly from Microsoft without the WebPI. The currently available version as of the publishing of this book is Workflow Manager Client Cumulative Update 4. This update may be installed without deploying previous versions of the Workflow Manager Client.

Note   The Workflow Manager Client Cumulative Update 4 is available from www. microsoft.com/en-us/download/details.aspx?id=55643. Download the file WorkflowManagerClient_x64.msi.

As Workflow Manager will need to communicate with SharePoint via HTTPS requests, we must grant the Workflow Manager service account, LAB\s-wfm in this case, with Full Control over the SharePoint Web Applications where Workflow Manager will be used. Because we only have a single Web Application for Team, Publishing, and other sites, we will only grant this right on https://sharepoint.learn-sp2016.com. Using the SharePoint Management Shell, grant the service account Full Control via the User Policy.

```
$wa = Get-SPWebApplication https://sp.cobaltatom.com
$zp = $wa.ZonePolicies("Default")
$policy = $zp.Add("i:0#.w|LAB\s-wfm", "Workflow Manager")
$policyRole = $wa.PolicyRoles.GetSpecialRole("FullControl")
$policy.PolicyRoleBindings.Add($policyRole)
$wa.Update()
```

Workflow Manager may only be configured with SharePoint via the SharePoint Management Shell. From the SharePoint Management Shell, register Workflow Manager using the load balanced URL on port 12290 (default SSL port for Workflow Manager).

```
Register-SPWorkflowService -SPSite https://sp.cobaltatom.com
-WorkflowHostUri https://calwfm.lab.cobaltatom.com:12290
```

Note that while Register-SPWorkflowService needs a validate SharePoint site to register against, once Workflow Manager has been registered successfully, it will be registered for the entire farm, not just the specified Site Collection.

Note   It may be necessary to restart the SharePoint servers in order to fully register the Workflow Manager binaries.

Now that Workflow Manager has been integrated into SharePoint, the next step will be to perform a simple test with SharePoint Designer 2013.

Testing Workflow Manager with SharePoint Designer 2013

For testing Workflow Manager with SharePoint Designer 2013, provision a new Site Collection using the classic Team Site template. If using an existing site, make sure the Site Feature "Workflow Task Content Type Feature" has been enabled.

On the site, create a new List named WorkflowTest. No additional configuration on the List needs to be performed for this test.

Using SharePoint Designer 2013 from a client computer, connect to the Site Collection and create a new List Workflow. Give the workflow a name and select the SharePoint 2013 Workflow under Platform Type as shown in Figure 10-8.

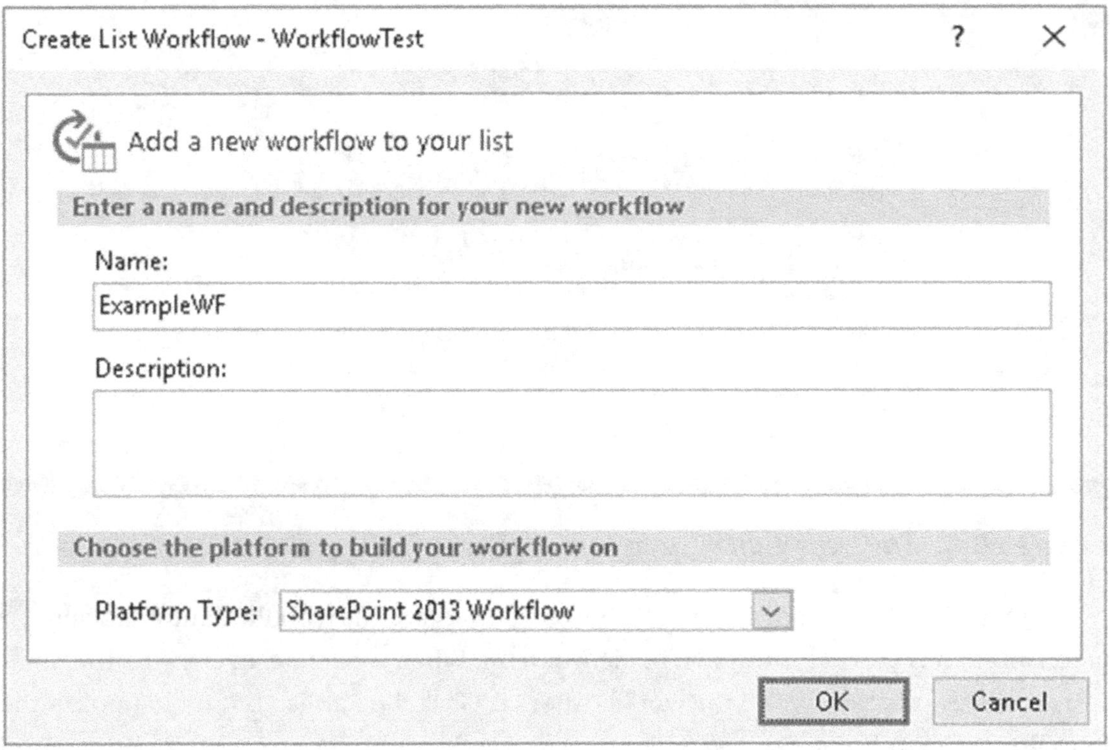

Create List Workflow - WorkflowTest   ?   ✕

⤴️ Add a new workflow to your list

Enter a name and description for your new workflow

Name:

ExampleWF

Description:

Choose the platform to build your workflow on

Platform Type: SharePoint 2013 Workflow   ⌄

OK   Cancel

Figure 10-8. *Creating a new SharePoint 2013 Workflow for testing*

Insert an Action of "Log to History List" and add text to the action. Under Transition to Stage, select End of Workflow. In Figure 10-9, the Log to History List text is "Workflow Testing."

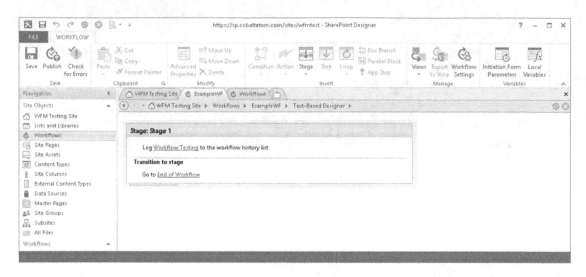

Figure 10-9. *The steps in the example workflow*

Under Workflow Settings, check the box next to "Start this workflow automatically when an item is created" as shown in Figure 10-10. When we create an entry on the new List, it will automatically start the workflow for us. Click the Publish button to publish the workflow to SharePoint.

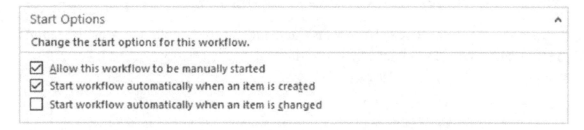

Figure 10-10. *Enabling the workflow to automatically start when a new item is created*

From SharePoint, navigate to the custom List. Create a new item, specifying any value for the title. The workflow will automatically start. Monitor the status by clicking the show actions button next to the List Item and navigate to More and Workflows. This page will display the workflow status along with allowing you to manually start it if needed, as shown in Figure 10-11.

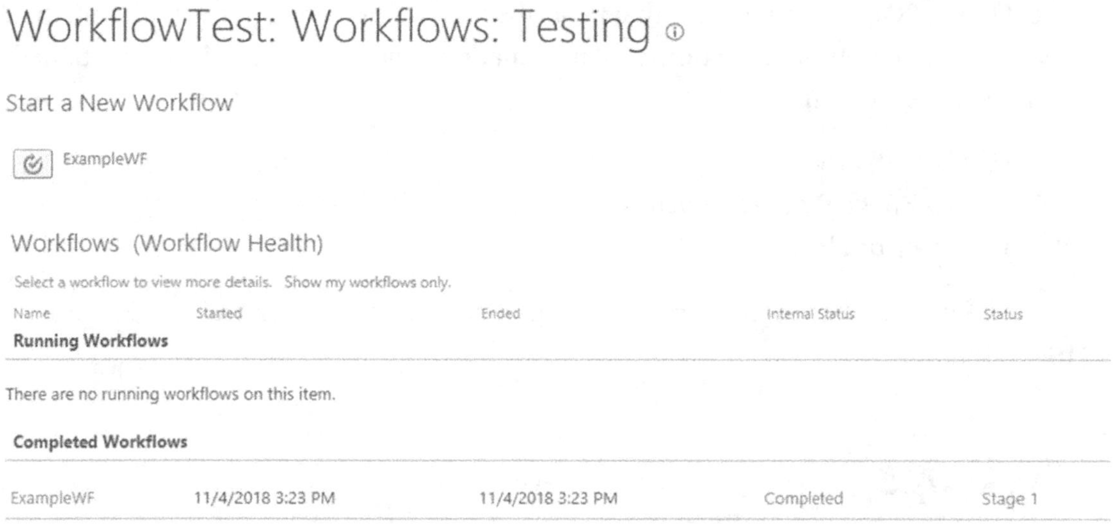

WorkflowTest: Workflows: Testing ⓘ

Start a New Workflow

[✓] ExampleWF

Workflows (Workflow Health)

Select a workflow to view more details. Show my workflows only.

Name	Started	Ended	Internal Status	Status
Running Workflows				

There are no running workflows on this item.

Completed Workflows				
ExampleWF	11/4/2018 3:23 PM	11/4/2018 3:23 PM	Completed	Stage 1

Figure 10-11. *The workflow completed without errors*

Clicking the ExampleWF link in Figure 10-11 will provide additional details about the workflow, including any potential errors during execution. Figure 10-12 displays a successful workflow execution, but if there were an error, an informational icon would be displayed next to the Internal Status. Hovering over the icon will display a pop-out with the error encountered.

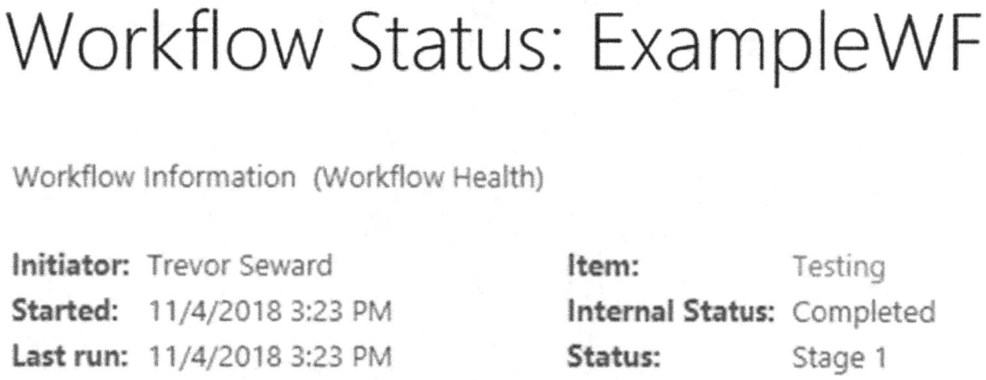

Workflow Status: ExampleWF

Workflow Information (Workflow Health)

Initiator: Trevor Seward		**Item:**	Testing
Started: 11/4/2018 3:23 PM		**Internal Status:**	Completed
Last run: 11/4/2018 3:23 PM		**Status:**	Stage 1

Figure 10-12. *Details about the successful execution of the workflow*

It may also be helpful to monitor the ULS logs across the farm. Using Microsoft's ULSViewer filter to the category "Workflow Services" which will provide detailed information regarding any potential errors. Errors are also logged in the Workflow Manager WFInstanceManagementDB database. Using SQL Server Management Studio, connect to the SQL Server instance that hosts the WFInstanceManagementDB. Run the following query to retrieve the additional information which will primarily be contained within the Message column:

```
Use [WFInstanceManagementDB]
SELECT * FROM DebugTraces (NoLock)
ORDER BY CreationTime DESC
```

This completes the deployment of the Workflow Manager and SharePoint Server 2016 integration.

Next Steps

With Workflow Manager configured to allow creation of SharePoint 2013 workflows, the next chapter will look at SharePoint Server 2019 and Exchange Server 2016 integration.

CHAPTER 11

SharePoint and Exchange Integration

While SharePoint Server 2019 alone provides great value to each company that decides to install it, it can offer more features when integrated with other servers from the Office suite such as Exchange Server 2019.

By integrating Exchange Server 2019 with SharePoint Server 2019, you enable features such as the Site Mailbox and Modern Attachments. If you are on SharePoint Server 2013 and skipped 2016, note that the Work Management Service from SharePoint 2013 does not exist in SharePoint Server 2019 as it has been removed since SharePoint Server 2016!

Site Mailbox Overview

The Site Mailbox was first introduced in Exchange 2013 / SharePoint 2013 and aims to increase collaboration as well as user productivity when dealing with both documents and e-mails for the same task. Traditionally, e-mails are stored in Exchange Server and consumed in Outlook, while documents are stored and consumed in SharePoint. This creates two different silos where users need to check for information. By implementing the Site Mailbox, you can create an Exchange Mailbox for specific SharePoint Sites, allowing your users to consume both SharePoint documents and Exchange e-mails from the same place.

Note Site Mailboxes have been deprecated in SharePoint Server 2019 but are still supported.

© Vlad Catrinescu and Trevor Seward 2019
V. Catrinescu and T. Seward, *Deploying SharePoint 2019*, https://doi.org/10.1007/978-1-4842-4526-2_11

After successfully being configured, the Site Mailbox will become an app (like a List or Document Library) that can be added in the Site Collection as seen in Figure 11-1.

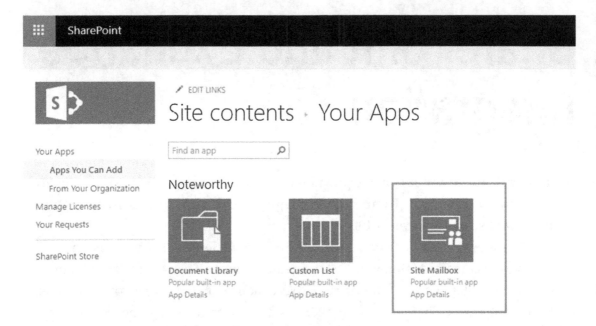

Figure 11-1. *Add a Site Mailbox to a SharePoint Site*

It's important to know that only one Site Mailbox can be added per SharePoint Site. Once created, the Site Mailbox will be assigned an e-mail address following the following naming convention: SM-SiteName@domain.tld. The Site Mailbox we created in a Site called Team Site is named "Team Site" and can be e-mailed at "SM-TeamSite@cobaltatom. com". The Site Mailbox can be accessed from the browser as seen in Figure 11-2.

Figure 11-2. *Viewing the Site Mailbox in the browser*

The Site Mailbox can also be accessed directly from Outlook. When a user has access to a Site Mailbox, it will automatically be added to that user's Outlook client as seen in Figure 11-3.

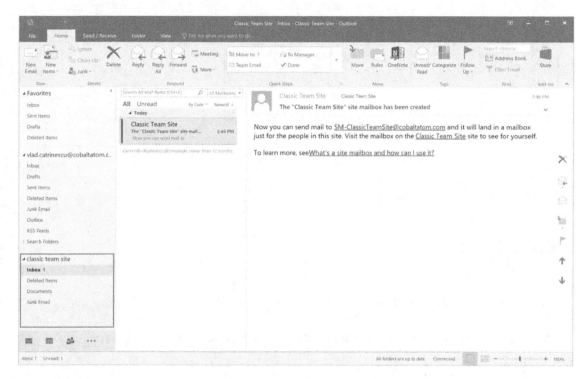

Figure 11-3. *The "Team Site" Site Mailbox in Outlook 2019*

Another advantage of the Site Mailbox is that document libraries that are displayed in the Quick Launch will also be available as a folder in your Outlook client. Users will be able to quickly open documents in their client applications, as well as drag and drop documents in Outlook, which will automatically be uploaded to their SharePoint document library. Figure 11-4 shows the "Presentations" document library inside Outlook 2019.

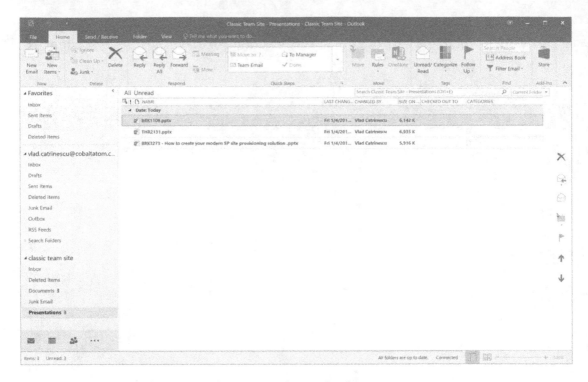

Figure 11-4. *A Document Library inside Outlook 2019*

Now that we know what a Site Mailbox is, in the next section we will learn how to configure it.

Configure SharePoint Server 2019 Site Mailbox

The process to configure the SharePoint Server 2019 Site Mailbox is pretty straightforward. We will first need to install the Exchange Web Services (EWS) Managed API 2.2 on all the servers in our farm. This will install the required tools that SharePoint will use to communicate with Exchange Server 2019. The next step will then be to create a trust between our SharePoint Server 2019 and Exchange Server 2019 so they can securely exchange information. Lastly, we will need to enable the Site Mailbox feature on the sites we want to use this feature on.

It's important to know that Site Mailboxes will only work on Web Applications that use SSL on their default Zone. Furthermore, in order for Site Mailboxes to work, the User Profile Service Application needs to work and users need to be synchronized from Active Directory. Lastly, the App Management Service Application should be configured. We covered both those requirements in previous chapters.

Installing Exchange Web Services Managed API

To get our SharePoint Servers ready, we will need to download the Exchange Web Services (EWS) Managed API on every server in our SharePoint Server Farm. You can download EWS Managed API 2.2 from the Microsoft Download Center:

- Microsoft Exchange Web Services Managed API 2.2 (`www.microsoft.com/en-ca/download/details.aspx?id=42951`)

Once downloaded, run the following cmd either from an elevated Command Prompt or PowerShell Window:

`msiexec /i EwsManagedApi.msi addlocal="ExchangeWebServicesApi_Feature, ExchangeWebServicesApi_Gac"`

After the install finishes successfully, you will have to do an IIS Reset on every server in the farm. With the Prerequisites configured, it's time to configure SharePoint 2019 to trust the Exchange Server.

Establish OAuth Trust and Permissions on SharePoint

In this section, we will configure our Exchange Server as a new SP Trusted Security Token Issuer, as well as add a property in the Web Application Property Bag. We will do this by using PowerShell scripts provided by Microsoft. There are two scripts that we need to create on any one of our SharePoint Servers. The first script is named Set-SiteMailboxConfig.ps1 and can the second script is called Check-SiteMailboxConfig.ps1. Both scripts can be downloaded from the Github site of this book.

Note   Both scripts can be downloaded from TechNet at the following link:
`https://docs.microsoft.com/en-us/sharepoint/administration/configure-site-mailboxes-in-sharepoint`.

The Set-SiteMailboxConfig script is the script that will configure everything, while the Check-SiteMailboxConfig.ps1 will simply verify that the configuration is valid before enabling the CollaborationMailbox Farm Feature.

To run the Set-SiteMailboxConfig, open SharePoint Management Shell as an administrator, and run the following cmdlet:

```
.\Set-SiteMailboxConfig.ps1 -ExchangeSiteMailboxDomain <Domain Name>
-ExchangeAutodiscoverDomain <Exchange Server FQDN>
```

Where the `<Domain Name>` is the Domain Name that your Exchange Mailbox addresses should be created in, and the `<ExchangeAutodiscoverDomain>` is the FQDN of your Exchange Server. The -ExchangeAutodiscoverDomain parameter is only required if Autodiscover is not properly configured in your DNS. If the parameter is left blank, the script will default it to *Autodiscover.<Exchange Site Mailbox Domain>*. A simple way to test it is navigating to *https://autodiscover.<mailbox domain>/autodiscover/metadata/ json/1* . For example, in our environment we validated it by navigating to `https:// autodiscover.cobaltatom.com/autodiscover/metadata/json/1` .

Here is the cmdlet that we ran in our environment, and we did not specify the ExchangeAutodiscoverDomain since Autodiscover is properly setup inside the DNS:

```
.\Set-SiteMailboxConfig.ps1 -ExchangeSiteMailboxDomain cobaltatom.com
```

If you only want to enable it on a certain Web Application, you can add the – WebApplication parameter to the script, for example:

```
.\Set-SiteMailboxConfig.ps1 -ExchangeSiteMailboxDomain cobaltatom.com  –
WebApplication https://sp.cobaltatom.com
```

With everything configured on the SharePoint side, we need to configure Exchange Server as well.

Configure Exchange Server 2019 for Site Mailboxes

The last part of the Site Mailbox configuration is to configure Exchange Server 2019 for Site Mailboxes. The scripts required for the configuration are included with ever Exchange Server installation, and you will find them at the following path: "C:\Program Files\Microsoft\Exchange Server\V15\Scripts".

As we have enforced the use of TLS 1.2 for SharePoint, we must enable strong crypto as outlined in Microsoft Security Advisory 2960358. Per the advisory, it may be necessary to enable TLS 1.2 support on Windows Server via a registry entry. Save the following text as a UseStrongCrypto.reg and import it into each Office Online Server. Once imported, restart each Exchange in your Exchange Organization. A reboot is required for the change to take effect.

```
Windows Registry Editor Version 5.00
[HKEY_LOCAL_MACHINE\SOFTWARE\Microsoft\.NETFramework\v4.0.30319]
"SchUseStrongCrypto"=dword:00000001
```

After the reboot, open Exchange Management Shell as an Administrator and make sure you are in that script location and run the following PowerShell cmdlet:

```
.\Configure-EnterprisePartnerApplication.ps1 -ApplicationType Sharepoint
-AuthMetadataUrl https://<SP Site Collection>/_layouts/15/metadata/json/1
```

Where <SP Site Collection> is the Root Site Collection of the Web Application where you enabled Site Mailbox. In our environment, the cmdlet we ran was

```
.\Configure-EnterprisePartnerApplication.ps1 -ApplicationType Sharepoint
-AuthMetadataUrl https://sp.cobaltatom.com/_layouts/15/metadata/json/1
```

The Script should output that the Configuration has succeeded. To test the Site Mailbox feature, navigate to a SharePoint Site and try to add a new Site Mailbox from the "Add an app" page. After adding the Site Mailbox, SharePoint will display a note that it might take up to 30 minutes for the Site Mailbox to be created as seen in Figure 11-5.

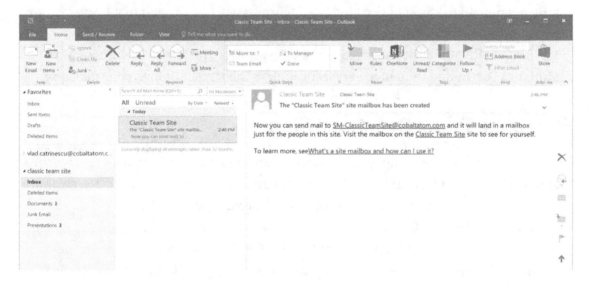

Figure 11-5. *Site Mailbox has been created*

Once the Site Mailbox is ready to use, every Site Owner will receive an e-mail notifying them of the Site Mailbox e-mail address as well as a link to learn more about what a Site Mailbox is. An example of this welcome e-mail can be seen in Figure 11-6.

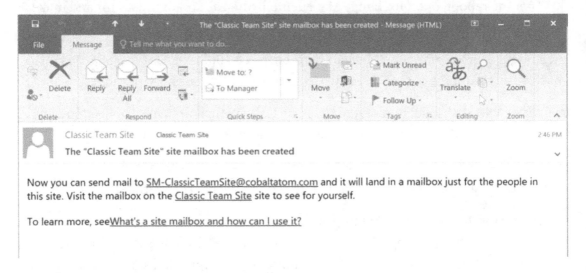

Figure 11-6. *Site Mailbox welcome e-mail*

By default, all the Site Owners and Site Members will have access to the Site Mailbox and will be able to view and send e-mails.

With the Site Mailbox configured, another feature we can enable by integrating SharePoint Server and Exchange Server together is Exchange Photo Synchronization.

Exchange Photo Synchronization

The User Profile Service is capable of synchronizing photos from Exchange Server 2013, Exchange Server 2016, or Exchange Server 2019 instead of the `thumbnailPhoto` attribute in Active Directory. This provides significantly higher-quality pictures.

As we've already performed the preceding prerequisites by installing the Exchange Web Services API on SharePoint and configuring OAuth between Exchange Server and SharePoint using the Configure-EnterprisePartnerApplication.ps1 script, those steps will not be repeated here. Instead, only the necessary steps for Exchange Photo Synchronization will be present.

First, validate the Autodiscovery domain for Exchange Server. This can be done using the Exchange Management Console. In this example, the Exchange Server name is CAEXCH02.

```
(Get-AutodiscoverVirtualDirectory -Server CAEXCH02).InternalUrl.AbsoluteUri
```

This will provide the full path for the Autodiscovery URL.

On SharePoint, using the SharePoint Management Shell, configure the Security Token Service, setting the HybridStsSelectionEnabled property to true.

```
$sts=Get-SPSecurityTokenServiceConfig
$sts.HybridStsSelectionEnabled = $true
$sts.AllowMetadataOverHttp = $false
$sts.AllowOAuthOverHttp = $false
$sts.Update()
```

The next step is to retrieve the Exchange Trusted Security Token Issuer and apply the App Principal to our MySite Host. In this farm, the MySite Host is https://sp-my.cobaltatom.com.

```
$exchange = Get-SPTrustedSecurityTokenIssuer -Identity "Exchange"
$app = Get-SPAppPrincipal -Site https://sp-my.cobaltatom.com
-NameIdentifier $exchange.NameId
$site = Get-SPSite https://sp-my.cobaltatom.com
Set-SPAppPrincipalPermission -AppPrincipal $app -Site $site.RootWeb -Scope
SiteSubscription -Right FullControl -EnableAppOnlyPolicy
```

Continuing to use the SharePoint Management Shell, place the MySite Web Application into a variable, set the ExchangeAutodiscoverDomain property to the Autodiscovery URL, the photo expiration properties, and finally enable the user photo import.

```
$wa.Properties["ExchangeAutodiscoverDomain"] = https://autodiscover.
cobaltatom.com
$wa.UserPhotoErrorExpiration = 1
$wa.UserPhotoExpiration = 12
$wa.UserPhotoImportEnabled = $true
$wa.Update()
```

Once this is completed, each user must visit the About Me page to establish the OAuth session between Exchange and SharePoint to import the picture into the MySite host.

There can be a variety of errors present in the ULS log for picture import. To filter to just the specific errors, set the Category to "Exchange Integration". This will narrow the scope to the import process when a user visits their About Me page.

As previously mentioned, pictures are imported when a user visits their own About Me (profile) page. If the import process runs into an error, SharePoint will not retry for the number of hours specified in `UserPhotoErrorExpiration`. Likewise, if the photo import is successful, SharePoint will not look for a new photo for the number of hours specified in `UserPhotoExpiration`. The value for when the last import took place is the timestamp of the photo in the MySite Host. This includes the generic person image when a photo import fails.

When a photo has been successfully imported, it will be displayed for that user. If you search for the user's profile in the User Profile Service Application, as shown in Figure 11-7, the picture cannot be changed by the administrator via editing the User Profile.

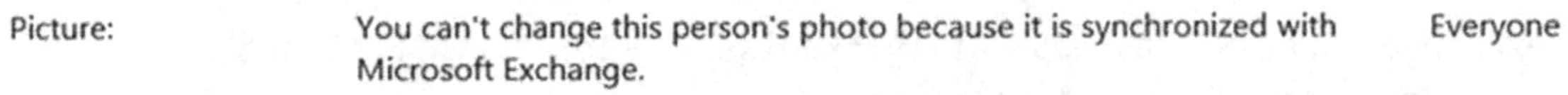

Picture: You can't change this person's photo because it is synchronized with   Everyone
                            Microsoft Exchange.

Figure 11-7. *The Picture property when a user's profile photo is synchronized from Exchange*

Additionally, if the user edits their own profile via the MySite Host to change their picture, they will be redirected to Outlook on the Web.

Next Steps

With the integration between Exchange and SharePoint now completed, in the next chapter we will learn how to deploy Business Intelligence Services in SharePoint 2019.

CHAPTER 12

Business Intelligence with SharePoint 2019

Business Intelligence is one of the categories that has seen the most features removed in SharePoint Server 2019. Whereas SharePoint Server was the recommended platform to publish Business Intelligence reports, most of technologies depended on Silverlight to render results, and reports were not user friendly to build. With Silverlight support officially ending in October 2021, most Business Intelligence features that we are used to in SharePoint are no longer available. Table 12-1 gives a summary of features that are deprecated and removed from SharePoint Server 2019.

Table 12-1. *Removed and Deprecated Features in SharePoint Server 2019*

Feature	Status
PowerPivot management dashboard	Removed
PowerPivot Gallery	Removed
Power Pivot for SharePoint	Removed
Power View	Removed
BISM file connections	Removed
PerformancePoint – Decomposition Trees	Removed
Scheduled workbook data refresh	Removed
Workbook as a data source	Removed
SQL Server Reporting Services Integrated Mode	Removed
PerformancePoint	Deprecated

© Vlad Catrinescu and Trevor Seward 2019
V. Catrinescu and T. Seward, *Deploying SharePoint 2019*, https://doi.org/10.1007/978-1-4842-4526-2_12

While some features have been deprecated, we can still publish Business Intelligence reports in SharePoint to integrate important reports, with the rest of our digital workplace. Let's look at the two main options!

Configuring SQL Server Reporting Services

While SQL Server Reporting Services (SSRS) – Integrated Mode has been removed, you can still install SSSRS in Native mode and integrate it with SharePoint. One major limitation of the web part that Microsoft provides for integrating SSRS into SharePoint 2019 only support classic pages and will not work on Modern Pages found in modern team or Communication Sites. Another requirement is for the Claims to Windows Token Service (C2WTS) needs to be started and configured for Kerberos Constrained delegation.

Tip   You can learn more about configuring Claims to Windows Token Service (C2WTS) and Reporting Services at the following link: `https://docs.microsoft.com/en-us/sql/reporting-services/install-windows/claims-to-windows-token-service-c2wts-and-reporting-services?view=sql-server-2017`.

Microsoft SQL Server 2017 Reporting Services can be downloaded from the Microsoft Download Center at `www.microsoft.com/en-us/download/details.aspx?id=55252`. After the binaries are downloaded, open the executable and click Install Reporting Services as seen in Figure 12-1.

Figure 12-1. *SQL Server 2017 Reporting Services Splash Screen*

Installing the SQL Server 2017 Reporting Services Server is quite easy and only requires a few clicks as well as the product key which can be obtained from your licensing center. Once the binary installation is done, you might have to reboot the server as you can see in Figure 12-2.

Figure 12-2. *Reboot Warning*

Once the server has been rebooted, you need to open the Report Server Configuration Manager and configure the SQL Report Server as seen in Figure 12-3.

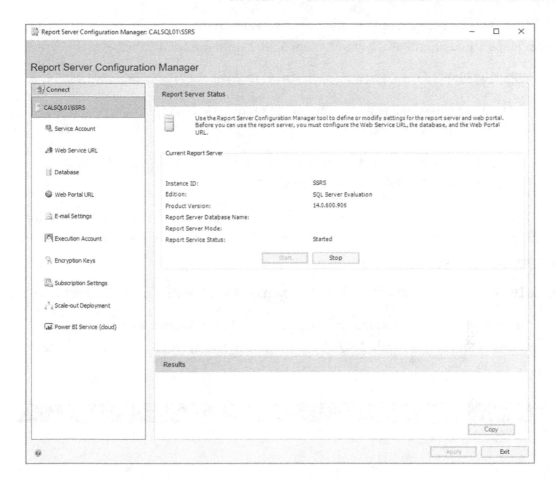

Figure 12-3. *SQL Report Server Configuration Manager*

Since this book focuses on SharePoint, we will not go through all the different possible configurations of SSRS in Native mode. Before moving on, you need to make sure that the SSRS server is up and running, and both Web Service and Web Portal URLs can be accessed from clients and SharePoint Servers. We also recommend configuring SSRS Web Services and Web Portal URLs to use https.

The next task will be to install the Report Viewer farm solution on our farm. Since this will be deployed as a farm solution, it's recommended to do the installation during a maintenance period.

Note   The Microsoft Report Viewer Web Part for Microsoft SharePoint can be downloaded from the Microsoft Download Center at www.microsoft.com/en-us/download/details.aspx?id=55949.

Once you download the WSP file on the server, run the following PowerShell cmdlet from an elevated SharePoint Management Shell to add the farm solution to the farm:

```
Add-SPSolution -LiteralPath "{path to file}\ReportViewerWebPart.wsp"
```

Next up, we will install the solution on the required Web Applications with the PowerShell cmdlet as follows:

```
Install-SPSolution -Identity ReportViewerWebPart.wsp -GACDeployment
-WebApplication {URL to web application}
```

You can then enable the *Report Viewer Web Part* manually on each Site Collection in the Web Application, or you can also do it via PowerShell with the Enable-SPFeature PowerShell cmdlet as seen in the following:

```
Enable-SPFeature -identity "ReportViewerWebPart" -URL {Site Collection URL}
```

Once the feature is activated, you will have the Report Viewer webpart available in a new Web Part category called SQL Server Reporting Services (Native mode) as seen in Figure 12-4.

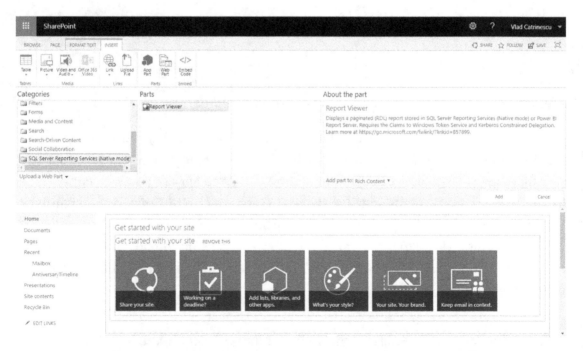

Figure 12-4. *The Report Viewer Web Part*

Once the Web Part is added, from the Web Part properties seen in Figure 12-5, you need to add the information for both the SSRS server as well as the report, and any other information such as the Parameters that is needed in order to correctly display the report.

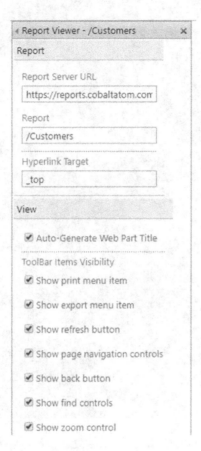

Figure 12-5. *Configuring the Report Viewer Web Part*

That is it for SQL Server Reporting Services in Native Mode! Now let's look at Power BI Server.

Power BI Server

Another option to create Business Intelligence reports on-premises is Power BI Server, a version of Microsoft's Power BI service from Office 365 that runs completely On-Premises. Installing Power BI Server is very similar to SQL Server Reporting Services and shares most of the same configurations. Once installed, it will require a server reboot as seen in Figure 12-6.

Figure 12-6. *Installing Power BI Report Server*

Once configured, users can use Power BI Desktop to create beautiful and responsive reports and publish them in Power BI Report Server. In SharePoint, you can use the Embed Web Part in Modern Sites or the Content Editor in Classic sites to embed a Power BI Report iframe inside a SharePoint page. In Figure 12-7, I use the following iframe code in order to embed a PowerBI Report in a modern SharePoint Communication Site using the Embed Web Part:

```
<iframe width="800" height="600" src="https://calsql02/Reports/powerbi/
FIrstReport?rs:Embed=true" frameborder="0" allowFullScreen="true"></iframe>
```

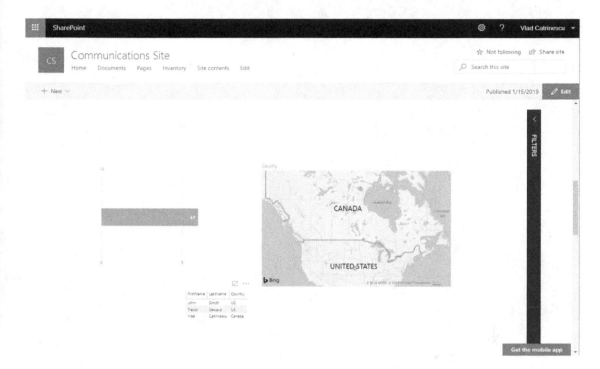

Figure 12-7. *Power BI Server Report inside SharePoint Server 2019*

The embed web part in modern SharePoint sites only supports secured iframes, so your Power BI Report Server needs to be configured with HTTPS and both the SharePoint farm and clients in the organization need to trust the certificate.

Next Steps

In this chapter, we have learned what Business Intelligence services have been removed from SharePoint Server 2019, as well as learned how to configure SQL Server Reporting Services in Native mode and how to embed Power BI Server reports in modern SharePoint Sites! In the next chapter, we will learn how to create Web Applications and Site Collections.

CHAPTER 13

Creating Web Applications and Site Collections

In previous chapters, we have learned how to create Service Applications in order to enable additional functionality for our users. In this chapter, we will learn how to create Web Applications and Path-based as well as Host Named Site Collections and how to customize Alternate Access Mappings, create Content Databases for our Site Collections, and enable Fast Site Collection Creation.

SharePoint Web Architecture

When talking about SharePoint sites, we usually talk about three different levels: Web Applications, Site Collections, and Webs. The first two are actually simply containers; as there is no content stored directly in the Web Application and Site Collection, all the content is stored in the actual Web, which can be the root Web of your Site Collection.

The Web Applications can only be created by SharePoint Administrators who have Farm Administrator privileges as well as Local Administrator permissions on the SharePoint Servers. Creating a Web Application will create a new site in IIS on every server running the Microsoft SharePoint Foundation Web Application service, as well as a new database in SQL. While two SharePoint Web Applications can be hosted in the same IIS Application Pool, they cannot have the same URL or be hosted in the same database. A Web Application can have one, or many Content Databases attached to it. All the Site Collections created in that Web Application will go to one of those Content Databases. Every Web Application needs to have a root Site Collection, which is a Site Collection with the same URL as the Web Application. This is not created automatically, but is a requirement for supportability and stability of your SharePoint system. A Site Collection can be placed into its own Content Database and can be moved between

V. Catrinescu and T. Seward, *Deploying SharePoint 2019*, https://doi.org/10.1007/978-1-4842-4526-2_13

content databases that are attached in the same Web Application. Under the site collection, we find Webs. Those Webs can either be at the root of the Site Collection, meaning they have the same URL as the Site Collection, or they can be a subsite of the Root Web. Those Webs cannot be moved in a different Content Database individually; they all reside in the same Site Collection container. In Figure 13-1, you can see en example SharePoint Web Architecture.

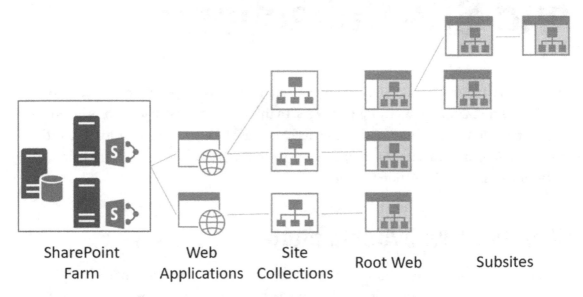

Figure 13-1. *SharePoint Web Architecture*

Modern Sites and the Flat Architecture

If you have followed the latest news in Office 365, you should already have a good base of knowledge around Modern SharePoint Team Sites and Communication Sites. With Modern SharePoint sites, Microsoft recommends only staying at the Site Collection level and not creating any subsites at all, as they aren't as flexible as Site Collections. However, in Office 365, the Hub Site concept allows us to "tie" Site Collections together and share the same branding, security and navigation in multiple Site Collections. Sadly, the Hub Site concept is not available in SharePoint Server 2019, at least at launch, making the design of your modern Information Architecture more difficult. The decision to go with a standard or a flat information architecture will ultimately rely on your business requirements.

Not that we know a bit more of the architecture behind, let's start creating Web Applications in SharePoint 2019.

Web Applications

Web Applications in SharePoint 2019 can be created either from the SharePoint Central Administration, or by PowerShell. Before creating a Web Application, you need to know the business requirements for creating that Web Application and have that information ready. Since Web Applications consume significant resources on the SharePoint server, it is recommended to keep the number of Web Applications to a minimum. According to the Software boundaries and limits for SharePoint Server 2019, there is a supported limit of 20 Web Applications per SharePoint farm.

You will first need the information for the IIS Site seen in Figure 13-2.

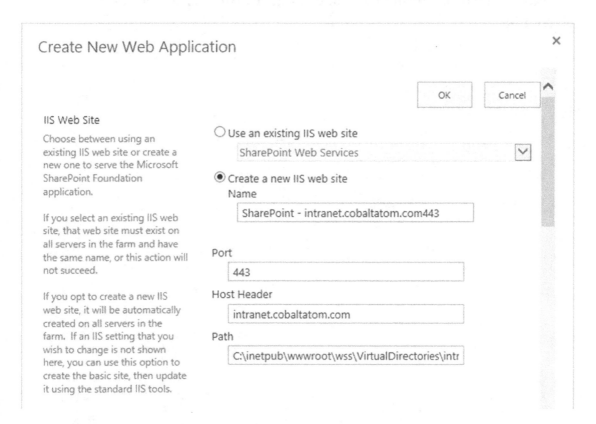

Figure 13-2. *IIS Web Site information when creating a new Web Application*

- **URL of the Web Application**

  This will be the host header of the web application, for example intranet.company.com. This information should be taken from the business requirements and can be changed later if needed.

- **Port**

  The port that the site will be accessed on. Usually port 80 for sites on HTTP and port 443 for sites using HTTPS. While it's possible to choose any port, we recommend keeping either 80 or 443 for an improved user experience, as users won't have to specify the port when entering the URL when using those two. You can have multiple Web Applications using the same port.

In the next portion of the Web Application creation process, you will need to enter the information on the Security and Authentication of the Web Application as seen in Figure 13-3.

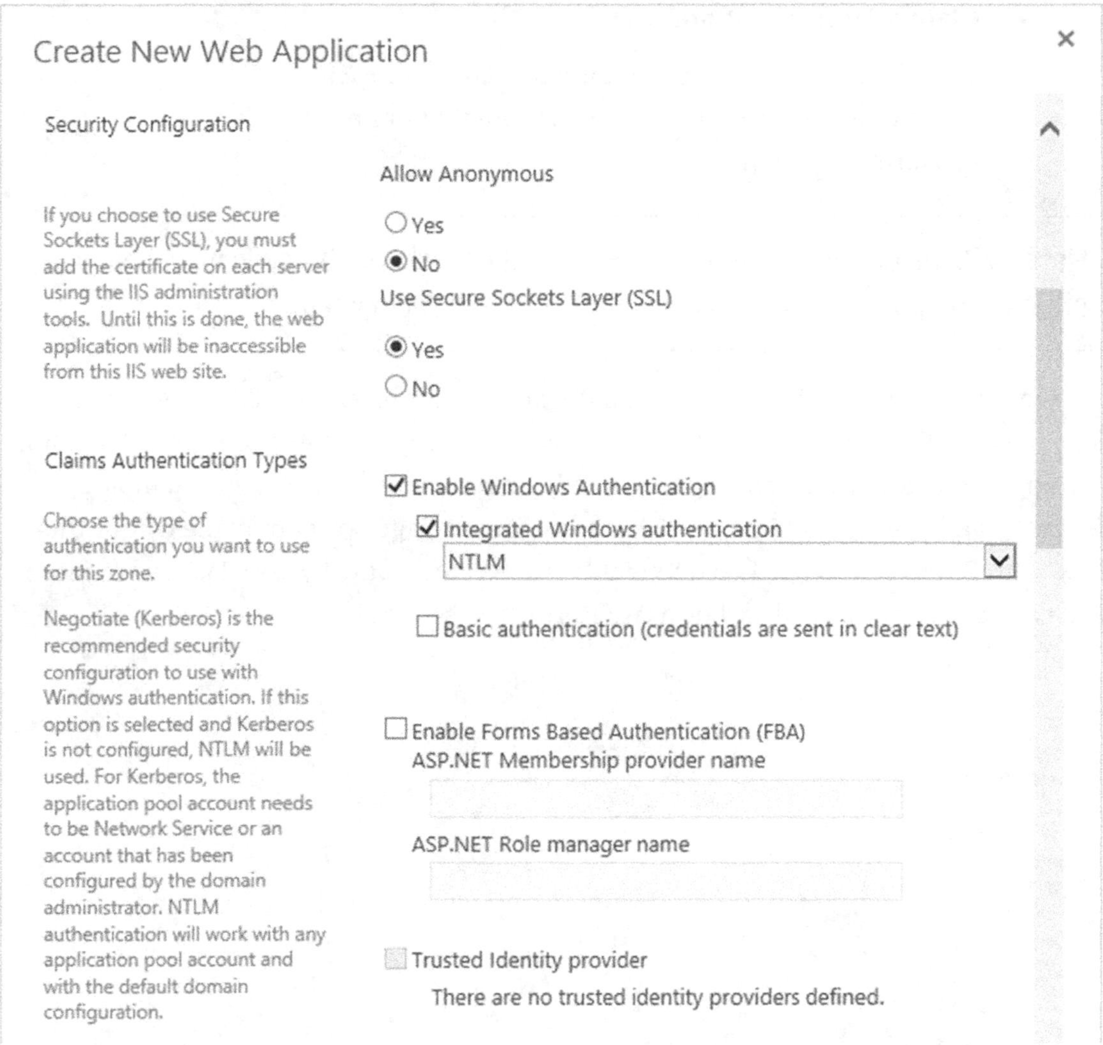

Create New Web Application   ✕

Security Configuration

If you choose to use Secure Sockets Layer (SSL), you must add the certificate on each server using the IIS administration tools. Until this is done, the web application will be inaccessible from this IIS web site.	**Allow Anonymous** ◯ Yes ⦿ No **Use Secure Sockets Layer (SSL)** ⦿ Yes ◯ No

Claims Authentication Types
 	
Choose the type of authentication you want to use for this zone.
 	
Negotiate (Kerberos) is the recommended security configuration to use with Windows authentication. If this option is selected and Kerberos is not configured, NTLM will be used. For Kerberos, the application pool account needs to be Network Service or an account that has been configured by the domain administrator. NTLM authentication will work with any application pool account and with the default domain configuration.
	☑ Enable Windows Authentication
	    ☑ Integrated Windows authentication
	    `NTLM                                    ▾`
	
	    ☐ Basic authentication (credentials are sent in clear text)
	
	☐ Enable Forms Based Authentication (FBA)
	ASP.NET Membership provider name
	
	ASP.NET Role manager name
	
	▢ Trusted Identity provider
	    There are no trusted identity providers defined.

Figure 13-3. *Security Configuration Information when creating a new Web Application*

- **Allow Anonymous**

    Select Yes if you want this Web Application to serve a public site, where users will not have to log in to see information.

- **Use Secure Sockets Layer (SSL)**

    Select Yes if your Web Application will use HTTPS.

- **Claims Authentication Types**

  This is the authentication method that your users will use to authenticate to SharePoint. Those possibilities have been explained in Chapter 4.

Note   We recommend using SSL throughout on every Web Applications that you create to increase the security of your SharePoint deployment.

On the next part of the Web Application creation process, we need to specify the Sign in Page URL as well as the Public URL as seen in Figure 13-4. The Sign in Page URL would be changed when creating a custom login page for your users, for example an Extranet, and you want them to use this personalized page rather than the Out-of-the-Box SharePoint login page. The Public URL will be automatically populated from the Host Header you specified earlier, as well as the SSL checkbox.

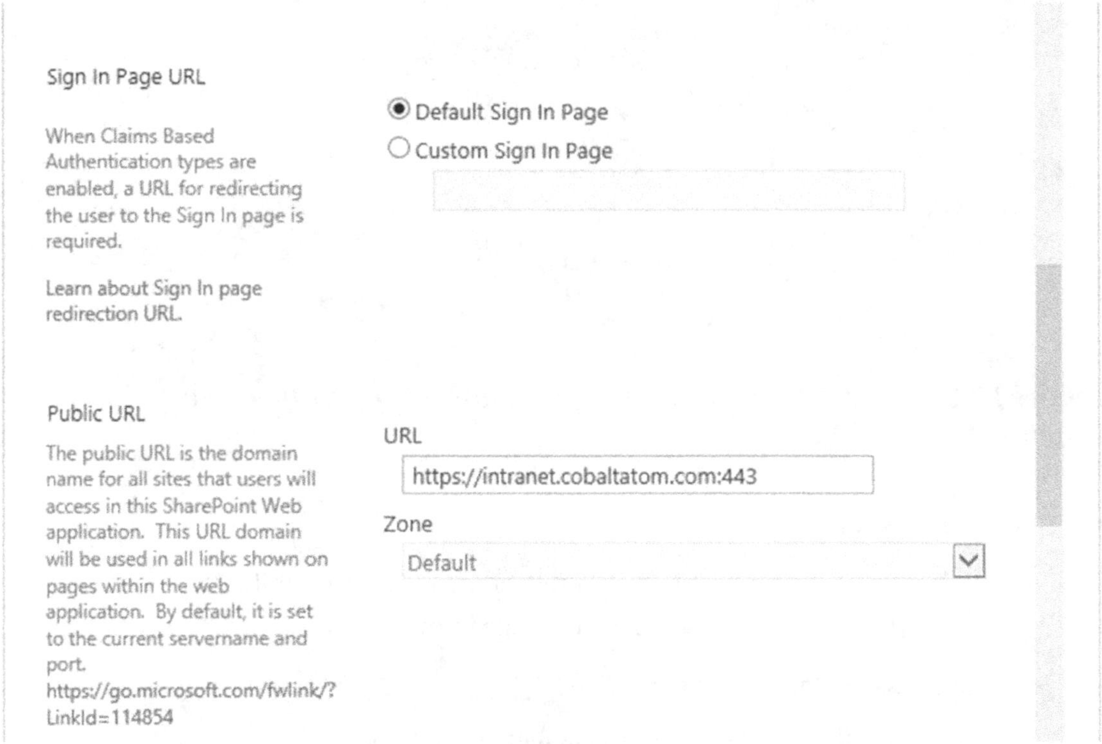

Sign In Page URL

When Claims Based Authentication types are enabled, a URL for redirecting the user to the Sign In page is required.

Learn about Sign In page redirection URL.

◉ Default Sign In Page
◯ Custom Sign In Page

Public URL

The public URL is the domain name for all sites that users will access in this SharePoint Web application. This URL domain will be used in all links shown on pages within the web application. By default, it is set to the current servername and port.
https://go.microsoft.com/fwlink/?
LinkId=114854

URL

https://intranet.cobaltatom.com:443

Zone

Default

Figure 13-4.   *Sign in Page URL and Public URL*

We will then need to select if we create a new Web Application Pool for this Web Application, or use an existing one. Unless you have specific business or security requirements to create a new application pool, we suggest using the same one as the rest of your Web Applications. In Figure 13-5, we selected the existing *SharePoint* Application pool, which runs under the *LAB\S-Web* account.

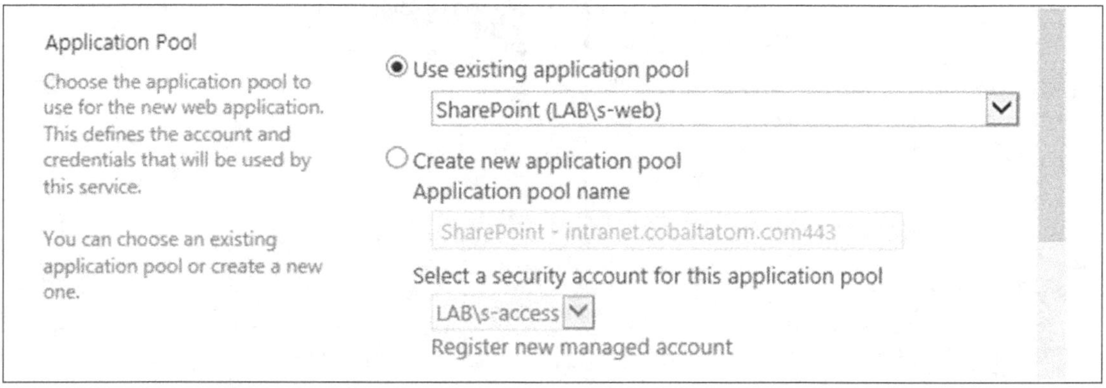

Figure 13-5. *Application Pool Selection*

The Next Step is to enter the information about the Database Server and database name as seen in Figure 13-6. The Database Server will be automatically populated with your main SQL Server from your farm configuration. The Failover Server is only required when using SQL Mirroring and not required when using AlwaysOn Availability Groups or SQL Server Clustering. In both AlwaysOn Availability Groups and Mirroring, you must manually add the database to the secondary replica or Availability Group after it has been created.

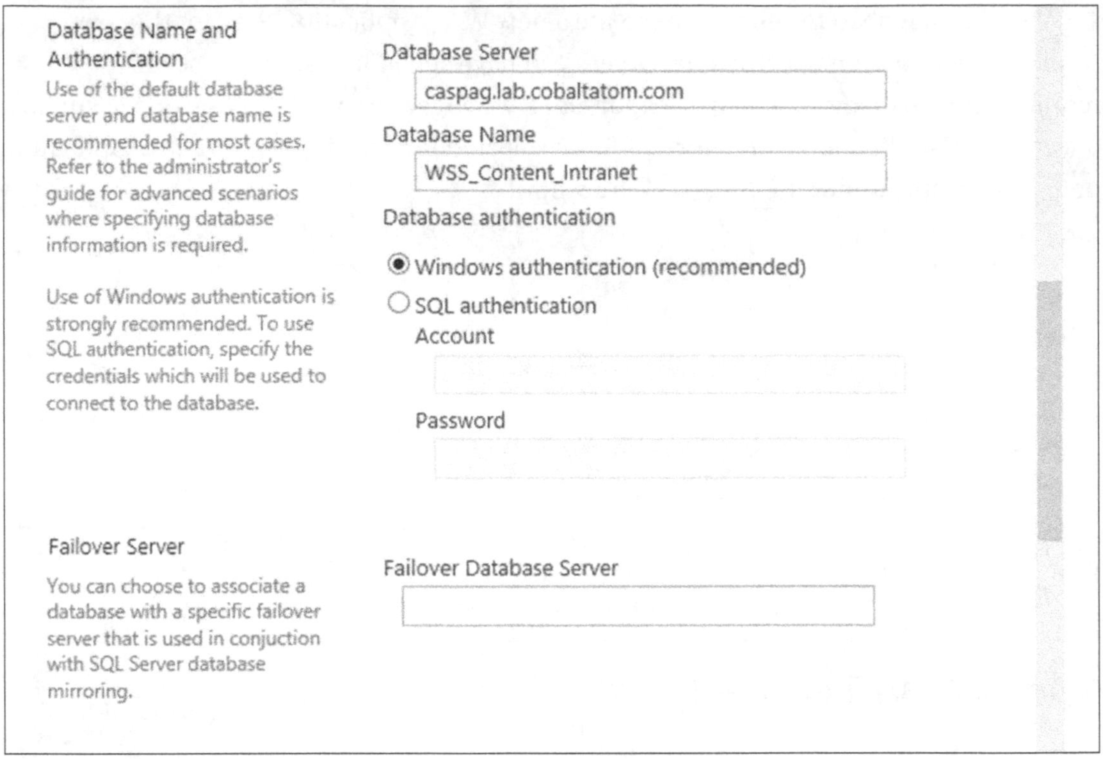

Database Name and Authentication

Use of the default database server and database name is recommended for most cases. Refer to the administrator's guide for advanced scenarios where specifying database information is required.

Use of Windows authentication is strongly recommended. To use SQL authentication, specify the credentials which will be used to connect to the database.

Database Server

caspag.lab.cobaltatom.com

Database Name

WSS_Content_Intranet

Database authentication

● Windows authentication (recommended)

○ SQL authentication

Account

Password

Failover Server

You can choose to associate a database with a specific failover server that is used in conjuction with SQL Server database mirroring.

Failover Database Server

Figure 13-6. *Database Information for the Web Application*

The Final step to create the Web Application is to select the Service Application Connections. Those are what Service Applications will serve this Web Application. By default, the Web Application will be connected to the Default proxy group; however, you can select custom, and only select the Service Applications you want for this Web Application as seen in Figure 13-7.

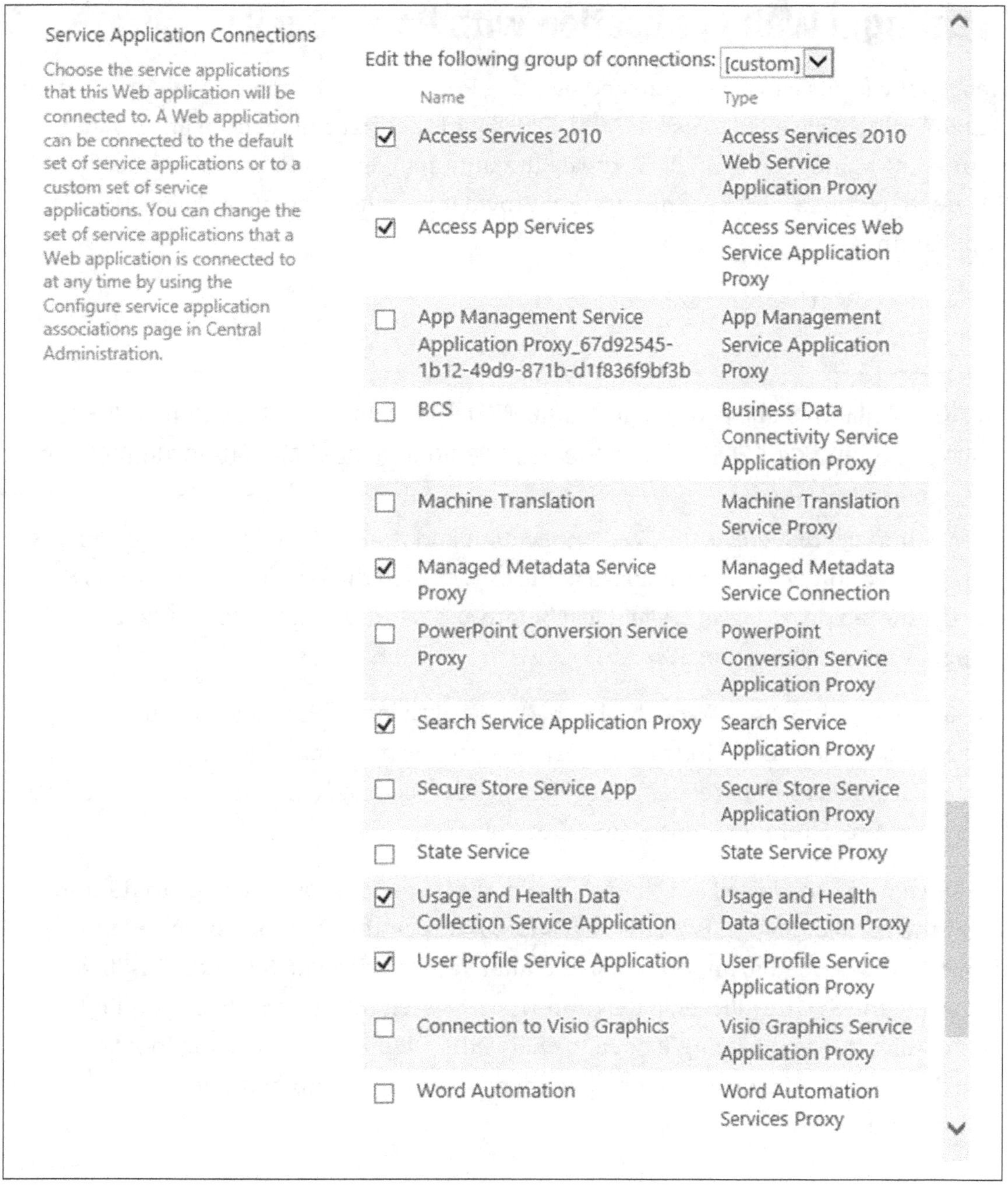

Service Application Connections

Choose the service applications that this Web application will be connected to. A Web application can be connected to the default set of service applications or to a custom set of service applications. You can change the set of service applications that a Web application is connected to at any time by using the Configure service application associations page in Central Administration.

Edit the following group of connections: [custom] ⌄

	Name	Type
☑	Access Services 2010	Access Services 2010 Web Service Application Proxy
☑	Access App Services	Access Services Web Service Application Proxy
☐	App Management Service Application Proxy_67d92545-1b12-49d9-871b-d1f836f9bf3b	App Management Service Application Proxy
☐	BCS	Business Data Connectivity Service Application Proxy
☐	Machine Translation	Machine Translation Service Proxy
☑	Managed Metadata Service Proxy	Managed Metadata Service Connection
☐	PowerPoint Conversion Service Proxy	PowerPoint Conversion Service Application Proxy
☑	Search Service Application Proxy	Search Service Application Proxy
☐	Secure Store Service App	Secure Store Service Application Proxy
☐	State Service	State Service Proxy
☑	Usage and Health Data Collection Service Application	Usage and Health Data Collection Proxy
☑	User Profile Service Application	User Profile Service Application Proxy
☐	Connection to Visio Graphics	Visio Graphics Service Application Proxy
☐	Word Automation	Word Automation Services Proxy

Figure 13-7. Service Application Connections

After clicking OK, the Web Application will be created.

Creating a Web Application with PowerShell

Web Applications can also be created by using PowerShell. To create a Web Application via PowerShell, we need to use the New-SPWebApplication cmdlet from an elevated SharePoint Management Shell. To create the Intranet Web Application, we would first need to create a New Authentication Provider in order to create a Claims Web Application.

```
$ap = New-SPAuthenticationProvider
```

Note   While it is still possible to create Web Application in classic authentication mode in SharePoint 2019, this mode has been deprecated and not recommended.

We then need to create the Web Application and give it the Name, HostHeader, URL, Port, Application Pool, and Database name as we did in the User Interface. We also specify the $ap provider we created just before and use the SecureSocketsLayer switch to specify that it will run on SSL.

```
New-SPWebApplication -Name "Cobalt Atom Intranet" -HostHeader "intranet.
cobaltatom.com" -URL "https://intranet.cobaltatom.com" -Port 443
-ApplicationPool "SharePoint"  -AuthenticationProvider $ap  -DatabaseName
"WSS_Content_Intranet" -SecureSocketsLayer
```

Since we have created a Web Application that uses SSL, we need to go to IIS, and select the certificate for this Web Application. If this certificate is not imported into IIS yet, you will need to import it first and afterward from the IIS Site, Edit Bindings, and select the SSL Certificate in the drop-down as seen in Figure 13-8. Depending of your configurations, you might need to enable the "Require Server Name Indication" checkbox. Server Name Indication allows you to host sites with multiple SSL Certificates, on the same IP.

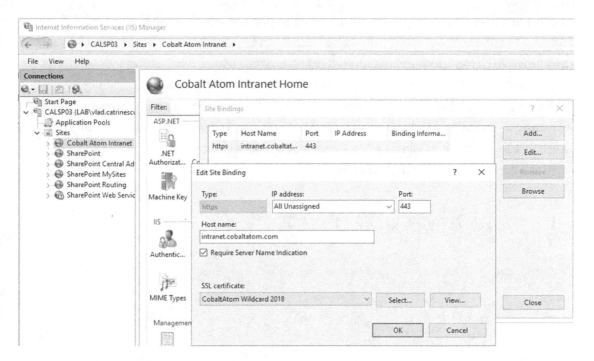

Figure 13-8. *Edit Bindings in IIS*

Note   This needs to be done on all the servers running the Foundation Web Application Service. In a MinRole Farm configuration, this service runs on all the roles except the standalone Search.

Furthermore, if you haven't already, make sure to add this new entry to your company DNS as well as configure your load balancer if you have multiple Web Front Ends. With our Web Application created, let's see how we can add other URLs to this Web Application.

Alternate Access Mappings

SharePoint includes a feature called Alternate Access Mappings which allows you to create multiple URLs for the same Web Application. An alternative to Alternate Access Mappings would be Host Named Site Collections, which we will cover later in this chapter. Common uses for Alternate Access Mappings are to allow users from the internal company network to access the intranet by simply using `https://intranet`, but forcing users accessing from the Internet to use the FQDN, which is `https://intranet.cobaltatom.com`. From a User Experience point of view, it's preferable to have the same URL from both inside and outside the organization.

To create an Alternate Access Mapping from Central Administration, navigate to the Application Management page and choose "Configure Alternate Access Mappings." SharePoint will show you all the Alternate Access Mappings from all the Web Applications as seen in Figure 13-9. By using the top right drop-down, you can select only the Web Application that you wish to view.

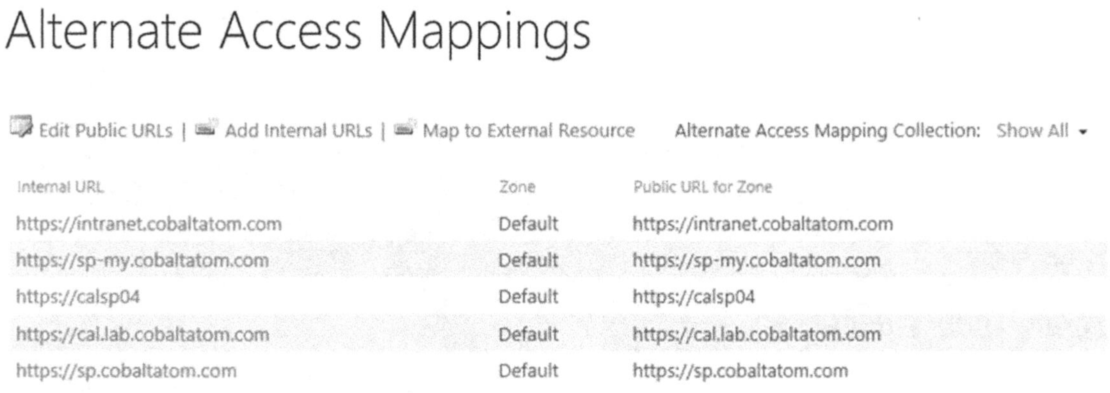

Alternate Access Mappings

Internal URL	Zone	Public URL for Zone
https://intranet.cobaltatom.com	Default	https://intranet.cobaltatom.com
https://sp-my.cobaltatom.com	Default	https://sp-my.cobaltatom.com
https://calsp04	Default	https://calsp04
https://cal.lab.cobaltatom.com	Default	https://cal.lab.cobaltatom.com
https://sp.cobaltatom.com	Default	https://sp.cobaltatom.com

Edit Public URLs | Add Internal URLs | Map to External Resource   Alternate Access Mapping Collection: Show All ▾

Figure 13-9. *Alternate Access Mappings*

There are two types of Alternate Access Mappings that we can add in SharePoint Server 2019:

- **Internal URL**

  The Internal URL is simply an alias for the same site. For example, you could call me Vlad, or Vlad Catrinescu, and I will answer to both names, since I know you are talking to me. However, it's the same person (Vlad Catrinescu) that will answer back to you. When creating an internal SharePoint URL, users will be able to access the SharePoint site by typing this URL in the browser; however, they will be redirected to the Public URL of the Web Application.

- **Public URL**

    A public URL is another URL for the Web Application. For
    example, I would have an identity Vlad Catrinescu and another
    one John Smith. Depending on what name you call, still the same
    person will answer; however, the identity displayed, in our case
    the URL, will be the one you called. Every URL that a user sees in
    his browser should be registered as a Public URL. An alternative
    to creating Public URLs, which will also allow us to change
    authentication modes, is extending the Web Application, which
    we cover a bit later in this chapter.

    To create a new public URL or change existing ones, use the "Edit
    Public URLs" button at the top right. SharePoint offers five Zones
    for five different URLs. There is no technical difference between the
    Intranet, Internet, Custom and Extranet zones. The exception here
    is the Default zone, which is used internally by SharePoint. One
    example is Search, where in order to get results displayed with the
    correct URL, you absolutely need to crawl the Default Public URL of
    the Web Application. In Figure 13-10, we have added a second public
    URL https://publishing.cobaltatom.com in the Intranet Zone.

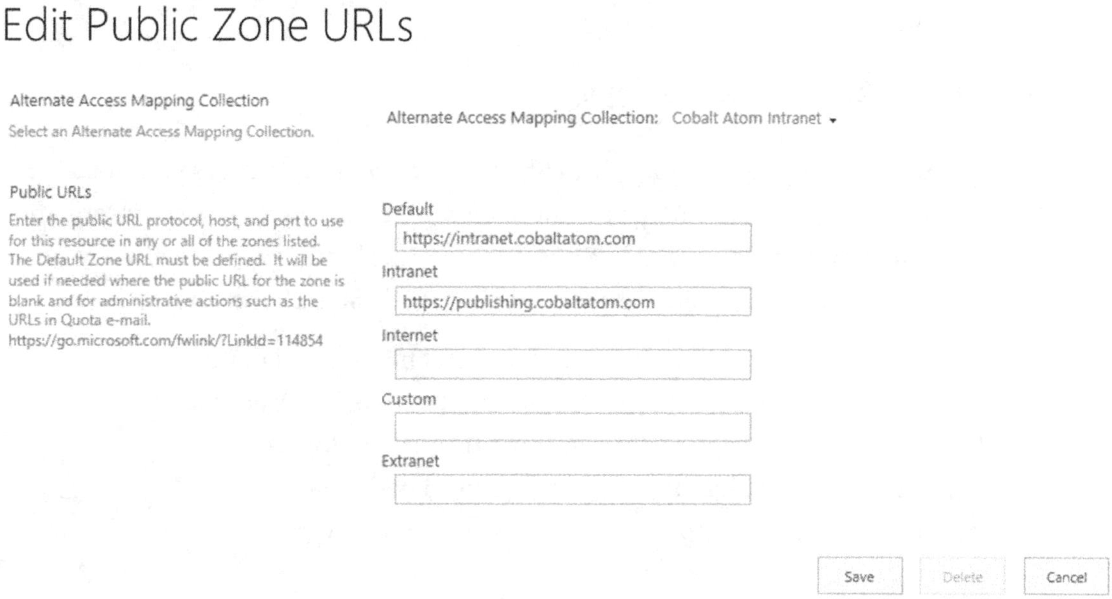

Edit Public Zone URLs

Alternate Access Mapping Collection

Select an Alternate Access Mapping Collection.

Alternate Access Mapping Collection: Cobalt Atom Intranet ▾

Public URLs

Enter the public URL protocol, host, and port to use
for this resource in any or all of the zones listed.
The Default Zone URL must be defined. It will be
used if needed where the public URL for the zone is
blank and for administrative actions such as the
URLs in Quota e-mail.
https://go.microsoft.com/fwlink/?LinkId=114854

Default

https://intranet.cobaltatom.com

Intranet

https://publishing.cobaltatom.com

Internet

Custom

Extranet

Save   Delete   Cancel

Figure 13-10. *New Public URL*

This can also be done by PowerShell by using the New-SPAlternateURL PowerShell cmdlet from an elevated SharePoint Management Shell. To create a new Public URL as we did in the preceding, we would run the following cmdlet:

```
New-SPAlternateURL -Url https://publishing.cobaltatom.com -Zone "Intranet"
-WebApplication https://intranet.cobaltatom.com
```

To create an Internal URL that would redirect https://intranet to https://intranet.cobaltatom.com, we would still use the New-SPAlternateURL cmdlet, but add the -Internal switch.

```
New-SPAlternateURL -Url https://intranet -Zone "Default" -WebApplication
https://intranet.cobaltatom.com -Internal
```

The result seen in Figure 13-11 will be that this SharePoint Web Application is able to be accessed by those three URLs.

Alternate Access Mappings

Edit Public URLs | Add Internal URLs | Map to External Resource   Alternate Access Mapping Collection: Cobalt Atom Intranet ▾

Internal URL	Zone	Public URL for Zone
https://intranet.cobaltatom.com	Default	https://intranet.cobaltatom.com
https://intranet	Default	https://intranet.cobaltatom.com
https://publishing.cobaltatom.com	Intranet	https://publishing.cobaltatom.com

Figure 13-11. *Alternate Access Mappings*

Alternate Access Mappings only apply to SharePoint, and any changes you make here do not automatically make changes to the Web Application in IIS. Furthermore, the new hostnames also need to be added in DNS. Figure 13-12 better explains where your new URL needs to be resolved, before a user can get to your SharePoint Site.

1. When requesting an URL, that URL must first be resolved in the Domain Name System (DNS). The DNS will tell the browser what IP or server it should go to. Depending on your topology, it will either directly to a SharePoint Server, or to a Load Balancer that will then forward the request to one of your Web Servers.

2. IIS receives the request and looks for a binding that matches. This is why it's important to always make sure to update your URLs not only in SharePoint but in IIS as well.

3. Once IIS matches the request to one of the sites, the request will go to SharePoint, which will match it against one of the Web Applications and return the SharePoint site to the user.

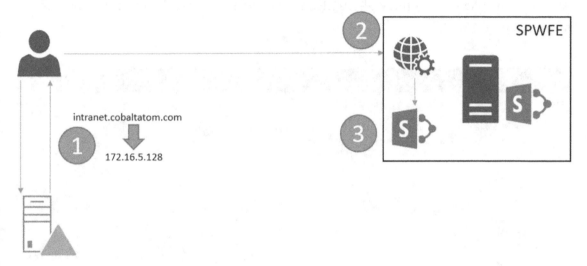

Figure 13-12. *SharePoint Site Resolution*

It's important to remember that whenever you add, or change an URL in SharePoint, the change must be done in all three places: DNS, IIS and SharePoint. Instead of adding multiple Alternate Access Mappings, best practice would be to extend the Web Application.

Extending a Web Application

In the previous section we saw how to add a new Public URL to our Web Application in order to allow users to access it under another name. A different way to achieve the same result, as well as provide more options is to extend the Web Application. When you extend a Web Application, not only you do have a new URL to access that Web Application, but the process also creates a different IIS site, as well as allowing you to set a different authentication method.

Take, for example, a Web Application used for an extranet that internal user's access with `http://extranet` and uses NTLM authentication. Since we don't want external users to have an AD account, we need to enable Form-Based Authentication. By extending the Web Application to `https://extranet.cobaltatom.com` we can get the new URL, as well as enable another form of authentication, in our case Form-Based Authentication.

To extend a Web Application from the Central Administration, from the Web Applications page, select the Web Application you want to extend and click Extend as seen in Figure 13-13.

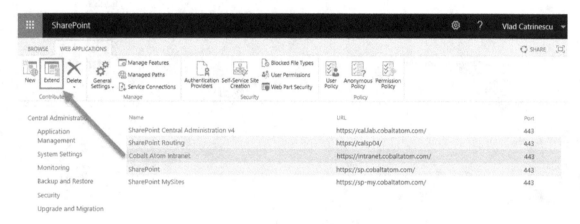

Figure 13-13.   *Extend Web Application*

The Extend screen seen in Figure 13-14 is very similar to the new Web Application. We first need to enter the Port and Host header of the new IIS Web Site.

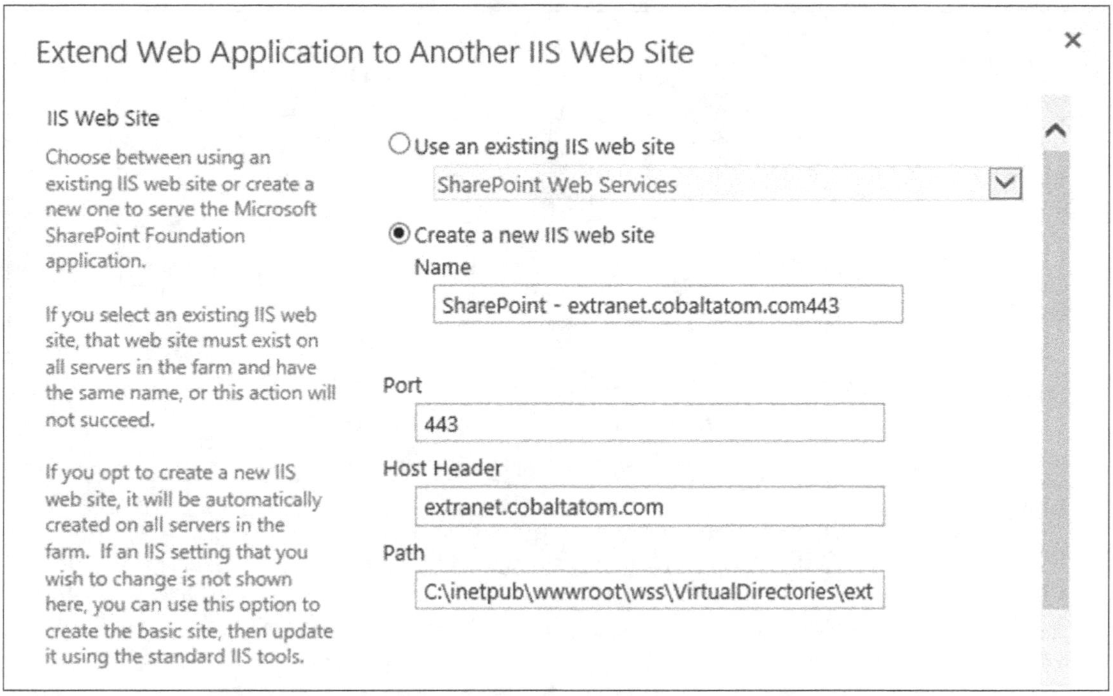

Extend Web Application to Another IIS Web Site   ✕

IIS Web Site

Choose between using an
existing IIS web site or create a
new one to serve the Microsoft
SharePoint Foundation
application.

If you select an existing IIS web
site, that web site must exist on
all servers in the farm and have
the same name, or this action will
not succeed.

If you opt to create a new IIS
web site, it will be automatically
created on all servers in the
farm. If an IIS setting that you
wish to change is not shown
here, you can use this option to
create the basic site, then update
it using the standard IIS tools.

○ Use an existing IIS web site

> SharePoint Web Services   ⌄

◉ Create a new IIS web site
   Name

> SharePoint - extranet.cobaltatom.com443

Port

> 443

Host Header

> extranet.cobaltatom.com

Path

> C:\inetpub\wwwroot\wss\VirtualDirectories\ext

Figure 13-14. *Extend Web Application to another IIS Web Site*

We then need to specify the Security Configuration as well as the Claims
authentication types we want to use. In Figure 13-15 we selected to use SSL, and allow
users to connect to the Web Application with both NTLM and FBA.

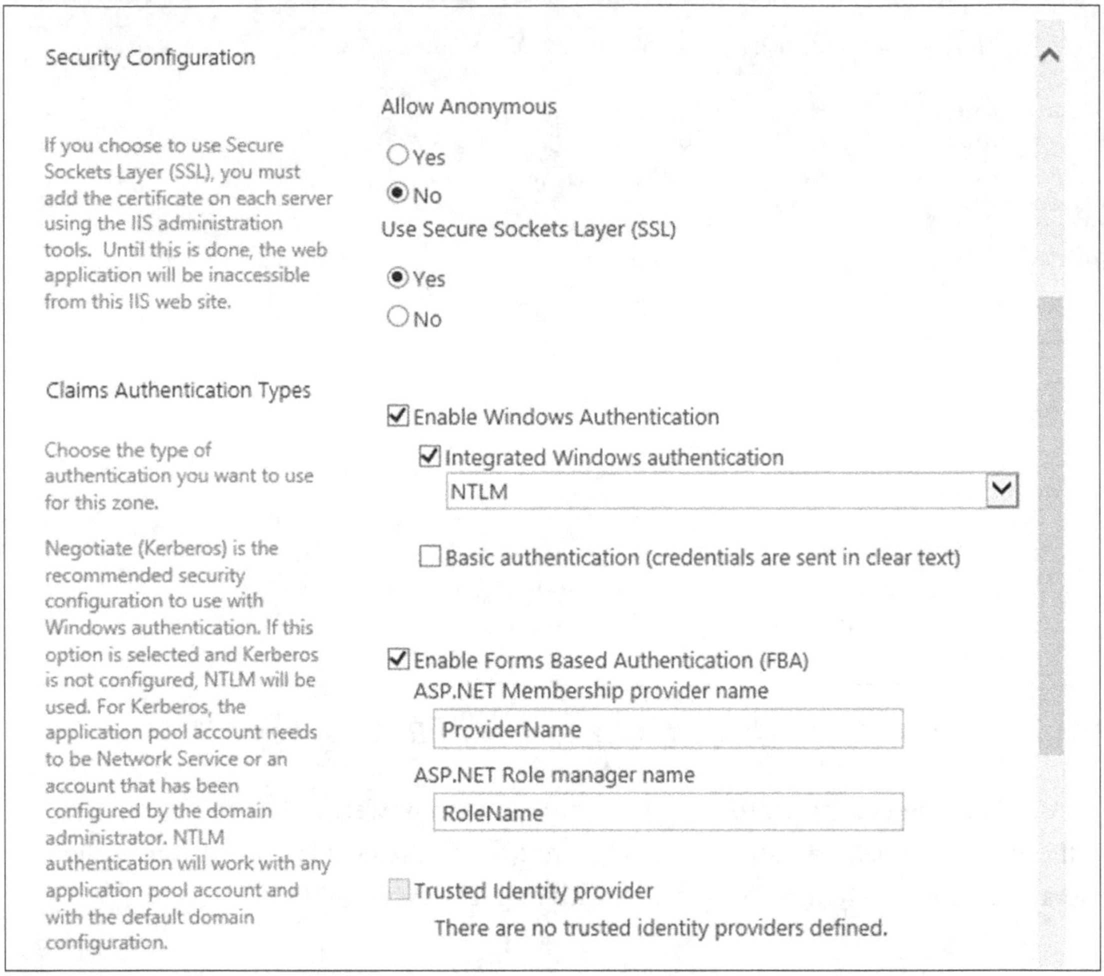

Security Configuration

If you choose to use Secure
Sockets Layer (SSL), you must
add the certificate on each server
using the IIS administration
tools. Until this is done, the web
application will be inaccessible
from this IIS web site.

Allow Anonymous

○ Yes
◉ No

Use Secure Sockets Layer (SSL)

◉ Yes
○ No

Claims Authentication Types

Choose the type of
authentication you want to use
for this zone.

Negotiate (Kerberos) is the
recommended security
configuration to use with
Windows authentication. If this
option is selected and Kerberos
is not configured, NTLM will be
used. For Kerberos, the
application pool account needs
to be Network Service or an
account that has been
configured by the domain
administrator. NTLM
authentication will work with any
application pool account and
with the default domain
configuration.

☑ Enable Windows Authentication
   ☑ Integrated Windows authentication
      | NTLM   ▼ |

   ☐ Basic authentication (credentials are sent in clear text)

☑ Enable Forms Based Authentication (FBA)
ASP.NET Membership provider name
| ProviderName |
ASP.NET Role manager name
| RoleName |

☐ Trusted Identity provider
   There are no trusted identity providers defined.

Figure 13-15. *Extend Web Application Security Configuration*

A new site will be created in IIS with the extranet.cobaltatom.com binding
already there; however, we need to set the certificate manually as well as enter it
in the DNS. To extend a Web Application via PowerShell, we need to run the New-
SPWebApplicationExtension cmdlet from an elevated SharePoint Management Shell. To
extend our Intranet Web Application with the URL https://extranet.cobaltatom.com
on port 443 and using SSL, we would run the following cmdlet:

```
Get-SPWebApplication https://intranet.cobaltatom.com |  New-
SPWebApplicationExtension -Name "Extranet" -URL "https://extranet.
cobaltatom.com"  -SecureSocketsLayer -Zone "Extranet" -HostHeader
"extranet.cobaltatom.com" -Port 443
```

Web Application User Policy

SharePoint allows us to give certain permissions to users, directly at the Web Application level. This is very useful for SharePoint Administrators who need access to all the Site Collections in a Web Application, but don't want to add themselves manually. Those permissions are not seen trough the "Check Permissions" in each Site Collection and apply before any Site Collection permission is applied. SharePoint also uses Web Application policies to give certain accounts permissions to the Web Application. For example, the Search Crawl account has Full Read permissions on every Web Applications in the farm it needs to crawl. There are four available permissions at the Web Application level:

1. **Full Control**

   Full Control to all the Site Collections in the Web Application.

2. **Full Read**

   Can read all the content in the Web Application, but not modify or add content, unless given rights directly in the Site.

3. **Deny Write**

   This policy will not allow the user or group to modify or add any content in the Web Application, even if given rights directly in a SharePoint Site.

4. **Deny All**

   This policy will not allow the user or group to access any site in the Web Application, even if given rights directly in a SharePoint site in that Web Application.

You can also create custom policies in the Web Application Permission Policy; however, it's recommended to only use the default ones if possible.

To add users to the Web Application Policy, from the Web Application page in Central Administration, select the Web Application you want to apply the policy to, and select *User Policy* from the ribbon. A window similar to Figure 13-16 will open, displaying all the current policies for the Web Application.

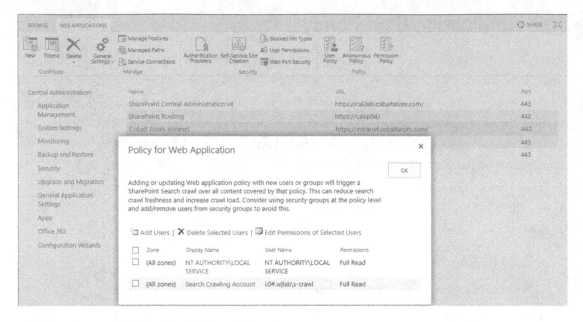

Figure 13-16. *Policy for Web Application*

As noted in Chapter 6, adding or deleting users from the Web Application policies will make the search engine crawl the whole content of the Web Application on the next crawl, in order to recalculate the item Access Control List.

To add a User to the Web Application Policy, click Add Users at the top left of the window and if the Web Application has more than one zone, select the zone you want to apply this policy to. On the next window seen in Figure 13-17, enter the users or groups that you wish to add to the Web Application policy, as well as what permissions you want to give them. The "Account operates as System" checkbox is only recommended for service accounts, as their actions will be marked as "System" in the logs, and not the actual username.

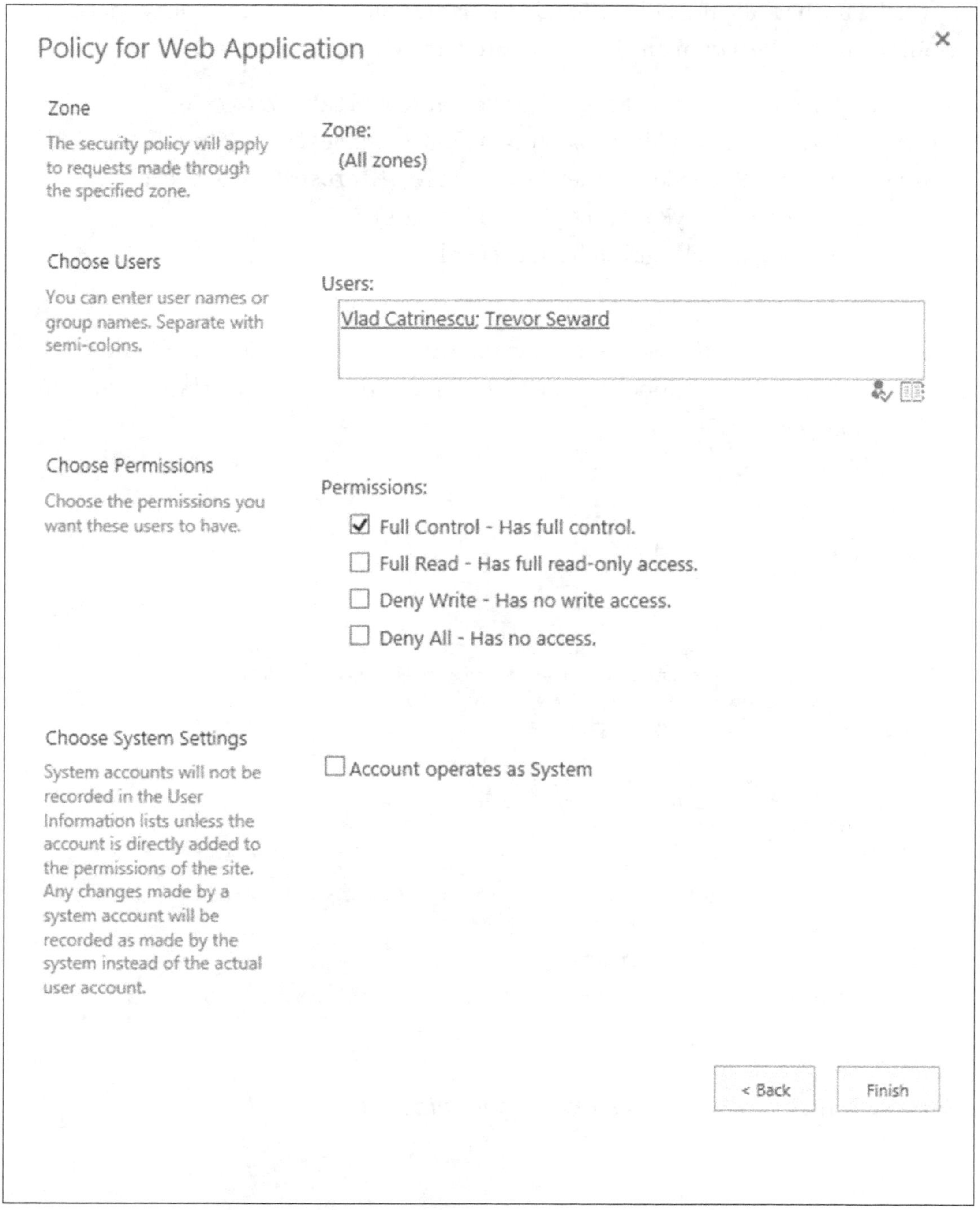

Policy for Web Application   ×

Zone

The security policy will apply   Zone:
to requests made through   (All zones)
the specified zone.

Choose Users

You can enter user names or   Users:
group names. Separate with
semi-colons.   Vlad Catrinescu; Trevor Seward

Choose Permissions

Choose the permissions you   Permissions:
want these users to have.
                                       ☑ Full Control - Has full control.

                                       ☐ Full Read - Has full read-only access.

                                       ☐ Deny Write - Has no write access.

                                       ☐ Deny All - Has no access.

Choose System Settings

System accounts will not be   ☐ Account operates as System
recorded in the User
Information lists unless the
account is directly added to
the permissions of the site.
Any changes made by a
system account will be
recorded as made by the
system instead of the actual
user account.

                                                          < Back   Finish

Figure 13-17. *New Web Application Policy*

Click Finish to add the Policy. To add the same policy via PowerShell, we need to run the following cmdlets from an elevated SharePoint Management Shell:

```
$w = Get-SPWebApplication https://intranet.cobaltatom.com/
$policy = $w.Policies.Add("i:0#.w|LAB\vlad.catrinescu", "SharePoint Admin")
$policyRole = $w.PolicyRoles.GetSpecialRole([Microsoft.SharePoint.
Administration.SPPolicyRoleType]::FullControl)
$policy.PolicyRoleBindings.Add($policyRole)
$w.Update()
```

Where LAB\vlad.catrinescu is the account we want to add, and SharePoint Admin is the display name that will appear in the Web Application Policy. The result of this cmdlet can be seen in Figure 13-18.

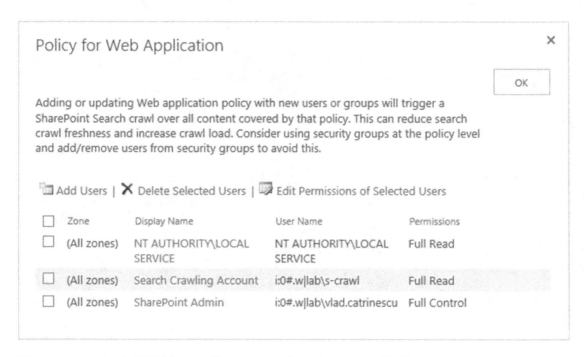

Figure 13-18. *Add Web Application Policy via PowerShell*

Object Cache Accounts

SharePoint publishing sites use two Object Cache Accounts to improve page rendering speeds on publishing pages and reduce load on the SQL Server. Those accounts are often referred to Portal Super User and Portal Super Reader accounts. The Portal Super User account will have Full Control on the Web Application, while the Portal Super Reader account will only have Full Read on the Web Application. SharePoint will use those cache accounts, to create two versions of the object cache, one with the Portal Super Reader account, which will only see published items, and one with the Portal Super User account, which will see both published items and drafts. When a user queries a publishing page, the object cache will check that user's permissions and will return the appropriate cached object depending on if he can see draft items or not. The Object Cache accounts are only needed for Web Applications that will run publishing sites, but there is no harm in setting them on all your Web Applications.

The Portal Super User and Portal Super Reader accounts must be two separate service accounts, and they must not be used to login on the site. We must first add them to the Web Application property bag by using the following cmdlets:

```
$wa = Get-SPWebApplication https://intranet.cobaltatom.com/
$wa.Properties["portalsuperuseraccount"] = "i:0#.w|LAB\s-su"
$wa.Properties["portalsuperreaderaccount"] = "i:0#.w|LAB\s-sr"
$wa.Update()
```

Afterward, we must give them the required permissions. The Super User account needs to have full control at the Web Application level, while the Super Reader must have full read.

```
$w = Get-SPWebApplication https://intranet.cobaltatom.com/
$policy = $w.Policies.Add("i:0#.w|LAB\s-su", "Portal Super User")
$policyRole = $w.PolicyRoles.GetSpecialRole([Microsoft.SharePoint.
Administration.SPPolicyRoleType]::FullControl)
$policy.PolicyRoleBindings.Add($policyRole)
$policy = $w.Policies.Add("i:0#.w|LAB\s-sr", "Portal Super Reader")
$policyRole = $w.PolicyRoles.GetSpecialRole([Microsoft.SharePoint.
Administration.SPPolicyRoleType]::FullRead)
$policy.PolicyRoleBindings.Add($policyRole)
$w.Update()
```

After running those scripts, the accounts will be seen in the Web Application properties as seen in Figure 13-19.

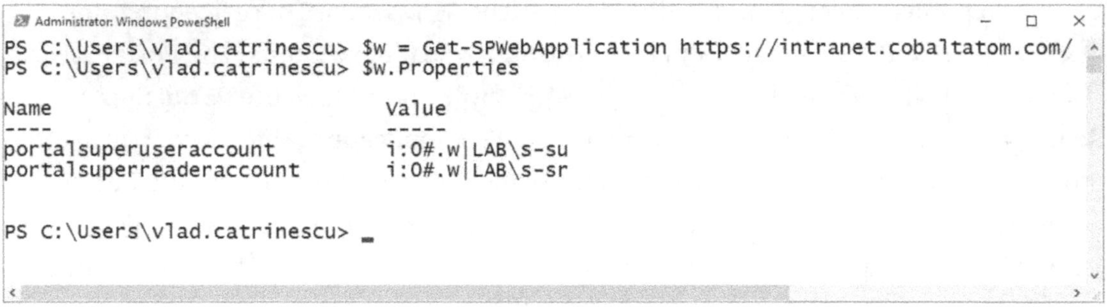

```
Administrator: Windows PowerShell                                          —    □    ×
PS C:\Users\vlad.catrinescu> $w = Get-SPWebApplication https://intranet.cobaltatom.com/
PS C:\Users\vlad.catrinescu> $w.Properties

Name                                Value
----                                -----
portalsuperuseraccount              i:0#.w|LAB\s-su
portalsuperreaderaccount            i:0#.w|LAB\s-sr


PS C:\Users\vlad.catrinescu> _
```

Figure 13-19. *Web Application Properties*

The two Object Cache accounts will also be seen in the Web Application Policy with the required permissions.

Note   In order for the Object Cache Accounts changes to take effect, you will need to perform an IISReset.

Content Databases

A Web Application can have one, or many Content Databases attached to it. By creating multiple content databases, you can isolate Site Collections from one another, making database management easier. To view or create databases from Central Administration, navigate to the Application Management Page, and then click Manage Content Databases. The page seen in Figure 13-20 will show all the databases attached to this Web Application, as well as how many Site Collections they have inside.

Content Databases ⓘ

Add a content database					Web Application:	https://intranet.cobaltatom.com/ ▾	
Database Name	Database Status	Database Read-Only	Current Number of Site Collections	Site Collection Level Warning	Maximum Number of Site Collections	Preferred Timer Server	
WSS_Content_Intranet	Started	No	0	2000	5000		

Figure 13-20. *Content Databases*

To create a new Content Database, click the "Add a Content Database" button on the top left. You will first need to enter the Database Server where to add the database as well as its name. In Figure 13-21, we kept our default database server and named the database WSS_Content_Intranet_2.

Add Content Database ⓘ

Web Application

Select a web application.

Web Application: https://intranet.cobaltatom.com/ ▾

Database Name and Authentication

Use of the default database server and database name is recommended for most cases. Refer to the administrator's guide for advanced scenarios where specifying database information is required.

Use of Windows authentication is strongly recommended. To use SQL authentication, specify the credentials which will be used to connect to the database.

Database Server

caspag.lab.cobaltatom.com

Database Name

WSS_Content_Intranet_2

Database authentication

◉ Windows authentication (recommended)

○ SQL authentication

Account

Password

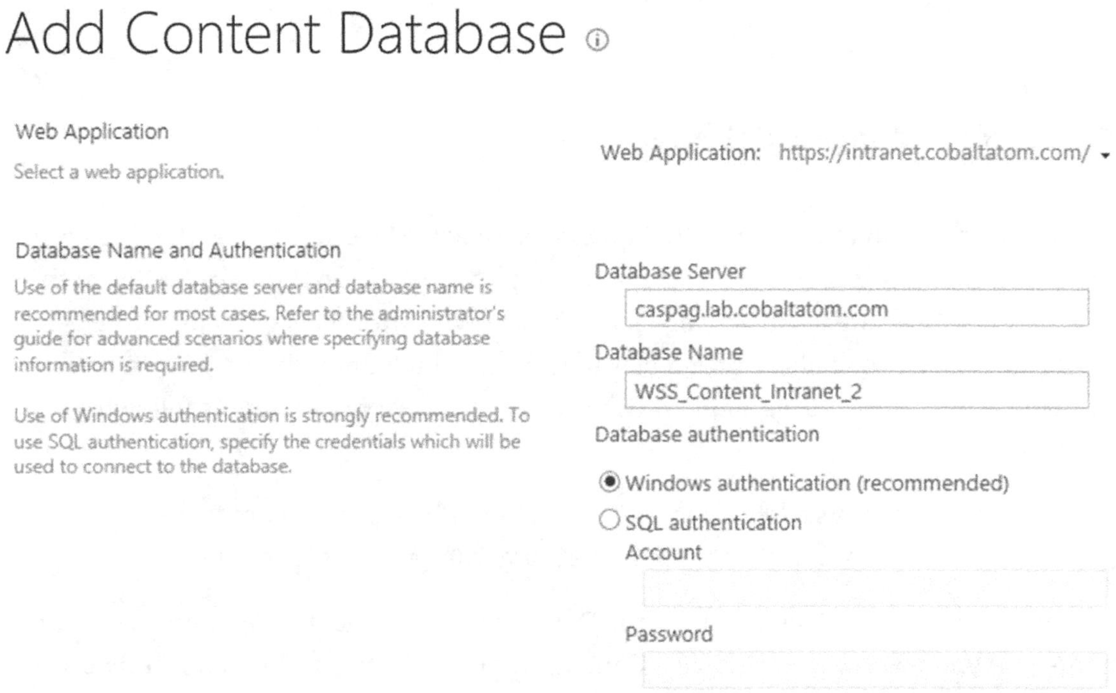

Figure 13-21. *New Content Database Server and Name*

We then need to enter the Failover Database Server if we are running SQL Mirroring. This is not required if you are running SQL Server AlwaysOn Availability groups, or SQL Server Clustering. Finally you will need to enter the maximum number of Site Collections that can be created in this database, as well as a number where a warning event will be generated in the event log. If you set this maximum to the current number of Site Collections in the Content Database, SharePoint will simply not create any more Site Collections in this Content Database. In Figure 13-22, we set the warning at 10 and maximum number at 15.

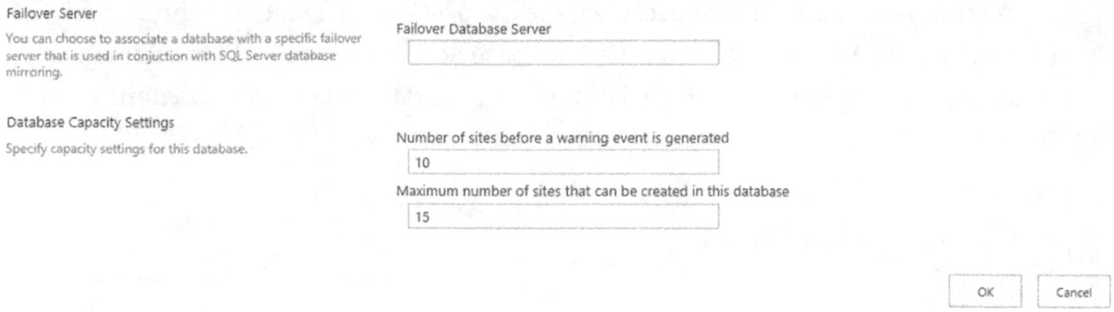

Failover Server

You can choose to associate a database with a specific failover server that is used in conjuction with SQL Server database mirroring.

Failover Database Server

Database Capacity Settings

Specify capacity settings for this database.

Number of sites before a warning event is generated

10

Maximum number of sites that can be created in this database

15

OK   Cancel

Figure 13-22. *Database Capacity Settings*

Simply press on OK to create the Content Database. Make sure to add the database to your Availability group or to the secondary replica if you have High Availability at the SQL tier. The Content Database can also be created via PowerShell by using the New-SPContentDatabase cmdlet from an elevated SharePoint Management Shell. To create a database with the same parameters as the one before, we would run the following PowerShell cmdlet:

```
New-SPContentDatabase "WSS_Content_Intranet_3" -WebApplication https://
intranet.cobaltatom.com/ -WarningSiteCount 10 -MaxSiteCount 15
```

To Edit a Content Database, from the Database Management page, simply click the name and you will get to the Manage Content Database Settings. The Name and Server of the database cannot be changed; however, you can change the status of the database from *Ready* to *Offline* as seen in Figure 13-23. Changing the Database status to Offline, will not actually put the database offline, it will only tell SharePoint not to put any new Site Collections in this database. Furthermore, databases in Offline mode cannot be retrieved trough the Get-SPContentDatabase PowerShell cmdlet, you would have to use the Get-SPDatabase cmdlet to retrieve them. All the existing Site Collections in those databases will work as before.

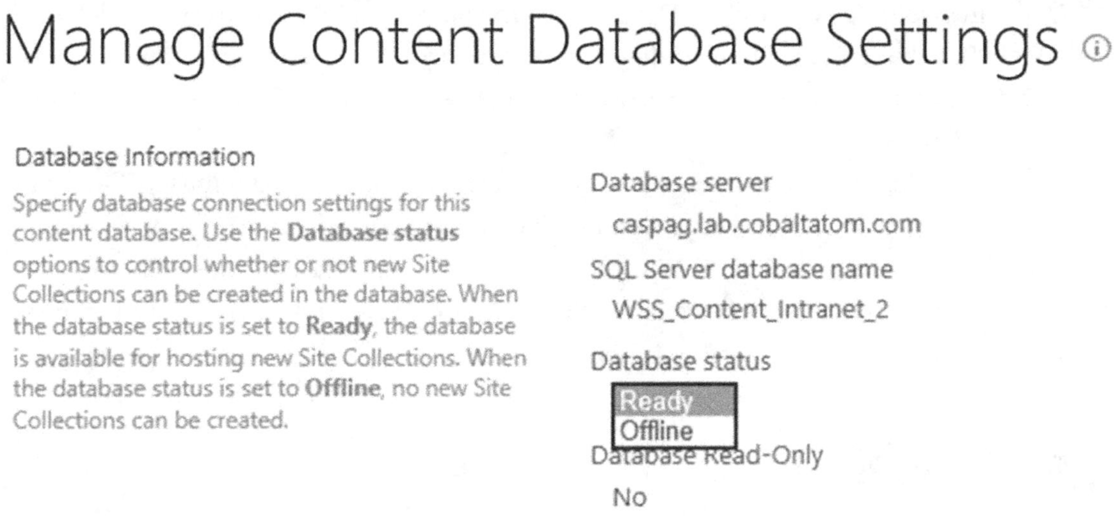

Manage Content Database Settings ⓘ

Database Information

Specify database connection settings for this content database. Use the **Database status** options to control whether or not new Site Collections can be created in the database. When the database status is set to **Ready**, the database is available for hosting new Site Collections. When the database status is set to **Offline**, no new Site Collections can be created.

Database server

   caspag.lab.cobaltatom.com

SQL Server database name

   WSS_Content_Intranet_2

Database status

   Ready
   Offline

Database Read-Only

   No

Figure 13-23. *Database Status*

You can also change the Maximum Number of Site Collections in the database from this page. To Remove a Content Database, check the "Remove Content Database" checkbox seen in Figure 13-24. This will not delete the database, but it will simply detach it from the farm, and all the Site Collections in that database will not be available in the SharePoint farm anymore. The data will still be kept in the database, until you delete it from SQL Server.

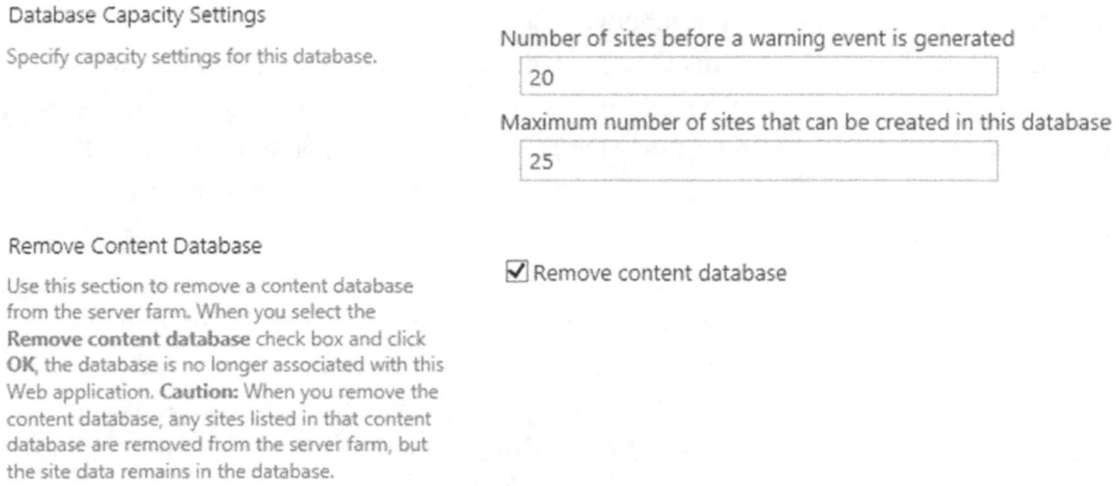

Database Capacity Settings

Specify capacity settings for this database.

Number of sites before a warning event is generated

   20

Maximum number of sites that can be created in this database

   25

Remove Content Database

Use this section to remove a content database from the server farm. When you select the **Remove content database** check box and click **OK**, the database is no longer associated with this Web application. **Caution:** When you remove the content database, any sites listed in that content database are removed from the server farm, but the site data remains in the database.

☑ Remove content database

Figure 13-24. *Remove Content Database*

You can also detach a Content Database from SharePoint by using the `Dismount-SPContentDatabase` PowerShell cmdlet. To remove a Content Database from both SharePoint and delete it from SQL Server, you can use the `Remove-SPContentDatabase` PowerShell cmdlet.

When Site Collections are created without specifying a Content Database, SharePoint will create the Site Collection in the Content Database that is available and has the lowest number of Site Collections inside. With this algorithm, Content Databases will grow evenly. You can also implement a custom Site Creation Provider by using custom code to analyze what type of Site Collection is being created and route it to a certain database.

Site Collections

With our Web Application created and ready, we now need to create Site Collections. There are two strategies to create Site Collections. The first one is called Path-Based Site Collection and is the traditional approach we have used since SharePoint 2010. A Path-Based Site Collection always has the same URL as the Web Application it is under. For example, if my Web Application URL is `https://intranet.cobaltatom.com`, all my Site Collections in that Web Application will start with `https://intranet.cobaltatom.com`. Therefore, if a team asks you to create a Site Collection that is at `https://communications.cobaltatom.com`, you would need to create a new Web Application. Remember that for performance reasons, we should have a maximum of 20 Web Applications, so this approach can be very limited in scalability.

Since SharePoint 2013, Microsoft has encouraged the use of Host Named Site Collections. Host Named Site Collections do not necessarily share the same URL as the Web Application they are in; therefore, I could have my Site Collection with the URL `https://communications.cobaltatom.com` in my `https://intranet.cobaltatom.com` Web Application.

But what is the problem with Web Applications? Web Applications consume a lot more resources on your Web Front End than a Site Collection. In the SharePoint 2019 Software Boundaries and Limits, Microsoft lists 20 as the maximum supported number of Web Applications per SharePoint farm. While having fewer Web Applications and using Host Named Site Collections is definitely better for your server performance, creating and managing Host Named Site Collection is more difficult and a lot less user friendly. We will get more into details in the section covering Host Named Site Collections.

Path-Based Site Collections

Path-Based Site Collections are still the most common Site Collections across On-Premises SharePoint deployments because they are easier to create and manage. To create a Site Collection from Central Administration, navigate to the Application Management page and under Site Collections, click Create Site Collections. On the top of the screen, you need to select in which Web Application you want to create this site collection. You will have to first enter the Title of the Site Collection and optionally the description as well. You then have to choose the URL of your Site Collection. Since our Web Application doesn't have any Site Collections at the root, meaning with the same URL as the Web Application, we can create either a Root Site Collection, or a site collection that is under /sites/url. The Sites part of the URL is what we call a managed path, and we are able to customize those to include sites after /teams/ for example, or even create a site collection that is the (Web Application URL)/HR, for example `https://intranet/HR`. We will look at Managed Paths later in this chapter. In our example seen in Figure 13-25, we will create a root Site Collection with the title Intranet Home.

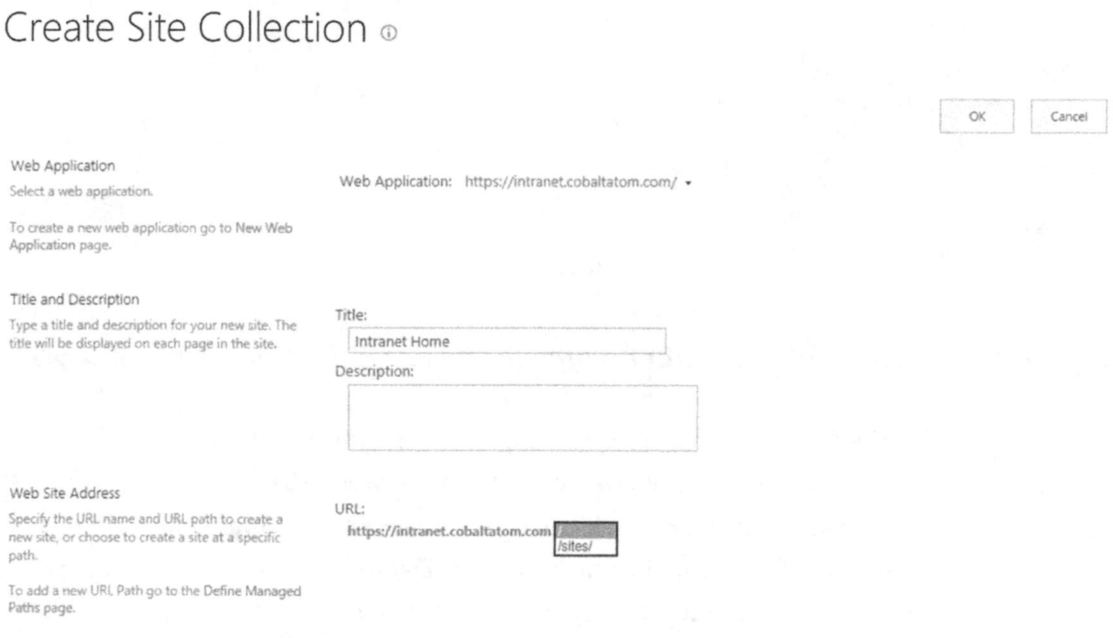

Figure 13-25. New Site Collection

On the second part of the form, you need to select the Template, as well as the Primary and Secondary Site Collection Administrators as seen in Figure 13-26. If you have multiple language packs installed, you will also have a drop-down field where you can select the language of the site collection. Lastly, not seen in Figure 13-26 is the Quota Template selection. We will talk about Quota Templates a bit later in the chapter. To create modern sites, you can choose the Team Site template under collaboration as seen in Figure 13-26, or the Communication Site under the publishing tab.

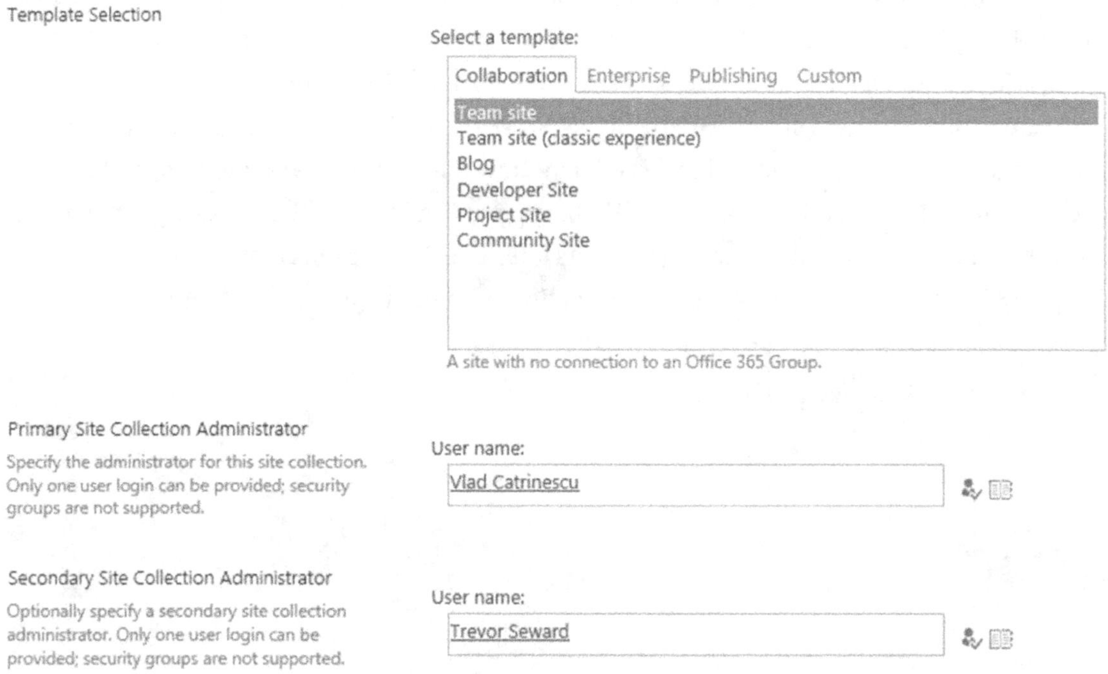

Template Selection

Select a template:

| Collaboration | Enterprise | Publishing | Custom |

Team site
Team site (classic experience)
Blog
Developer Site
Project Site
Community Site

A site with no connection to an Office 365 Group.

Primary Site Collection Administrator

Specify the administrator for this site collection. Only one user login can be provided; security groups are not supported.

User name:

Vlad Catrinescu

Secondary Site Collection Administrator

Optionally specify a secondary site collection administrator. Only one user login can be provided; security groups are not supported.

User name:

Trevor Seward

Figure 13-26. *New Site Collection Template and Site Collection Administrators*

To create the Site Collection, simply press on OK at the bottom of the screen. To create a Site Collection by PowerShell, we need to use the New-SPSite cmdlet from an elevated SharePoint Management Shell. By using the SharePoint Management Shell, we also have the possibility of selecting in which Content Database we want to put this Site Collection in. In the following cmdlet we specify the URL, name, and description of the Site Collection. We also pass the usernames of the first and secondary owners. Lastly, we specify the Modern Team Site template ID (STS#3) and the Content Database in which we want to create the Site Collection.

```
New-SPSite -url "https://intranet.cobaltatom.com/sites/team1" -Name "Team 1
Home" -Description "Team 1 SharePoint Site" -OwnerAlias "LAB\vlad.
catrinescu" -SecondaryOwnerAlias "LAB\trevor.seward" -Template "STS#3"
-ContentDatabase WSS_Content_Intranet_2
```

Note   When creating a Site Collections through PowerShell, the default SharePoint groups will not be created.

If you do not specify a template, the Site Collection will be created without a Root Web, and SharePoint will ask you to select a template the first time you browse to the site as seen in Figure 13-27.

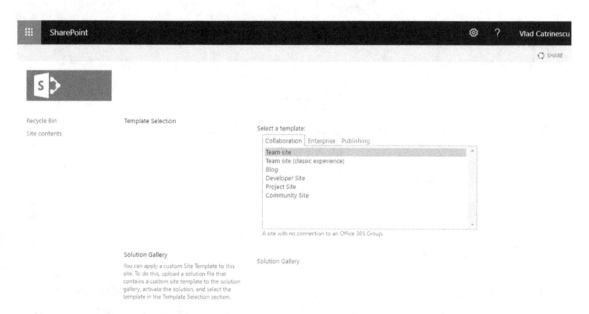

Figure 13-27.   *Site Collection Template Selection*

Site Quotas

SharePoint allows administrators to specify a quota for each Site Collection. Quotas will not allow users to use more than a certain amount of storage, as well as limit the number of resources that can be consumed by Sandboxed Solutions. The Sandbox Solutions with Code Limits are still there in the User Interface but are irrelevant as Sandbox Solutions with code are removed from SharePoint 2019. Once the quota is reached, a "No Free Space" message appears to users when they try to create new items in SharePoint, and a red bar is displayed at the top of the site. To create a new Site Quota by Central Administration, navigate to the Application Management page, and then, Specify Quota templates. You will see a page similar to Figure 13-28.

Quota Templates ⓘ

Template Name

Edit an existing quota template, or create a new template. For a new template, you can start from a blank template or modify an existing template.

○ Edit an existing template
   Template to modify
   Personal Site [⌄]

◉ Create a new quota template
   Template to start from
   [new blank template] [⌄]
   New template name:
   Bronze Team Site

Storage Limit Values

Specify whether to limit the amount of storage available on a Site Collection, and set the maximum amount of storage, and a warning level. When the warning level or maximum storage level is reached, an e-mail is sent to the site administrator to inform them of the issue.

☑ Limit site storage to a maximum of:
   500 MB

☑ Send warning E-mail when Site Collection storage reaches:
   300 MB

Sandboxed Solutions With Code Limits

Specifies whether sandboxed solutions with code are allowed for this site collection. When the warning level is reached, an e-mail is sent. When the maximum usage limit is reached, sandboxed solutions with code are disabled for the rest of the day and an e-mail is sent to the site administrator.

Limit maximum usage per day to: 0 points
☑ Send warning e-mail when usage per day reaches: 0 points

[OK]   [Cancel]

Figure 13-28. *New Quota Template*

The Quota Template can also be created via PowerShell. In the next script, we will create a quota named "Silver Team Site" with a 1024 MB maximum storage limit and a warning sent at 750 MB. Note that the StorageMaximumLevel and StorageWarningLevel variables need to be in bytes.

```
$Template = New-Object Microsoft.SharePoint.Administration.SPQuotaTemplate
$Template.Name = "Silver Team Site"
$Template.StorageMaximumLevel = 1073741824
$Template.StorageWarningLevel = 786432000
```

```
$ContentService = [Microsoft.SharePoint.Administration.
SPWebService]::ContentService
$ContentService.QuotaTemplates.Add($Template)
$ContentService.Update()
```

Assigning a Quota Template to a Site Collection can be done by using the `Set-SPSite` cmdlet and specifying the URL and name of the `QuotaTemplate` as seen in the following example:

```
Set-SPSite -Identity https://intranet.cobaltatom.com/sites/team1
-QuotaTemplate "Silver Team Site"
```

You can also use the `Set-SPSite` cmdlet to change the quota to another template later on.

Managed Paths

Managed Paths allow you to customize the URL of your sites in order to make them more user friendly and to align with your business requirements and to allow us to host multiple Site Collections in the same Web Application. Managed Paths are what is between the Web Application URL and the part of your URL you want to give to your Site Collection. By Default, every SharePoint Web Application contains the /sites/ Managed Path as well as the (root) Managed Path, allowing you to create the root Site Collection. There are two types of Managed Paths that you can create in SharePoint:

- **Wildcard Inclusion**

   A Wildcard Inclusion is a managed path that allows you to create multiple Site Collections using the path you specify. For example, if you create a /teams/ managed path, you could create URLs like `https://intranet.cobaltatom.com/teams/engineering`, `https://intranet.cobaltatom.com/teams/HR`, `https://intranet.cobaltatom.com/teams/Marketing` and so on. However, you cannot create a site with the URL `https://intranet.cobaltatom.com/teams`.

   The default /sites/ Managed Path is of type Wildcard Inclusion.

- **Explicit Inclusion**

  An Explicit Inclusion only allows you to create a Site Collection with the specified address. For example, we could create a /HR Managed path in Explicit Inclusion, you could only create a Site Collection at `https://intranet.cobaltatom.com/HR`. You will not need to add anything after the HR as you would have to do with a Wildcard Inclusion.

Note   For performance reasons, Microsoft recommends a maximum of 20 Managed Paths per Web Application.

To create a Managed Path via Central Administration, navigate to the Web Application Management Page, and from the Ribbon click Managed Paths as seen in Figure 13-29.

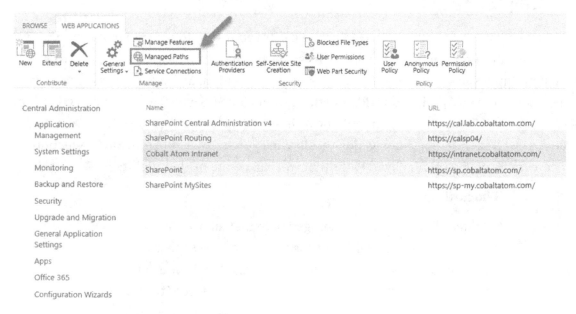

Figure 13-29.   *Managed Paths*

Simply enter the path that you wish to create, as well as the Type from the drop-down, and click the "Add Path" button. After the path is added to the included paths, you can click OK to close the pop-up window. In Figure 13-30 we have created a Managed Path called "Teams" of type Wildcard.

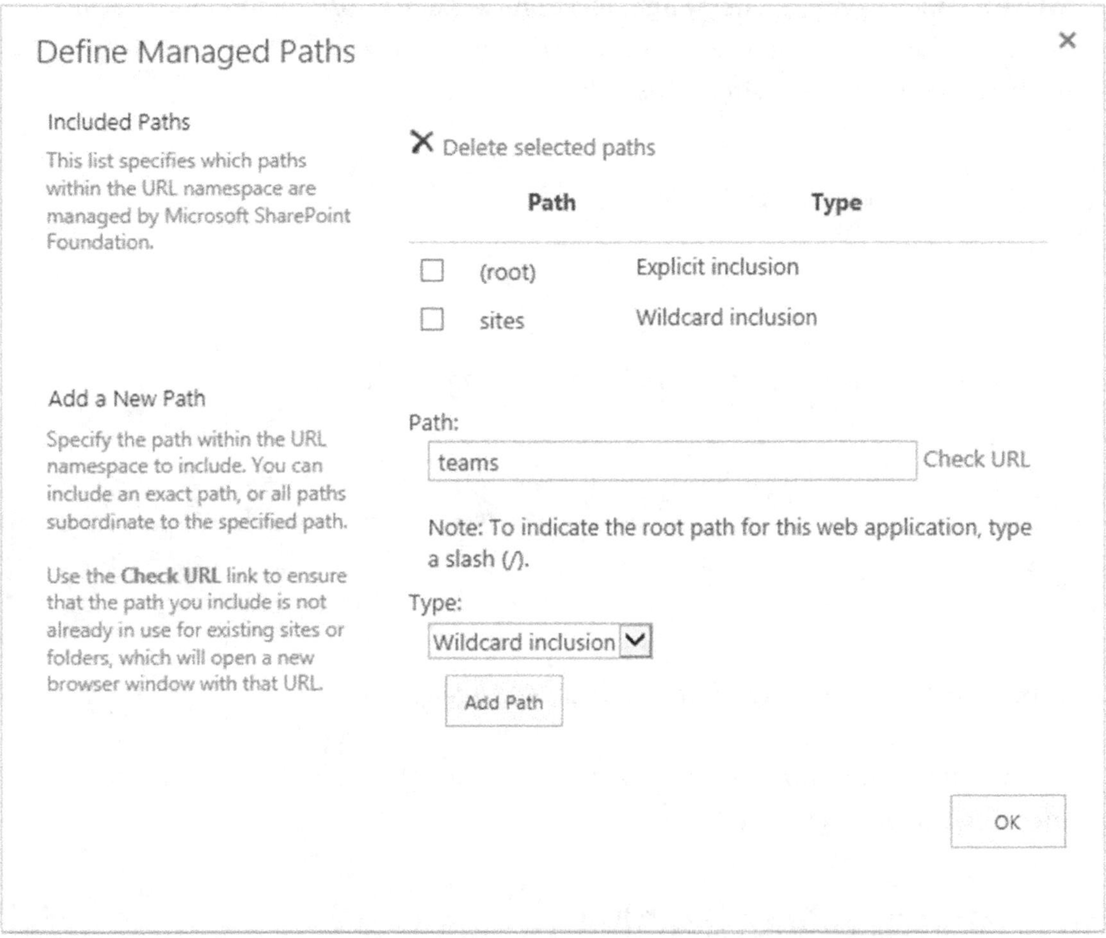

Figure 13-30.   *Teams Managed Path*

To create a Managed Path with PowerShell, we need to run the New-SPManagedPath PowerShell cmdlet from an elevated SharePoint Management Shell. For example, to create a new Wildcard inclusion Managed Path with the "department" path, we would run the following PowerShell cmdlet:

```
New-SPManagedPath "department" -WebApplication https://intranet.cobaltatom.com
```

If we want to create an Explicit Managed Path, we need to add the –Explicit switch, as in the following example:

```
New-SPManagedPath "communications" -WebApplication "https://intranet.
cobaltatom.com" –Explicit
```

If we go back to create a new Site Collection via Central Administration, we will see both the /teams Managed Path as seen in Figure 13-31 and the /communications Explicit Managed Path seen in Figure 13-32.

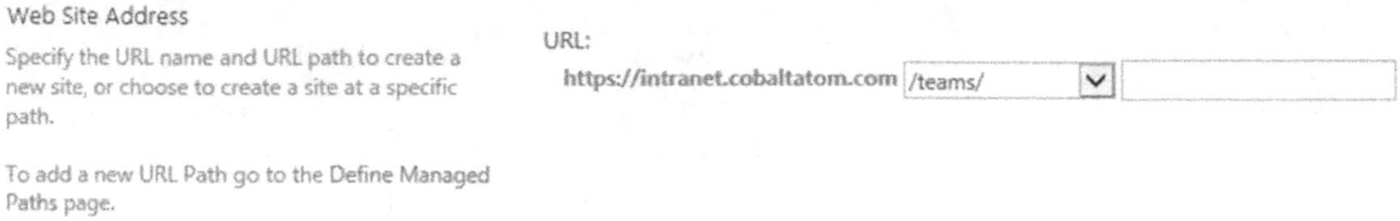

Figure 13-31. *Teams Wildcard Inclusion Managed Path*

Figure 13-32. *Communications Explicit Managed Path*

Now that we know how to create Path-Based Site Collections, let's take a look at Host Named Site Collections.

Host Named Site Collections

As discussed previously, Host Named Site Collections allow you to host multiple hostnames in the same Web Application. Although this approach is the best practice approach according to Microsoft, don't embark on a Host Named Site Collections journey without the proper planning. The Web Application in which you will create Host Named Site Collections will need to have an IIS Binding that answers to all the traffic on a specific port. For example, if we want to create Host Named Site Collections in the `https://sp.cobaltatom.com` Web Application, you need to add a binding that listens on *:443, which has a certificate assigned to it that is either a wildcard or has all the Host Named Site Collection URLs in the SAN.

Since in Chapter 5 we have configured Add-ins to listen on *:443, we cannot have another site listen to the exact same binding, so we have configured another IP Address for our server. If you are running multiple Web Front Ends, you will need to configure an additional IP for every Web Front End in your farm. It is recommended to have an additional IP and correctly configure every server running the Microsoft SharePoint Foundation Web Application service in the farm. For every Web Application that you want to use for Host Named Site Collections, you will need to add another IP, since that one as well will need to listen on *:443, or *:80 if you do not use SSL.

To prepare our `https://sp.cobaltatom.com` we have added the binding in IIS that listens to all requests on the 172.16.5.207 IP address and port 443 on our first Front End. We have also used the *.cobaltatom.com wildcard certificate, which means all the Host Named Site Collections we will create will need to be in the cobaltatom.com domain. The IIS Binding can be seen in Figure 13-33.

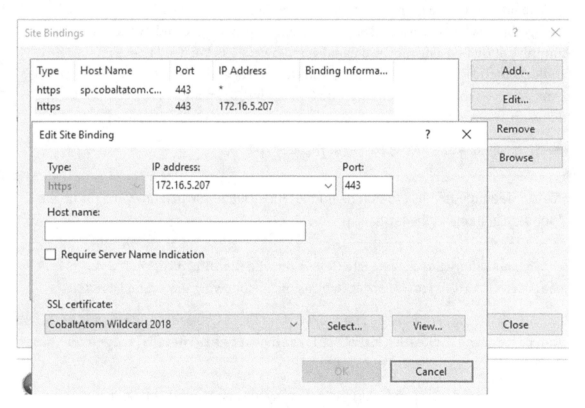

Figure 13-33. *Host Named Site Collection Binding*

With IIS Configured, we can now create our Host Named Site Collection. Unlike Path-Based Site Collections, we cannot use Central Administration to create them, so PowerShell is mandatory. We still use the `New-SPSite` cmdlet and most parameters are the same; however, when creating Host Named Site Collections, we need to specify the `–HostHeaderWebApplication` parameter, in order to tell SharePoint what Web Application to put it in.

```
New-SPSite https://Team1.cobaltatom.com –OwnerAlias "LAB\vlad.catrinescu"
–HostHeaderWebApplication https://sp.cobaltatom.com –Name "Team Site 1"
-Template "STS#3"
```

The other difference with Host Named Site Collections is the Managed Paths. Managed Paths for Host Named Site Collections cannot be created by Central Administration and can only be created with PowerShell. We need to use the same cmdlet, which is `New-SPManagedPath,` and we need to add the `–HostHeader` switch to make it available for Host Named Site Collections. To create a "Projects" Wildcard Inclusion Managed Path, we need to use the following PowerShell cmdlet:

```
New-SPManagedPath "projects" -HostHeader
```

Note   Managed Paths created using the –HostHeader switch are valid for all the Web Applications in the farm.

We could afterward create a Site Collection with the URL `https://Team1.cobaltatom.com/Projects/Project1` by using the following PowerShell cmdlet:

```
New-SPSite https://Team1.cobaltatom.com/Projects/Project1 -OwnerAlias "LAB\
vlad.catrinescu" –HostHeaderWebApplication https://sp.cobaltatom.com –Name
"Project Site 1" -Template "STS#3"
```

Alternate Access Mappings also do not apply to Host Named Site Collections. Alternate URLs can be set individual to each Host Named Site Collection by using the `Set-SPSiteUrl` PowerShell cmdlet. To make our `https://Team1.cobaltatom.com` Site Collection also accessible with the URL `https://ProjectCenter.cobaltatom.com` we would run the following PowerShell cmdlets:

```
$site = Get-SPSite https://Team1.cobaltatom.com
Set-SPSiteUrl $site -Url 'https://ProjectCenter.cobaltatom.com' -Zone Intranet
```

Similar to how Alternate Access Mappings work, you will need to assign the URL to one of the five zones. To view all the current URLs for a Host Named Site Collection, you need to use the `Get-SPSiteURL` cmdlet and give the `$site` variable we saved earlier. In Figure 13-34 we can see the URLs we set for the Team1 Site Collection.

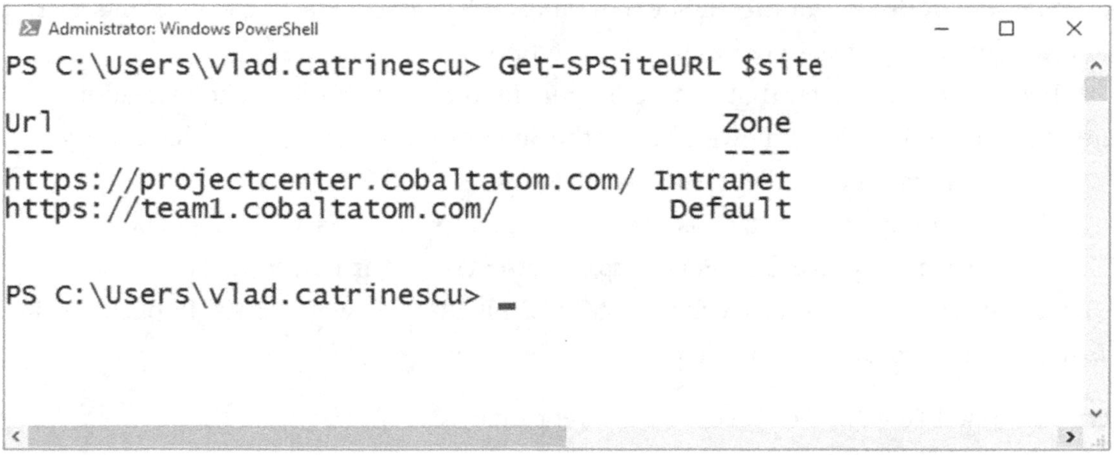

Figure 13-34. *Get-SPSiteURL*

While Host Named Site Collections are recommended by Microsoft and do have performance advantages over using multiple Web Applications, there are some disadvantages that stop companies from using them. First of all, there are no management tools for Host Named Site Collections in Central Administration. Also, mixing MySites and Content Site Collections in the same Web Application can cause disorganization in Content Database, since you will have both MySites Site Collections, as well as Content Site Collections in mixed Databases, and they might not all have the same requirement for backups and management. Lastly, you cannot create Host Named Site Collections using the built in Self Service Site Creation feature. Users will still be able to use the feature and create Path-Based Site Collections under an existing Managed Path.

Ultimately, the decision between Host Named Site Collections and Path-Based Site Collections will depend on your business requirements.

Fast Site Collection Creation

Fast Site Collection Creation is a new feature in SharePoint Server 2019 that allows administrators to create Site Collections faster than the traditional method. When creating a Site Collection, SharePoint creates a blank site and activates all the features necessary to get to your desired template. With Fast Site Collection Creation, a copy of a template would be saved in the database, and every time you create a Site Collection with that template by using Fast Site Collection Creation, SharePoint will copy the site directly in the Content Database, making the site creation a lot faster. SharePoint enables this by default for the MySite template, and all the MySite Site Collections that SharePoint automatically creates use this method.

It's important to know that in order to benefit from Fast Site Collection Creation, you need to create sites trough PowerShell as the Site Collections that are created through Central Administration will not use this new engine.

The first thing we need to do is to enable the template for Fast Site Collection Creation by using the `Enable-SPWebTemplateForSiteMaster` PowerShell cmdlet. Throughout the examples, we will use CMSPUBLISHING#0, which is the Publishing Site Template. The cmdlet we will use is

```
Enable-SPWebTemplateForSiteMaster -Template CMSPUBLISHING#0
-CompatibilityLevel 15
```

Note   Templates for Modern Team Sites (STS#3) , Modern Communication Sites (#SITEPAGEPUBLISHING#0) are enabled by default. To see all the templates currently enabled in your farm run the Get-SPWebTemplatesEnabledForSiteMaster PowerShell cmdlet.

While "15" is usually associated with SharePoint 2013, SharePoint 2019 uses the same Compatibility level

We then need to create the Site Master in the Content Database by using the New-SPSiteMaster cmdlet. You will need to do this for every Content Database that you wish to create those types of Site Collections in. In our case, the Content Database name is WSS_Content_Intranet_2 and we ran the following cmdlet:

```
New-SPSiteMaster -ContentDatabase WSS_Content_Intranet_2 -Template
SITEPAGEPUBLISHING#0
```

With everything ready, we can now create our site using the `New-SPSite` PowerShell cmdlet as seen previously, but we need to add the `-CreateFromSiteMaster` switch in order to tell SharePoint to use Fast Site Collection Creation to create this Site Collection. An example cmdlet to create the Site Collection will be

```
New-SPSite -url "https://intranet.cobaltatom.com/sites/CommmSite"
-Name "Communication Site" -OwnerAlias "LAB\vlad.catrinescu" -Template
"SITEPAGEPUBLISHING#0" -ContentDatabase WSS_Content_Intranet_2
-CreateFromSiteMaster
```

To compare the speed of site provisioning side by side, we have created two Site Collections using the same template. The first one was created without the –CreateFromSiteMaster switch, while the second one was created with the switch. The results seen in Figure 13-35 show that the Site Collection provisioned using the traditional method took 19.83 seconds to create, while the Site Collection provisioned with Fast Site Collection creation took 3.93 seconds.

Figure 13-35. *Measuring Fast Site Collection Creation*

Depending on the site template you want to enable for Fast Site Collection, the increase in speed might not be noticeable. For example, Classic Team Sites that do not have many features to activate can be created slower using Fast Site Collection than normal provisioning. Also, remember that Fast Site Collection can only be used by PowerShell or by code, and all the Site Collections created via Central Administration will use the standard provisioning engine.

Next Steps

In this chapter, we have learned how to create Web Applications, as well as Path-Based and Host Named Site Collections. We have also learned how to enable Fast Site Collection Creation for the templates that we use the most often. In the next chapter, we will cover how to implement a Hybrid SharePoint Infrastructure between SharePoint 2019 and Office 365.

CHAPTER 14

Hybrid Scenarios

Deploying a hybrid SharePoint infrastructure can provide great benefits to your enterprise and enable your business users to be more productive, while using the latest and greatest technologies that Microsoft offers.

In this chapter, we will look at how to deploy a hybrid SharePoint Server 2019 infrastructure from the requirements to the Hybrid Sites, OneDrive for Business, Hybrid Taxonomy, and the Cloud Search Service Application.

What Is a Hybrid Deployment?

Before going into technical details, let's first understand what a SharePoint hybrid deployment is. A hybrid SharePoint deployment is a link between a SharePoint Server farm and Office 365. The SharePoint Server farm can be hosted in our own datacenter, in a private cloud, or in a public cloud such as Azure or AWS.

There are multiple reasons to deploy a hybrid SharePoint Server 2019 Infrastructure. As you probably heard countless times already, Microsoft's vision is Cloud-First, Mobile-First, meaning that all the newest features come in the cloud first and then make their way in the next On-Premises release. Furthermore, some features such as Delve, Office 365 Groups, Flow, PowerApps, and Stream will not be available as purely on-premises servers.

At the same time, there are multiple reasons to keep using SharePoint On-Premises. Companies can easily customize SharePoint 2019 to fit their business requirements with farm solutions and timer jobs, as well as keeping control of all the SharePoint settings and configurations. Furthermore, due to legal, compliance, or security reasons, some companies simply cannot store some of their data in Office 365 as the data must be protected in certain ways.

© Vlad Catrinescu and Trevor Seward 2019
V. Catrinescu and T. Seward, *Deploying SharePoint 2019*, https://doi.org/10.1007/978-1-4842-4526-2_14

This is why a Hybrid deployment is the best of both worlds. By using the right system for the right business need, your business users will be able to have the custom SharePoint solutions and control they need On-Premises, as well as the latest and greatest features in the cloud.

Authentication and Authorization

A big part of setting up a hybrid Microsoft environment is setting up the user synchronization between the On-Premises Active Directory and Azure Active Directory, which is the directory used by Office 365. Microsoft provides DirSync, now deprecated, Azure AD Connect, and a Microsoft Identity Manager Management Agent. Third parties also provide synchronization agents.

The next topic is providing Single Sign on (SSO). An SSO solution will make sure that your users only log in once on the local Active Directory and don't have to re-enter their credentials when trying to use a cloud service. Microsoft offers Active Directory Federation Services (ADFS) as well as Azure AD Connect SSO to achieve SSO functionality, which is the preferred solution. Providing an SSO solution is optional (but highly recommended) for your user experience and is not mandatory for setting up a hybrid SharePoint 2019 Infrastructure.

In this book, we will not cover the differences between User Synchronization solutions and how to configure them since this action is typically implemented by a Domain Administrator and not by the SharePoint Administrator. In the context of this book we have used Azure AD Connect to sync our On-Premises users to Office 365. Let's look at the high-level architecture of a hybrid SharePoint deployment.

Architecture Overview

In a Hybrid Infrastructure we have both a SharePoint 2019 On-Premises Farm as well as a SharePoint Online tenant. There is a Server-To-Server Authentication (S2S Trust) setup between the two different systems so that they could authenticate to each other and communicate securely.

For inbound features such as Hybrid BCS and Inbound Hybrid Federated Search, a Reverse Proxy is needed to secure inbound communication from SharePoint Online to our SharePoint On-Premises farm. This can be visualized in Figure 14-1.

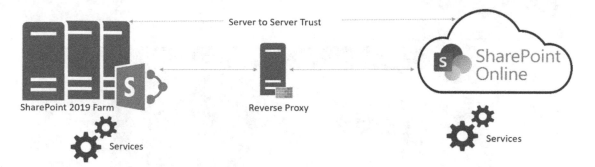

Figure 14-1. *Hybrid SharePoint 2019 Infrastructure high-level overview*

Inbound features such as Hybrid Business Connectivity Services and inbound federated search are not part of a classic hybrid deployment so we will not cover those in detail in this book.

Hybrid Features Overview

Before starting the configuration, we will do an overview of what features are available in hybrid and what each one offers!

Hybrid App Launcher

The Hybrid App launcher modifies the SharePoint 2019 app launcher to be more in sync with the app launcher part of Office 365. The hybrid app launcher, seen in Figure 14-2 shows Office 365 only apps such as Delve and Office 365 video, as well as any custom apps you pin to your Office 365 app launcher such as "Testing Tile" in Figure 14-2.

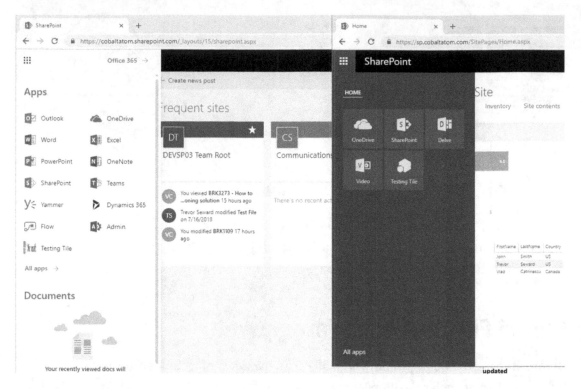

Figure 14-2.   *The Hybrid App Launcher*

Hybrid Sites

The Hybrid Sites functionality in SharePoint 2019 and SharePoint Online allows a user's Followed Sites from both On-Premises and Online to display in a single location; their SharePoint Home in Office 365. In Figure 14-3, I have followed the site called "Communication Site," and it shows up in my SharePoint Online Home page.

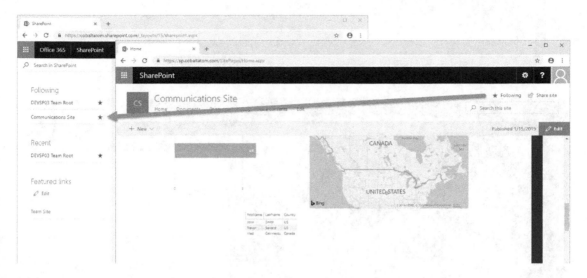

Figure 14-3. *Hybrid Sites*

Hybrid OneDrive for Business

Once enabled, Hybrid OneDrive for Business will create user's OneDrive for Business in SharePoint Online instead of SharePoint On-Premises. From an integration point of view, the OneDrive icon inside SharePoint On-Premises app launcher will now redirect users to their OneDrive inside Office 365. In Figure 14-4 you can see the OneDrive icon in the SharePoint 2019 app launcher redirecting me to my SharePoint Online OneDrive for Business site.

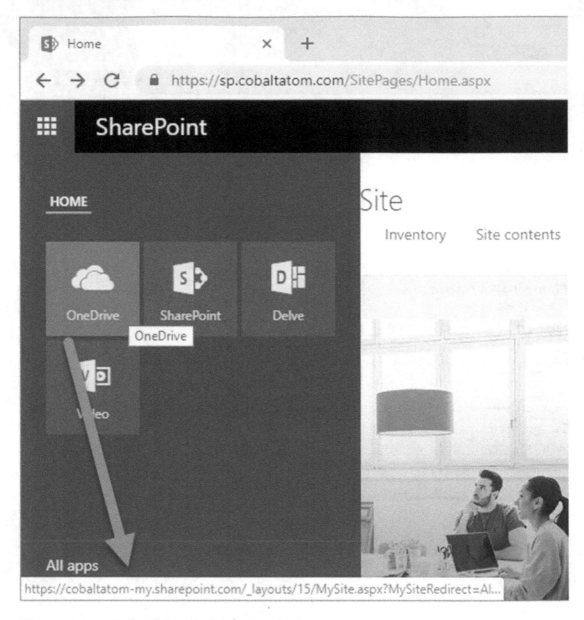

Figure 14-4. *Hybrid OneDrive for Business*

Hybrid Business to Business (B2B) Sites

While you will see this feature in the hybrid configuration wizard, which we will talk about later, this feature does not really create any integrations between your SharePoint On-Premises farm and Office 365 tenant. It's only there as a reminder of the extranet features in SharePoint Online and how you can benefit from hosting your external collaboration sites in Office 365 rather than On-Premises.

Note   You can learn more about using SharePoint Online as a business-to-business (B2B) extranet solution on Microsoft Docs at the following link: `https://docs.microsoft.com/en-us/sharepoint/create-b2b-extranet`.

Hybrid Self-Service Site Creation

Hybrid self-service site creation allows you to redirect the default self-service site creation page in SharePoint Server (if you have it enabled) to SharePoint Online. By enabling this feature, you can make sure all newly created sites are in SharePoint Online, therefore having less content to migrate in an eventual migration to Office 365.

Hybrid Taxonomy and Content Types

The hybrid taxonomy and content types feature allow you to have a shared taxonomy and set of Content Types between your SharePoint Online tenant and SharePoint On-premises farm. After the initial term store migration is done via PowerShell, managed metadata terms and Content Types will be synced to SharePoint On-Premises via a daily timer job.

Hybrid Business Connectivity Services

Hybrid Business Connectivity Services allows you to securely display data from external system, as a SharePoint list in Office 365. Users can then view and edit the data from wherever they are in the world, without needing to be connected to their on-premises infrastructure. In Figure 14-5, you can see information from a SQL Server database being displayed in a SharePoint Online list.

Figure 14-5. *Hybrid Business Connectivity Services*

Hybrid Search

SharePoint Server 2019 offers us two options to integrate search between SharePoint On-Premises and SharePoint Online. The first option is called Federated Search. In a Federated Search setup, SharePoint Server 2019 can show results from SharePoint Online by making a Remote SharePoint query, and users can also search SharePoint On-Premises directly from SharePoint Online. What is important to understand is that in a Federated Search scenario, the index stays on the same system as the data. The SharePoint Server 2019 index remains On-Premises while the SharePoint Online index remains in the cloud.

The second option is called Cloud Hybrid Search. This option requires a different type of Search Service Application called the Cloud Search Service Application, and the main difference between Federated Search and Cloud Hybrid Search is that in a Cloud Hybrid Search scenario, SharePoint Server 2019 pushes the index of On-Premises items and documents to Office 365, where it's merged with the SharePoint Online index. By having the index of both On-Premises and Cloud documents merged in the cloud, your users will have access to Office 365–only features such as Delve and the Office Graph.

Hybrid Federated Search Overview

In a Hybrid Federated Search setup, the index of SharePoint On-Premises documents remains On-Premises, and all the SharePoint Online index remains in Office 365. When configuring Hybrid Federated Search, we have three possible topologies we can choose from.

One-Way Outbound Topology

In a One-Way Outbound Topology, SharePoint Server can query SharePoint Online; however, SharePoint Online cannot query SharePoint Server. Therefore, a user who logs on to SharePoint On-Premises and performs a search query will be able to retrieve both SharePoint On-Premises and SharePoint Online results. However, a user performing a query on SharePoint Online will not be able to get results from SharePoint On-Premises.

One-Way Inbound Topology

In a One-Way Inbound Topology, SharePoint Online can query SharePoint Server 2019; however, SharePoint On-Premises cannot query SharePoint Online. Therefore, a user that logs on to SharePoint Online and performs a query will be able to see results from both SharePoint Online and SharePoint On-Premises. However, a user performing a query in SharePoint On-Premises will only see results from SharePoint On-Premises and not SharePoint Online.

Two-Way (Bidirectional) Topology

In a Two-Way (Bidirectional) topology, we basically configure both the One-Way Inbound and One-Way Outbound topologies. In this topology, both systems can query each other and therefore return results from the other system.

Hybrid Cloud Search Overview

The main difference in the Hybrid Cloud Search topology is that the Cloud Search Service Application does not store the index on the SharePoint On-Premises; instead, it pushes it to Office 365. Out of the six Search components in the Search Service Application, only the Admin, Crawl and Query components are active. The Index, Content Processing and Analytics components do need to exist, but they are not used in a Hybrid Cloud Search scenario. All the Content Processing and Analytics are done in Office 365, where the Index is stored.

The Cloud Search Service Application can crawl the same type of Content Sources as a normal Search Service Application; therefore, you can push items from Remote SharePoint Sites, File Shares, BCS, and more in the SharePoint Online Index.

One of the disadvantages of the Hybrid Cloud Search topology is that you are limited to the Search customization options of SharePoint Online, since that is where the content processing is done and Index is stored. Therefore, some options like Custom Entity Extraction and Content Enrichment Web Service are not available. The big advantage of the Hybrid Cloud Search is having homogeneous results when doing a query, whether those results come from SharePoint Online or SharePoint On-Premises.

Which Option Should You Choose?

The choice between Federated Search and Hybrid Cloud Search will ultimately depend on your business requirements and on the regulation applicable to your data. In a Federated Search scenario, the index of your On-Premises documents remains On-Premises. In a Cloud Hybrid Search scenario, your index, and therefore the content of all your documents, will be in Office 365. Some regulations about the data and the documents might not allow your business to put the content of your documents in Office 365.

Furthermore, in a Cloud Hybrid Search topology, since the index is stored in the SharePoint Online, all your SharePoint users will have to be licensed in Office 365 even if they only want to search SharePoint On-Premises and never use SharePoint Online. With Hybrid Federated Search, users who are only licensed On-Premises can still search all the SharePoint On-Premises items.

Microsoft recommends using the Cloud Hybrid Search whenever possible since it will provide a better experience for your users, enable cloud-only features on On-Premises content, and save disk space and maybe even SharePoint Server 2019 licenses On-Premises, since you need a small search footprint in your On-Premises SharePoint Server 2019 infrastructure. This is the option that will be covered in this chapter.

Prerequisites

Before starting to configure different Hybrid features, there are a few requirements that you need to have.

SharePoint Server Prerequisites

In order to start configuring Hybrid, you need to configure the following Service Applications on your SharePoint Server 2019 Server:

1. Managed Metadata Service Application

2. User Profile Service Application

3. App Management Service

4. Subscription Settings Service Application

Furthermore, you also need to have MySites configured inside your User Profile Service Application. As we already covered how to create those service applications, we will not cover that again in this chapter. One important thing to note is that the *Work Email* user property needs to contain the e-mail address that you configured for the user in Active Directory, and the User Principal Name property must be mapped to the *userPrincipalName* attributed in Active Directory.

Licensing Prerequisites

In order to be able to use hybrid functionalities your users must have licenses assigned in Office 365. By default, when Azure AD Connect synchronizes new users in Office 365, the users are synchronized but no licenses are assigned automatically. You can use group-based licensing in Azure Active Directory to make sure your users are automatically licensed!

Tip   Learn more about group-based licensing in Azure Active Directory over here: `https://docs.microsoft.com/en-us/azure/active-directory/fundamentals/active-directory-licensing-whatis-azure-portal`.

Note   If you plan to use the SharePoint 2019 Data Loss Prevention feature and want it to work in a Cloud Hybrid Search mode, you will need to synchronize and assign a license to the SharePoint Farm account as well.

Reverse Proxy Requirements

If you plan to implement hybrid Business Connectivity Services, or Inbound Federated Search, you will need to configure a reverse proxy so Office 365 can securely access your SharePoint 2019 On-Premises farm. The reverse proxy is also required to show document previews of On-Premises documents in SharePoint Online when using Cloud Hybrid Search if you are using Office Online Server. At the time of writing this book, there are four supported Reverse Proxy tools; however, more might be added in the future. The four supported ones by Microsoft are

- Windows Server 2012 R2 with Web Application Proxy

- Forefront Threat Management Gateway (TMG) 2010

- F5 BIG-IP

- Citrix NetScaler

Note   To view the up-to-date list of supported Reverse Proxies for a hybrid SharePoint infrastructure, visit the following TechNet article. `https://docs.microsoft.com/en-us/SharePoint/hybrid/configure-a-reverse-proxy-device-for-sharepoint-server-hybrid#supported-reverse-proxy-devices`.

While the preceding Reverse Proxies are the recommended ones by Microsoft, you can make SharePoint work in hybrid mode with a reverse proxy that supports the following features:

- Support client certificate authentication with a wildcard or SAN SSL certificate.

- Support pass-through authentication for OAuth 2.0, including unlimited OAuth bearer token transactions.

- Accept unsolicited inbound traffic on TCP port 443 (HTTPS).

- Bind a wildcard or SAN SSL certificate to a published endpoint.

- Relay traffic to an On-Premises SharePoint Server 2019 farm or load balancer without rewriting any packet headers.

Accounts Needed for Hybrid Configuration and Testing

To configure all the hybrid SharePoint 2019 features described in this chapter, you will need to have access to accounts with the following roles:

- Office 365 Global Administrator

- SharePoint Farm Admin

For the Office 365 Global Administrator account, we recommend having a **cloud-only** account that does not have multifactor authentication enabled during the setup of your hybrid environment. In this book, we will use a dedicated service account named sphybrid@cobaltatom.com.

If you don't plan to deploy Hybrid SharePoint features to all the users in your organization, consider creating a Security Group in Active Directory with all the accounts that will have access to Hybrid Features. This group should also be replicated to Azure Active Directory. By creating a Security Group, we will easily be able to create an audience in the SharePoint User Profile Service Application and only offer Hybrid Features to those users, while the rest of the users will still be able to use features such as OneDrive for Business Fully On-Premises.

Domain User Requirements

You must create an UPN domain suffix for your On-Premises users that matches the public domain you are using in Office 365. To give a concrete example, in our book we use the lab.cobaltatom.com domain for all our users and computers; therefore, usernames are under the LAB\Username format. For the synchronization and user mapping to work, we set up our users to use the username@cobaltatom.com format as well. This is done in the "User Logon Name" property as seen in Figure 14-6.

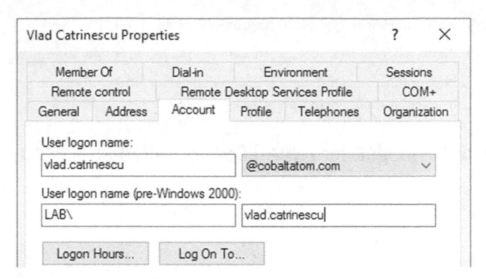

Figure 14-6. *User Logon Name is the same as our Office 365 domain*

Certificate Requirements

To configure secure communication between your SharePoint 2019 On-Premises farm and SharePoint Online from Office 365, you will need to update your SharePoint Server Security Token Service (STS) certificate. This certificate is only used to configure Server-to-Server trust between SharePoint Online and your SharePoint 2019 Server farm. Following Microsoft's best practices, in this book we will use the ***Hybrid Picker***, a Graphical User Interface tool that makes it easier to setup a hybrid environment. This tool will create a self-signed certificate for the Server-To-Server trust. The expiration of the certificate is in year 9999, so you won't have to worry about replacing it anytime soon.

Software

If you plan to configure Hybrid Search, you will need to install the following tools on the server that will be used for hybrid configuration:

- Microsoft Online Services Sign-In Assistant (www.microsoft.com/en-us/download/details.aspx?id=39267)

- MSOnline PowerShell for Azure Active Directory (www.powershellgallery.com/packages/MSOnline/)

Migrate Your Taxonomy and Content Types to SharePoint Online

If you plan to use the Hybrid Taxonomy and Content Types feature as part of your hybrid deployment, it's recommended to migrate your Terms and Content Types to SharePoint Online before starting to configuration process. This can be done later, after the feature has been implemented, but it would require you to re-run the configuration wizard.

The copy process will preserve most information about the term sets such as owner and stakeholders, however only users can be copied over; Active Directory groups assigned as owners or stakeholders will not be copied over to Office 365.

Copying taxonomy groups is done with the `Copy-SPTaxonomyGroups` PowerShell cmdlet. The following parameters will be needed:

- **LocalSiteUrl**: The URL of the site where you want to migrate Content Types from. This could be your local Content Type Hub.

- **LocalTermStoreName**: The name of the Term Store from your local Managed Metadata Service Application.

- **RemoteSiteUrl**: The URL of your SharePoint Online tenant (https://<tenant>.sharepoint.com).

- **GroupNames**: The name of the Term Groups you want to migrate to SharePoint Online.

- **Credentials**: A credential object with the credentials of your Office 365 Global Administrator.

To start the copy, we will first get our Office 365 Admin credentials and save them into a variable called $cred:

```
$cred = Get-Credential
```

We will then run the Copy-SPTaxonomyGroups PowerShell cmdlet specifying the required parameters. In our following example, we are copying the Engineering and Marketing Term Groups over to SharePoint Online:

```
Copy-SPTaxonomyGroups `
    -LocalTermStoreName "Managed Metadata Service Proxy" `
    -LocalSiteUrl "https://sp.cobaltatom.com" `
    -RemoteSiteUrl "https://cobaltatom.sharepoint.com" `
```

```
    -GroupNames "Engineering","Marketing" `
    -Credential $cred
```

Migrating Content Types is done via the `Copy-SPContentTypes` PowerShell cmdlet, which will copy Content Types to your SharePoint Online Content Type hub located at https://<tenant>.sharepoint.com/sites/contentTypeHub. If the site does not exist before running the PowerShell cmdlet, it will be automatically created for you and the Site Collection Feature Content Type Syndication Hub will be enabled. The following parameters will be needed:

- **LocalSiteUrl**: The URL of the site where you want to migrate Content Types from. This could be your local Content Type Hub.

- **LocalTermStoreName**: The name of the Term Store from your local Managed Metadata Service Application.

- **RemoteSiteUrl**: The URL of your SharePoint Online tenant (http://<tenant>.sharepoint.com).

- **ContentTypeNames**: The name of the Content Types you want to migrate to SharePoint Online.

- **Credentials**: A credential object with the credentials of your Office 365 Global Administrator.

In order to migrate the *Customers* and *Doctors* Content Types from our On-Premises Content Type Hub to SharePoint Online, we would run the following PowerShell cmdlet:

```
Copy-SPContentTypes `
    -LocalSiteUrl https://sp.cobaltatom.com/sites/ContentTypeHub `
    -LocalTermStoreName "Managed Metadata Service Proxy" `
    -RemoteSiteUrl https://cobaltatom.sharepoint.com/ `
    -ContentTypeNames @("Customers", "Doctors") `
    -Credential $cred
```

Configuring Hybrid SharePoint

The first step we need to do is to get the SharePoint hybrid picker, also sometimes called the SharePoint hybrid configuration wizard. To get it, navigate to the SharePoint Online admin center, and under Configure Hybrid, click Go to Hybrid Picker download page as seen in Figure 14-7. Make sure you are on the SharePoint Server you wish to configure SharePoint Hybrid on, as clicking the link will start downloading the application.

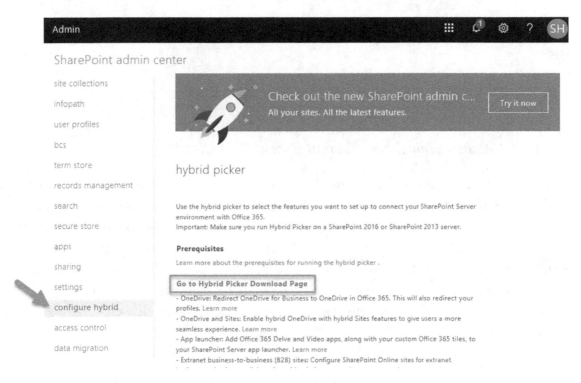

Figure 14-7. *The Hybrid Picker Download Location*

Once prompted with the Security Warning seen in Figure 14-8, click Install in order to install the application.

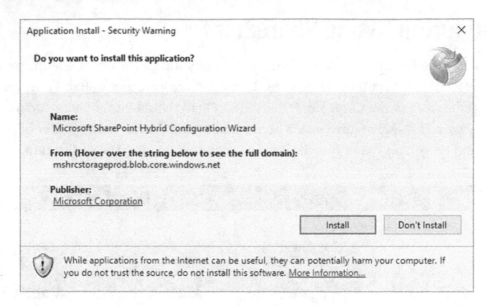

Figure 14-8. *Installing the SharePoint Hybrid Configuration Wizard*

Once the application is installed, the SharePoint Hybrid Configuration Wizard will start. After the splash screen, the first step you will have to do is enter both your on-premises and Office 365 credentials. In Figure 14-9, we have chosen to connect to our On-Premises farm with the currently logged in User and to connect to Office 365 using the sphybrid@cobaltatom.com service account we have previously created. Once this information is entered, click the Validate Credentials button. If the information was entered correctly, you should see a Succeeded message like the one in Figure 14-9.

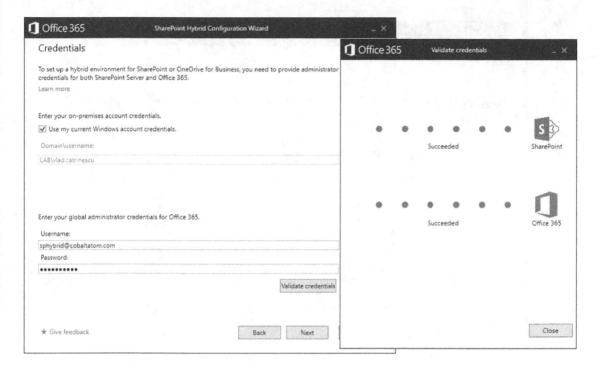

Figure 14-9. *Credential Validation in the SharePoint Hybrid Picker*

The wizard will then check the prerequisites needed for configuring hybrid on your farm. If you have configured the Service Applications mentioned earlier in this chapter and have installed the required modules, you should see green marks next to each category like in Figure 14-10.

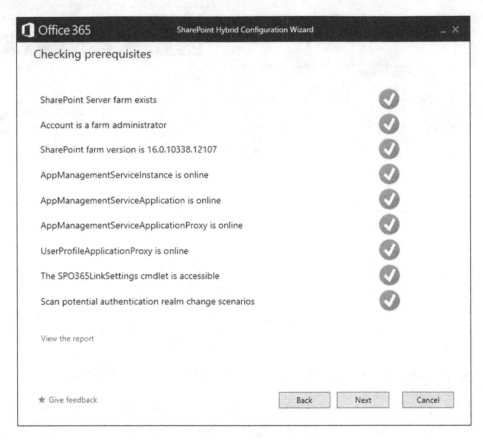

Figure 14-10. *SharePoint Hybrid Prerequisite Checker*

In the next screen you can choose the hybrid features that you want the wizard to configure for you. Depending on what version you are on, some options might be grayed out. For example, in Figure 14-11 you can see that Hybrid Auditing is grayed out since it was not available on SharePoint 2019 at the time of writing this book.

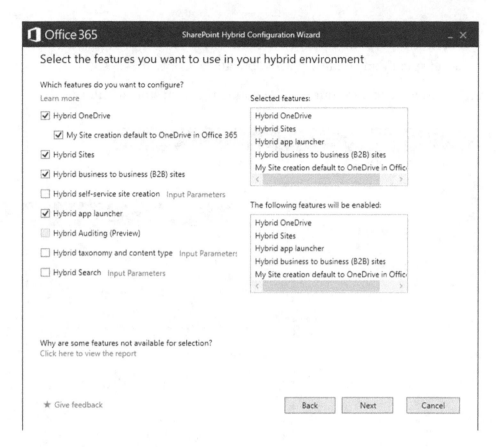

Figure 14-11. *Hybrid Feature Selection*

Some features, such as hybrid taxonomy and content types require extra parameters to be configured. Once you select the checkbox, and you click Input Parameters, a form like Figure 14-12 will appear where you can enter the required information. For the Hybrid Taxonomy and Content Types, the following parameters are needed:

- **Local Site URL**: URL of a Root Site Collection inside your on-premises SharePoint Farm.

- **Local Term Store Name**: The name of the Term Store from your local Managed Metadata Service Application. This might be different than the name of your Service Application!

- **Remote Group Names:** The names of the taxonomy groups that you want to replicate from SharePoint Online to On-Premises. If you don't specify any names, it will replicate all groups except system ones.

- **Remote Content Type Names**: The names of the content types that you want to replicate from SharePoint Online to On-Premises. If you don't specify any names, it will replicate all Content Types.

You will also need to add your Farm Account as a term store administrator.

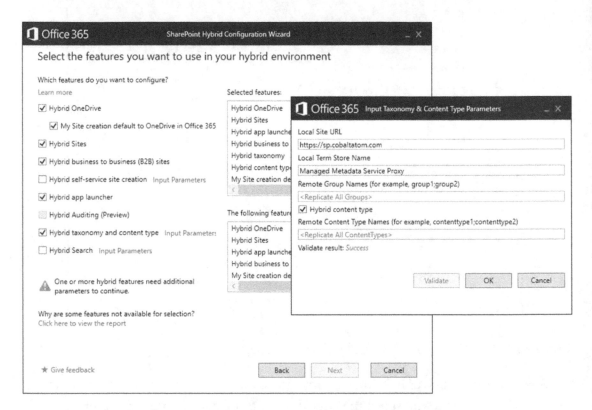

Figure 14-12. *Configuring Hybrid Taxonomy and Content Types*

Another feature that requires Input Parameters is Hybrid Cloud Search seen in Figure 14-13. While you can configure this feature via the SharePoint Hybrid Configuration Wizard, we recommend configuring the Cloud Search Service via PowerShell, which we will cover later in this chapter. By configuring it via PowerShell, you will have more control around the topology, application pools, and accounts used by this service application.

Figure 14-13. *Hybrid Search Parameters in the SharePoint Hybrid Configuration Wizard*

After you have selected all the features you want to configure, you can click Next. The SharePoint Hybrid Configuration Wizard will start configuring the settings, and you will be able to monitor the progress in the wizard. Once the configuration is complete, you will see a report of all the features that were successfully configured, as well as those that weren't. In Figure 14-14, you can see that most Hybrid features have been successfully configured, except Hybrid Search. To see the error, you can click View Failure Report, and you will get more details.

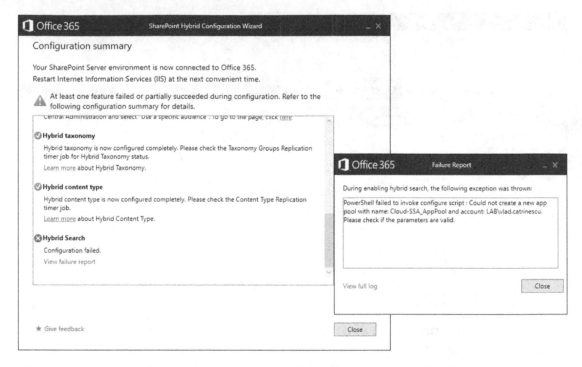

Figure 14-14. *Configuration Summary of the SharePoint Hybrid Configuration Wizard*

After the Wizard finishes running, an IISReset must be performed on all SharePoint servers of the farm.

Now that we have configured all Hybrid OneDrive for Business, Hybrid Sites, the Hybrid App Launcher as well as Hybrid Taxonomy and Content Types, let's verify that they work properly and view other configuration options that we have for those features. Afterwards, we will configure the Cloud Search Service Application via PowerShell.

Hybrid OneDrive for Business

To view or change the settings of Hybrid OneDrive for Business, you need to go in the SharePoint Server 2019 Central Administration in the **Office 365 ➤ Configure hybrid OneDrive and Sites features** section and you should reach a page similar to Figure 14-15.

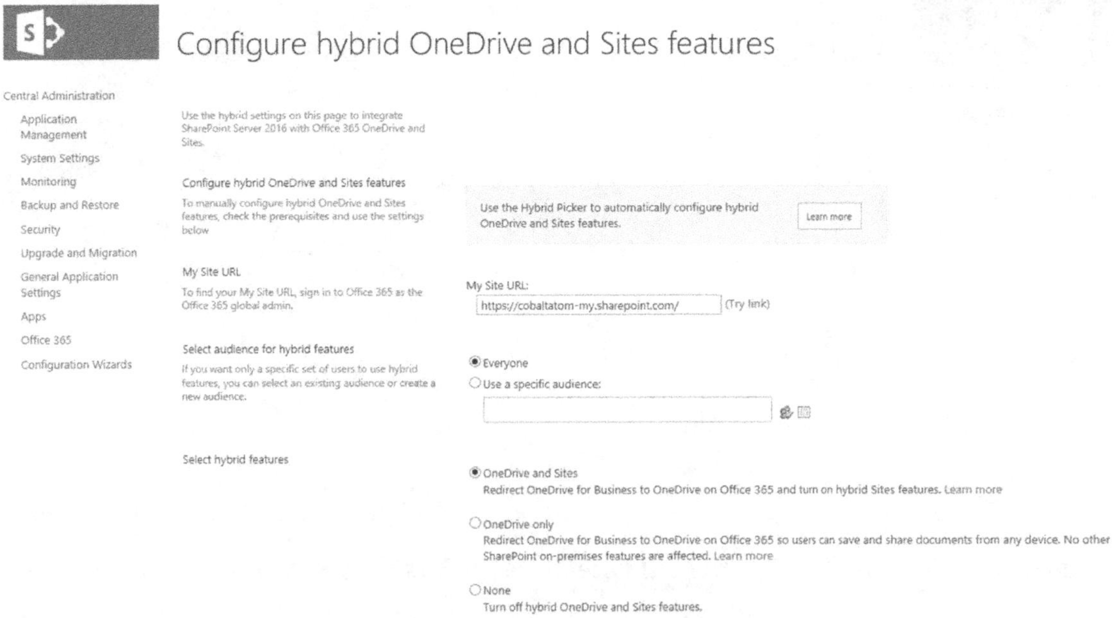

Figure 14-15. *Configure Hybrid OneDrive and Sites features in Central Administration*

In the My Site URL section, the SharePoint Hybrid Picker has automatically entered the My Site URL of your SharePoint Online Tenant. This can be found in the SharePoint Online Admin Center and is the one under the format `https://tenantName-my.sharepoint.com`.

One of the great features of Hybrid OneDrive for Business is that you can enable this feature for only certain users inside the organization, while the rest would be using OneDrive for Business On-Premises. If you want to enable this feature for only select users, you need to create an audience of those users and specify it as seen in Figure 14-16.

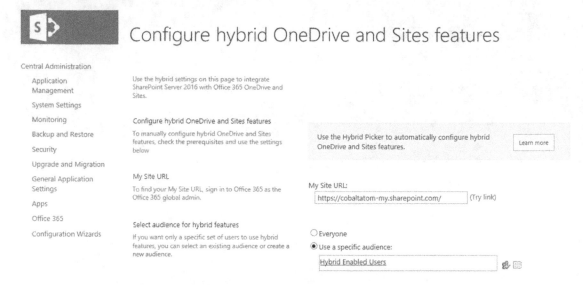

Figure 14-16. *Configuring Hybrid OneDrive for Business Settings*

In the next section of the page pictured in Figure 14-17, you can change what feature we want to activate. Our choices are

- OneDrive and Sites

- OneDrive only

- None

Figure 14-17. *Hybrid Feature Selection Radio Boxes*

Since we have decided to activate both features in the hybrid picker, the OneDrive and Sites feature is selected. If you want to disable the Hybrid Sites feature and only keep OneDrive for Business, you could select OneDrive Only.

To test the Hybrid OneDrive for Business functionality, log in as a user in the Hybrid Users audience, and in the App Launcher, when you click the "OneDrive" icon, you should be redirected to their OneDrive in Office 365. Furthermore, hybrid-enabled users will also see the Delve and Video in the App Launcher as seen in Figure 14-18. Furthermore, the OneDrive for Business link will also link to the user's OneDrive for Business in SharePoint Online.

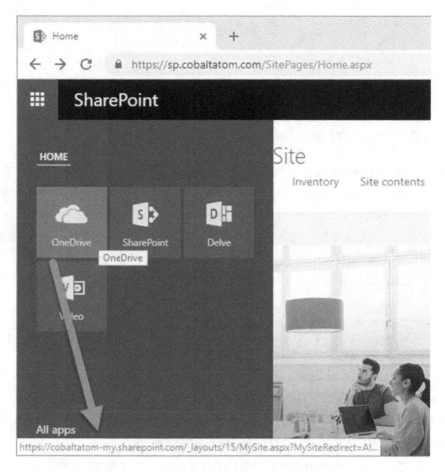

Figure 14-18. *Hybrid-Enabled App Launcher and Hybrid OneDrive for Business*

Users that are not in the Hybrid Users audience will see a Ribbon without the "Delve" and "Video" as seen in Figure 14-19.

Apps

 OneDrive    SharePoint

Figure 14-19. *Out-of-the-box SharePoint 2019 App Launcher*

An important aspect to remember when configuring Hybrid OneDrive for Business is that if you had implemented OneDrive for Business On-Premises before and your users had already put documents in their SharePoint 2019 OneDrive for Business, those files will not be automatically migrated to Office 365. You will need to migrate those files manually, by using PowerShell or a third-party product. The original My Site and OneDrive are still accessible for your users if they access it by entering the URL in the browser. Make sure to educate your users to use the version in Office 365 for business after you have successfully migrated their content.

Tip   If you want to avoid users having the "Welcome" screen and wait for their OneDrive for Business to be created in Office 365 on their first use, you can preprovision them by following this TechNet article: `https://docs.microsoft.com/en-us/onedrive/pre-provision-accounts`.

Hybrid Sites

The Hybrid Sites configuration is really tied with OneDrive for Business as you have seen from the preceding screenshots. The Configuration is done via the SharePoint Server 2019 Central Administration in the **Office 365 ➤ Configure hybrid OneDrive and Sites features** section. You cannot enable Hybrid Sites without enabling hybrid OneDrive for business, and both Hybrid Sites and Hybrid OneDrive for Business share the same audience

To test the functionality, log in as a member of the Hybrid Users audience, and follow an On-Premises Site by using the "Follow" button at the top right of a site seen in Figure 14-20.

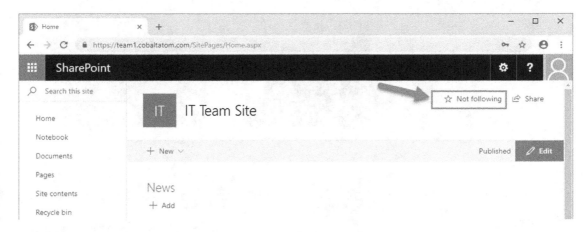

Figure 14-20. *The Follow Site button*

Afterward, when you go in the Ribbon and click the SharePoint icon, you should be redirected to the SharePoint Home in Office 365.

On the Sites Page seen in Figure 14-21, you should see the site you just followed from your On-Premises SharePoint Server 2019 Farm. In our case, that site is called "IT Team Site" and you can see it in Office 365.

Tip   It can take a few minutes until the site shows up in the SharePoint Home.

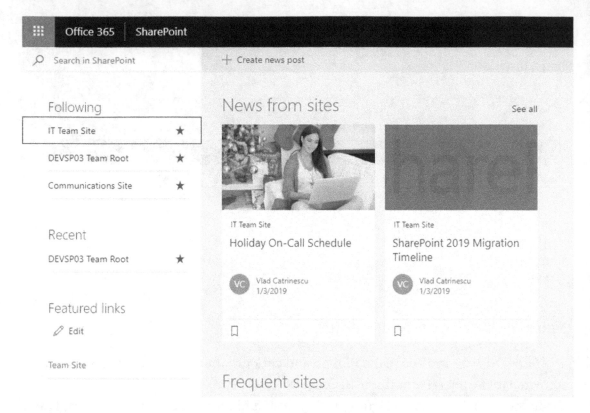

Figure 14-21. *On-Premises and SharePoint Online sites in the Office 365 Sites Page*

Hybrid Taxonomy and Content Types

Once Hybrid Taxonomy and Content Types are setup in your SharePoint Server farm, a new timer job called "Taxonomy Groups Replication" will be added to your farm. The job of this timer job is to copy all the specified terms groups from SharePoint Online to SharePoint On-Premises. The timer job schedule, seen in Figure 14-22, is set by default to run once daily.

Figure 14-22. *The Taxonomy Groups Replication Timer Job*

This Timer Job is configurable, so if your business requirements require, you could change it to run hourly for example. To test the timer job, you can click Run Now, and if it runs successfully, you will see all the specified Term Groups have been copied from SharePoint Online to your On-Premises farm, keeping the same name, owner and GUID. In Figure 14-23 you can see my Departments Group got copied over, as well as the different terms inside.

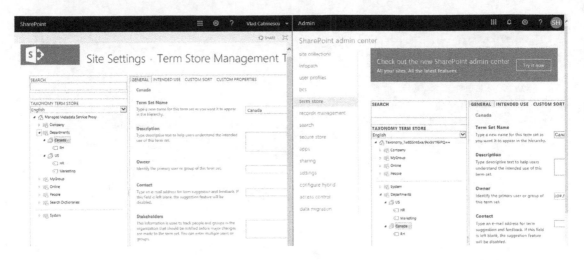

Figure 14-23. *Synchronized Terms*

It is very important to train your delegated taxonomy administrators (anyone who is allowed to modify terms, Term Group or Term Set) to use SharePoint Online to create Term Groups, Term Sets and terms and not to create, or modify those On-Premises. If terms are created, modified, or deleted On-Premises, they will *not* be replicated to SharePoint Online. Furthermore, if the same term is added On-Premises first and in SharePoint Online After, it will be synced with a GUID inside the name on the next run of the timer job.

Tip   You can set the Term Set On-Premises to "Closed" while leaving it "Open" in SharePoint Online. When a term set is closed, only metadata managers can add terms to this term set. This will block users on-premises from adding terms to an existing Term Set.

Hybrid Cloud Search

The Hybrid Cloud Search is a feature that we recommend you manually do, as it will allow you to better control the parameters of your new Search Service Application!

Setting Up the Cloud Search Service Application

In Order to use the Hybrid Cloud Search, you first need to set up the Cloud Search Service Application. The Cloud Search Service Application is very similar to a normal Search Service Application; the only difference is that the CloudIndex property is equal to True. This Property is ReadOnly after a Service Application is created; therefore, you cannot convert a normal Search Service Application. You can create it via the Central Administration, the only difference being you need to check the checkbox "Cloud Search Service Application" pointed in Figure 14-24.

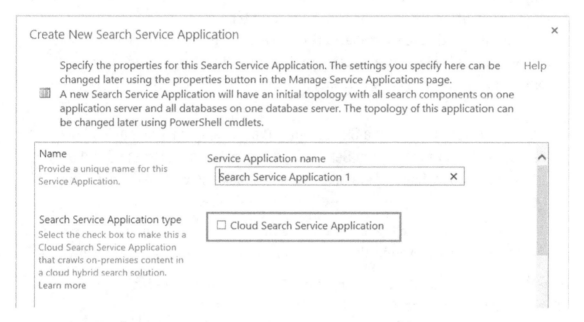

Figure 14-24. The Cloud Search Service Application checkbox

However, creating it via the Central Administration will cause your database name to have GUIDs, which we do not want. The other way is of course PowerShell. In this chapter, we will reuse the PowerShell code we saw in Chapters 3 and 6; the only difference is that you need to add the -CloudIndex $true Parameter when running the New-SPEnterpriseSearchServiceApplication Cmdlet.

First, let's create the Cloud Search Service Application via PowerShell, by running the following script on a Search MinRole server, or on a server that runs the Search components.

```
$sa = New-SPEnterpriseSearchServiceApplication -Name "Cloud Search Service
Application" -DatabaseName "CloudSearchDB" -ApplicationPool "SharePoint Web
Services Default" -AdminApplicationPool "SharePoint Web Services Default"
-CloudIndex $true
New-SPEnterpriseSearchServiceApplicationProxy -Name "Cloud Search Service
Application Proxy" -SearchApplication $sa
$sa = Get-SPEnterpriseSearchServiceApplication
$si = Get-SPEnterpriseSearchServiceInstance | ?{$_.Server -match "CALSP03"}
Start-SPEnterpriseSearchServiceInstance -Identity $si
$clone = $sa.Active Topology.Clone()
```

Note   If you are running on a SharePoint server running the Custom MinRole, make sure you start the Search Service Instance before creating the Cloud Search Service Application. Starting the Search Service Instance was covered in Chapter 6.

We then need to create the Initial Topology and add all the required components to our new Search Service Application by running the following PowerShell Script:

```
New-SPEnterpriseSearchAdminComponent -SearchTopology $clone
-SearchServiceInstance $si
New-SPEnterpriseSearchContentProcessingComponent -SearchTopology $clone
-SearchServiceInstance $si
New-SPEnterpriseSearchAnalyticsProcessingComponent -SearchTopology $clone
-SearchServiceInstance $si
New-SPEnterpriseSearchCrawlComponent -SearchTopology $clone
-SearchServiceInstance $si
New-SPEnterpriseSearchIndexComponent -SearchTopology $clone
-SearchServiceInstance $si -IndexPartition 0
New-SPEnterpriseSearchQueryProcessingComponent -SearchTopology $clone
-SearchServiceInstance $si
```

The next step is to add the components on the second Search Server as well, with Server Name CALSP04, and to activate the topology.

```
$si2 = Get-SPEnterpriseSearchServiceInstance | ?{$_.Server -match
"CALSP04"}
New-SPEnterpriseSearchAdminComponent -SearchTopology $clone
-SearchServiceInstance $si2
New-SPEnterpriseSearchAnalyticsProcessingComponent -SearchTopology $clone
-SearchServiceInstance $si2
New-SPEnterpriseSearchContentProcessingComponent -SearchTopology $clone
-SearchServiceInstance $si2
New-SPEnterpriseSearchCrawlComponent -SearchTopology $clone
-SearchServiceInstance $si2
New-SPEnterpriseSearchIndexComponent -SearchTopology $clone
-SearchServiceInstance $si2 -IndexPartition 0
New-SPEnterpriseSearchQueryProcessingComponent -SearchTopology $clone
-SearchServiceInstance $si2
$clone.Activate()
```

Lastly, get rid of all the Inactive Topologies and set the Crawl Account to the right one.

```
$sa = Get-SPEnterpriseSearchServiceApplication
foreach($topo in (Get-SPEnterpriseSearchTopology -SearchApplication $sa |
?{$_.State -eq "Inactive"})){Remove-SPEnterpriseSearchTopology -Identity
$topo -Confirm:$false}
$sa = Get-SPEnterpriseSearchServiceApplication
$content = New-Object Microsoft.Office.Server.Search.Administration.
Content($sa)
$content.SetDefaultGatheringAccount("LAB\s-crawl", (ConvertTo-SecureString
"<Password>" -AsPlainText -Force))
```

After the script finishes running successfully, you can navigate to the Central Administration and go to your Cloud Search Service Application. Everything should be exactly the same as a normal Search Service Application and your Servers should show all green check marks. The only difference is a gray box at the top of the screen advising you that this is a Cloud Search Service Application, as seen in Figure 14-25.

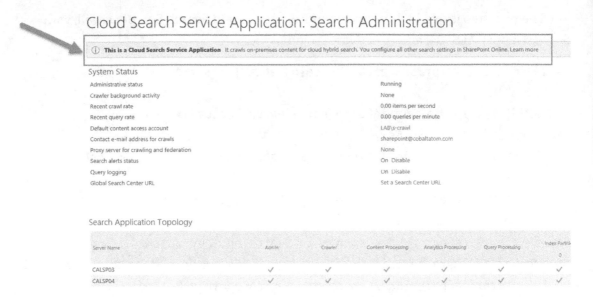

Figure 14-25. *The Cloud Search Service Application information box*

You then need to create your Content Sources, but do not start the crawl yet as we need to set up the connection between our Cloud Search Service Application and SharePoint Online. This Process is called On-Boarding.

On-Boarding Process

The On-Boarding Process is done by a script provided by Microsoft in the Download Center. This download called "Windows PowerShell scripts to configure cloud hybrid search for SharePoint" can be found at `www.microsoft.com/en-us/download/details.aspx?id=51490`.

Note   The OnBoarding process is only needed if you configured the Cloud Search Service Application via PowerShell or the Central Administration. You do not need to do this if you configured it with the Hybrid Configuration Wizard.

The zip file contains two scripts. The first script called CreateCloudSSA.ps1 is used to create the Cloud Search Service Application, but we already created it so you can discard it. The important script that we will use is called Onboard-CloudHybridSearch.ps1.

To run the Onboard-CloudHybridSearch.ps1 you need to have the Microsoft Online Services Sign-In Assistant as well as the Microsoft Azure AD PowerShell installed on the server on which you wish to run it. We have previously installed those prerequisites when we set up the Server-to-Server Authentication earlier in the chapter, so we will use the same server to run this Onboard script.

The Onboard-CloudHybridSearch takes three parameters:

1. **PortalURL**: The Root Site Collection of your SharePoint Online Tenant

2. **CloudSsaId**: The GUID or Name of your Cloud Search Service Application

3. **Credential**: A PSCredential object containing the credential of a Global Office 365 Administrator

The script is doing four main things:

1. **Get-HybridSSA**

   This section validates that the CloudSsaId you gave is a valid Cloud Search Service Application.

2. **Prepare-Environment**

   This section validates you have the Microsoft Online Services Sign-In Assistant and Microsoft Azure AD PowerShell installed on the server.

3. **Connect-SPFarmToAAD**

   This section checks if you already have a Server-to-Server Authentication setup and use it, or else it will create one for you. Since we have created one previously in this chapter, it just used the existing one. This section also creates a new SharePoint Online connection proxy to allow the farm to communication with the external endpoint of the cloud Search Service.

4. **Add-ServicePrincipal**

   This section will add the Office 365 Service Principal ID as well as create four new service Principals.

Now that we know what the script does, we first need to create the three variables we will pass as parameters to the script. We explained those variables earlier.

```
$PortalUrl = "https://cobaltatom.sharepoint.com"
$CloudSsaId = "Cloud Search Service Application"
$Credential = get-credential
```

Afterward, we need to navigate to the folder where the Onboard-CloudHybridSearch.ps1 script is and run the following PowerShell cmdlet:

```
.\Onboard-CloudHybridSearch.ps1 $PortalUrl $CloudSsaId $Credential
```

The script should finish without any errors and without breaking any existing Hybrid Configurations.

Note   The script might throw an error on "Restarting SharePoint Server Search…" if you did not run it from a Search MinRole server or a server running the Search Services. Make sure to run the `Restart-Service OSearch16` cmdlet or manually restart the Search service on all the Search Servers in your Cloud SSA topology.

When the On-Boarding Process is done, it's time to crawl our content and see if everything worked.

Crawling and Testing

In order to get the data in Office 365, we must first crawl it. Navigate to the Central Administration and to your Cloud Search Service Application. Afterward, go in Content Sources and start a Full Crawl on one of your content sources with SharePoint Content.

Wait for the Crawl to finish and verify the Crawl Log to make sure that there is a high Success Rate and no Top-Level Errors.

Tip   With the Cloud Search Service Application, the Searchable items row in the Search Administration screen will always show 0. You need to check the Crawl Log to see how many items have been marked as successfully crawled.

Once the crawl is done and you verified that documents have been successfully crawled, navigate to your Office 365 Search Center and search for the following query: *isexternalcontent:1*. The isexternalcontent property is a managed property part of the SharePoint Online search schema. This Property gets automatically set to TRUE for On-Premises content (External from SharePoint Online) and FALSE for SharePoint Online content. This property will allow us to filter On-Premises or SharePoint Online results in our Result Sources. When you search for *isexternalcontent:1* in the SharePoint Online Search Center you should content from your On-Premises SharePoint Farm as seen in Figure 14-26.

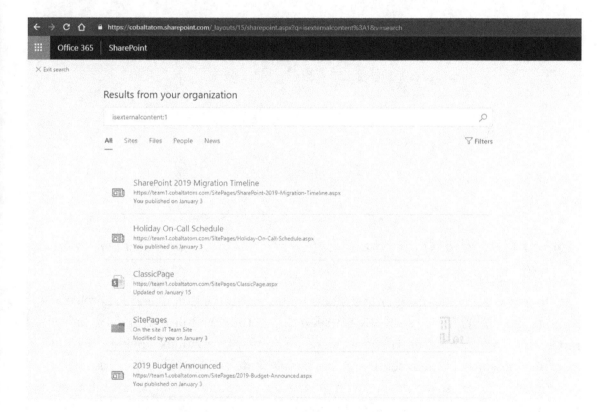

Figure 14-26. *Testing the Cloud Search Service Application*

You can easily verify the content is from On-Premises by looking at the URL. SharePoint Online content always ends with ".sharepoint.com".

If you do a query for content that you know exists in both locations, you should see results from both systems, as seen in Figure 14-27. The first two results come from SharePoint Online while the next two come from SharePoint 2019 On-Premises.

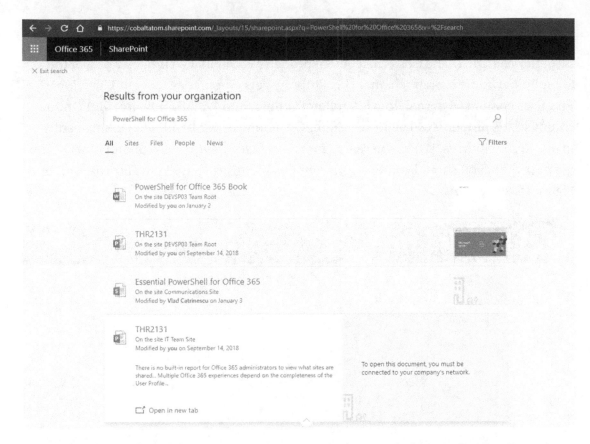

Figure 14-27. *Results from both SharePoint Online and SharePoint On-Premises are shown*

Once you get results from both systems it means that the Cloud Search Service Application is functioning correctly, and you can set the schedule and crawl your remaining Content Sources. However, since we don't have an index On-Premises anymore, all your On-Premises Search boxes and Search Center will not work at this point. Let's fix them so our users have a great experience and are able to search content from both SharePoint Online and Office 365.

Searching from SharePoint On-Premises

The default result source for Cloud Search Service Application remains the local SharePoint index, the same as a regular Search Service Application. However, since the Cloud Search Service application pushes all the crawled items in the SharePoint Online index, all our On-Premises Queries stop returning results, including the Search Boxes in document Libraries.

What we will need to do is change the default Result Source of the Cloud Search Service Application to use a new Result Source that queries SharePoint Online for the results. This is using the same technique as the Outgoing Federated Search.

To create the result source, open Central Administration, navigate to the Cloud Search Service Application, and go to the Result Sources Page. Click the "New Result Source" button to create a new Result Source.

Give a Name to the Result Source, for example "Combined Results," as well as a meaningful description. The Protocol should be "Remote SharePoint" and the Remote Service URL should be the root site collection of your SharePoint Online tenant as seen in Figure 14-28.

Cloud Search Service Application: Add Result Source

(i) **Note:** This result source will be available to all sites. To make one for just a specific site, use the query rules page in its Site Settings.

General Information

Names must be unique at each administrative level. For example, two result sources in a site cannot share a name, but one in a site and one provided by the site collection can.

Descriptions are shown as tooltips when selecting result sources in other configuration pages.

Name

| Combined Results |

Description

| This Result Source will return results from both SharePoint Online and the local farm |

Protocol

Select Local SharePoint for results from the index of this Search Service.

Select OpenSearch 1.0/1.1 for results from a search engine that uses that protocol.

Select Exchange for results from an exchange source.

Select Remote SharePoint for results from the index of a search service hosted in another farm.

○ Local SharePoint
● Remote SharePoint
○ OpenSearch 1.0/1.1
○ Exchange

Remote Service URL

Type the address of the root site collection of the remote SharePoint farm.

| https://cobaltatom.sharepoint.com |

Figure 14-28. *Creating a Combined Results result source*

The Type will be "SharePoint Search Results" and we will not transform the Query for this Result Source as we want all the results, both On-Premises and Online. In the Credentials Information choose "Default Authentication" as seen in Figure 14-29.

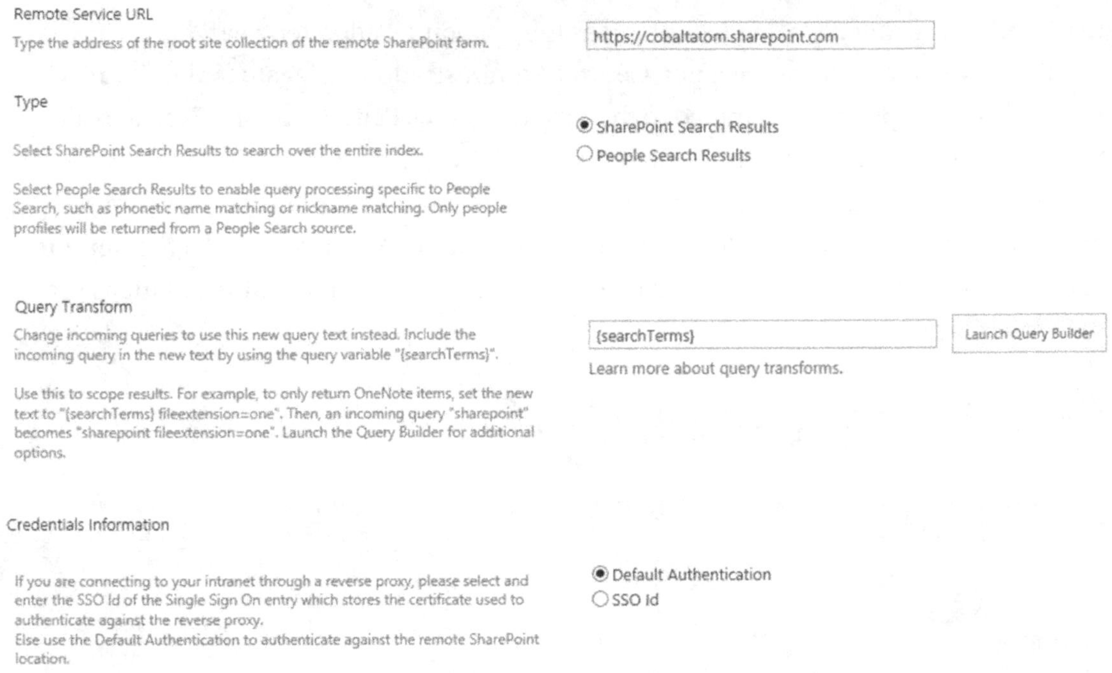

Remote Service URL

Type the address of the root site collection of the remote SharePoint farm.

https://cobaltatom.sharepoint.com

Type

Select SharePoint Search Results to search over the entire index.

Select People Search Results to enable query processing specific to People Search, such as phonetic name matching or nickname matching. Only people profiles will be returned from a People Search source.

⦿ SharePoint Search Results
◯ People Search Results

Query Transform

Change incoming queries to use this new query text instead. Include the incoming query in the new text by using the query variable "{searchTerms}".

Use this to scope results. For example, to only return OneNote items, set the new text to "{searchTerms} fileextension=one". Then, an incoming query "sharepoint" becomes "sharepoint fileextension=one". Launch the Query Builder for additional options.

{searchTerms} | Launch Query Builder |

Learn more about query transforms.

Credentials Information

If you are connecting to your intranet through a reverse proxy, please select and enter the SSO Id of the Single Sign On entry which stores the certificate used to authenticate against the reverse proxy.
Else use the Default Authentication to authenticate against the remote SharePoint location.

⦿ Default Authentication
◯ SSO Id

Figure 14-29. *Creating a Combined Results result source*

Click Save and you will be redirected back to the Results Source Page. Click the drop-down for the Result Source you just created and click "Set as Default" as seen in Figure 14-30.

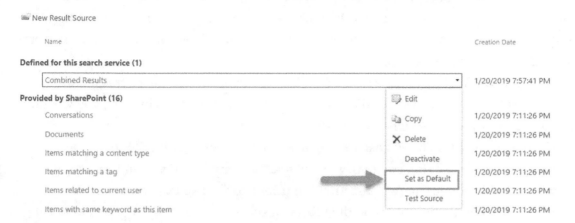

Figure 14-30. *Setting the Default Result Source*

Your On-Premises Search Boxes as well as Search Center will now show results from both On-Premises and SharePoint Online, exactly as if a user searched from the SharePoint Online Search Center.

While having results from both systems combined is an amazing feature, your users might want to target only certain systems. In the next section, we will learn how to customize our Search Results.

Customizing Your Search Results

By creating Result Sources both in SharePoint Online and SharePoint Server 2019, you can create different pages in your Search Centers to show for example only On-Premises results, or only SharePoint Online results.

To create different pages that show results only from certain systems, you can create different tabs in your SharePoint Search Centers with different result sources. The result sources would use the Query Builder and the `isexternalcontent` managed property to return the appropriate results. For example, you could have the following Query text to return only SharePoint Online results:

```
{searchTerms} NOT(IsExternalContent:1)
```

Or the following Query text for On-Premises only results:

```
{searchTerms}(IsExternalContent:1)
```

Something that will also need to be planned is People Search. By default, all the users in the SharePoint Online User Profile Service Application will be indexed by the Office 365 crawler. If you also crawl On-Premises users using your Cloud Search Service Application, your search results will return duplicate data. There are two options you can go with to go around this challenge.

The first option is to use the Office 365 User Profile service as the primary source of user information and let Office 365 search take care of crawling it. This way, you will not need to crawl people data On-Premises.

The second option if you wish to keep the On-Premises User Profile service as primary source of user information, you will need to crawl that On-Premises people data, and then use the Query transformation rules to only display results from On-Premises. This could be done by adding a new result source for People Search and using the `isexternalcontent` managed property to filter results.

Next Steps

In this chapter, we have learned how to configure a Hybrid SharePoint 2019 Infrastructure and offer additional features to your users. In the next chapter, we will learn how we can use other cloud-only features such as PowerApps and Microsoft Flow with your On-Premises content!

CHAPTER 15

PowerApps and Flow

We will begin looking at how to use Microsoft PowerApps and Microsoft Flow with SharePoint Server 2019 via the Microsoft On-Premises Data Gateway. Microsoft Flow and PowerApps are the recommended way of automating business processes and creating apps for SharePoint 2019 hybrid environments and SharePoint Online. Those services are still cloud-only services, meaning they only run in the cloud, but you can integrate them with on-premises data. This chapter will cover the installation of a highly available Data Gateway as well as examples of using PowerApps and Flow with on-premises SharePoint data.

Microsoft On-Premises Data Gateway

The Microsoft Data Gateway can be deployed on one or more servers in your on-premises environment. The Data Gateway may be configured to run under a specified Active Directory managed service account, Domain User account, or the default service account. Our scenario will be using a highly available, two node Data Gateway implementation using the default service account, NT SERVICE\PBIEgwService. You may need use an alternate Active Directory account if you have an upstream proxy server that requires authentication. If you do encounter this scenario, use an Active Directory Managed Service account, like what was configured for SQL Server in Chapter 3 of this book.

© Vlad Catrinescu and Trevor Seward 2019

V. Catrinescu and T. Seward, *Deploying SharePoint 2019*, https://doi.org/10.1007/978-1-4842-4526-2_15

Note   The Data Management Gateway can be downloaded from `https://go.microsoft.com/fwlink/?LinkID=820925` or via the PowerApps site at `https://web.powerapps.com`.

Installation

In this scenario, we will be deploying the Data Management Gateway to CALDMG01 and CALDMG02. These servers are joined to the Active Directory domain and do not require any firewall ports to be open inbound from the public Internet. The servers are running Windows Server 2016. While Microsoft recommends an 8 core CPU and 8GB RAM, the exact sizing of the server will depend on your usage of the service.

As the gateway requires you to log into Office 365 from the server where it is installed, you may want to turn off the IE Enhanced Security Configuration for Users in the Server Manager, Local Server settings.

After downloading the gateway installer, run it on the first Data Management Gateway server. The installation will only ask you for the path to install the gateway to. Once the installation is complete, you will be prompted to enter an e-mail address associated with the gateway, as shown in Figure 15-1.

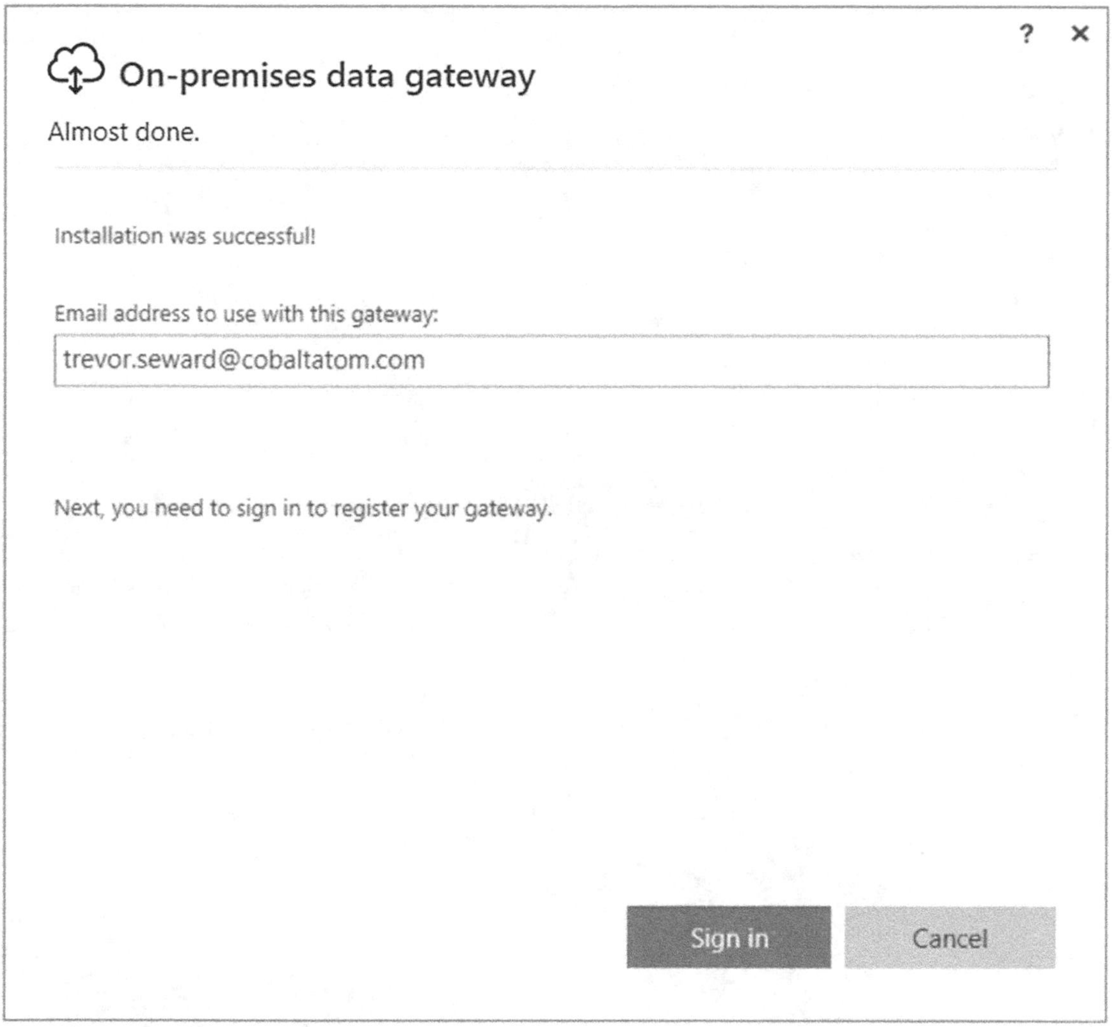

On-premises data gateway

Almost done.

Installation was successful!

Email address to use with this gateway:

trevor.seward@cobaltatom.com

Next, you need to sign in to register your gateway.

Sign in   Cancel

Figure 15-1. *Specifying an e-mail address for the data gateway*

You will be prompted to sign into Office 365 using the e-mail address in Figure 15-1. Once the sign in has completed, we will be configuring the gateway. You will be prompted to create the name of the gateway. This is how the name will appear when connecting to the gateway from PowerApps or Flow. You will also need to specify a recovery key for the gateway, as shown in Figure 15-2. Keep this key in a safe location.

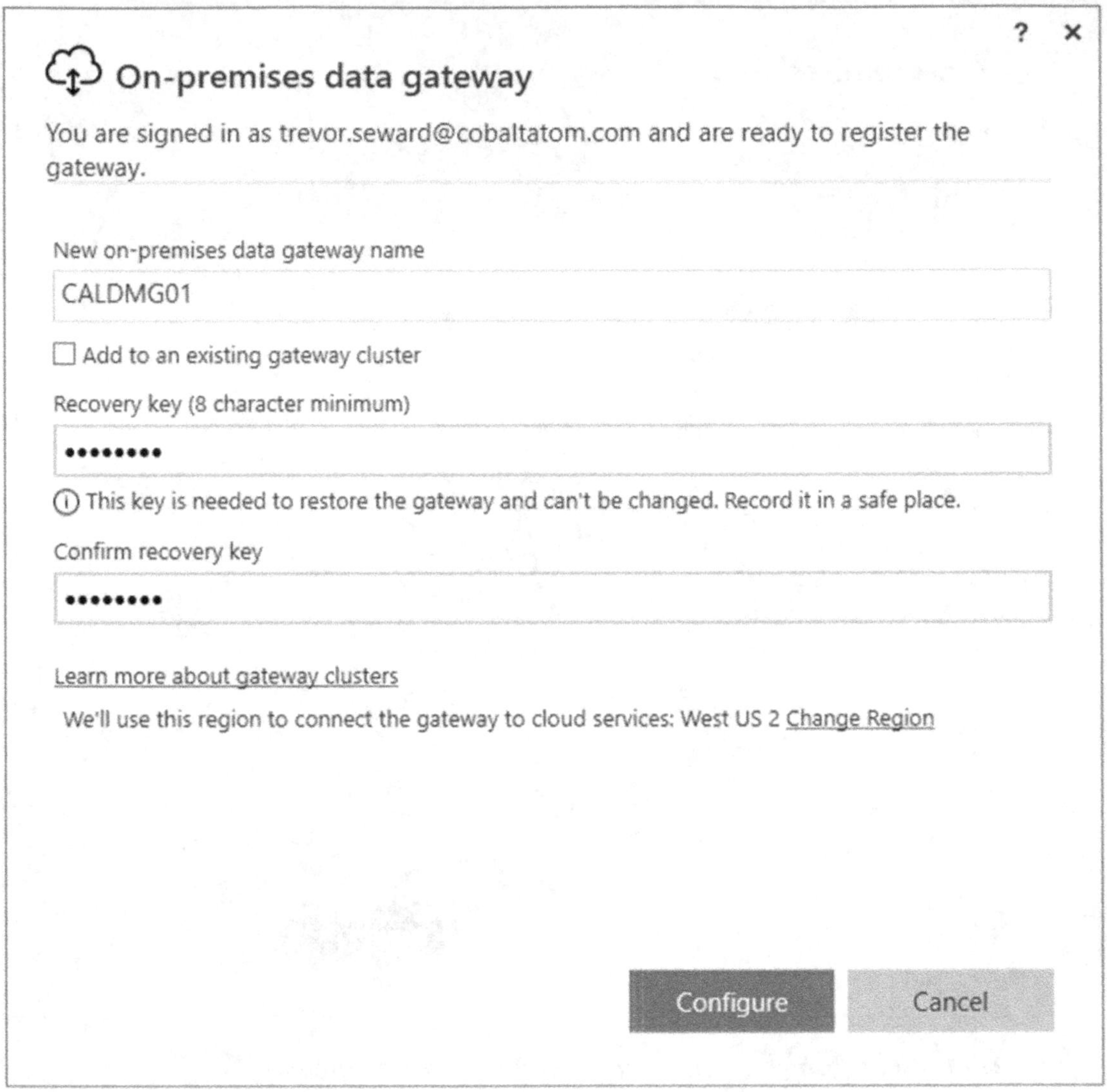

Figure 15-2. Configuring the data gateway

The on-premises gateway is configured at this point and the PowerApps, Microsoft Flow status should be green, as shown in Figure 15-3.

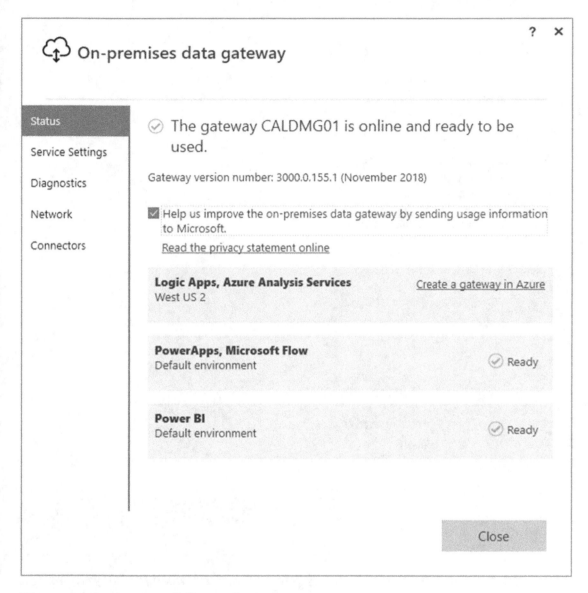

Figure 15-3. A successfully configured gateway

Additional options are available in the gateway settings, such as under Network, we can configure Azure Service Bus to use TLS 1.2.

To add an additional server to the Data Management Gateway, start the installation on the second server. Use the same sign in when prompted for an e-mail address as previously shown in Figure 15-1. After signing into the service, you will see a prompt to register a new gateway or migrate a gateway, as shown in Figure 15-4. Choose the option to register a new gateway.

Figure 15-4. When another gateway is detected, you will need to choose an option to register the gateway as new or migrate an existing gateway

Enter a new gateway name and select the option to Add to an existing gateway cluster. Select the previous gateway we created and then enter the same recovery key we used to create the initial gateway, as shown in Figure 15-5.

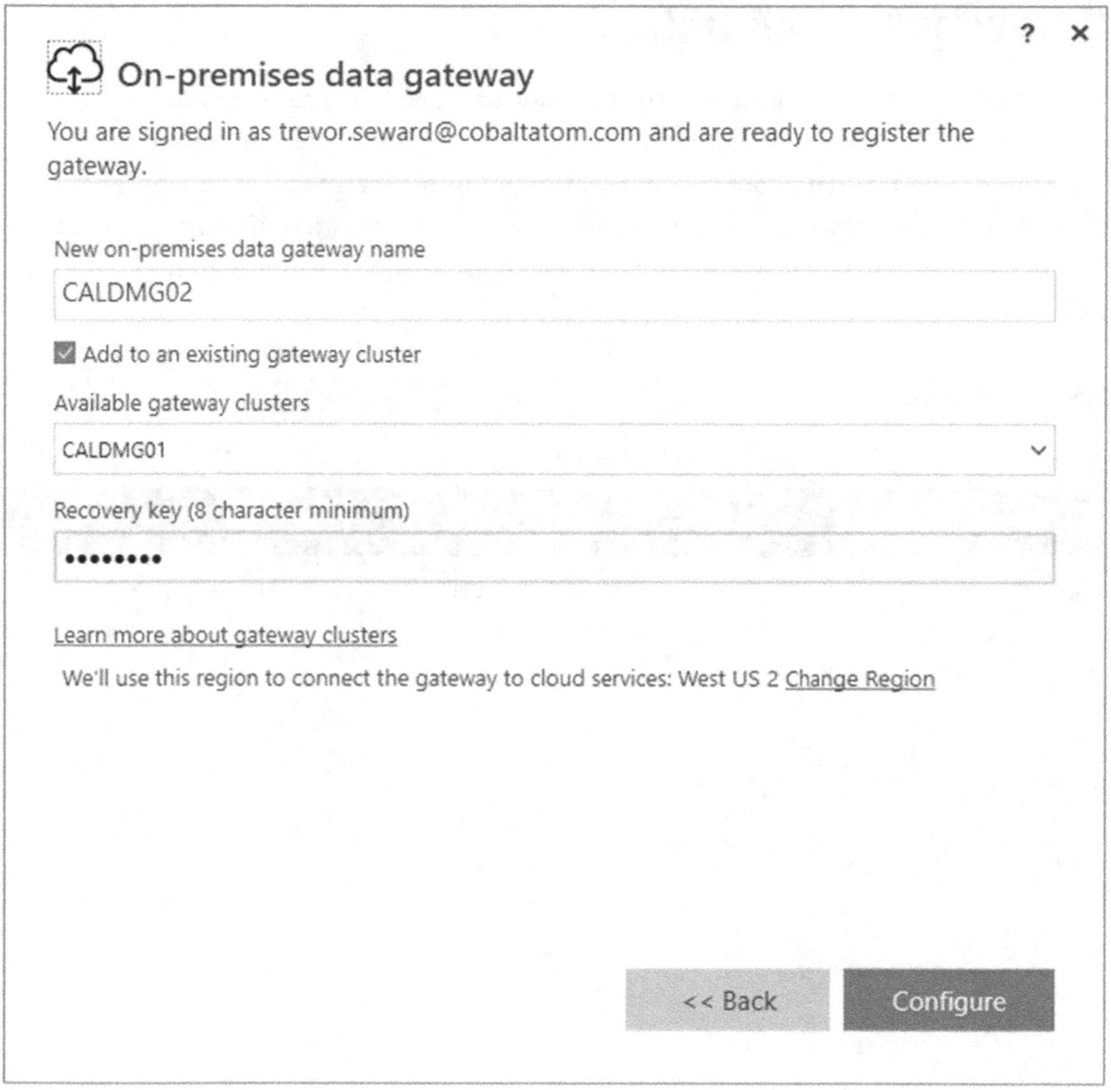

Figure 15-5. *Configuring the second data gateway*

As previously shown in Figure 15-3, a successfully configured gateway will show as ready for PowerApps and Microsoft Flow. Note that if you configured the first gateway to use TLS 1.2 under the Network tab, you will also need to set that on any subsequently deployed gateways.

Gateway Administration

To check the status and administer the gateway, navigate to `https://web.powerapps.com` or `https://flow.microsoft.com` and sign in with the same account used to register the gateways with Office 365. On either service, in the left-hand navigation under Data, then Gateways you can administer all on-premises gateways. If you navigated to Microsoft Flow, you will be redirected to PowerApps to administer the gateway, as shown in Figure 15-6.

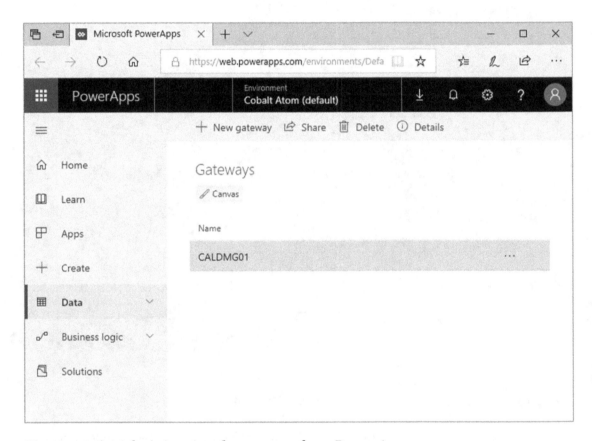

Figure 15-6. *Administering the gateway from PowerApps*

Clicking the Share button, you can add individual users with the capability to use the gateway including what type of services they may connect to. You can also allow the user to use the gateway but also share it. Finally, you can make them an administrator of the gateway. You can also share the gateway with all users in your organization who are synchronized to Azure AD and who are licensed for PowerApps, Power BI, or Flow, as shown in Figure 15-7.

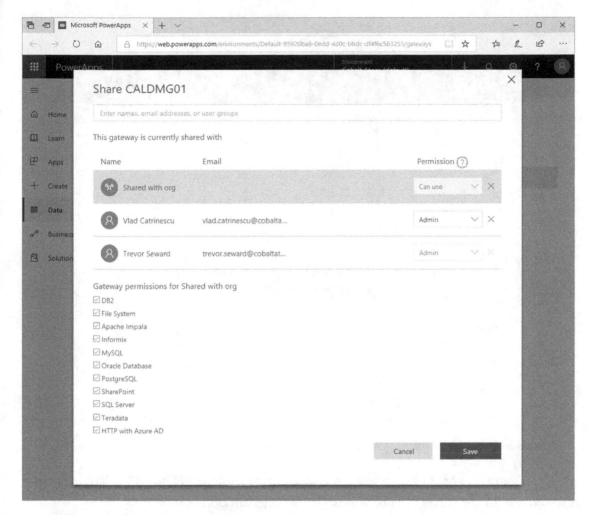

Figure 15-7. *Adding all users in the organization to the gateway*

Clicking Details will show you the status of the connection to the gateway. If one or more gateways are online, the status will be Live, as shown in Figure 15-8.

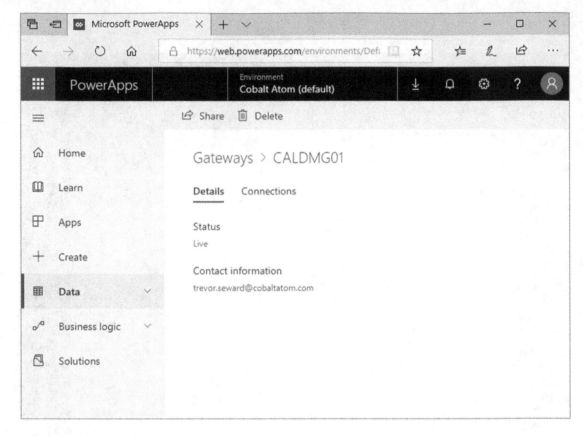

Figure 15-8. *One or more gateways are online*

If all gateways are down, you will see an error, as shown in Figure 15-9. This may be caused due to the server or gateway service being in an offline state.

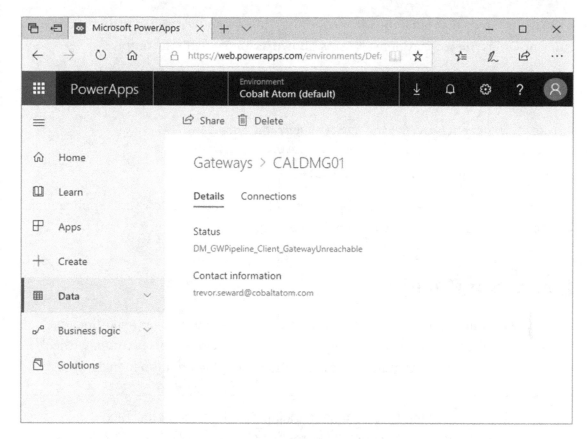

Figure 15-9. *All gateways are in an unavailable state*

PowerShell

The gateways may also be configured via PowerShell. By default, the PowerShell module is installed to "C:\Program Files\On-premises data gateway\ OnPremisesDataGatewayHAMgmt.psm1". You must first log into the gateway via PowerShell prior to using the other cmdlets available using Login-OnPremisesDataGateway. Use Get-OnPremisesDataGatewayClusters to retrieve the objectID (also called the ClusterObjectId) and the gatewayObjectId. There will be one gatewayObjectId per gateway server in the cluster. In this example, the output of Get-OnPremisesDataGatewayClusters shows my objectID as 12558961-deac-4142-9952-4e9325d63ad5 and my secondary servers gatewayObjectId as 6dc96cc6-70a8-48f9-90aeb1305780841f. To find out if the Microsoft Data Gateway software is up to date, I can then run Get-OnPremisesDataGatewayStatus, shown as follows with the output:

```
Get-OnPremisesDataGatewayStatus -ClusterObjectId 12558961-deac-4142-9952-
4e9325d63ad5 -GatewayObjectId 12558961-deac-4142-9952-4e9325d63ad5

gatewayStatus gatewayVersion gatewayUpgradeState
------------- -------------- -------------------
Live          3000.0.155.1   UpToDate
```

Now that our Gateway is setup, let's start building some workflows and applications, but before that, check if we have the right licensing!

Licensing Requirements

Effective February 1, 2019, Microsoft has implemented some changes regarding the licensing requirements to use Flow and PowerApps with On-Premises content. Check out the current licensing requirements at the time of implementation to make sure that

---

Note   You can view the blog post announcing the changes on the Tech Community site at the following link: `https://techcommunity.microsoft. com/t5/Office-Retirement-Blog/UPDATED-Updates-to-Microsoft- Flow-and-PowerApps-for-Office-365/ba-p/289589`.

As always, we recommend talking to your Microsoft Licensing expert about the cases specific to your organization.

Workflows with Microsoft Flow

Microsoft Flow is the recommended way of doing workflows in Office 365, as well as hybrid SharePoint scenarios. Before creating our Flows, we need to create a connection to our On-Premises SharePoint 2019 Server. To create the connection, open the Flow Menu on the left, and navigate to Data, and then Connections as seen in Figure 15-10.

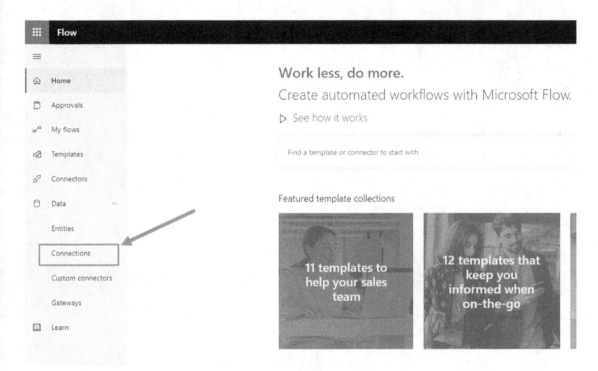

Figure 15-10. *Connections In Microsoft Flow*

At the top of the page, click **New Connection** and select SharePoint from the list of available Connections. In the radio buttons, select the **Connect using on-premises data gateway** option as seen in Figure 15-11, and select **Windows** as the Authentication Type.

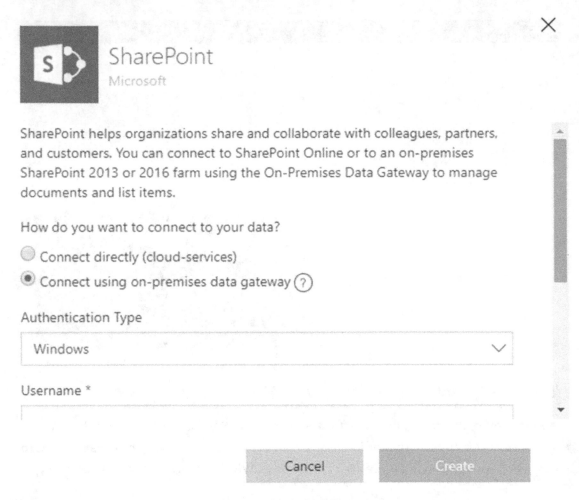

Figure 15-11. *Creating a new connection for SharePoint On-Premises*

After scrolling down, enter your on-premises Username and Password and select the Gateway you want to use when connecting on-premises as seen in Figure 15-12.

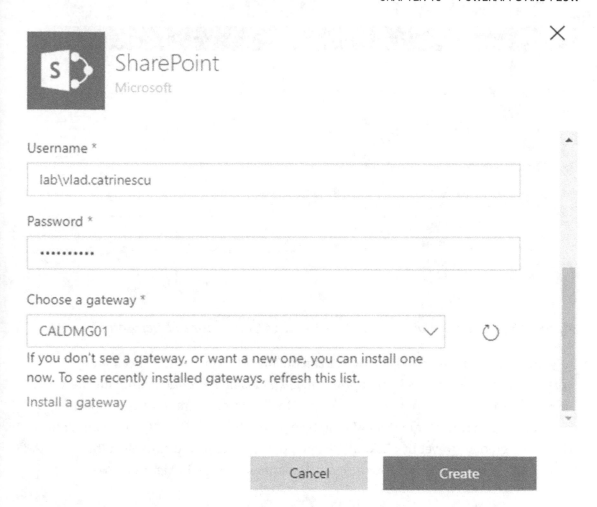

Figure 15-12. *Creating a new connection to SharePoint On-Premises Part 2*

Once the connection is done, you will see a SharePoint connection with your domain credentials in the Connections tab in Microsoft Flow, like Figure 15-13. Depending on your prior usage of Microsoft Flow, you might have more or less connections than Figure 15-13.

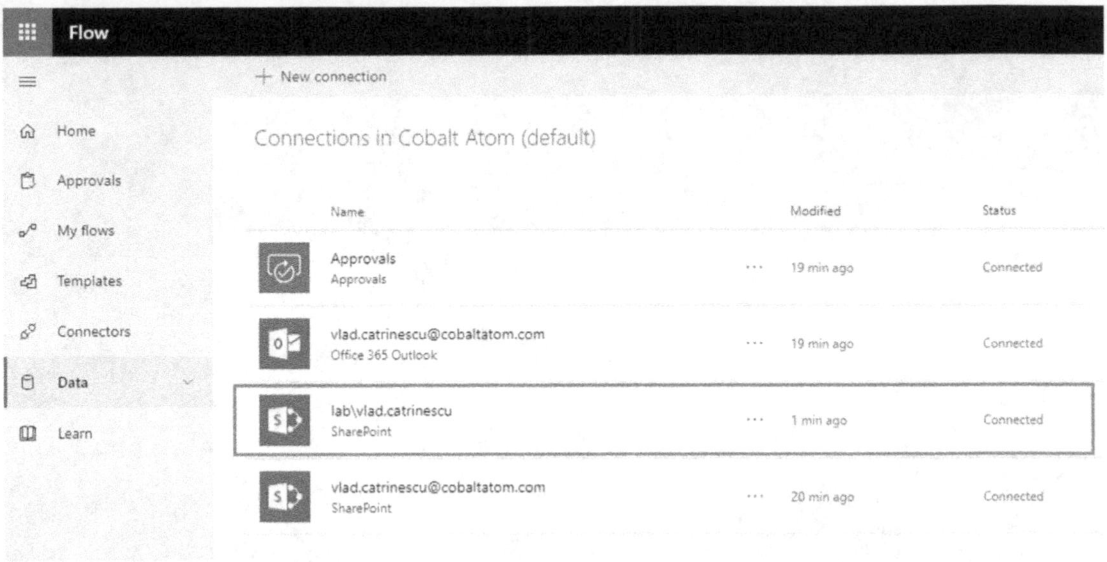

Figure 15-13. *The newly created On-Premises Connector in Microsoft Flow*

Now that our connector is ready, we can create our workflows. I will create a workflow starting from the *Start approval when a new item is added* template offered by Microsoft, and since I want to connect to my On-Premises SharePoint, it's important to select the right connector for SharePoint. By default, the SharePoint Online connector will be selected, however by clicking the three dots next to it, you can select the SharePoint Connection with your domain credentials as seen in Figure 15-14.

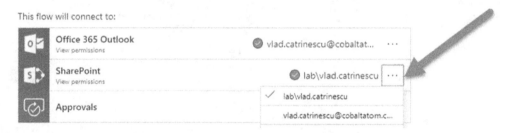

Figure 15-14. *Selecting the right connector when creating the Flow*

You can then start creating your Flows as usual, and when entering an On-Premises Site Collection, Flow will be able to propose dynamic values as the Inventory list suggestion seen in Figure 15-15.

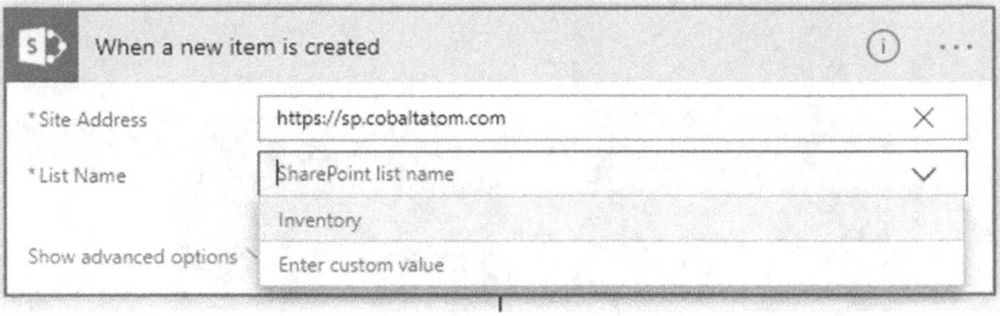

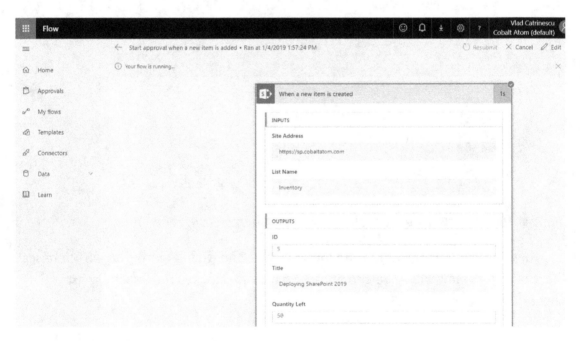

Figure 15-15. *Flow proposes an On-Premises list*

You can then test it out by adding an item on your On-Premises list, or the trigger that you configured, and the Flow should kick off within the SLA specified by your Flow Licensing. In Figure 15-16 you can see our Flow got triggered when a new item got added in the Inventory list of our On-Premises Site Collection.

Figure 15-16. *Flow triggered successfully*

Even if the integration with Microsoft Flow and On-Premises SharePoint is great, something that is missing from SharePoint 2019 in comparison to SharePoint Online is the ability to manually trigger Flows from On-Premises. There is no Flow button in SharePoint

On-premises lists and Document Libraries, so triggers such as *On Selected Item* are available in Flow, but cannot be used with SharePoint On-Premises.

Now that we can create Workflows with Microsoft Flow, let's look at PowerApps.

Business Apps with PowerApps

PowerApps is the recommended tool to create business applications in Office 365 and hybrid SharePoint Deployments. PowerApps shares a lot of back-end with Microsoft Flow, so if you have created the connection for our On-Premises SharePoint environment in Flow as we have done earlier in this chapter, you should also see it in your PowerApps Connections as seen in Figure 15-17.

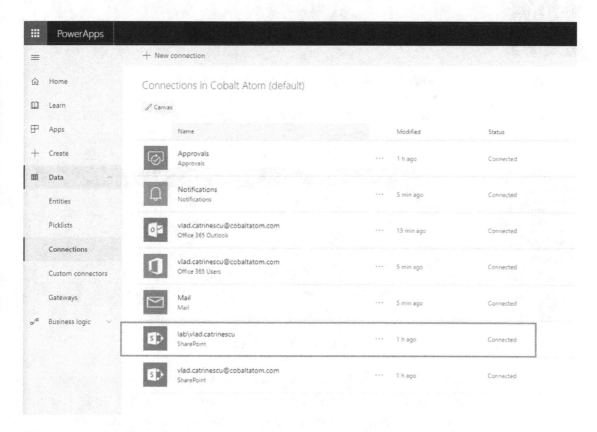

Figure 15-17. SharePoint On-Premises connection in PowerApps

We can then start creating a blank application, or starting from a template, and in the Data Connections, both the SharePoint Online as well as SharePoint On-Premises connections will be displayed. Select the one that displays your on-premises domain credentials and enter the URL of your SharePoint On-Premises Site collection as seen in Figure 15-18, then click Go.

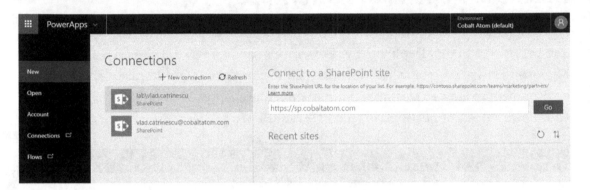

Figure 15-18. *SharePoint On-Premises and Online connections*

PowerApps should then be able to automatically suggest the lists available in that Site Collection as seen in Figure 15-19.

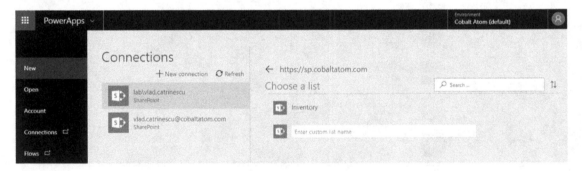

Figure 15-19. *Lists in our On-Premises Site Collection*

You are now able to create your business application using PowerApps with your On-Premises data. You can use the same knowledge as if the data was fully in SharePoint Online. You can view the PowerApps designer showing items from SharePoint On-Premises in Figure 15-20.

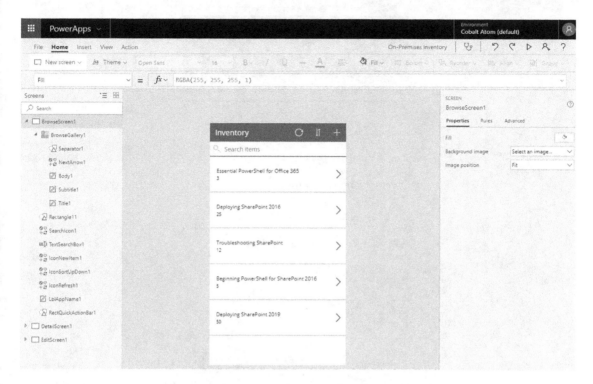

Figure 15-20. *PowerApps Designer with SharePoint On-Premises items*

After the app is published, you can also consume it from your mobile phone. In Figure 15-21, you can view the same application displaying On-Premises items on my Android phone.

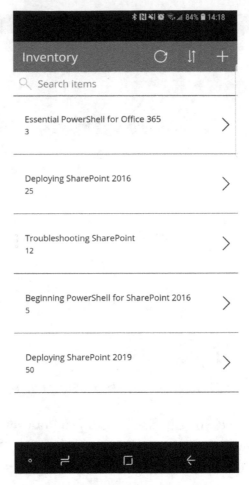

Figure 15-21. *On-Premises Items in PowerApps on an android phone*

Like Microsoft Flow, while the integration between PowerApps and SharePoint Server 2019 is great, there are some features missing. One of the biggest one is the ability to customize SharePoint list forms using PowerApps and displaying those forms directly in the list.

We have now successfully created both workflows with Microsoft Flow and Business apps with PowerApps that consume content from our On-Premises SharePoint implementation.

Next Steps

In this chapter, we have learned how to install the On-Premises Data Gateway which allows us to use the latest business applications such as Flow and PowerApps in order to create workflows and applications with our on-premises content. With the connection done, users can simply consume those services without needing any additional knowledge other than the basics of Flow and PowerApps. If you want to learn more about Flow and PowerApps, Apress has a book on each subject that you can learn from.

Our next chapter will cover how to migrate content to SharePoint Server 2019.

CHAPTER 16

Migrating to SharePoint Server 2019

In previous chapters, we have installed SharePoint and configured our Web Applications and Service Applications. If your company is currently running a previous version of SharePoint such as SharePoint 2013, SharePoint 2016, or even earlier, you will probably want to migrate this data to your new SharePoint 2019 farm.

In this chapter, we will learn how to migrate sites from SharePoint 2016 to SharePoint 2019 as well as the Managed Metadata, User Profile, Search, and App Management Service Applications.

Migration Path

Similar to previous versions of SharePoint, the only direct path to migrate to SharePoint Server 2019 is from its previous version, which is SharePoint 2016. If you are currently on SharePoint Server 2013 and want to migrate to SharePoint Server 2019, you will need to migrate to a SharePoint Server 2016 farm then subsequently migrate from SharePoint Server 2016 to SharePoint Server 2019. This high-level path can be seen in Figure 16-1. There are third-party tools created by Microsoft Partners that allow you to directly migrate from almost any version of SharePoint to SharePoint 2019; however, those come with a price.

© Vlad Catrinescu and Trevor Seward 2019
V. Catrinescu and T. Seward, *Deploying SharePoint 2019*, https://doi.org/10.1007/978-1-4842-4526-2_16

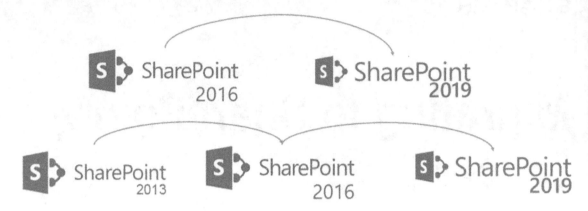

Figure 16-1. *Migrating from SharePoint 2013/2016 to SharePoint 2019*

There is no required SharePoint 2016 patch level in order to upgrade databases from SharePoint 2016 to SharePoint Server 2019, but it's recommended to be on the latest Public Update available. You should also make sure that all site collections are in 15 mode and all Web Applications are using Claims, and not classic authentication. If you have any Web Applications still in classic mode, you can convert them using the Convert-SPWebApplication PowerShell cmdlet.

Now that we understand the requirements and migration path, in the next section we'll look at how to migrate Service Applications from SharePoint 2016 to SharePoint 2019.

Migrating Service Applications

The first step in learning how to migrate from SharePoint 2016 to SharePoint Server 2019 is to migrate Service Applications.

Managed Metadata Service Application

To migrate the Managed Metadata Service Application, the first thing you will need to do is to back up the Service Application database from SharePoint 2016, and restore it onto our SharePoint 2019 SQL Server. Once it's on the SQL Server, the way to upgrade the Managed Metadata Service Application is to create a new Service Application as we learned in Chapter 8 but specify the database we just brought over from SharePoint Server 2016. In our environment, we named this database ManagedMetadataDB, and we will create the Service Application with PowerShell as we learned in Chapter 8. To create the Service Application, use the New-SPMetadataServiceApplication with the database name we restored from SharePoint Server 2016. This is the cmdlet that we have used in our environment. We have also created the Service Application proxy using the New-SPMetadataServiceApplicationProxy cmdlet.

```
$sa = New-SPMetadataServiceApplication -Name "Managed Metadata Service"
-DatabaseName "ManagedMetadataDB" -ApplicationPool "SharePoint Web Services
Default" -SyndicationErrorReportEnabled
New-SPMetadataServiceApplicationProxy -Name "Managed Metadata
Service Proxy" -ServiceApplication $sa -DefaultProxyGroup
-ContentTypePushdownEnabled -DefaultKeywordTaxonomy
-DefaultSiteCollectionTaxonomy
```

By Migrating the Service Application database, you ensure that the term IDs do not change; therefore, all the connections between the content migrated and the terms will remain intact.

Search Service Application

The next Service Application we will migrate to SharePoint 2019 is the Search Service Application. The Search Service Application has four databases; however, we only need to get the Administration database from the old SharePoint, and restore it on our SharePoint 2019 SQL Server.

SharePoint has a PowerShell cmdlet that we will use named Restore-SPEnterpriseSearchServiceApplication, which takes the name of your old Administration database, as well as the database server with the Service Application name and Application Pool. SharePoint will then create a Search Service Application from your database, which will keep your content sources, Search Center settings, Search Schema and crawl rules from your SharePoint 2016 Search Service Application. This Service Application will also keep the same crawl account, however, and we recommend having different crawl accounts between your farms; therefore, make sure to change afterward.

Make sure to run the following script on a server running the Search MinRole role. We will first get the local Search Service Instance and then save it into a variable called $si.

```
$si = Get-SPEnterpriseSearchServiceInstance -local
```

Afterward, we will create the Search Service Application using the `Restore-SPEnter priseSearchServiceApplication` cmdlet and specifying the database we have restored, in this case it's named `SharePoint_2016_Search`.

```
$sa = Restore-SPEnterpriseSearchServiceApplication -Name
'SearchServiceApplication' -applicationpool "SharePoint Web Services
Default" -databasename SharePoint_2016_Search -databaseserver caspag.lab.
cobaltatom.com -AdminSearchServiceInstance $si
```

Lastly, we will create a new Search Service Application Proxy and assign it to the Service Application that we just created.

```
New-SPEnterpriseSearchServiceApplicationProxy -Name "Search Service
Application Proxy" -SearchApplication $sa
```

You have now migrated your Service Application from SharePoint 2016, to SharePoint Server 2019. Note that you will need to define the Search Service Application topology by using PowerShell. We have learned how to do so in Chapter 6.

User Profile Service Application

The first thing we must do is back up two out of the three User Profile Databases from SharePoint Server 2016. We need to back up the Social database as well as the Profile database. There is no use of bringing the Sync database over to SharePoint 2019 since the mappings between properties and Active Directory are stored in Microsoft Identity Manager, and not in the SharePoint Sync database.

We will then create a new User Profile Service Application by using the `New-SPProfileServiceApplication` cmdlet as learned in Chapter 7 and specify the name of those two databases in the parameters as well as a name for the Sync database. Since this database does not exist, SharePoint will create it. The cmdlet we used in our environment is the following:

```
$sa = New-SPProfileServiceApplication -Name "User Profile Service
Application" -applicationpool "SharePoint Web Services Default"
-ProfileDBName 'Profile_DB_2016' -SocialDBName 'Social_DB_2016'
-ProfileSyncDBName 'Sync_DB'
```

We then need to create Service Application Proxy by using the following cmdlet:

```
New-SPProfileServiceApplicationProxy -Name "User Profile Service
Application Proxy" -ServiceApplication $sa –DefaultProxyGroup
```

With the Service Application in place, you need to update Microsoft Identity Manager as learned in Chapter 7 for it to send profile information to the new SharePoint Server 2019 farm. If you are using Active Directory import, configure the User Profile Service Application as learned in Chapter 7.

Add-ins

SharePoint Add-ins (Apps) were a new development method introduced with SharePoint Server 2013 and your company might have taken advantage of this development method to deploy solutions onto your SharePoint sites. We have already covered how to configure Add-ins in Chapter 5, and all the DNS setup as well as configuring the Add-in URLs needs to be done before continuing this step.

Note   Your Add-in URL doesn't have to be the same in SharePoint 2019 as it is in SharePoint 2016.

From the SharePoint Server 2016 farm, we will need to back up the databases of both the App Management Service Application as well as the Subscription Service Application and restore them on the SharePoint Server 2019 farm database server.

We will then create those Service Applications as learned in Chapter 5, and specify to use the name of the restored databases. We will first create the Subscription Service Application and Proxy with the following PowerShell cmdlets:

```
$SubscriptionSA = New-SPSubscriptionSettingsServiceApplication -
ApplicationPool "SharePoint Web Services Default" –Name "Subscription
Settings Service Application" -DatabaseName SharePoint_2016_
SubscriptionSettings

$proxySub = New-SPSubscriptionSettingsServiceApplicationProxy -
ServiceApplication $SubscriptionSA
```

Afterward, we will create the App Management Service Application) and its proxy using the following cmdlets:

```
$AppManagementSA = New-SPAppManagementServiceApplication -ApplicationPool
"SharePoint Web Services Default" -Name "App Management Service
Application" -DatabaseName SharePoint_2016_AppManagement

$proxyApp = New-SPAppManagementServiceApplicationProxy -ServiceApplication
$AppManagementSA
```

On the App Licenses page in the Central Administration, you will see the Add-ins you have installed, as well as the license types that you have as seen in Figure 16-2.

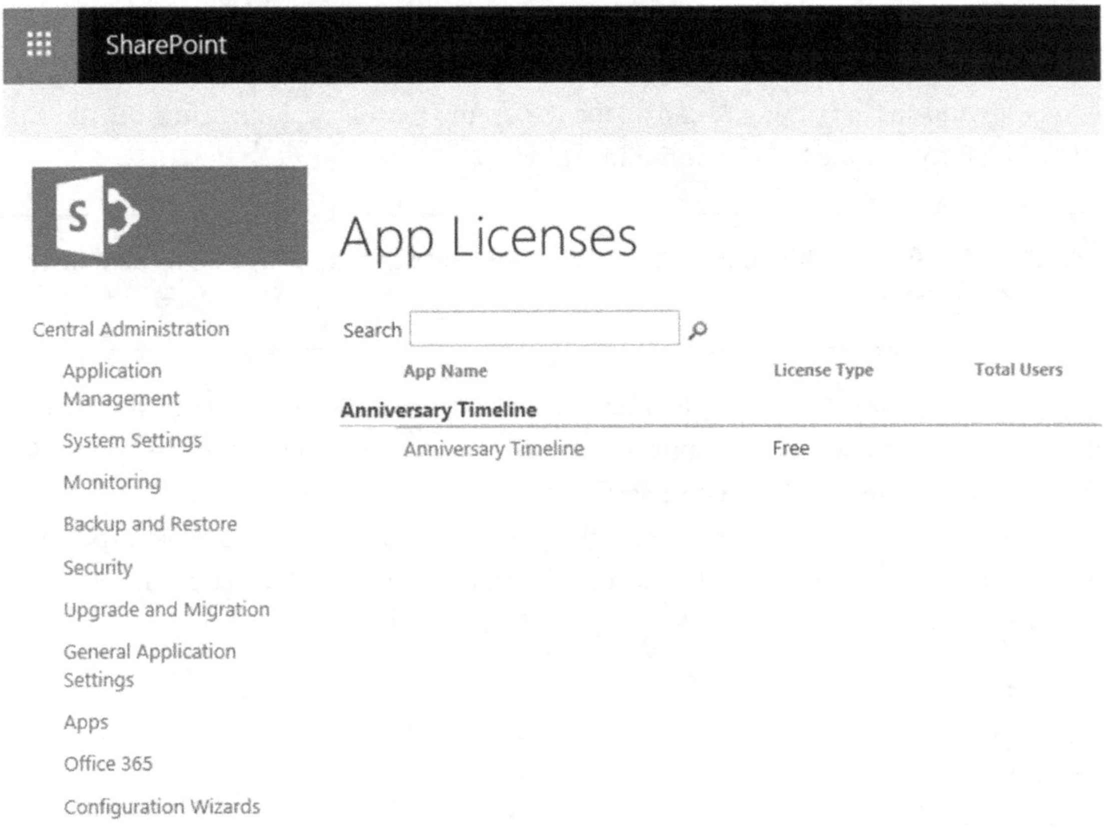

Figure 16-2.   SharePoint 2019 App Licenses

When restoring the content databases that included those Add-ins, the Add-ins) will be installed and you will be able to use them as you did in your SharePoint 2016 environment.

With the Service Applications migrated, the next step is to learn how to migrate our SharePoint sites from SharePoint 2016 to SharePoint 2019.

Migrating Content

Migrating Content from SharePoint Server 2016 to SharePoint Server 2019 is done by migrating databases from SharePoint 2016 to SharePoint 2019, and attaching them to a Web Application. The first step is to identify what Site Collections you want to migrate from SharePoint 2016 to SharePoint 2019. You can migrate all databases in a Web Application or particular databases containing particular Site Collections; the important thing to remember is that content migrations are done at the Content Database level. Therefore, if you only want to migrate a few Site Collections from your Web Application, make sure to group them into the same content database. You can move Site Collections between databases in the same Web Application by using the Move-SPSite PowerShell cmdlet. Something to remember is that if you only migrate certain Site Collections within a Web Application, you might have to use a different URL in SharePoint 2019 in order to keep the rest of the Site Collections accessible.

Back up the database from the SQL Server in use by SharePoint and restore it with the name you wish on the SQL Server in use by SharePoint Server 2019 as seen in Figure 16-3. The database does not need to exist prior to restoration, and you can enter a new name for this database in the Database field.

Tip   It's recommended to back up the databases using the COPY ONLY option. This will make sure that the backup plan on the source environment remains consistent.

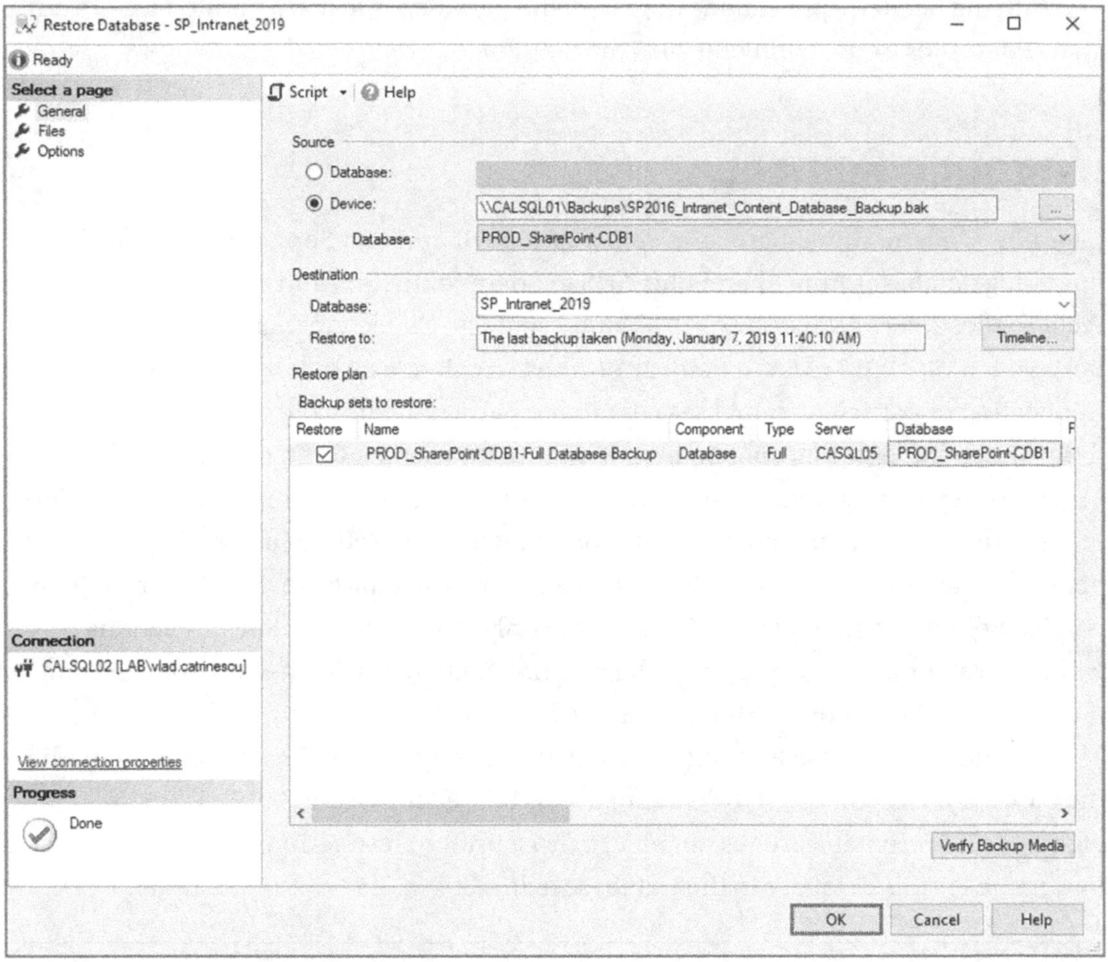

Figure 16-3. *Restore Content Database*

After the database is restored, create your Web Application on SharePoint Server 2019 if you have not already done so. When creating your Web Application, you need to create a new Content Database as well, but you can give it a temporary name as we will delete that database after the Web Application is created. We have covered how to create Web Applications in Chapter 13, and for this test we have created a Web Application with the URL https://intranet.cobaltatom.com and a database called "WSS_TempDB". To remove this database, we will use the Remove-SPContentDatabase PowerShell cmdlet. To remove all the content databases from the intranet.cobaltatom.com Web Application, we need to run the following cmdlet:

```
Get-SPContentDatabase -WebApplication
https://intranet.cobaltatom.com |Dismount-SPContentDatabase
```

Our Web Application is now ready to mount the Content Database restored to the SQL Server in use by SharePoint Server 2019. Before attaching the database, we can use the `Test-SPContentDatabase` PowerShell cmdlet. To test our database against the intranet.cobaltatom.com Web Application, we would run the following cmdlet:

```
Test-SPContentDatabase -Name SP_Intranet_2019 -WebApplication https://
intranet.cobaltatom.com
```

This will give us a report of the possible problems we may encounter when doing the migration. Some examples are Missing Features in the SharePoint 2016 farm that were referenced in the site collection. The report will show both errors and warnings, as well as inform us if the error is "Upgrade Blocking". If the error is Upgrade Blocking, it means that SharePoint might not be able to upgrade this database to SharePoint 2019. If the error is not error blocking, SharePoint will be able to upgrade the database, but your users might get unexpected behaviors when navigating to parts of the site. For our example seen in Figure 16-4, our database currently has Power View and SSRS features; however, those features do not exist in the Web Application.

Figure 16-4.   *Test-SPContentDatabase Results*

The two choices we have to avoid those issues are either to remove those features from SharePoint 2019 or activate them and have those features ready on the farm. Removing them would be a valid option when we would not use those features anymore in SharePoint 2019. When everything is ready and the `Test-SPContentDatabse` does not return any more blocking errors, we can proceed with the upgrade. The upgrade is done automatically when you attach the content database to the Web Application. This is done via PowerShell with the `Mount-SPContentDatabase` cmdlet. The parameters are the same as the Test-SPContentDatabase cmdlet, the database name and the Web Application. To attach our content database, we ran the following cmdlet:

```
Mount-SPContentDatabase -Name SP_Intranet_2019 -WebApplication https://
intranet.cobaltatom.com
```

PowerShell will output a warning that progress and details will be in the same location as your ULS log files as seen in Figure 16-5. The upgrade process creates two log files under the format:

- Upgrade-<date>-<guid>. Log

- Upgrade-<date>-<guid>-**error**. Log

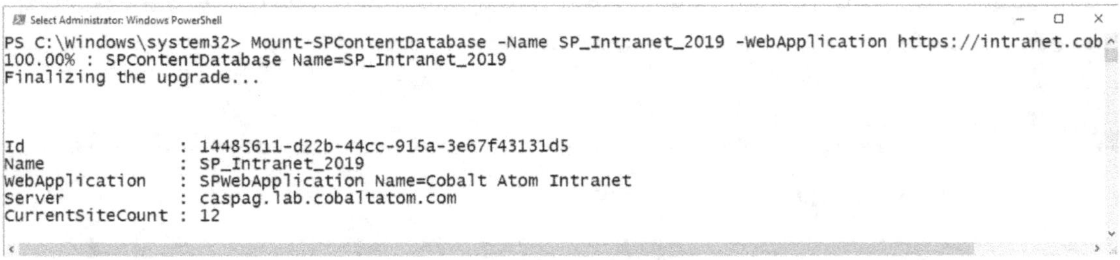

```
Select Administrator: Windows PowerShell                                           –  □  ×
PS C:\Windows\system32> Mount-SPContentDatabase -Name SP_Intranet_2019 -WebApplication https://intranet.cob
100.00% : SPContentDatabase Name=SP_Intranet_2019
Finalizing the upgrade...


Id                : 14485611-d22b-44cc-915a-3e67f43131d5
Name              : SP_Intranet_2019
WebApplication    : SPWebApplication Name=Cobalt Atom Intranet
Server            : caspag.lab.cobaltatom.com
CurrentSiteCount  : 12
```

Figure 16-5. *Mount-SPContentDatabase*

The error file will show any errors that might have occurred during the upgrade process. The duration of the upgrade will depend on the number of Site Collections you have in your database, as well as the amount of content in those sites.

After the database is successfully attached, you will be able to navigate to the Site Collections you have migrated and test out the functionality of the site. Permissions on the SharePoint site and content will not have changed between SharePoint 2016 and SharePoint 2019.

We have now learned how to migrate content, as well as the most popular Service Applications from SharePoint Server 2016, to SharePoint Server 2019. Now, let's take a look in what order we should do those migrations.

Migration Order

It is recommended to always migrate your Service Applications before you migrate your Web Applications and SharePoint sites. The reason is that SharePoint content has references to Service Applications, and those references will be broken if the site will not be able to find the Service Application once it's restored.

Next Steps

In this chapter, we have learned how to migrate SharePoint sites and Service Applications to SharePoint Server 2019. In the next chapter, we will learn how to implement High Availability and Disaster Recovery for your SharePoint farm.

CHAPTER 17

Implementing High Availability and Disaster Recovery

SharePoint Server 2019 has a variety of options for High Availability and Disaster Recovery. We will examine the options available at the farm and SQL Server level, which will help you choose the most appropriate option for your business.

Unsupported Methods

SharePoint has a variety of methods of replication and recovery that are not supported by Microsoft. In this chapter, we will cover the supported methods, but it is important to note methods that are not supported by Microsoft in order to avoid them when implementing Disaster Recovery.

Farms must have a 99% 1 ms round-trip time on average over 10 minutes. Exceeding this design limitation may cause object synchronization issues, including timer job failures. Farms also must have 1 Gbps connectivity between all farm members and SQL Servers that are serving the farm in a read-write capacity or are in a synchronous form of replication with the read-write SQL Server. Overall, the limitation for this means each farm member or SQL Server in a synchronous replica mode must be within approximately 186 miles or 299.33 km.

Virtual replication, which is either replicating an underlying virtual machine (such as using Hyper-V Replica or third-party products) is not supported as there may be consistency issues upon bringing the Disaster Recovery environment online. This is especially important for the Search index and timer jobs. The exclusion to this rule is

© Vlad Catrinescu and Trevor Seward 2019
V. Catrinescu and T. Seward, *Deploying SharePoint 2019*, https://doi.org/10.1007/978-1-4842-4526-2_17

Azure Site Recovery, which does support replication of virtual machines into Azure for the purposes of Disaster Recovery as this is a scenario Microsoft is specifically able to test.

Like virtual machine replication, backing up online virtual machines and saving them to tape or transporting the backup via other means is not supported.

SQL Server High Availability

SharePoint Server 2019 supports a variety of options for SQL Server high availability. These include SQL Clustering, Database Mirroring, and Always On Availability Groups. Each has their strengths and weaknesses. Let's look at each one individually.

SQL Clustering

SQL Clustering is a common form of high availability where the goal is to have rapid failover when the SQL Server acting as the primary fails within the environment. SharePoint fully supports all databases residing on a SQL Cluster.

The strengths of SQL Clustering include the ability to use SQL Clustering with the Standard Edition of SQL Server, as well as the Enterprise edition. SQL Clustering also uses a set of shared disks to store data, which reduces storage costs. As SharePoint connects to the virtual name of the cluster, a failover of SQL is only a short and minor interruption of service.

A significant weakness with SQL Clustering is the shared disk subsystem. If the shared storage becomes unavailable, while the cluster may remain online, SharePoint will be offline.

Database Mirroring

Database Mirroring was introduced in SQL Server 2005, and while present in SQL Server 2016 and 2017, is now considered a deprecated technology. With that in mind, Database Mirroring is an effective way to provide high availability for SharePoint. The Database Mirroring failover partner must be within 1 ms and have 1Gbps connectivity to the SharePoint farm; however, it does not need to be within the same building as long as these two requirements are met. Database Mirroring involves configuring two servers with automatic or manual failover. Automatic failover requires a witness, either a file share or a SQL Server witness (SQL Server Express may be used as a witness). This is a third server, often running at a remote site or alongside the failover partner.

Database Mirroring also supports three modes of operation. High-Safety with Automatic failover is a topology where a witness is involved and transactions are first committed to the Failover Partner prior to the Principal Partner.

High-Safety without automatic failover is where transactions are still committed to the Failover Partner first, but the failover event is a manual process that requires administrator intervention.

The last operating mode, High-Performance Mode, is a mode primarily meant for replicating a database over a high latency network connection. In this mode, transactions are *not* guaranteed to make it to the Failover Partner server. Because of this, this mode cannot be used for SharePoint Failover purposes, but may be suitable in certain Disaster Recovery scenarios.

When creating SharePoint Content Databases or many of the SharePoint Service Application databases, one can specify a Failover Partner.

However, not all databases may be configured through the GUI to use a Failover Partner *or* if you need to add a Failover Partner after the fact, you will need to set the Failover Partner SQL Server name via PowerShell. For example, our SharePoint Configuration database is named "Configuration." Here is how we would set the Failover Partner through the SharePoint Management Shell:

```
$db = Get-SPDatabase | ?{$_.Name -eq "Configuration"}
$db.FailoverServer = "SQLO2"
$db.Update()
```

It is up to SharePoint to detect that a failover has taken place. It does this by first querying the primary partner, followed up by the failover partner. If the primary is unavailable but the failover is available, SharePoint then leverages the failover partner.

Database Mirroring may also not be automatic. Without a witness, Database Mirroring failover is a manual process. This significantly increases downtime for SharePoint while the administrator intervenes to fail over the databases.

Lastly, with Database Mirroring, each database is treated as a singular object to failover. It is possible to have, for example, the Configuration database on one of the failover partners while a Content Database resides on the other failover partner. While this configuration would be uncommon, the fact that databases are treated independently of one another does increase maintenance investment into using Database Mirroring.

Always On Availability Groups

Always On Availability Groups are what were used throughout this book to provide high availability to the SharePoint databases. The configuration involves both Microsoft Clustering Services along with SQL Server Always On Availability Groups. Along with a witness server, provided by a file server or another SQL Server, failovers are seamless and quick. As with SQL Clustering, clients like SharePoint connect to Always On through a virtual name or fully qualified domain name.

With Always On Availability Groups, the storage space required is doubled. Each SQL Server must have an appropriate amount of storage to store the data files and log files for each SQL database. This may significantly increase the cost of the SQL Server implementation. In addition to the storage expense, only SQL Server Enterprise supports Always On Availability Groups. While SQL Server 2016 does bring "Basic Availability Groups," this feature is not appropriate for a SharePoint farm as it only supports a single database within the Basic Availability Group.

Always On Availability Groups also provide you with the ability to have additional Synchronous Availability Group members. Synchronous members are required for automatic failover for SharePoint. These members also have the same constraints of a 1 ms and 1Gbps network connection between the SharePoint farm and SQL Server. SQL Server 2016 and 2017 allow for up to eight replicas, three of which can participate in synchronous replication.

Always On Availability Groups do provide a function known as "read-only secondary" where read-only traffic is directed from the active member in the Availability Group to a secondary which is not serving write requests, but this function is not supported by SharePoint.

Disaster Recovery

Database Mirroring, Always On Availability Groups, and Log Shipping provide Disaster Recovery options for the SQL Server databases supporting the SharePoint farm. In this section, we will consider that the Disaster Recovery location is greater than 310 miles or 500 km away from the primary data center. This scenario prevents us from using synchronous connectivity to the remote SQL Server at the Disaster Recovery location.

Database Mirroring

Database Mirroring for Disaster Recovery involves adding a High-Performance Mode node to the existing SQL Server configuration. This member can coexist with a Database Mirroring High-Safety with or without automatic failover in place. As previously noted, failover to a High-Performance Mode partner is a manual process. Databases on this member will not be brought online automatically.

Log Shipping

Log Shipping is the shipping of transaction log backups from one SQL Server to another. The destination SQL Server then restores the transaction log backups to the target database. This method allows one to keep the databases up to date with additional replication options available outside of SQL Server. For example, it is possible to "ship" a transaction log backup to a Windows file server and, using Distributed File Services (DFS-R), replicate the transaction log backup to a Windows file server in the Disaster Recovery datacenter and have the DR SQL Server restore the transaction log backup to the destination database. This eliminates the SQL Server from being responsible for the replication of the transaction log backup. DFS-R also provides a faster and more reliable replication mechanism.

Always On Availability Groups

Always On Availability Groups provide the ability to add an asynchronous remote partner SQL Server to your Availability Group. This allows a highly available local Availability Group to also have a single SQL Server in a Disaster Recovery location. Unlike with the synchronous local Availability Group, the remote SQL Server must be set to Asynchronous mode. This mode has a manual failover process. This is the method we will be using in our Disaster Recovery example.

To add the SQL Server to the Always On Availability Group that will be the asynchronous member, duplicate the volume and directory structure for the SQL databases and log files. In our example, the M: and L: drives will be created using ReFS with 64Kb clusters.

Add the Windows Failover Clustering role along with the .NET 3.5 Framework feature. Using the Failover Cluster manager, add the new SQL Server to the existing Failover Cluster; we're using CALSQLClus in our environment. As shown in Figure 17-1, add the new SQL Server to the Failover Cluster.

Figure 17-1.   *Adding CALDRSQL01 to the existing Failover Cluster*

Install the same SQL Server version, edition, and patch level as the other SQL Servers in the cluster. As with the previous servers, use the same Service Account as the Synchronous members of the Availability Group.

As we previously used the Group Managed Service Account (GMSA) LAB\s-sql$, we will need to reconfigure it to support the additional SQL Server as well as add two new Service Principal Names (SPNs). We must perform this operation via PowerShell. Note that we are specifying all existing servers plus the new disaster recovery server to retrieve the password while specifying that we are adding additional SPNs to the service account.

```
Set-ADServiceAccount -Identity s-sql
-PrincipalsAllowedToRetrieveManagedPassword 'calsql01$','calsql02$','caldr
sql01$' -ServicePrincipalNames @{Add="MSSQLSvc/caldrsql01:1433","MSSQLSvc/
caldrsql01.lab.cobaltatom.com:1433"}
```

Using the SQL Server Configuration Manager or SQL PowerShell, enable Always On, as shown in Figure 17-2, then restart the SQL Server services as required.

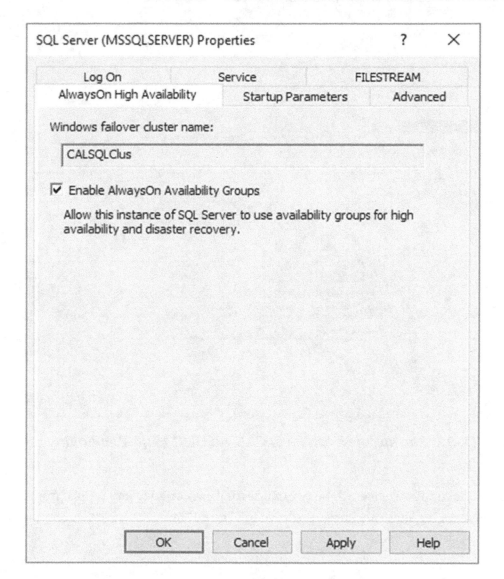

Figure 17-2. *Enabling Always On Availability Groups for the Disaster Recovery SQL Server*

Add the new server to the Availability Group in Asynchronous mode with no Automatic Failover, as shown in Figure 17-3. If you are intending to mount the content databases to the Disaster Recovery farm, set Readable Secondary to Yes for the Disaster Recovery SQL Server node.

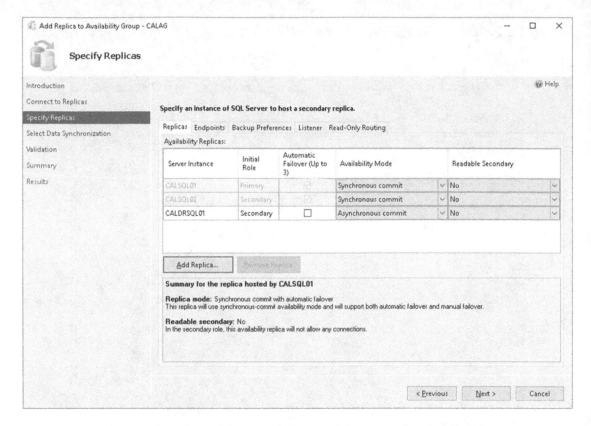

Figure 17-3.   *Starting the addition of CALDRSQL01 to the Availability*
Group

The Backup Preference will be to exclude the Disaster Recovery replica from taking
preference for database backups, as shown in Figure 17-4.

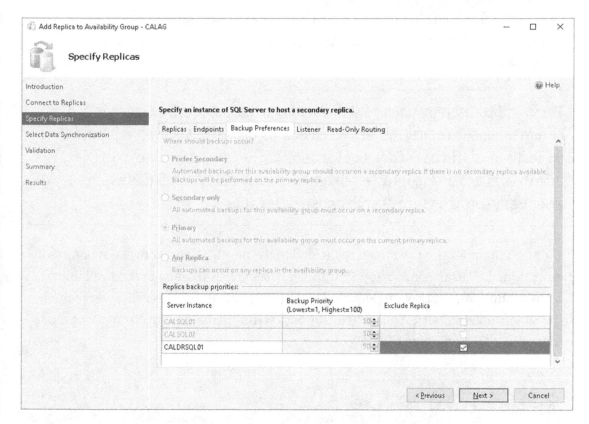

Figure 17-4.   *Removing preference for backups from CALDRSQL01*

We will not be using a listener endpoint for the disaster recovery SQL Server and instead using a SQL Alias (cliconfg.exe) to point the disaster recovery SharePoint farm at the disaster recovery SQL Server.

Make note that we have various databases in the Availability Group which are not candidates for replication: primarily the Search database as well as the Administration and Configuration databases. The State Service database is also not a good candidate for replication to the Disaster Recovery environment. This is due to the transient nature of the data. In previous versions of SharePoint, the User Profile Service Application Sync database also was not a candidate for being part of the Availability Group; however, in SharePoint Server 2019, this database is empty and will have minimal impact on the Availability Group.

If it is important to not synchronize databases such as the Search, Administration, or Configuration databases as part of the Availability Group ("farm-specific" databases), you must place them in a separate Availability Group on the two nodes in Synchronous replication. This allows you to synchronize just the databases that you require.

In a large environment, this is good practice in order to have multiple Availability Groups, separating out even various Content Databases across Availability Groups for independent replication.

Tip   Microsoft provides a list of databases that support synchronous and/ or asynchronous commit, as well as databases that do not support replication on TechNet, at `https://docs.microsoft.com/en-us/SharePoint/ administration/supported-high-availability-and-disaster- recovery-options-for-sharepoint-databas`.

Once the databases have been replicated to the new SQL Server over Asynchronous replication, the Disaster Recovery SQL Server will show as Healthy in the Availability Group dashboard, as shown in Figure 17-5. Note that the databases will always remain in a "Synchronizing" state, unless an error occurs during the synchronization, or the production SQL Servers go offline.

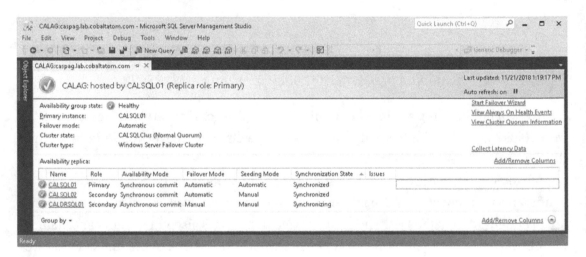

Figure 17-5. *CALDRSQL01 is now successfully synchronizing from the primary SQL Server*

Create a new SharePoint farm at the remote location. In our environment, this will be named CALDRSP01 and consist of a single SharePoint server; however, you may add as many SharePoint servers in any desired configuration as required.

Decide on if you will use Service Accounts unique to the Disaster Recovery environment or if you will use the same accounts as the production environment. If using new accounts for the Disaster Recovery environment, the accounts must be added to the replicated SQL databases with the appropriate permissions. In addition, Kerberos cannot be enabled as two separate accounts in Active Directory may not have the same SPN – this means the Disaster Recovery farm would be limited to using NTLM authentication. If using the same accounts as production, permissions are automatically added when attaching the SharePoint databases to the new farm; however, make note of any password changes that may take place on the account in Active Directory. The password must also be changed on the Disaster Recovery farm, independently of the production farm.

When creating the Disaster Recovery farm, do not point at the database at the Always On Listener, but instead at Disaster Recovery SQL Server directly. Alternatively, use a SQL alias using cliconfig.exe on the SharePoint Server for better mobility of databases should the need arise to change the Disaster Recovery SQL Server.

When building the new Disaster Recovery SharePoint farm, the Administration and Configuration database names will be unique as these are unique to the farm. We will also create unique Search databases, although should there be extensive Search customizations at the Search Service level, it may be advantageous to replicate the Search Administration database to preserve the schema. If using a Cloud Search Service Application in the production farm, do not use a Cloud Search Service Application on the Disaster Recovery farm to actively crawl content. Instead, only crawl content when an event has occurred that requires you to fail over to the Disaster Recovery farm.

Import the production SSL certificates into the Disaster Recovery SharePoint server.

As this environment will be similar to the production environment for security purposes, Kerberos will be enabled on Central Admin. As the Central Admin URL is unique to the farm, make sure to add an SPN for it.

```
Setspn -U -S https://dr-cal.lab.cobaltatom.com LAB\s-farm
```

Configure any remaining required settings in Central Administration, such as Outgoing E-mail, Rights Management Services configuration, and so forth.

Farm solutions must be deployed to the Disaster Recovery farm separate from the production farm. Keep farm solutions up to date as they are deployed to the production farm in order to have a well-prepared Disaster Recovery farm.

The Web Applications will use the *same* URL as in production, along with having Kerberos enabled. Because we are using the same Service Account, no changes are required. When creating the Web Applications in the Disaster Recovery farm, do not use the existing Content Database names. Instead, use a temporary Content Database name.

Once the Web Applications have been created, remove and delete the temporary Content Database. Using Central Administration or the Mount-SPContentDatabase cmdlet, mount the existing content databases. They will be in a read-only mode until a disaster occurs. Because of this the sites contained within the read-only Content Databases will display a banner on top indicating so, as shown in Figure 17-6.

Tip   Remember to set Readable Secondary to Yes on the Disaster Recovery SQL Server node in the Always On Availability Group if you are going to mount the databases outside of a failover event.

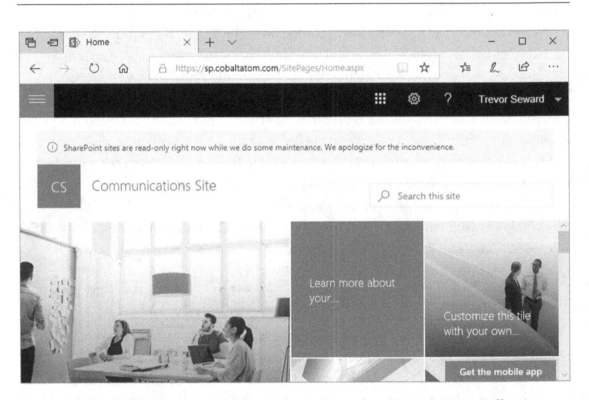

Figure 17-6.   While the Content Database is in read-only mode, Site Collections will display a maintenance banner

When creating new Site Collections in a database that is replicated to the Disaster Recovery farm, make note that in the Disaster Recovery farm, the Site Map will not automatically be updated. To update the Site Map manually, run the following cmdlet, passing in the Web Application URL:

```
Get-SPContentDatabase -WebApplication https://sp.cobaltatom.com |
% {$_.RefreshSitesInConfigurationDatabase()}
```

When creating Service Applications consuming the read-only databases, use the same database name. For example, with the User Profile Service Application or Secure Store Service, specify the database name for that Service Application that resides on the SQL Server. The Service Application will successfully create, although will not be fully functional. As an example, the User Profile Service Application cannot be managed, and the Secure Store Service will also run into an error when attempting to manage Secure Store keys. When the databases are changed from a read-only to an online mode, these options will become available.

The Managed Metadata Service Application is unique in that it cannot consume the read-only database. Unfortunately, one must wait for a failover to be invoked prior to creating the Managed Metadata Service Application using the existing database.

For the Search Service Application, Search may crawl read-only content. The Web Application URLs can continue to be part of the Content Source for Search to crawl. Implement hosts file entries on the Search server to properly direct the crawler to the local SharePoint server.

Tip   SharePoint Search Disaster Recovery is a complex topic: refer to the TechNet article at `https://docs.microsoft.com/en-us/SharePoint/search/best-practices-of-disaster-recovery-for-search`.

Initiating a Disaster Recovery Failover

As the Disaster Recovery SQL Server must be failed over manually, as soon as the link between production has been severed, the databases will enter a read-write state, showing "Not Synchronized" in the SQL Server Management Studio. At this point, a manual failover using the Always On Availability Group failover wizard, T-SQL, or

PowerShell is required. Once a failover has occurred to the Disaster Recovery SQL Server, the databases will be in a read-write state and show a status of "Synchronized."

The Managed Metadata Service Application can be created with the existing Managed Metadata Service database. If the production environment is a loss, the databases can be removed from the Availability Group on the Disaster Recovery SQL Server. With a change in DNS for the Web Applications, SharePoint should be fully functional at this point.

As we took only the necessary databases to our Disaster Recovery farm, this particular failover is relatively simple. But Disaster Recovery is a complex topic, and farms that are significantly more complex will take additional time, post-failover configuration, and potentially even troubleshooting to get the Disaster Recovery farm into a usable state.

Cloud Disaster Recovery

A Cloud Disaster Recovery is the concept of using an Infrastructure as a Service provider, such as Microsoft Azure, to host Virtual Machines in the Cloud for the Disaster Recovery farm. There are a few valid ways to achieve Disaster Recovery with Azure.

The first two methods are similar to existing On-Premises Disaster Recovery strategies. Both log shipping and Always On Availability Groups in Asynchronous mode serve as strategies which can be used with an Azure Site-to-Site VPN or ExpressRoute configuration.

Another method is to use physical or Virtual Machine–based backups. The Virtual Machines may reside on either Hyper-V or VMware ESXi. Using the Azure Site Recovery, an administrator can *replicate* an entire farm from On-Premises to Azure Infrastructure-as-a-Service (IaaS). This is the only supported product by Microsoft to perform full farm replication from one point to another. The caveat of this solution is that post-failover, you must clear the Configuration Cache on each SharePoint Server, as well as either establish a new Search Service Application *or* restore the Search Service Application from backup, for example, using Windows Azure Backup.

Tip   More information about Azure Site Recovery and SharePoint scenarios are available at `https://docs.microsoft.com/en-us/azure/site-recovery/site-recovery-sharepoint`.

Next Steps

Now that you've learned how to create a simple Disaster Recovery environment, we will take a look at the process of patching SharePoint Server 2019, including how to leverage Zero Downtime Patching.

CHAPTER 18

Patching SharePoint Server 2019

SharePoint Server 2019 has significantly improved the application of patches, along with the size of patches. This provides a faster, more reliable experience for SharePoint Administrators.

The Basics of Patching

Each patch will be delivered in an executable format. There will typically be one or two executables per month, called Public Updates. The primary executable is called "sts" while the secondary is "wssloc". The "sts" patch is the primary patch file, while the "wssloc" patch file contains locale-specific files for all languages, including English. Occasionally, Microsoft will not release a wssloc patch on a given month. If that is the case, use the latest available wssloc when patching your farm; if you have already applied the latest wssloc in a previous patch cycle, you may just apply the sts patch.

The basic steps to install an update are to install all binaries on each SharePoint server and then run the Configuration Wizard on each SharePoint server.

In larger environments, you may consider implementing a step in between the installation of binaries and running the Config Wizard. It is possible to run Upgrade-SPContentDatabase manually on each content database one by one or in parallel to speed up the final Config Wizard process time.

To begin the process, in Figure 18-1 we are installing the base patch, sts2019-kb4461513-fullfile-x64-glb.exe.

© Vlad Catrinescu and Trevor Seward 2019
V. Catrinescu and T. Seward, *Deploying SharePoint 2019*, https://doi.org/10.1007/978-1-4842-4526-2_18

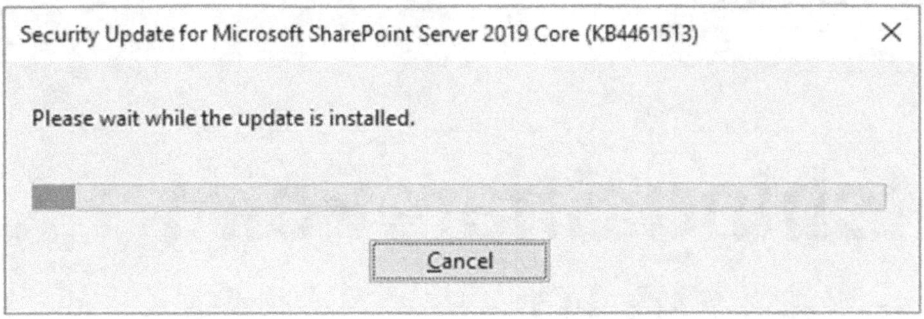

Security Update for Microsoft SharePoint Server 2019 Core (KB4461513)   ✕

Please wait while the update is installed.

Cancel

Figure 18-1. Beginning the installation of sts2019-kb4461513-fullfile-x64-glb.exe

When the base patch has been installed, install the locale-specific patch.

SharePoint does not require a specific order for servers to patch; for example, the server running Central Administration does not need to be patched first. Identify the order that suits your farm the best, as installing the binaries involves downtime for each particular SharePoint server.

Patching may require a reboot of the SharePoint Server, as shown in Figure 18-2. By having two or more SharePoint Servers running the same services, SharePoint Servers can be rebooted without incurring any downtime for end users, provided proper availability scenarios are in place such as having at least two web servers which can be rotated in and out of a load balancer.

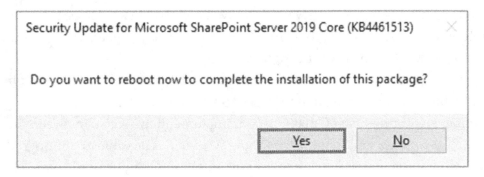

Security Update for Microsoft SharePoint Server 2019 Core (KB4461513)   ✕

Do you want to reboot now to complete the installation of this package?

Yes   No

Figure 18-2. Many SharePoint Server 2019 patches require reboots in order to complete

A SharePoint Server may be noted as "Upgrade Available" or "Upgrade Required" after installing a patch, as shown in Figure 18-3. If you see either of these messages, one or more databases require an upgrade or the SharePoint server requires the Configuration Wizard or psconfig.exe to be executed.

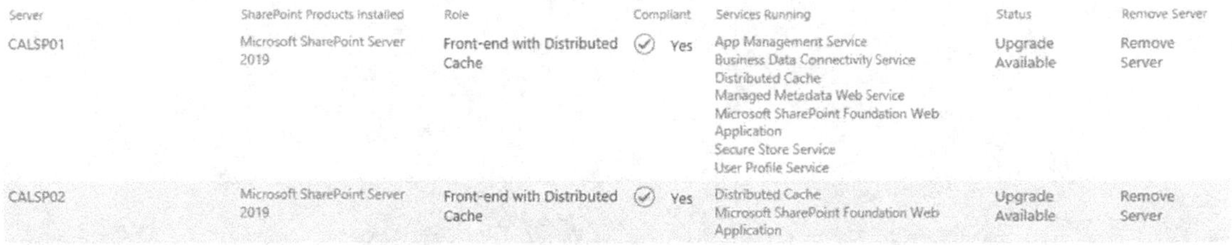

Server	SharePoint Products Installed	Role	Compliant	Services Running	Status	Remove Server
CALSP01	Microsoft SharePoint Server 2019	Front-end with Distributed Cache	✓ Yes	App Management Service Business Data Connectivity Service Distributed Cache Managed Metadata Web Service Microsoft SharePoint Foundation Web Application Secure Store Service User Profile Service	Upgrade Available	Remove Server
CALSP02	Microsoft SharePoint Server 2019	Front-end with Distributed Cache	✓ Yes	Distributed Cache Microsoft SharePoint Foundation Web Application	Upgrade Available	Remove Server

Figure 18-3. *Upgrade Available indicates the Configuration Wizard needs to be run*

If using psconfig.exe, run it from the SharePoint Management Shell (which puts psconfig.exe in the PATH). Use the following command:

```
PSConfig -cmd upgrade -inplace b2b -wait -cmd applicationcontent -install
-cmd installfeatures -cmd secureresources -cmd services -install
```

Otherwise, use the Configuration Wizard to complete the upgrade, as shown in Figures 18-4, 18-5, and 18-6.

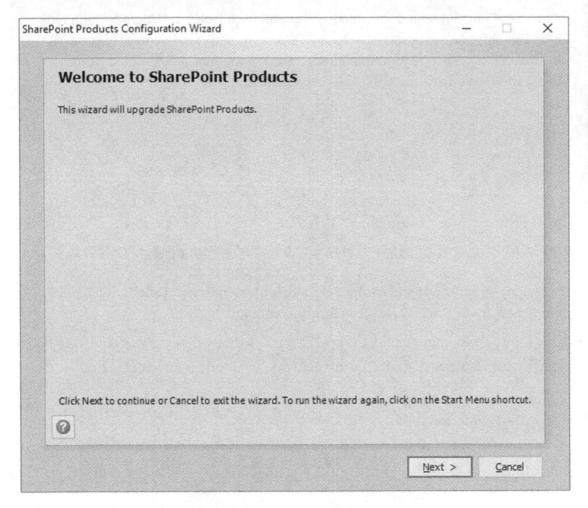

Figure 18-4. *Initiating the Configuration Wizard*

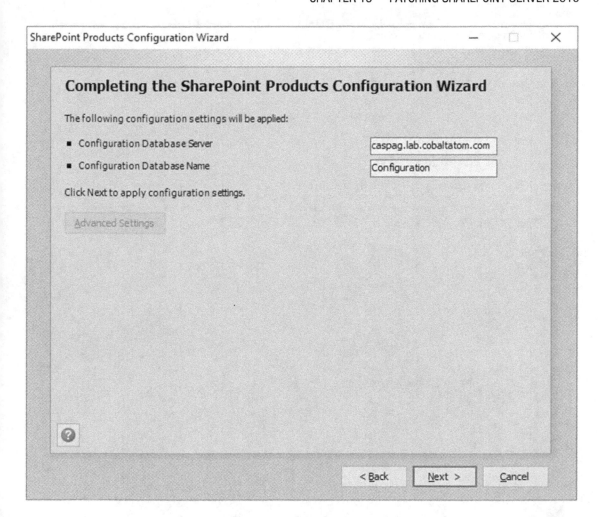

Figure 18-5. *Completing the Configuration Wizard, which will begin the upgrade*

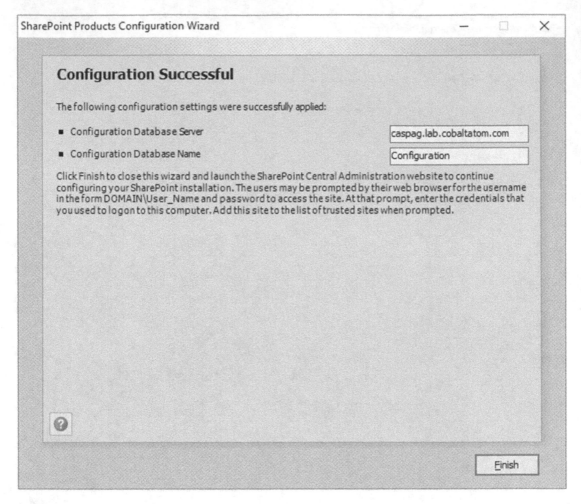

Figure 18-6. *The Configuration Wizard is complete and the SharePoint Server is now online*

With the completion of a SharePoint Server patch installation and configuration, let's examine the log files that provide additional information with the patching process. These logs will also provide information on any errors that may have taken place during the installation or configuration process.

Upgrade Log Files

There are two primary log files to work with. The PSConfig file and the Upgrade log file. PSConfig file is the format of PSCDiagnostics_mm_dd_YYYY_HH_mm_ss_fff while the

Upgrade log file has a format of Upgrade-YYYYmmdd-HHmmss-fff-<SPUpgradeSession_GUID>.log ("fff" stands for millisecond). An example of this format is Upgrade-20181120-165802-907-fc2cc387dc154d98bf4034d7c96bb047.log. Another type of log file, the PSC Diagnostics log, will look similar to PSCDiagnostics_11_20_2018_16_55_35_225_753447558.log, which ran on November 20, 2018 at 4:55:35.255 PM.

Log Files are located within the ULS log directory. In the environment outlined in this book, that is E:\ULS for each farm member, while by default, it would be located at %CommonProgramFiles%\Microsoft Shared\Web Server Extensions\16\LOGS\.

If an error is encountered during the upgrade process, there will also be an Upgrade-YYYYmmdd-HHmmss-fff-<SPUpgradeSession_GUID>-error.log file. This will help identify what errors and corrective actions need to be taken to successfully complete an upgrade. The ULS logs can provide additional details about any errors, as well.

Unlike previous versions of SharePoint, many patches will not increment the Farm Build number. Instead, under Upgrade and Migration in Central Administration, go to Check product and patch installation status to see the current state of patched products. In Figure 18-7, we can see that Microsoft SharePoint Server 2019 Core has been patched once. The base build, 16.0.10337.12109 was patched by build 16.0.10338.12107.

| CALSP01 | Microsoft SharePoint Server 2019 Core | 16.0.10337.12109 | Installed |
| CALSP01 | Security Update for Microsoft SharePoint Server 2019 Core (KB4461513) | 16.0.10338.12107 | Installed |

Figure 18-7. Patch applied to CALSP01

As with any SharePoint highly available farm, performing highly available upgrades is key. We will take a look at a strategy to maintain the high availability of the farm while patching.

Long Patch Times

SharePoint Server 2013 suffered from long patch times, but this has been resolved in SharePoint Server 2019. SharePoint Server 2019 patches take into account stopping and starting services as required. It is recommended that any Search Server instance be paused for the duration of the patching process when patching a server that runs any Search role(s). This prevents any crawls from executing while the patching takes place. This can be accomplished via the cmdlet Suspend-SPEnterpriseSearchServiceApplication.

Highly Available Upgrades

To upgrade a farm without taking it offline, follow this upgrade procedure for SharePoint patches.

Identify each server and the assigned role. Only one server for a given role will be offline at any given time. In the environment outlined by this book, we have the following configuration, as shown in Table 18-1.

Table 18-1. *Roles and Servers in the SharePoint Farm*

WebFrontEndWithDistributedCache	ApplicationWithSearch
CALSP01	CALSP03
CALSP02	CALSP04

Tip   Microsoft produced a video on the details of Zero Downtime Patching which also covers this process, available on TechNet at `https://docs.microsoft.com/en-us/SharePoint/upgrade-and-update/video-demo-of-zero-downtime-patching-in-sharepoint-server-2016`.

For the purposes of this environment, we will work down and across Table 18-1, starting with the WebFrontEndWithDistributedCache servers and finishing with the ApplicationWithSearch servers. But as noted, the order is not important. Except for special handling for Distributed Cache and Search, the process will be as follows.

Remove the first server, CALSP01, from the load balancer. Run the first patch, sts. Do not restart if prompted. Run the next patch if applicable, wssloc. Restart if either patch prompted you to do so.

These patches may also be run silently by passing the /passive switch to the patch executable, for example `sts2019-kb4461513-fullfile-x64-glb.exe /passive /norestart`.

This will install the sts and wssloc patches with a basic user interface and does not restart the computer. The patches are installed in the order specified. While a patch is being installed, one or more IIS resets may occur. Restart the computer manually through the UI or by using the Restart-Computer cmdlet once the patch installations have completed.

As CALSP01 and CALSP02 are running Distributed Cache, we need to take special steps to gracefully shutdown Distributed Cache. While the cmdlet Stop-SPDistributedCacheServiceInstance has a -Graceful switch, it is not a graceful shutdown of the cache node. Instead, use the following series of cmdlets to shutdown the cache cluster:

```
Use-CacheCluster
Stop-CacheHost -HostName <Fully Qualified Domain Name of Cache
Host>  -CachePort 22233 -Graceful
```

You can then monitor the shutdown process via Get-CacheHost, as shown in Figure 18-8. Note that this may take more than 10 minutes to transfer the cache fragments to another cache host in the farm.

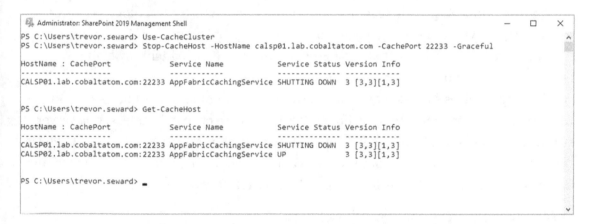

Figure 18-8. *Shutting down a cache node and monitoring service status*

Tip   Microsoft has provided a script to shutdown the Distributed Cache service. This can be found on the article Managing the Distributed Cache service in SharePoint Server at `https://docs.microsoft.com/en-us/sharepoint/administration/manage-the-distributed-cache-service#perform-a-graceful-shutdown-of-the-distributed-cache-service-by-using-a-powershell-script.`

Tip   If you interrupt a patch installation or the patch installation fails, IIS Application Pools or Sites may be in a Stopped state. Manually start them as required.

When the Distributed Cache shutdown has completed, the server can be restarted. The Distributed Cache service will automatically start when the server comes back online. If you need to restart the server again for any reason, make sure to shutdown Distributed Cache before doing so. Use Get-CacheHost to validate the host reports as "UP" before starting the patching process on the next Distributed Cache server. Once the server is back online, add it back to the Load Balancer.

Moving onto CALSP02, repeat the preceding steps; take the server out of the Load Balancer, install the patches, stop Distributed Cache, restart the server, then add it back to the Load Balancer.

For the Application with Search servers, as they are using the Topology Manager to maintain service availability, it is not necessary to rotate them in and out of the load balancer, but if you're running Central Administration in a highly available configuration, you may want to consider rotating them.

To keep services such as search online during the upgrade, at least one server in the farm must be running the specific service; in the case of Search, at least one server running any one specific role must be online. As an example, in Figure 18-9, CALSP03 is being patched, yet end users continue to be able to search for content. Prior to patching a server running a search role, first suspend the search service instance.

```
$ssa = Get-SPEnterpriseSearchServiceApplication
Suspend-SPEnterpriseSearchServiceApplication $ssa
```

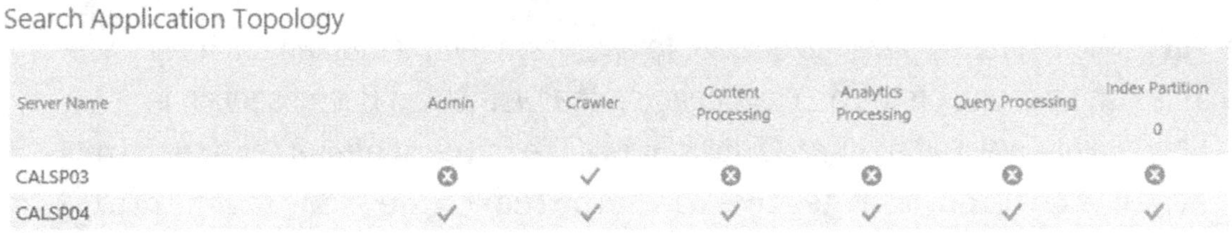

Search Application Topology

Server Name	Admin	Crawler	Content Processing	Analytics Processing	Query Processing	Index Partition 0
CALSP03	✗	✓	✗	✗	✗	✗
CALSP04	✓	✓	✓	✓	✓	✓

Figure 18-9. *CALSP03 is offline, while CALSP04 is still online and providing Search services*

> **Note** There is a bug on release of SharePoint Server 2019 where the Crawler component will show as online even if the server is unavailable.

When a Search server is back online from a reboot, validate in the Search Administration that all components are online. If you receive an HTTP 503 while viewing the Search Administration page, it may take the Topology Manager a few minutes to "fail over" the Search Administration component to the SharePoint Server that is online. You will also need to resume the search service instance. This can be accomplished via PowerShell.

```
$ssa = Get-SPEnterpriseSearchServiceApplication
Resume-SPEnterpriseSearchServiceApplication $ssa
```

When performing the Config Wizard or using psconfig.exe to update the farm after patching, remember to perform the same actions; remove Web Front Ends from the load balancer, gracefully stop Distributed Cache, then run the Config Wizard. Servers running a Search component, pause the Search service application prior to running the Config Wizard or psconfig.exe.

As SQL Server also has security hotfixes, rollups, and Service Packs, it will be important to maintain the highest availability possible. The next section briefly covers patching the SQL Servers that support the SharePoint Server farm.

Patching SQL Server

When patching SQL Server in a high-availability scenario, first patch the node that is currently in a secondary role (e.g., AlwaysOn Secondary Replica or the SQL Cluster passive node). Once completed, begin the failover process to that secondary SQL Server. Once the failover has completed, patch what was the primary SQL Server. You may or may not choose to failback to the original primary SQL Server. Note that as the Usage database is only active on the primary SQL Server and during the SQL Server outage, the Usage database will be unavailable, however that will not impact normal farm operations.

Next Steps

Now that you know how SharePoint can be patched in a highly available configuration, the next stage of administering is monitoring and maintenance of the SharePoint farm.

CHAPTER 19

Monitoring and Maintaining a SharePoint 2019 Deployment

In this chapter, we will look at how to monitor our SharePoint Server 2019 environment to assure stability as well as performance for your users. We will also look at how to monitor logs to make sure there are no issues and potential ongoing maintenance activities to keep your SharePoint farm running at peak performance.

Monitoring

SharePoint Server 2019 can be monitored with a variety of logs and tools. Logs include IIS logging, ULS logging, Event Logging (Event Viewer), and SQL Server log files. From a tools perspective, Performance Monitor will be the primary tool we will examine, in addition to the IIS Manager to look for potential long-running requests.

IIS Logging

IIS logs all web site activity to SharePoint. While not necessarily the primary place to examine for errors or performance, it can provide an indication of issues users are running into, including missing assets or server errors, such as HTTP 500 errors.

As IIS logs are plain text files and parsing them can be difficult with text editors like Notepad, Log Parser and Log Parser Studio from Microsoft makes finding specific types of log entries significantly easier.

© Vlad Catrinescu and Trevor Seward 2019
V. Catrinescu and T. Seward, *Deploying SharePoint 2019*, https://doi.org/10.1007/978-1-4842-4526-2_19

You may consider adding additional fields to log for each request. This can be done in IIS on a server or IIS web site level under Logging in the feature pane.

Tip   Log Parser 2.2 is available from Microsoft at `www.microsoft.com/en-us/download/details.aspx?id=24659` and Log Parser Studio is available on the TechNet Gallery at `https://gallery.technet.microsoft.com/office/Log-Parser-Studio-cd458765`.

In this example, we will start with Log Parser 2.2. We will be looking for any HTTP 404 errors, which indicate a missing file, from all files within an IIS Web Site.

```
LogParser "SELECT date, cs-uri-stem FROM E:\IIS\W3SVC548194741\u_ex*.log
WHERE sc-status = 500 GROUP BY date, cs-uri-stem"
date       cs-uri-stem
---------- -----------------------------------------------------------------
2018-11-03 /robots.txt
2018-11-06 /SitePages/none
2018-11-06 /_layouts/15/activitymonitor.js
2018-11-20 /SitePages/none
2018-11-20 /_layouts/15/activitymonitor.js
2018-11-20 /sites/team
2018-11-20 /favicon.ico

Statistics:
-----------
Elements processed: 6121
Elements output:    7
Execution time:     0.12 seconds
```

With this output, we can see there are 3 days where users received an HTTP 404 when requesting a resource. We know from this example that SharePoint does not include certain files, such as favicon.ico by default and can ignore these particular missing files.

Server errors are in the HTTP 500 range, and this output shows we have a few HTTP 500 errors across a few days. This output shows that the errors were primarily with the Publishing service.

```
LogParser "SELECT date, cs-uri-stem FROM E:\IIS\W3SVC548194741\u_ex*.log
WHERE sc-status = 500 GROUP BY date, cs-uri-stem"
date       cs-uri-stem
---------- -----------------------------------------------------------------
2018-11-04 /_vti_bin/publishingservice.asmx
2018-11-04 /_vti_bin/client.svc/SP.Directory.DirectorySession/me
2018-11-04 /_vti_bin/client.svc/social.following/IsFollowed
2018-11-04 /_vti_bin/client.svc/SP.Directory.DirectorySession/
           User(principalName='lab/trevor.seward')
2018-11-05 /_vti_bin/publishingservice.asmx
2018-11-06 /_vti_bin/publishingservice.asmx
2018-11-06 /_vti_bin/client.svc/social.following/IsFollowed
2018-11-06 /_vti_bin/client.svc/GroupSiteManager/GetGroupCreationContext
2018-11-07 /_vti_bin/publishingservice.asmx
2018-11-08 /_vti_bin/publishingservice.asmx
2018-11-09 /_vti_bin/publishingservice.asmx
2018-11-10 /_vti_bin/publishingservice.asmx
2018-11-11 /_vti_bin/publishingservice.asmx
2018-11-12 /_vti_bin/publishingservice.asmx
2018-11-13 /_vti_bin/publishingservice.asmx
2018-11-14 /_vti_bin/publishingservice.asmx
2018-11-15 /_vti_bin/publishingservice.asmx
2018-11-16 /_vti_bin/publishingservice.asmx
2018-11-17 /_vti_bin/publishingservice.asmx
2018-11-18 /_vti_bin/publishingservice.asmx
2018-11-19 /_vti_bin/publishingservice.asmx
2018-11-20 /_vti_bin/publishingservice.asmx

Statistics:
-----------
Elements processed: 6121
Elements output:    22
Execution time:     3.41 seconds
```

By default, IIS logging is in UTC format, so account for your local time zone. When finding a particular log entry that contains the HTTP 500, for example:

```
2018-11-18 09:02:22 172.16.5.128 POST /_vti_bin/publishingservice.asmx -
443 0#.w|lab\s-crawl 10.10.20.146 Mozilla/4.0+(compatible;+MSIE+4.01;+Windo
ws+NT;+MS+Search+6.0+Robot) - 500 0 0 78
```

We can directly correlate this entry with the ULS logs. In the ULS logs, which are local to your time zone, in this case, GMT-8, I will want to examine the ULS log from 1:02:22 AM. Examining this ULS log file, I can also identify the HTTP 500 from there:

```
11/18/2018 01:02:22.19    w3wp.exe (0x1044)    0x18DC    SharePoint
Server    Taxonomy    ca42    Medium    Exception returned from back
end service. System.ServiceModel.FaultException`1[System.ServiceModel.
ExceptionDetail]: Retrieving the COM class factory for component with CLSID
{BDEADF26-C265-11D0-BCED-00A0C90AB50F} failed due to the following error:
800703fa Illegal operation attempted on a registry key that has been marked for
deletion. (Exception from HRESULT: 0x800703FA). (Fault Detail is equal to An
ExceptionDetail, likely created by IncludeExceptionDetailInFaults=true, whose
value is: System.Runtime.InteropServices.COMException: Retrieving the COM class
factory for component with CLSID {BDEADF26-C265-11D0-BCED-00A0C90AB50F} failed
due to the following error: 800703fa Illegal operation attempted on a registry
key that has been marked for deletion. (Exception from HRESULT: 0x800703FA).
```

And finally, based on the correlation ID, using a tool such as ULS Viewer, we can further examine the errors generated. In the case of the preceding error, it was due to a registry key that was attempted to be used even though it was marked for deletion. Resolving this error typically involves simply restarting the server as Windows deletes registry keys during the reboot process.

ULS Logging

ULS provides a valuable source of information about your SharePoint farm. This is the core logging mechanism of SharePoint and is often the first place a SharePoint Administrator will look for any SharePoint-related errors. By default, ULS logs are located in C:\Program Files\Common Files\microsoft shared\Web Server Extensions\16\ LOGS\. ULS logs are in the format of ServerName-YYYYMMdd-hhmm.log, for example, CALSP01-20181114-0836.log.

Tip   ULS Viewer is available from Microsoft at `www.microsoft.com/en-us/download/details.aspx?id=44020`.

If the ULS logs have been relocated, you can use the cmdlet Get-SPDiagnosticConfig to identify where the logs have been relocated to.

```
(Get-SPDiagnosticConfig).LogLocation
```

The log location may also be found via Central Administration. Using Central Administration, navigate to Monitoring. Under Configure diagnostic logging, the Trace Log Path is where the ULS log is located, as shown in Figure 19-1.

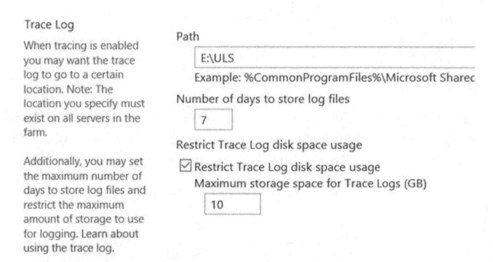

Figure 19-1. ULS log location

Users may encounter errors from SharePoint, which provides them the date and time the error occurred, as well as the ULS Correlation ID. An example of one such error is seen in Figure 19-2.

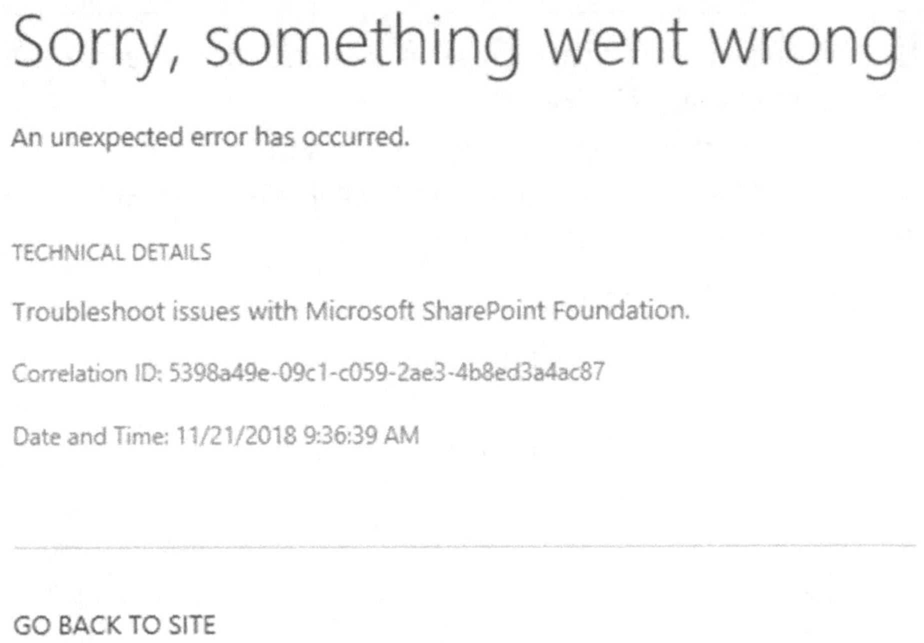

Sorry, something went wrong

An unexpected error has occurred.

TECHNICAL DETAILS

Troubleshoot issues with Microsoft SharePoint Foundation.

Correlation ID: 5398a49e-09c1-c059-2ae3-4b8ed3a4ac87

Date and Time: 11/21/2018 9:36:39 AM

GO BACK TO SITE

Figure 19-2. *A SharePoint error as seen by a user*

Using this information, the Correlation ID and Date and Time, and using Ulsviewer, open the appropriate ULS log file. By using Ulsviewer, we can filter by the preceding Correlation ID, as shown in Figure 19-3, to see the end user's request end to end.

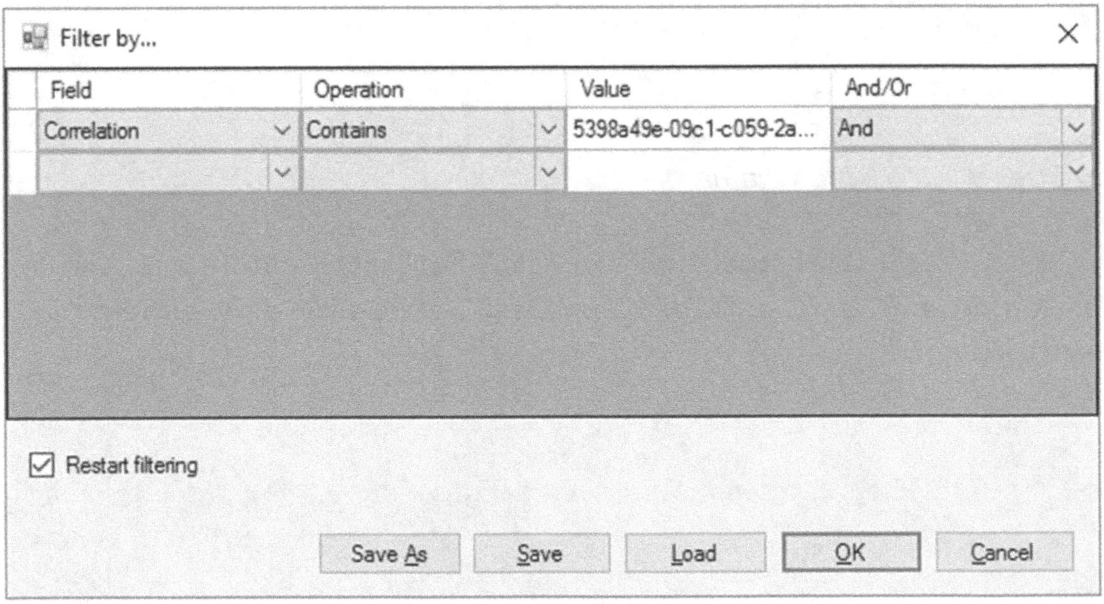

Field	Operation	Value	And/Or
Correlation	Contains	5398a49e-09c1-c059-2a...	And

☑ Restart filtering

Save As   Save   Load   OK   Cancel

Figure 19-3.   *Filtering the ULS log by Correlation ID*

The error may be identified within the list of entries once filtered. In this case, the error is generic, but the user had requested a Content Type that does not exist, seen in Figure 19-4.

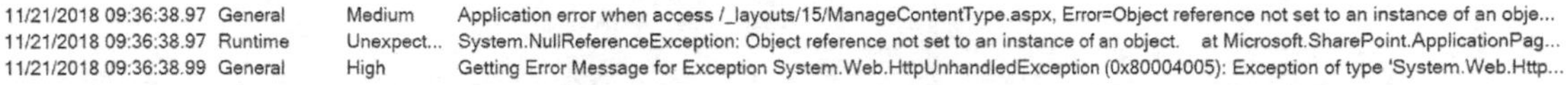

11/21/2018 09:36:38.97	General	Medium	Application error when access /_layouts/15/ManageContentType.aspx, Error=Object reference not set to an instance of an obje...
11/21/2018 09:36:38.97	Runtime	Unexpect...	System.NullReferenceException: Object reference not set to an instance of an object. at Microsoft.SharePoint.ApplicationPag...
11/21/2018 09:36:38.99	General	High	Getting Error Message for Exception System.Web.HttpUnhandledException (0x80004005): Exception of type 'System.Web.Http...

Figure 19-4. *Content Type errors in the ULS log*

The ULS log will display the date and time the log entry is from, the product (e.g., SharePoint, Project Server, PowerPivot, etc.), the Category (User Profiles, Search), the Event ID, the level (Unexpected are generally errors), Correlation ID, Message, the Request, and other information depending on the type of error.

Event IDs are used internally by Microsoft and the information of what message they're associated with is not generally published.

As many farms consist of multiple servers, sometimes it is difficult to locate an error as there may be more than one server that provides the service associated with an error, such as more than one server running Search or serving as a Web Front End. Using the cmdlet Merge-SPLogFile, one can use parameters to narrow down the search for specific errors across the farm. This is an example of how to merge all log files from all SharePoint servers in the farm by a Correlation ID.

```
Merge-SPLogFile -Path C:\error.log -CorrelationID "5398a49e-09c1-c059-2ae3-
4b8ed3a4ac87"
```

If the Correlation ID is found, it will output the matching ULS log entries to the C:\error.log file. When you do not specify a time range, the Merge-SPLogFile cmdlet will only look at the previous 60 minutes of logs. If the Correlation ID is not known, it is also possible to narrow down the log by time. Time will be formatted in military time (24 hours), for example, to merge the logs between 3 PM and 5 PM, you would use the following cmdlet:

```
Merge-SPLogFile -Path C:\error.log -StartTime "11/21/2018 15:00" -EndTime
"11/21/2018 17:00"
```

It is possible that errors may not be caught using the default logging settings. For this, we need to increase the verbosity of logs. The verbosity settings are based on Areas. These settings can be modified via Central Administration under Monitoring, Configuring diagnostic logging.

This page will list the current verbosity level for each Area, as shown in Figure 19-5, as well as provide two drop-downs to adjust the verbosity between None to Verbose or allowing you to Reset to Default.

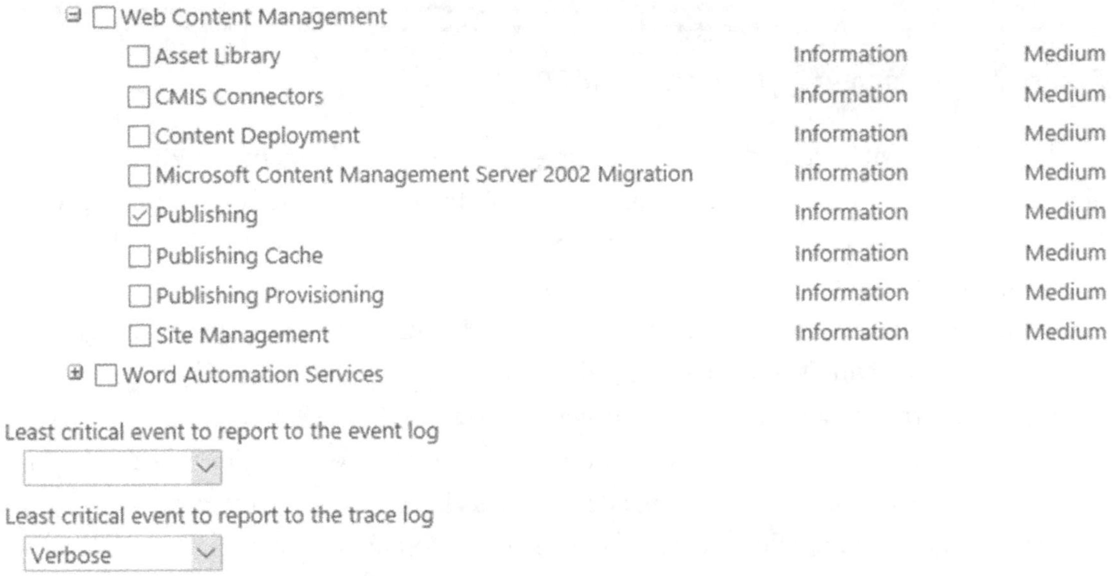

⊟ ☐ Web Content Management		
☐ Asset Library	Information	Medium
☐ CMIS Connectors	Information	Medium
☐ Content Deployment	Information	Medium
☐ Microsoft Content Management Server 2002 Migration	Information	Medium
☑ Publishing	Information	Medium
☐ Publishing Cache	Information	Medium
☐ Publishing Provisioning	Information	Medium
☐ Site Management	Information	Medium
⊞ ☐ Word Automation Services		

Least critical event to report to the event log

[⌄]

Least critical event to report to the trace log

[Verbose   ⌄]

Figure 19-5. *Adjusting the verbosity of an Area*

Verbosity can also be adjusted through the SharePoint Management Shell. In addition, setting the verbosity via PowerShell will allow you to set the verbosity up to VerboseEx, which has additional information not provided at the Verbose logging level. The format to setting a specific area is either by simply specifying the Area, or CategoryName:Area, or even CategoryName:*, which will set the entire Category to the specified Trace Severity. Here are a few examples:

```
Set-SPLogLevel -Identity "SharePoint Foundation:Asp Runtime" -TraceSeverity
VerboseEx
Set-SPLogLevel -Identity "Asp Runtime" -TraceSeverity VerboseEx
Set-SPLogLevel -Identity "SharePoint Foundation:*" -TraceSeverity VerboseEx
```

When using Verbose or VerboseEx trace levels, there may be a significant impact on farm performance. Because of this, you may want to run with these Trace Severities for a short period of time to reproduce a specific issue.

Once completed reproducing the issue, use Clear-SPLogLevel to reset all Areas back to their default Trace Severity.

ULS Viewer can be used for monitoring the live environment, as well. This is suitable when having a user reproduce a problem that does not necessarily surface an error, but will allow you to correlate the user's action with one or more messages within the ULS log. The latest version of ULS Viewer is also able to monitor logs over the entire farm. By selecting the farm icon, represented by a tree node in the toolbar, you can enter one or more server names into the farm, then using a UNC path, Ulsviewer will allow you to see the server logs intermixed, real time. This is useful in scenarios where a user may call a service on a backend server, but you must trace the action of the user through the frontend to the backend.

Event Viewer

SharePoint records a limited amount of information to the Event Viewer, but the Event Viewer is more useful for service-specific and ASP.NET errors.

Generally, Windows Services that run SharePoint, such as the SharePoint Timer or SharePoint Administration service, will show any startup or unexpected stops in the System Event Log. For example, if the SharePoint Timer service unexpectedly stops, it will show an error in the System Event Log as seen in Figure 19-6.

Figure 19-6. *The SharePoint Timer service has unexpectedly stopped*

The System Event Log is also useful for diagnosing Kerberos errors, along with any TLS/SSL errors that may occur.

The Application Event Log will show other more general SharePoint information, warnings, and error messages from a variety of sources. As an example, it will show when an IIS Application Pool has started, as shown in Figure 19-7.

Figure 19-7. *An IIS Application Pool starting up*

SharePoint also logs data in a few Applications and Services event logs. In the Operational log for SharePoint Products, Shared, log entries typically consist of Incoming E-mail statistics, Usage and Trace Log status, such as when the log reached the retention limit based on space used or date as shown in Figure 19-8, and InfoPath Forms Services messages.

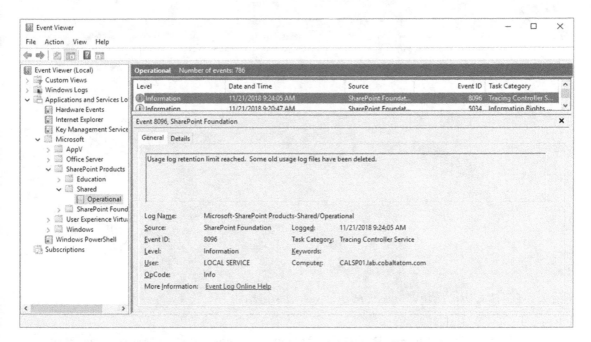

Figure 19-8.   Usage service logs reaching the retention limit

IIS Manager

The IIS Manager provides a limited amount of information on active requests in Application Pools. This information may be helpful for diagnosing the origins of long-running requests, for example, a large number of requests to a OneNote notebook residing on a SharePoint site.

Using IIS Manager, at the server level, go into "Worker Processes." From here, as shown in Figure 19-9, it will show a limited amount of information about each worker process.

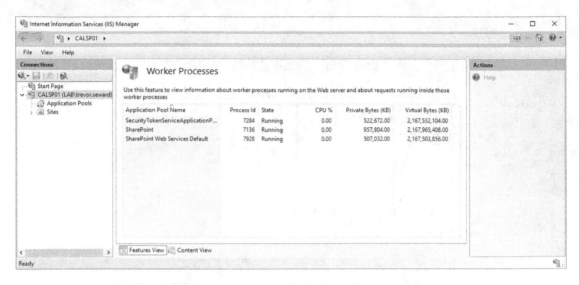

Figure 19-9. *Running Worker Process information*

By right-clicking a Worker Process and selecting View Current Requests, we can identify running requests as shown in Figure 19-10.

Figure 19-10. *Running requests to the Worker Process*

Usage Logging

SharePoint Usage Logging logs a variety of information to the Usage database. This database can be directly queried either through the tables or through the built-in Views. For example, the RequestUsage View can provide information on how long a particular request took, how many CPU megacycle it consumed, Distributed Cache reads and how long those Distributed Cache reads took, among other statistics.

Usage Logging can be configured in Central Administration under Monitoring, Configure usage and health data collection. There are a number of scenarios to gather data on, but only gather those scenarios you believe will be important for farm diagnostics. Logging more than is required may lead to farm performance issues as the data is transferred from the SharePoint farm into the Usage database, along with the Usage database size growth.

The Usage database may be queried directly via SQL Server Management Studio. Microsoft provisions Views for many common scenarios one may be interested in, as shown in Figure 19-11, but you may also construct your own Views within the database if needed.

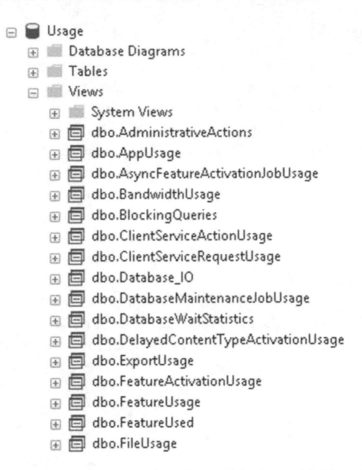

Figure 19-11. Many Views are provisioned out of the box with SharePoint

Querying the database is simple. As shown in Figure 19-12, construct your query of a View and select the columns you wish to display in the results, in the order you wish to display the results in. In this query, we are looking at the Administrative Actions View and select just the relevant columns that we're interested in, then sorting by the time the log entry was created in the database, with the newest entries appearing first.

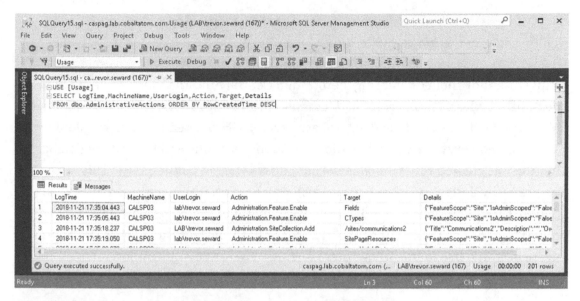

Figure 19-12. *A query of a View in the Usage database*

Central Administration Health Analyzer

The built-in SharePoint Health Analyzer is a set of rules that run periodically via the SharePoint Timer Service. These rules detect various issues, as shown in Figure 19-13, such as SharePoint Application Pools recycling, or databases with a large amount of free space, and other minor to major issues with the farm.

Review problems and solutions ⓘ

⊕ new item

All Reports   ⋯

✓	Severity	Title		Failing Servers	Failing Services	Modified

⊿ Category : Security (1)

| | 📖 | The server farm account should not be used for other services. | | | SPTimerService (SPTimerV4) | 15 hours ago |

⊿ Category : Performance (1)

| | 📖 | Search - One or more crawl databases may have fragmented indices. | | | SPTimerService (SPTimerV4) | 15 hours ago |

⊿ Category : Configuration (6)

| | 📖 | Product / patch installation or server upgrade required. | | | SPTimerService (SPTimerV4) | 15 hours ago |
| | 📖 | Missing server side dependencies. | | | SPTimerService (SPTimerV4) | 15 hours ago |

Figure 19-13. *Reviewing Health Analyzer issues*

While the Health Analyzer can be useful, there are rules which are out of date or Health Analyzer warnings which cannot be resolved. As these rules are written into SharePoint's codebase, it is not possible to modify the rules. We have the option of simply disabling them or ignoring them within Central Administration. An example of one of these rules is "Some content databases are growing too large." This rule looks at the size of the database. If the database exceeds 100 GB, the health analyzer rule shows a warning. However, we know that Microsoft supports multi-terabyte content databases. The rule was created when mechanical hard drives were in common use. This warning was primarily designed for backup and restore scenarios, where it may not have been possible to back up or restore a database exceeding 100 GB in a reasonable amount of time. With the wide deployment of either SSD or flash-based systems, these databases may be restored in a matter of minutes rather than hours. It is still important to monitor database size, but this should be done outside of the context of SharePoint with SQL Server database monitoring tools.

If there are rules which are not required, they can be disabled via the Review rule definitions, as shown in Figure 19-14. Each rule will have an Enabled checkbox. Simply uncheck it to disable the rule. You may then delete the Health Alert from the Health Analyzer and the raised issue will no longer appear.

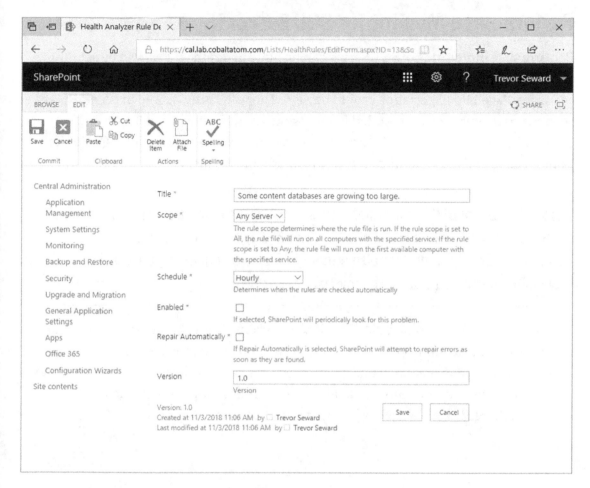

Figure 19-14. *Disabling a Rule Definition*

Performance Monitor for SharePoint

Performance Monitor may also be a useful tool for diagnosing server performance issues, such as examining outstanding ASP.NET requests, CPU usage by process, and so forth. The scenario in which Performance Monitor is used depends on the performance problem one is attempting to troubleshoot.

Performance Monitor for SQL Server

Performance monitoring of SQL Server can be quite in depth, but we will be skimming the surface here of "essential numbers." For example, within the SQL Server Buffer Manager, Page Life Expectancy should be high. The value is measured in seconds; 300 seconds or higher is recommended in most systems. In addition, the Buffer Cache Hit Ratio should be well over 70 (or 70%). DMVs are also used to monitor SQL Server performance and are generally preferred over other methods.

Tip   Additional DMV information, including scripts to monitor DMVs are available from Glenn Berry at `www.sqlskills.com/blogs/glenn/category/dmv-queries/`. Brent Ozar also offers DMV monitoring via sp_BlitzCache available at `www.brentozar.com/blitzcache/`.

Maintaining SharePoint database is also important. With SharePoint Server 2019, databases are set to auto-update statistics, but it is still good practice to implement a maintenance plan to manually update statistics on a periodic basis. In addition, a plan should be set in place to maintain database indexes. One popular script to handle these tasks is available from Ola Hallengren at `https://ola.hallengren.com/`.

Index

A

S

CPSIA information can be obtained
at www.ICGtesting.com
Printed in the USA
LVHW061655240519
619032LV00007B/114/P